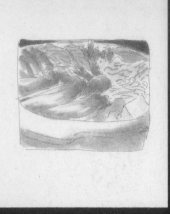

A hotpot dinner I'd planned with some friends around New Year's got pushed back to February because I was busy, then to March because I was getting ready to move, then to April because I was actually making the move. As I write this, April is almost over.

I wonder if my friends would be willing to come eat a hotpot dinner in early summer...?

-Tite Kubo

BLEACH is author Tite Kubo's second title. Kubo made his debut with *ZOMBIEPOWDER.*, a four-volume series for *WEEKLY SHONEN JUMP*. To date, *BLEACH* has been translated into numerous languages and has also inspired an animated TV series that began airing in the U.S. in 2006. Beginning its serialization in 2001, *BLEACH* is still a mainstay in the pages of *WEEKLY SHONEN JUMP*. In 2005, *BLEACH* was awarded the prestigious Shogakukan Manga Award in the *shonen* (boys) category.

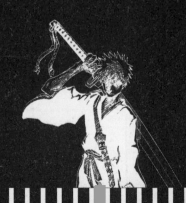

BLEACH
Vol. 45: THE BURNOUT INFERNO
SHONEN JUMP Manga Edition

STORY AND ART BY
TITE KUBO

English Adaptation/Lance Caselman
Translation/Joe Yamazaki
Touch-up Art & Lettering/Mark McMurray
Design/Yukiko Whitley, Kam Li
Editor/Alexis Kirsch

Printed in the U.S.A.

Published by VIZ Media, LLC
P.O. Box 77010
San Francisco, CA 94107

10 9 8 7 6 5 4 3 2 1
First printing, August 2012

www.viz.com

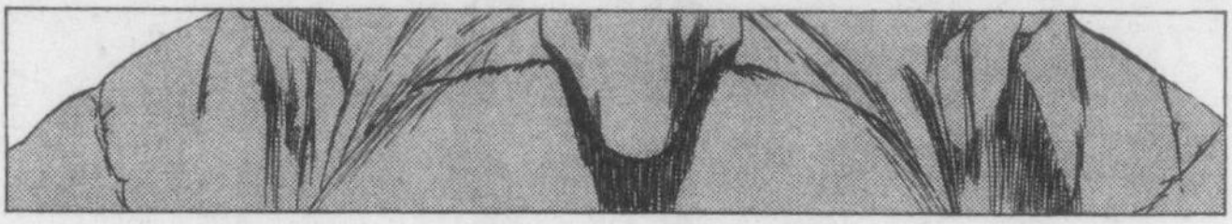

Do not live bowing down.
Die standing up.

BLEACH 45

THE BURNOUT INFERNO

Shonen Jump Manga

STARS AND

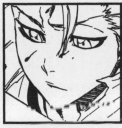

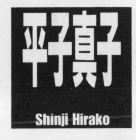

平子真子
Shinji Hirako

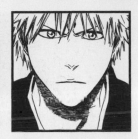

Tôshirô Hitsugaya

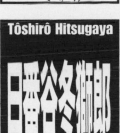

日番谷冬獅郎

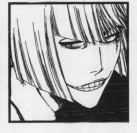

黒崎一護
Ichigo Kurosaki

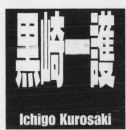

★ plot

When high school student Ichigo Kurosaki meets Soul Reaper Rukia Kuchiki his life is changed forever. Soon Ichigo is a soul-cleansing Soul Reaper too, and he finds himself having adventures, as well as problems, that he never would have imagined. Now Ichigo and his friends must stop renegade Soul Reaper Aizen and his army of Arrancars from destroying the Soul Society and wiping out Karakura as well.

After a fierce battle in Las Noches to save Orihime, Ichigo heads to Karakura Town for the final battle! But a coalition of the Thirteen Court Guard Companies and the Visoreds seem unable to defeat Aizen's minions. After a deadly duel, Komamura finds himself at Tôsen's mercy. But the finishing blow is preempted when Hisagi's sword pierces Tôsen's head!

BLEACH ALL

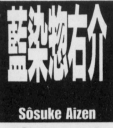

藍染惣右介
Sôsuke Aizen

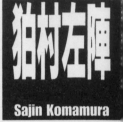

狛村左陣
Sajin Komamura

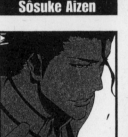

Genryusai Shigekuni Yamamoto

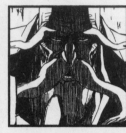

山本元柳斎重國

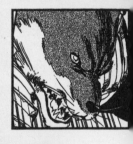

STORIES

BLEACH45

THE BURNOUT INFERNO

Contents

387. Ignited

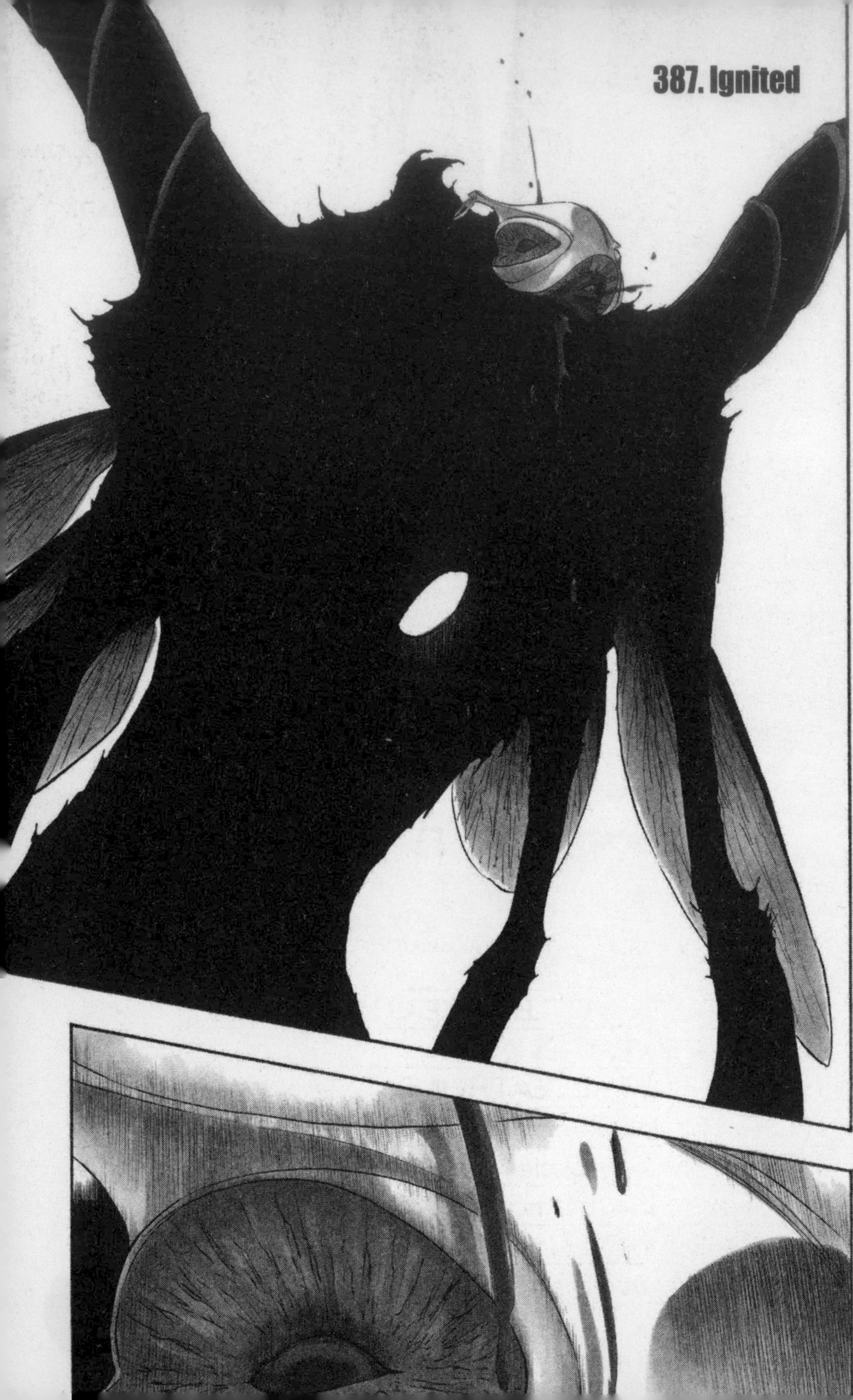

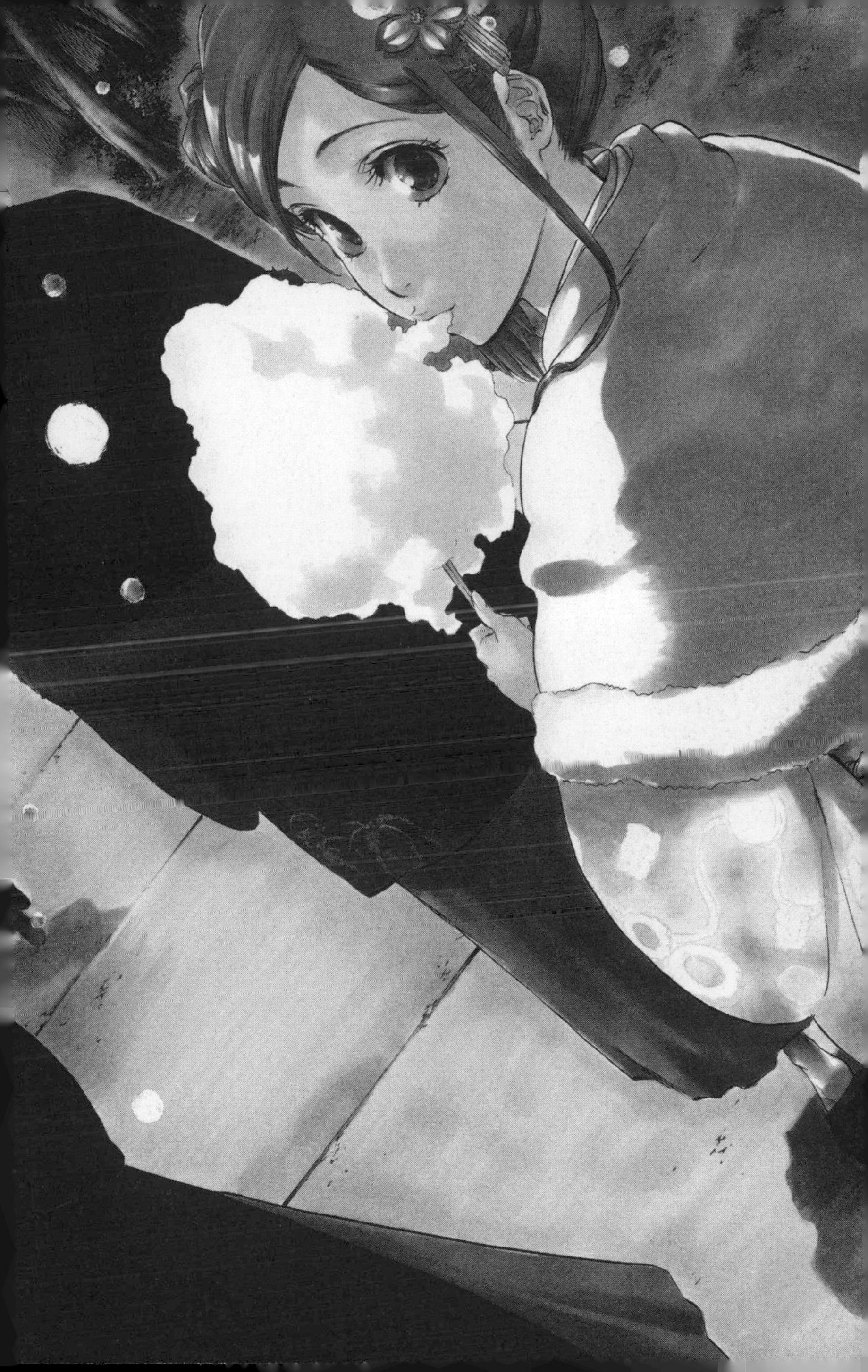

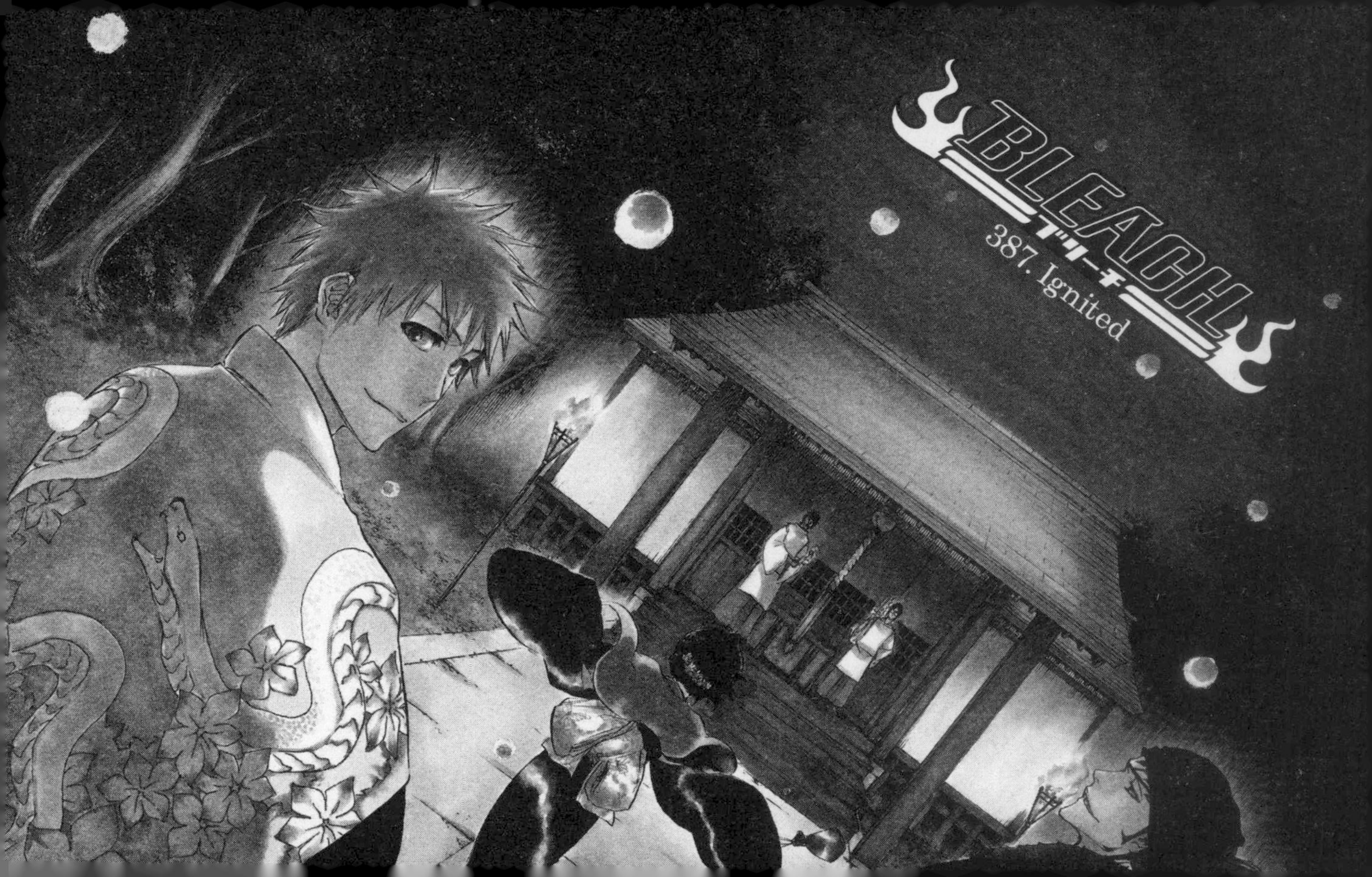
BLEACH
ブリーチ
387. Ignited

BLEACH
ブリーチ

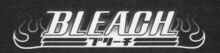

READ THIS WAY

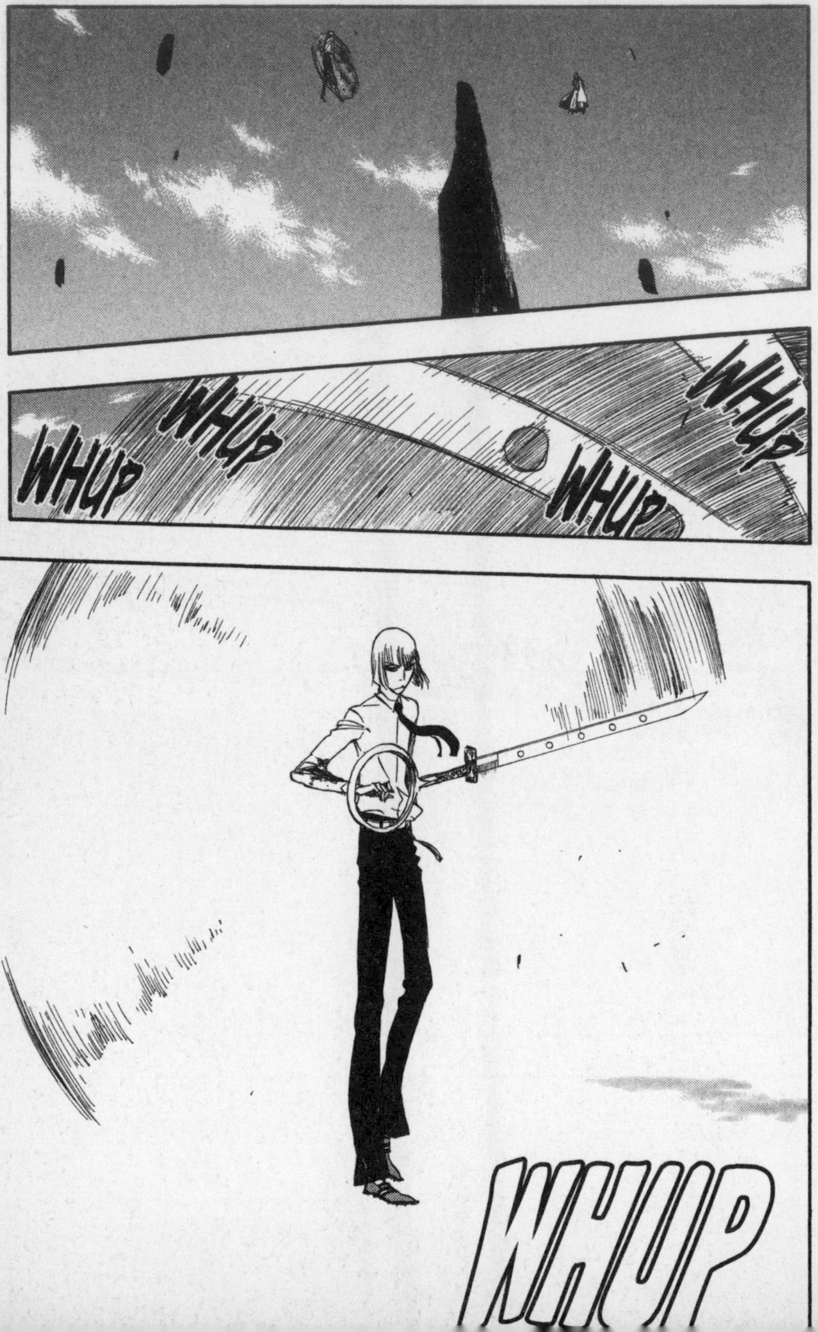
WHUP
WHUP
WHUP
WHUP
WHUP

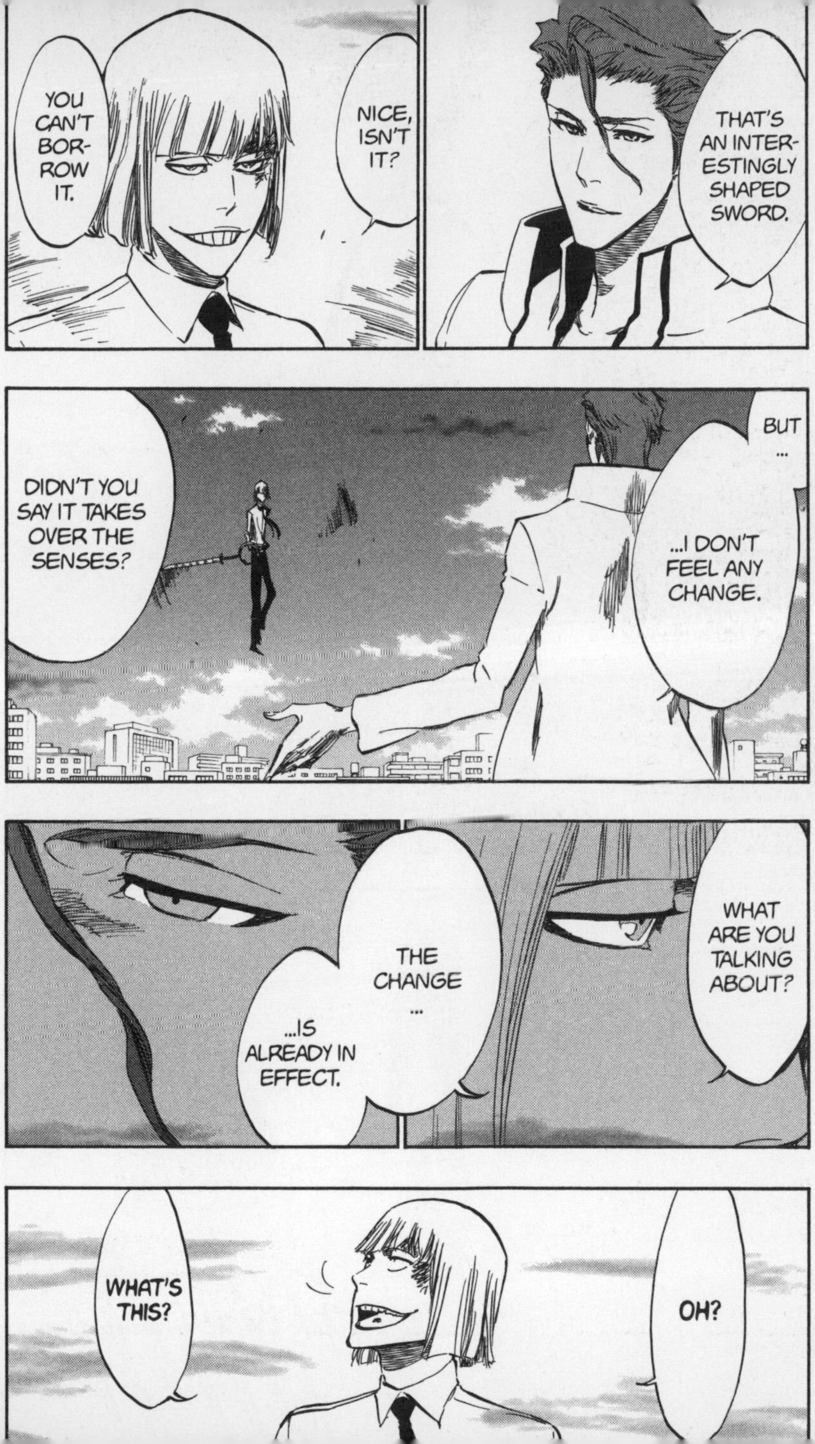
THAT'S AN INTER-ESTINGLY SHAPED SWORD.
NICE, ISN'T IT?
YOU CAN'T BOR-ROW IT.
BUT ...
...I DON'T FEEL ANY CHANGE.
DIDN'T YOU SAY IT TAKES OVER THE SENSES?
WHAT ARE YOU TALKING ABOUT?
THE CHANGE ...
...IS ALREADY IN EFFECT.
OH?
WHAT'S THIS?

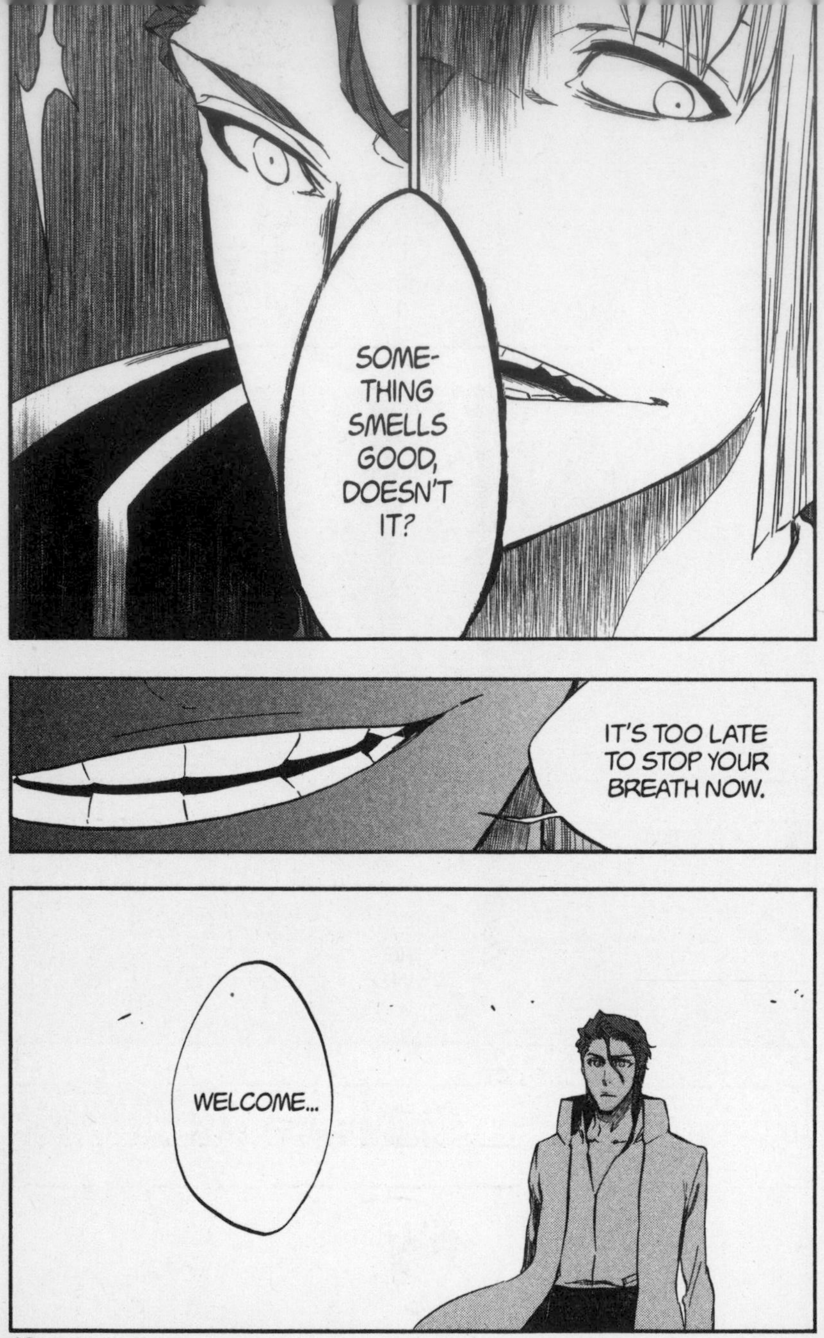
SOME-THING SMELLS GOOD, DOESN'T IT?
IT'S TOO LATE TO STOP YOUR BREATH NOW.
WELCOME...

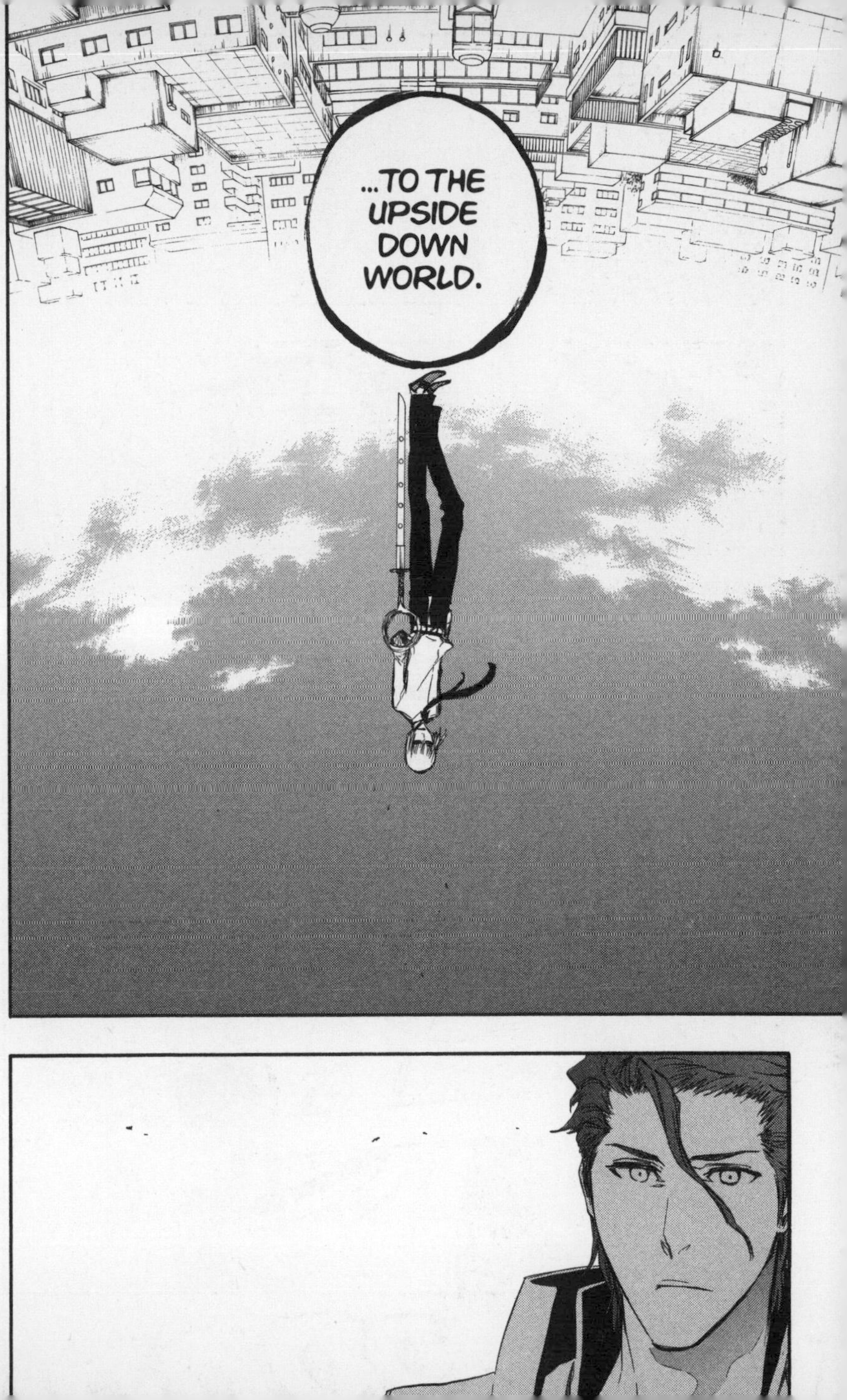
...TO THE UPSIDE DOWN WORLD.

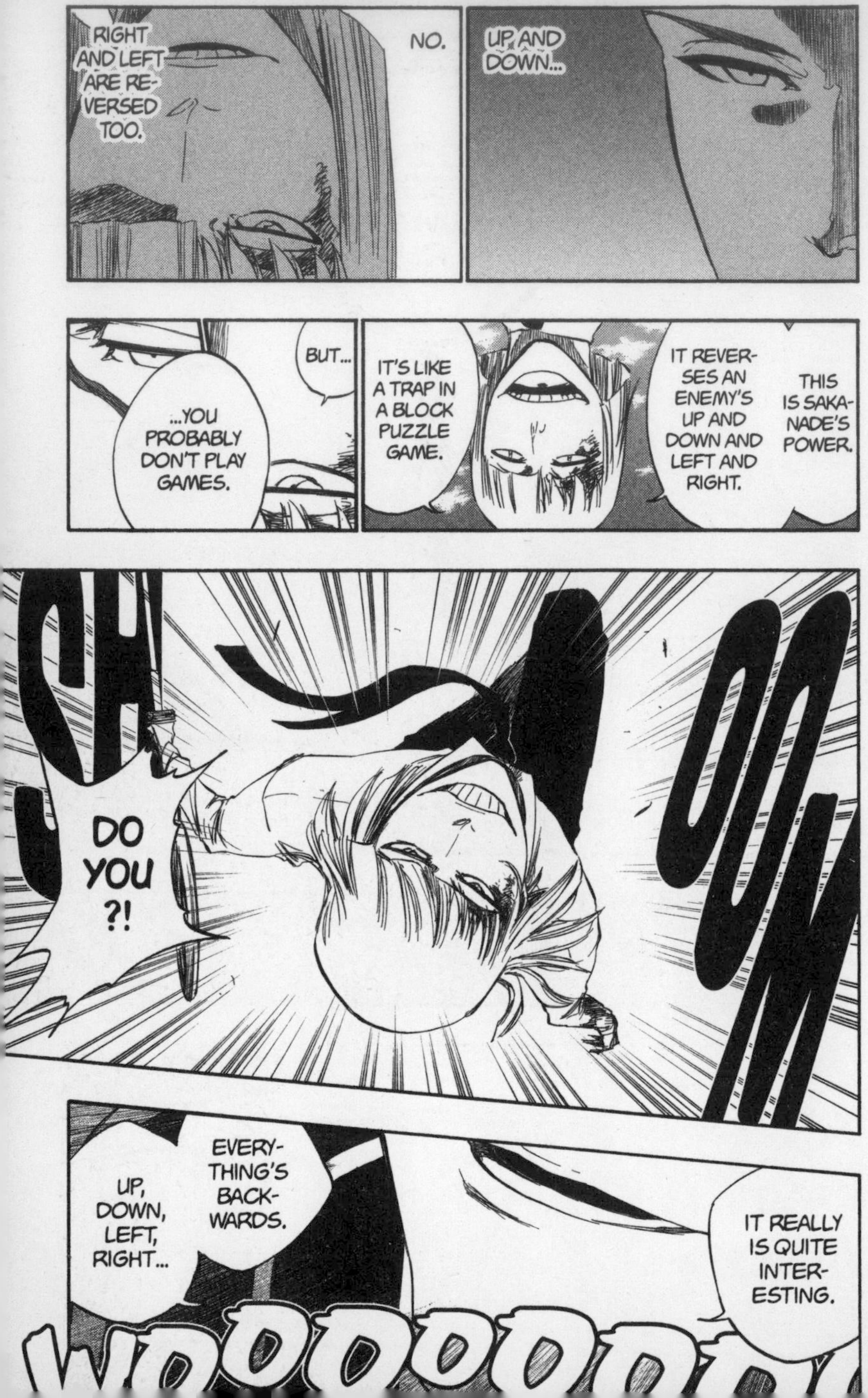
UP AND DOWN...
NO.
RIGHT AND LEFT ARE RE-VERSED TOO.
THIS IS SAKA-NADE'S POWER.
IT REVER-SES AN ENEMY'S UP AND DOWN AND LEFT AND RIGHT.
IT'S LIKE A TRAP IN A BLOCK PUZZLE GAME.
BUT...
...YOU PROBABLY DON'T PLAY GAMES.
DO YOU ?!
IT REALLY IS QUITE INTER-ESTING.
EVERY-THING'S BACK-WARDS.
UP, DOWN, LEFT, RIGHT...

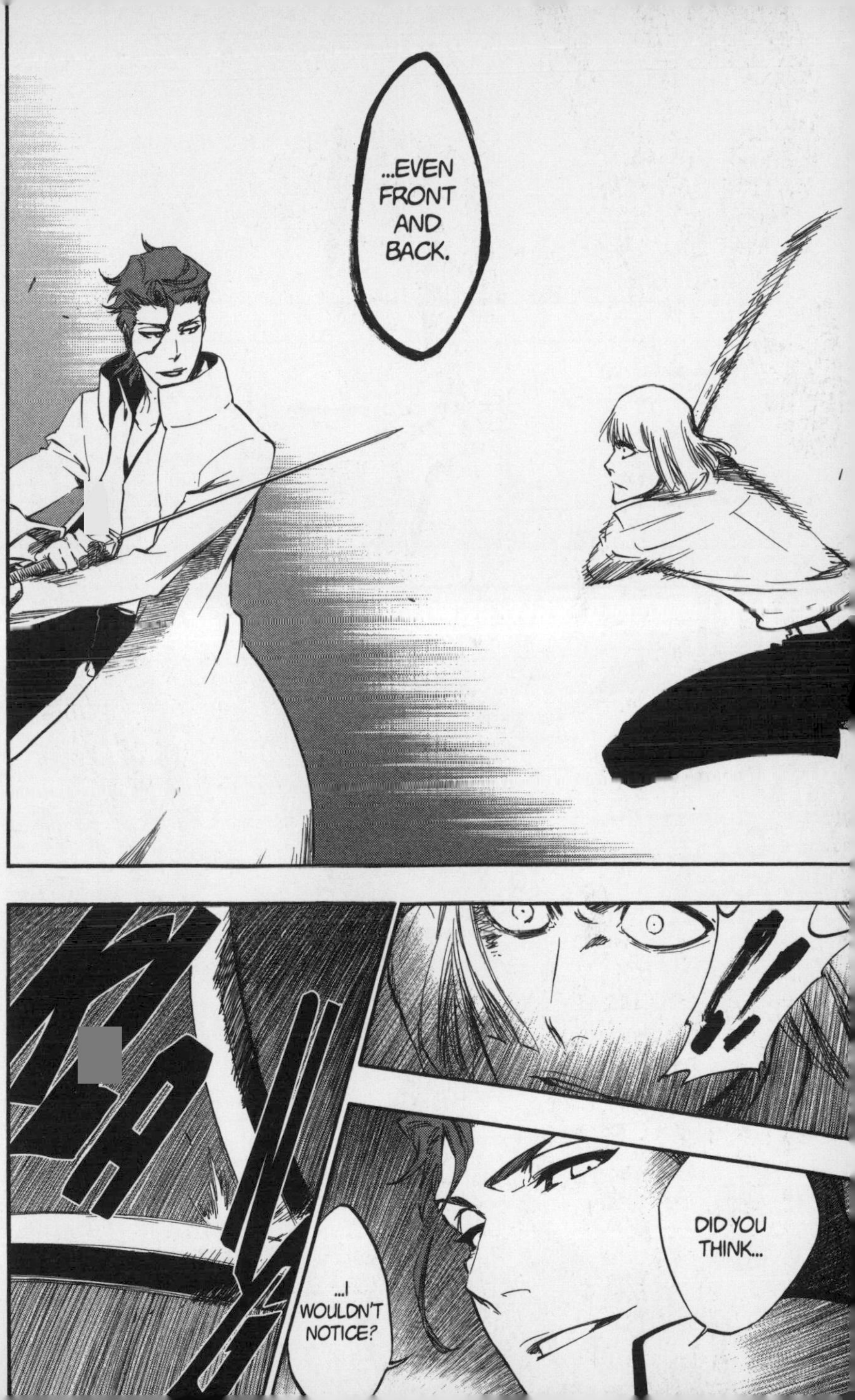
...EVEN FRONT AND BACK.
DID YOU THINK...
...I WOULDN'T NOTICE?

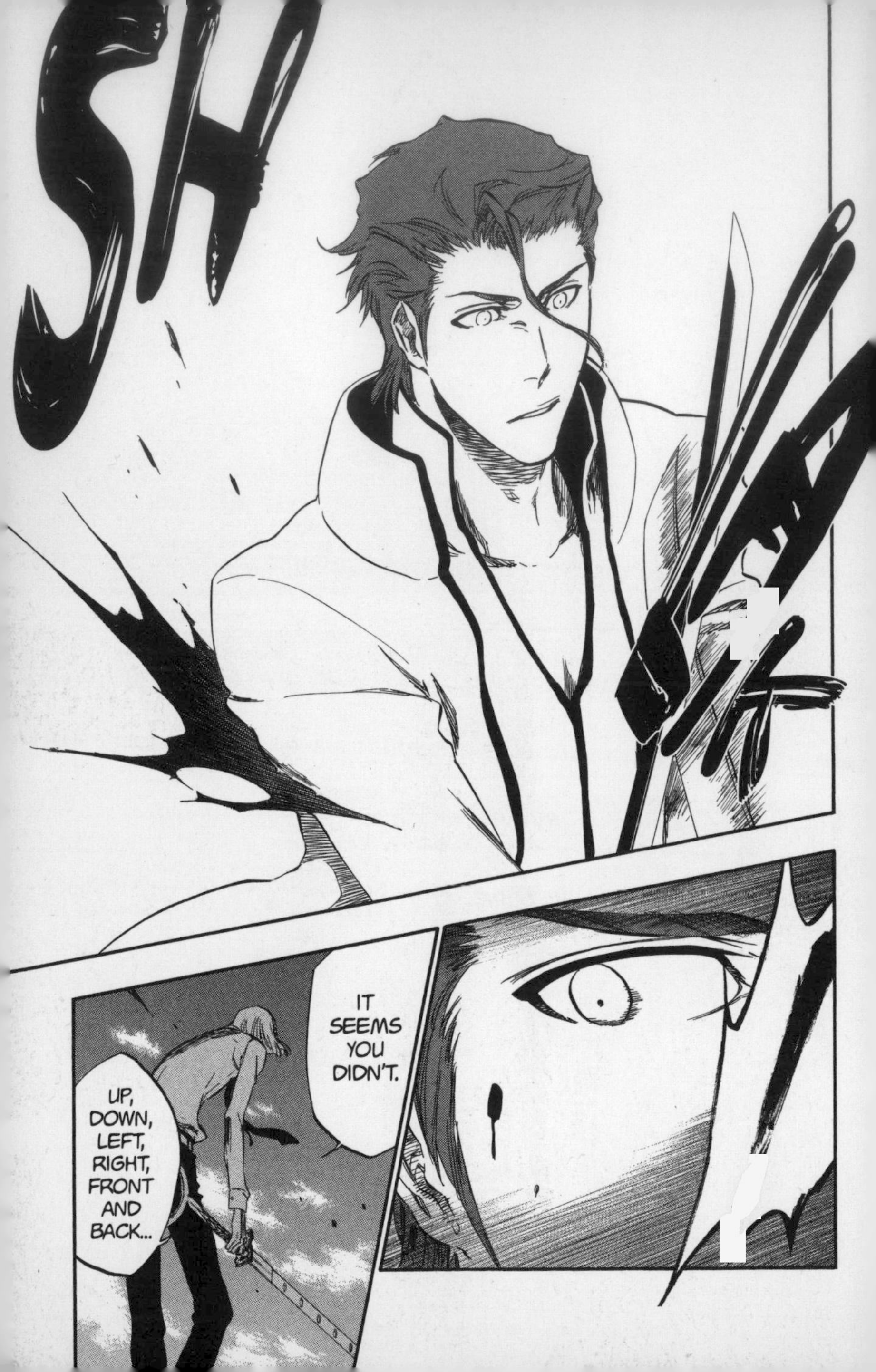
SH
IT SEEMS YOU DIDN'T.
UP, DOWN, LEFT, RIGHT, FRONT AND BACK...

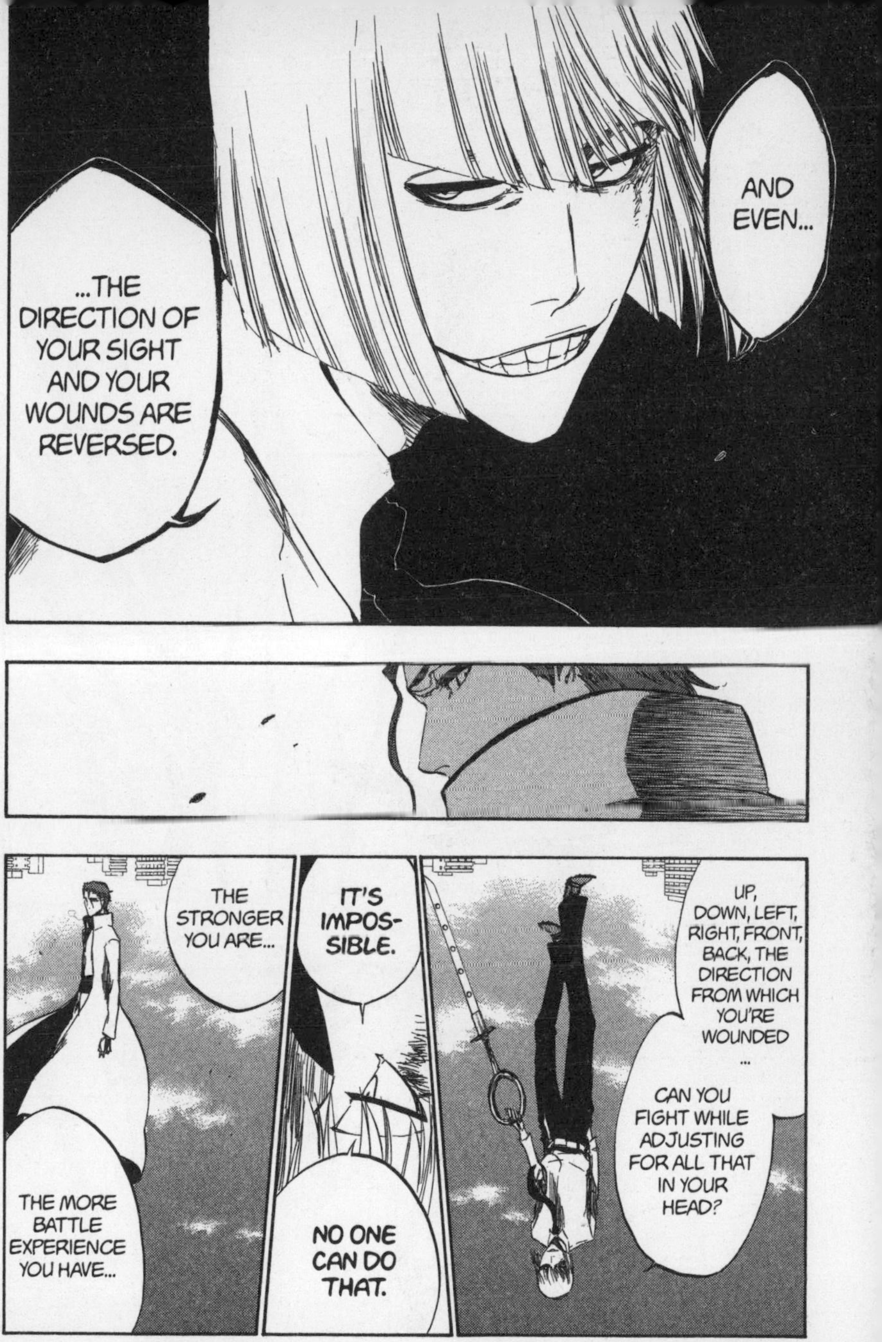
AND EVEN...
...THE DIRECTION OF YOUR SIGHT AND YOUR WOUNDS ARE REVERSED.
UP, DOWN, LEFT, RIGHT, FRONT, BACK, THE DIRECTION FROM WHICH YOU'RE WOUNDED ...
CAN YOU FIGHT WHILE ADJUSTING FOR ALL THAT IN YOUR HEAD?
IT'S IMPOSSIBLE.
NO ONE CAN DO THAT.
THE STRONGER YOU ARE...
THE MORE BATTLE EXPERIENCE YOU HAVE...

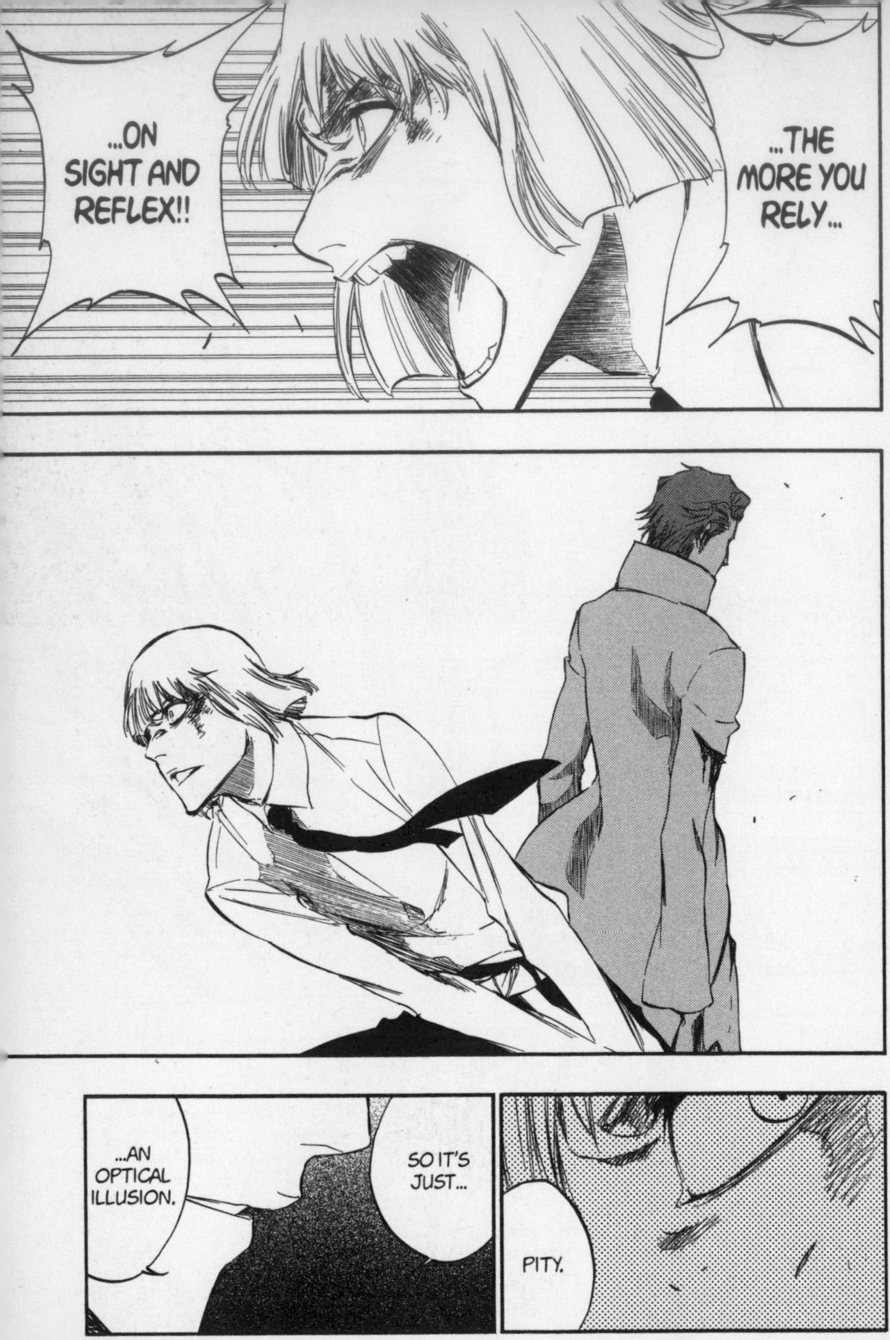
...THE MORE YOU RELY...
...ON SIGHT AND REFLEX!!
PITY.
SO IT'S JUST...
...AN OPTICAL ILLUSION.

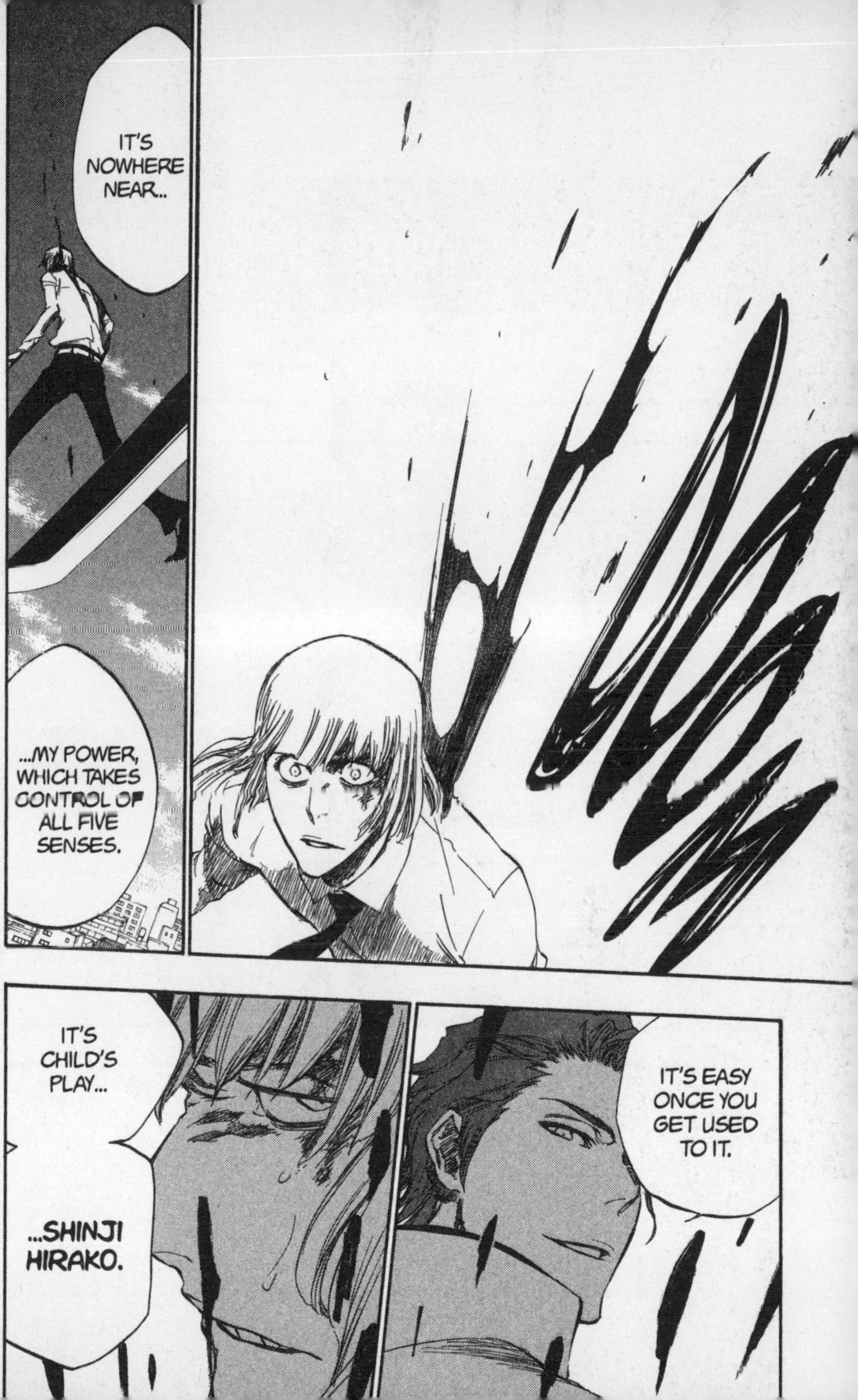
IT'S NOWHERE NEAR...
...MY POWER, WHICH TAKES CONTROL OF ALL FIVE SENSES.
IT'S EASY ONCE YOU GET USED TO IT.
IT'S CHILD'S PLAY...
...SHINJI HIRAKO.

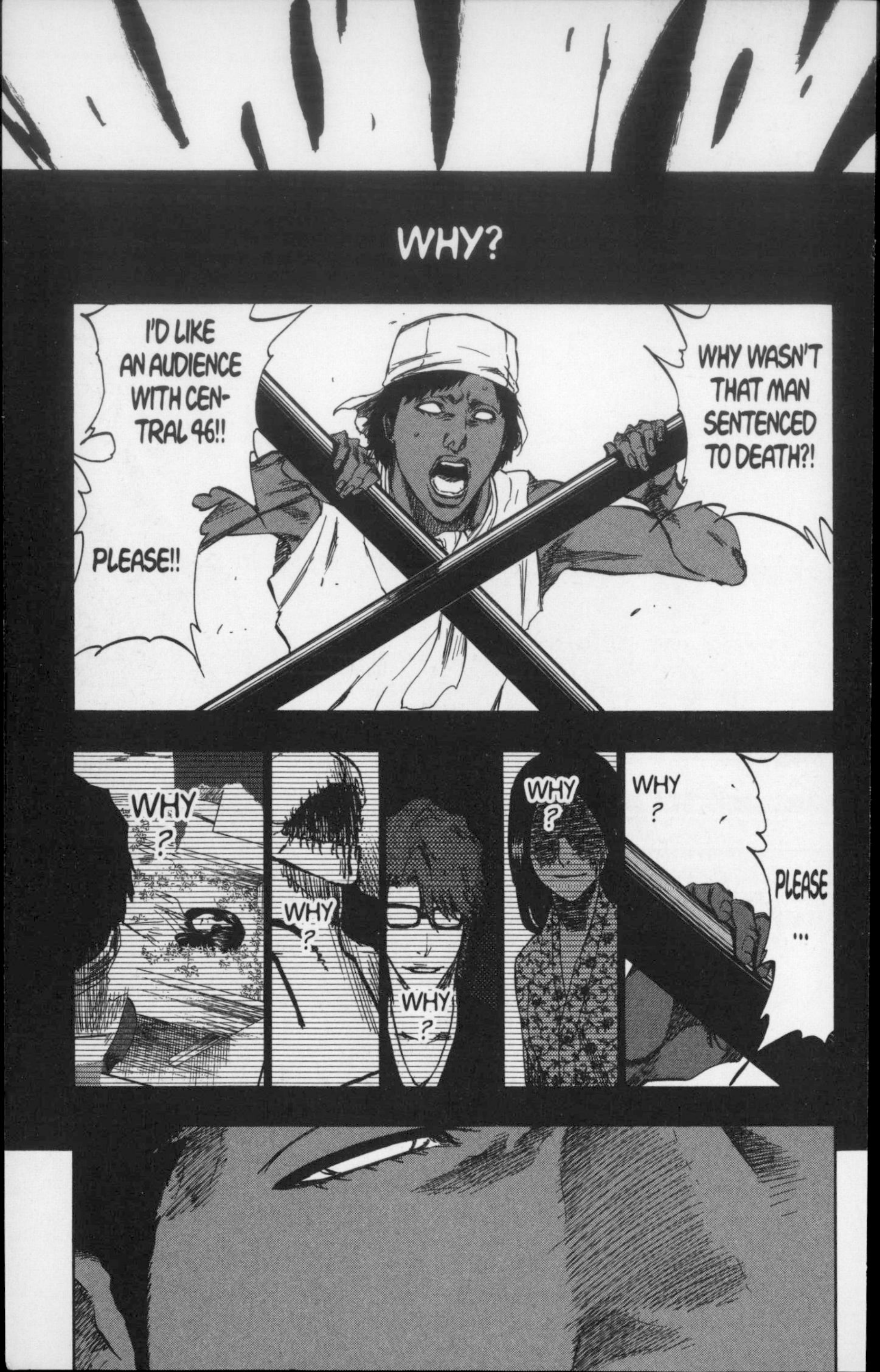
WHY?
WHY WASN'T THAT MAN SENTENCED TO DEATH?!
I'D LIKE AN AUDIENCE WITH CEN-TRAL 46!!
PLEASE!!
WHY ?
PLEASE ...
WHY ?
WHY ?
WHY ?
WHY ?

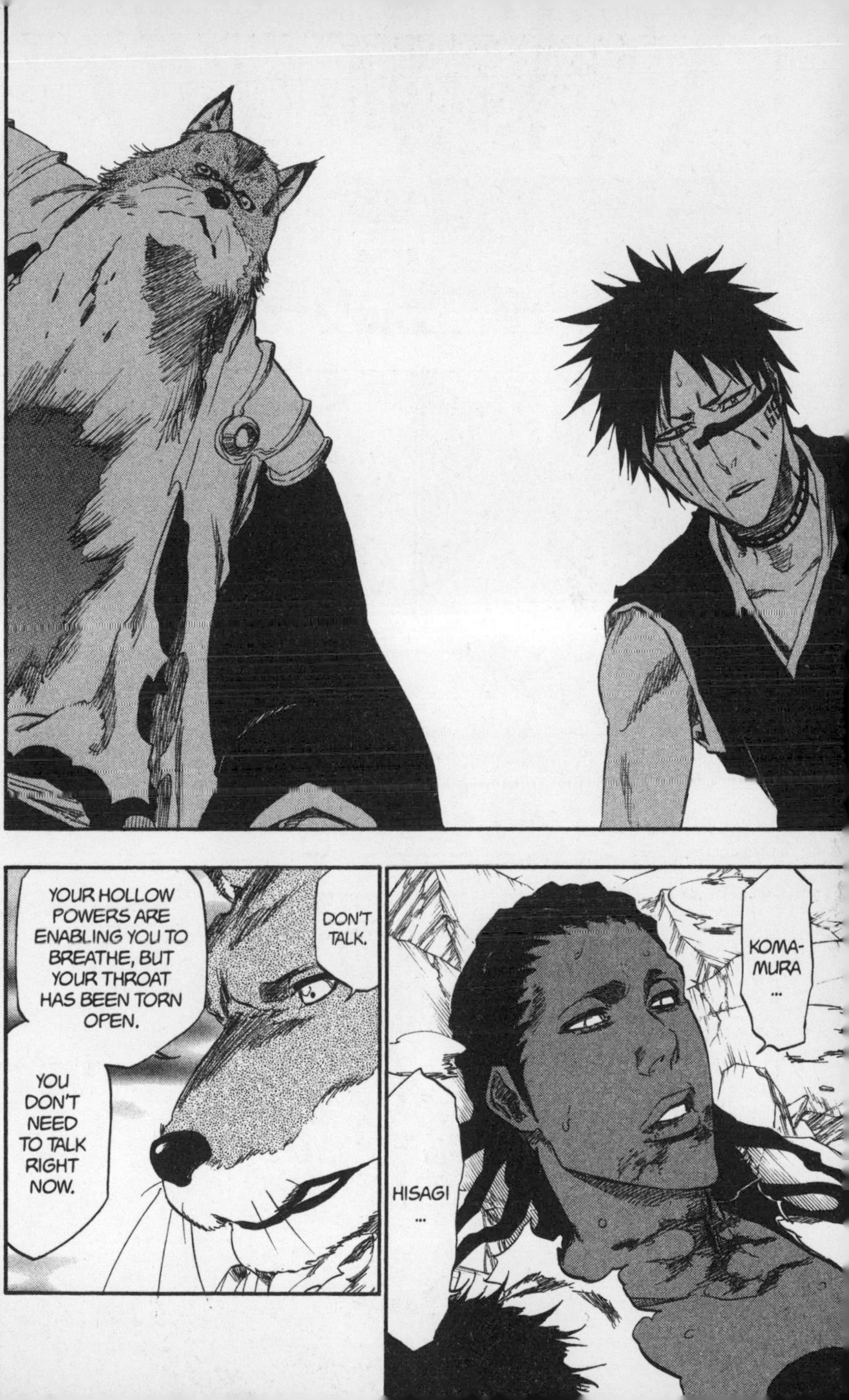
KOMAMURA...
HISAGI...
DON'T TALK.
YOUR HOLLOW POWERS ARE ENABLING YOU TO BREATHE, BUT YOUR THROAT HAS BEEN TORN OPEN.
YOU DON'T NEED TO TALK RIGHT NOW.

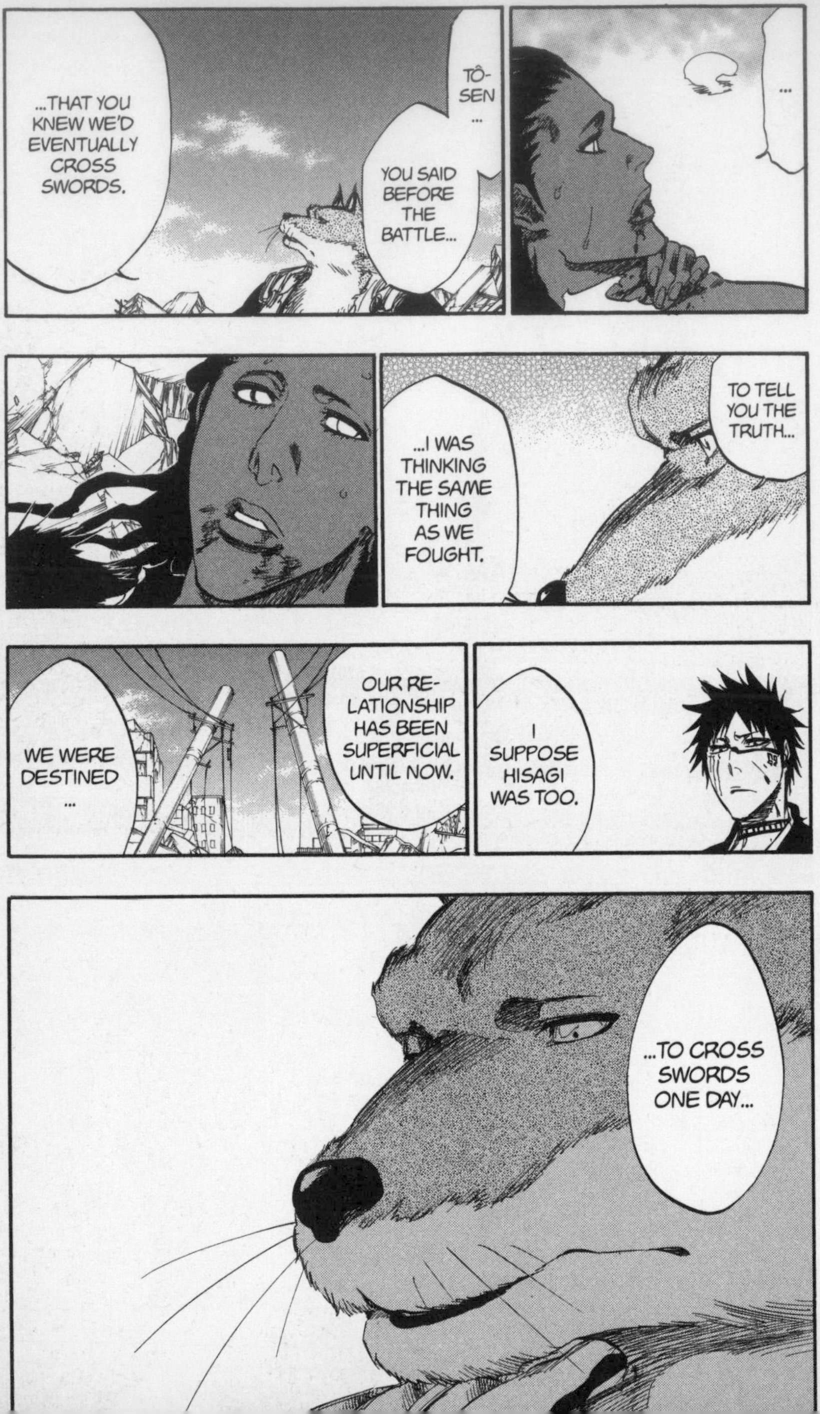
...
TÔ-SEN ...
YOU SAID BEFORE THE BATTLE...
...THAT YOU KNEW WE'D EVENTUALLY CROSS SWORDS.
TO TELL YOU THE TRUTH...
...I WAS THINKING THE SAME THING AS WE FOUGHT.
I SUPPOSE HISAGI WAS TOO.
OUR RELATIONSHIP HAS BEEN SUPERFICIAL UNTIL NOW.
WE WERE DESTINED ...
...TO CROSS SWORDS ONE DAY...

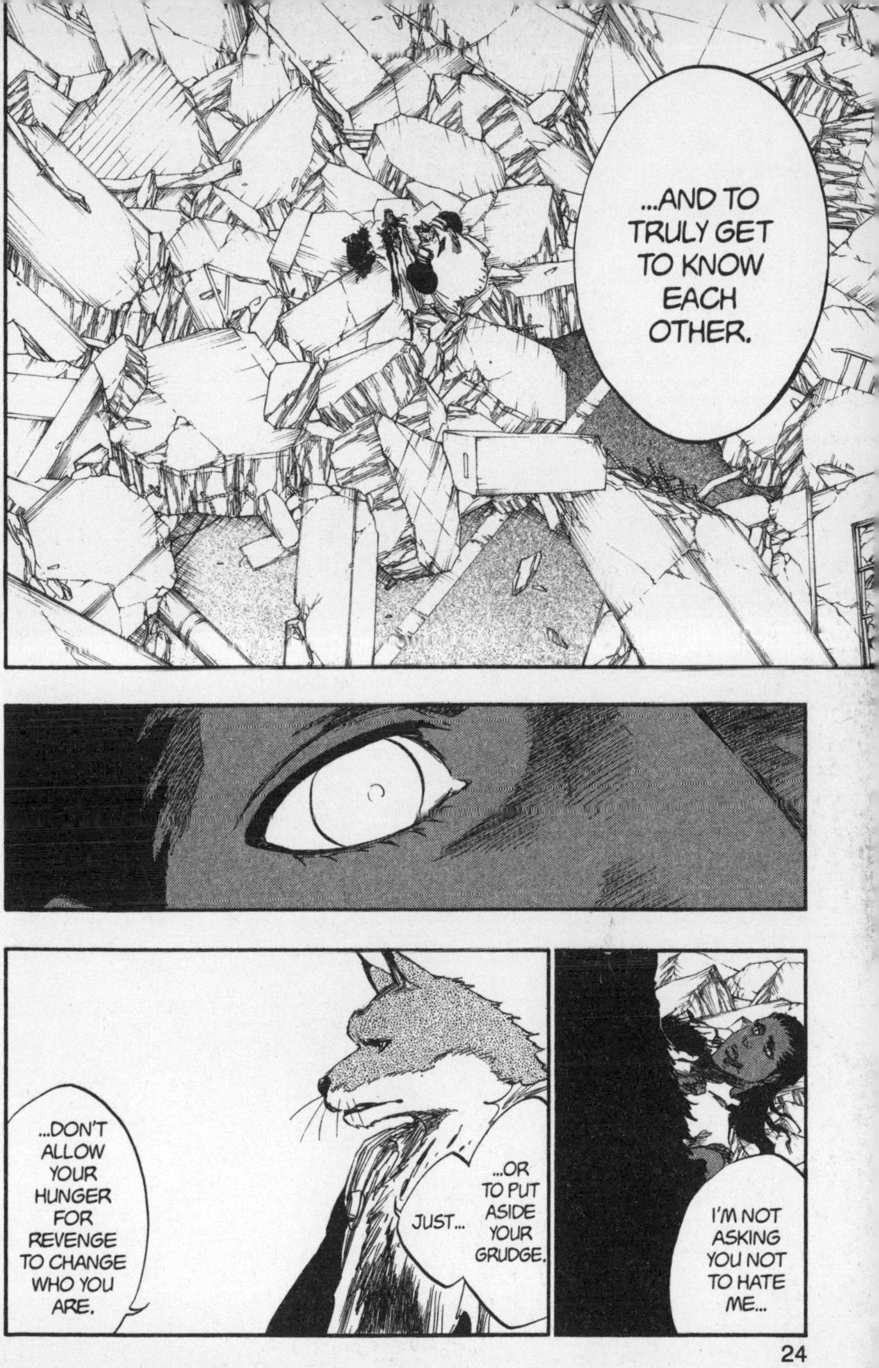
...AND TO TRULY GET TO KNOW EACH OTHER.
I'M NOT ASKING YOU NOT TO HATE ME...
...OR TO PUT ASIDE YOUR GRUDGE.
JUST...
...DON'T ALLOW YOUR HUNGER FOR REVENGE TO CHANGE WHO YOU ARE.

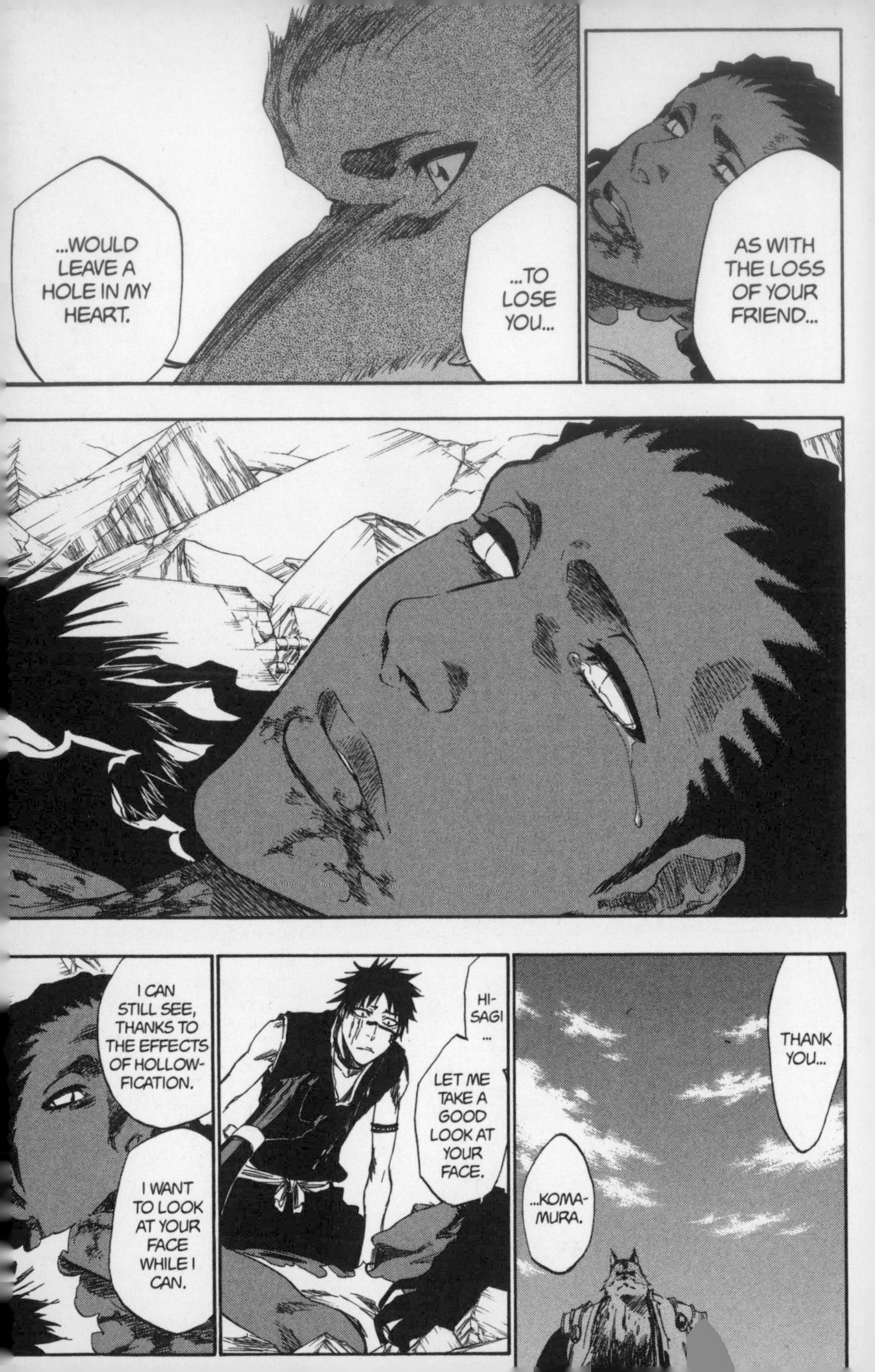
AS WITH THE LOSS OF YOUR FRIEND...
...TO LOSE YOU...
...WOULD LEAVE A HOLE IN MY HEART.
THANK YOU...
...KOMAMURA.
HI-SAGI...
LET ME TAKE A GOOD LOOK AT YOUR FACE.
I CAN STILL SEE, THANKS TO THE EFFECTS OF HOLLOW-FICATION.
I WANT TO LOOK AT YOUR FACE WHILE I CAN.

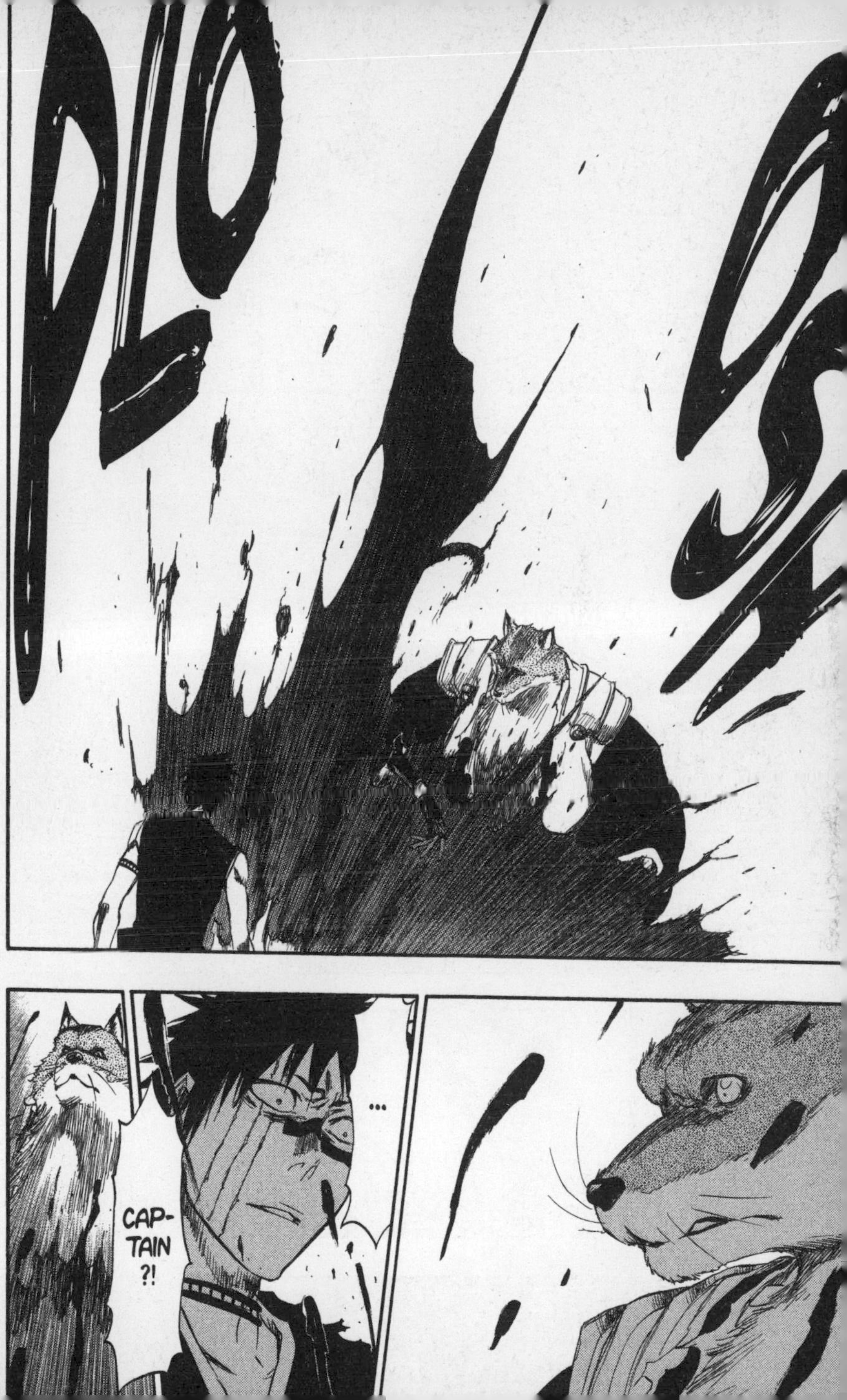
...
CAP-TAIN ?!

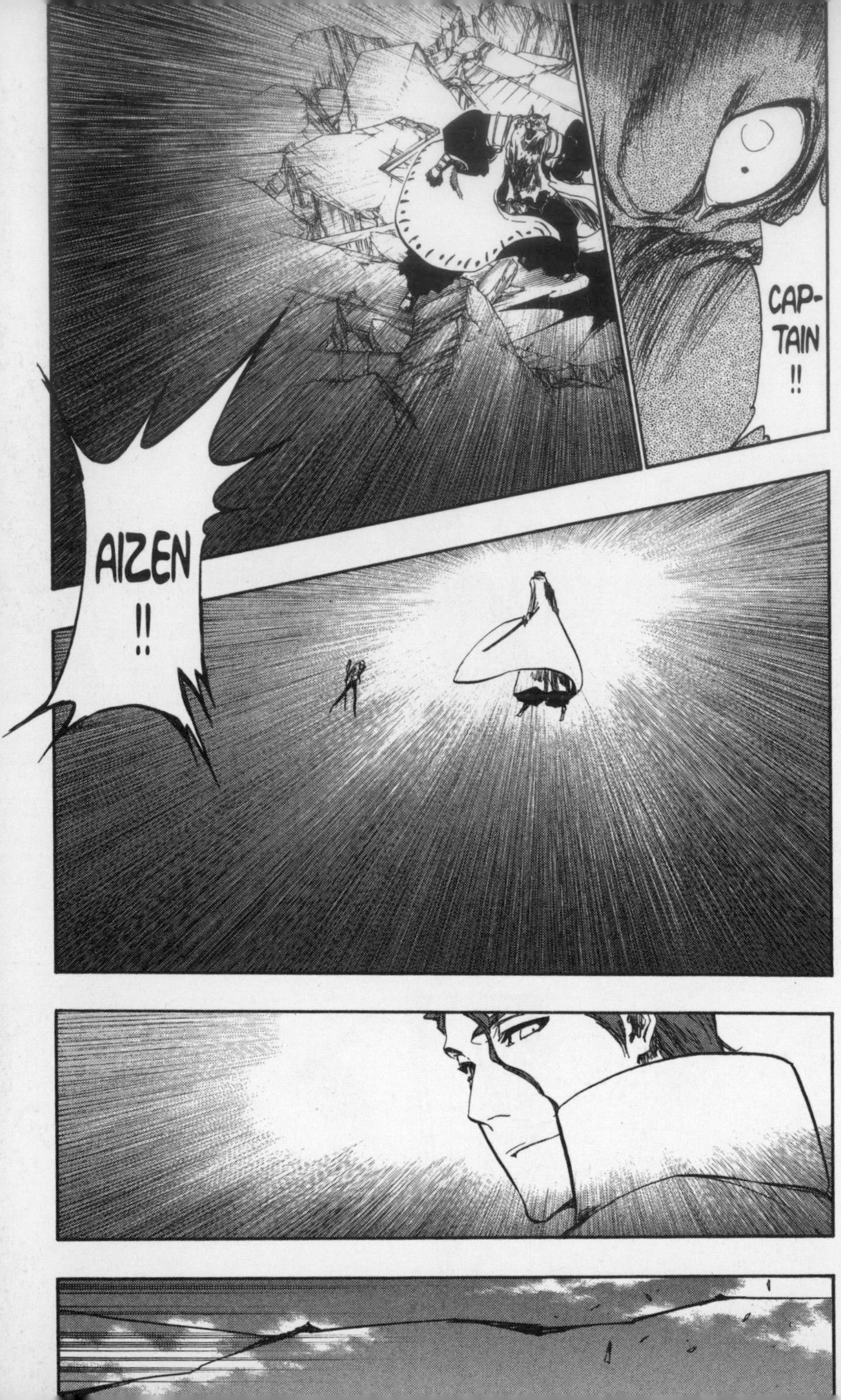
CAP-
TAIN
!!
AIZEN
!!

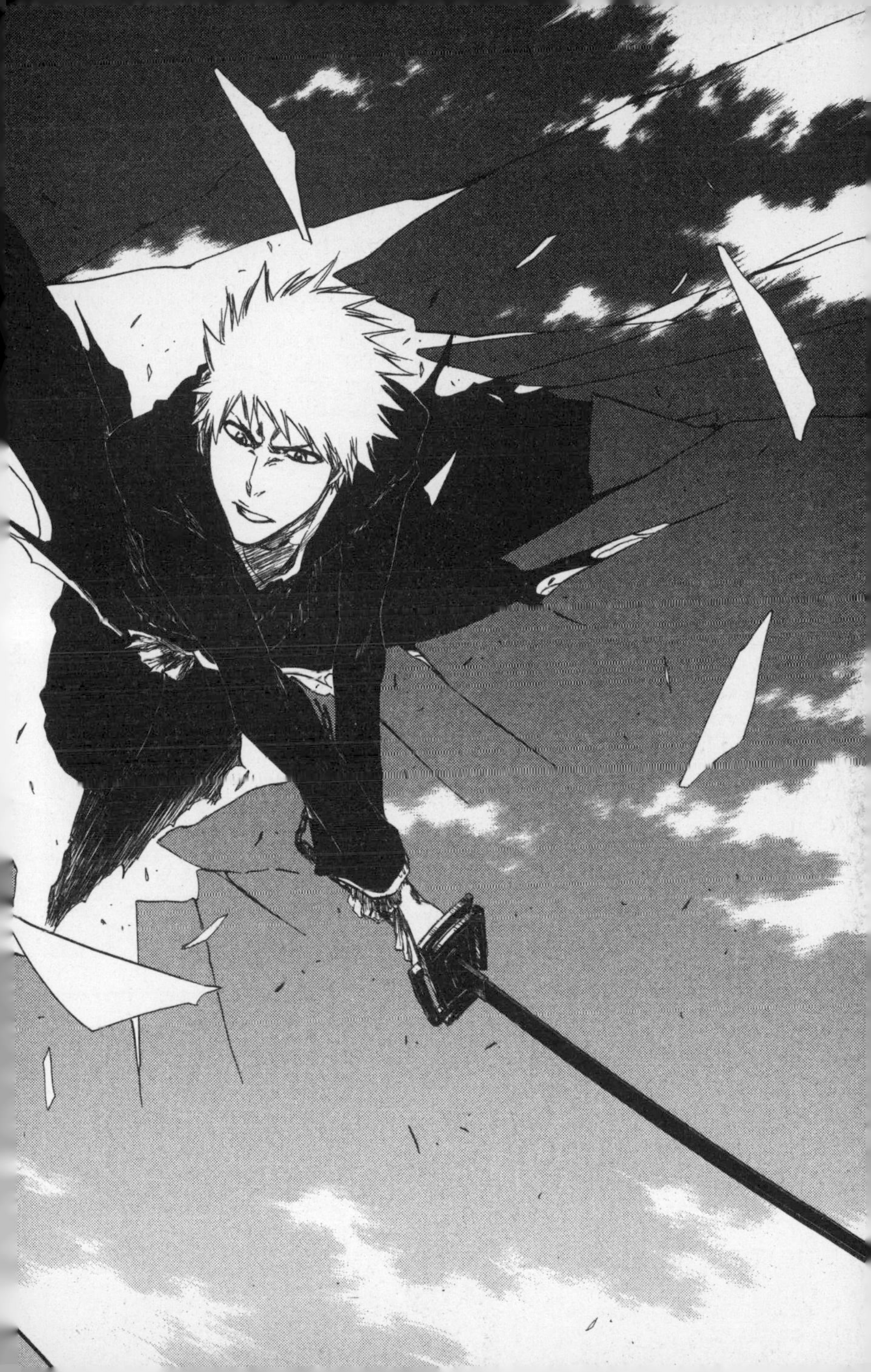

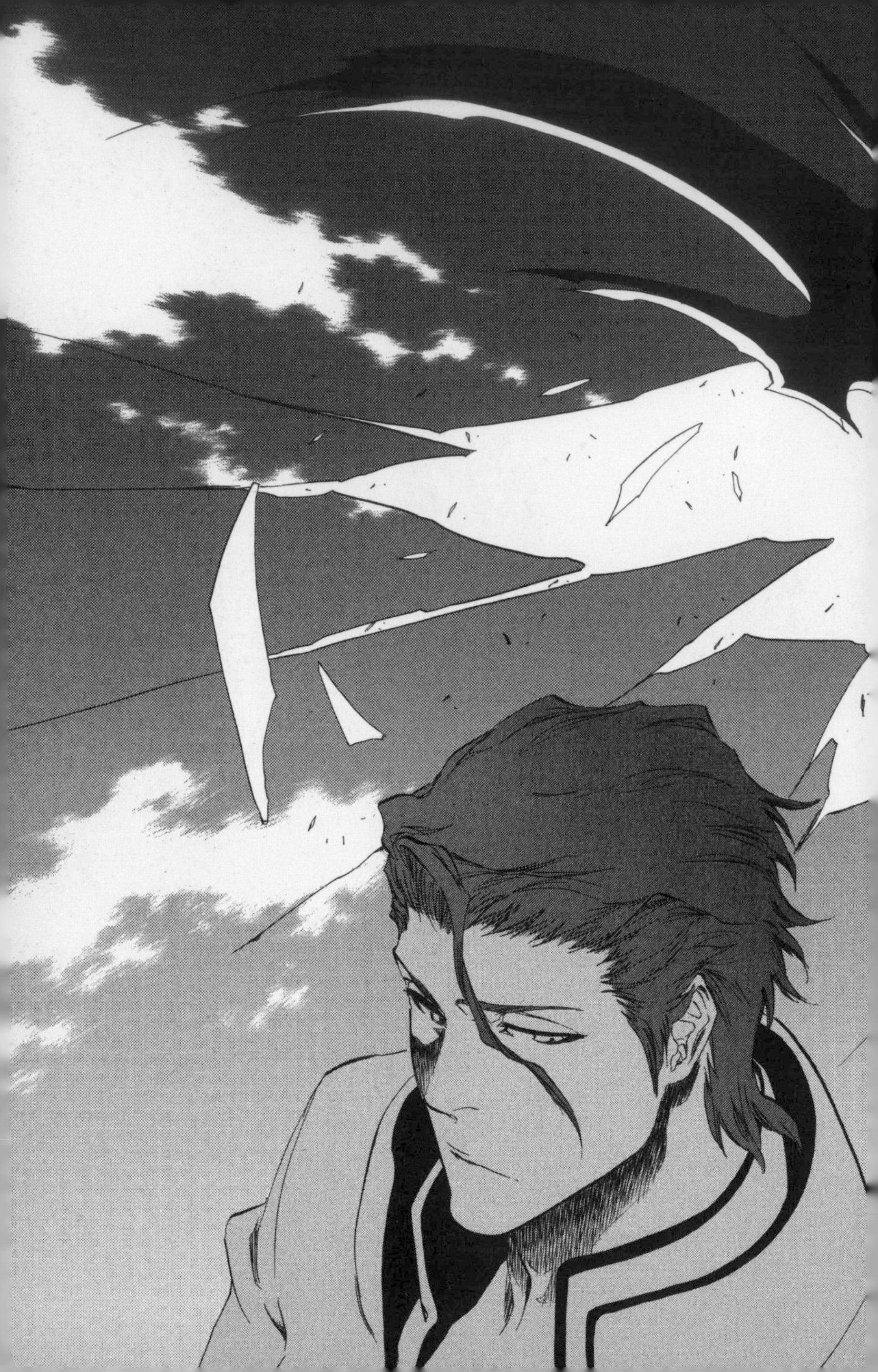

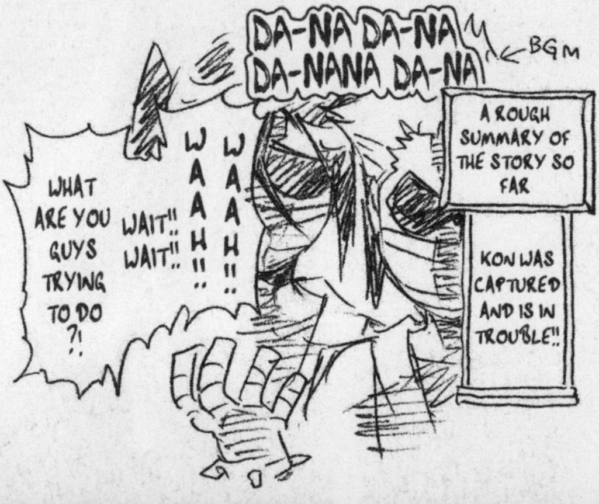
BGM
DA-NA DA-NA DA-NANA DA-NA
A ROUGH SUMMARY OF THE STORY SO FAR
KON WAS CAPTURED AND IS IN TROUBLE!!
WAAAH!!
WAAAH!!
WAIT!! WAIT!!
WHAT ARE YOU GUYS TRYING TO DO?!

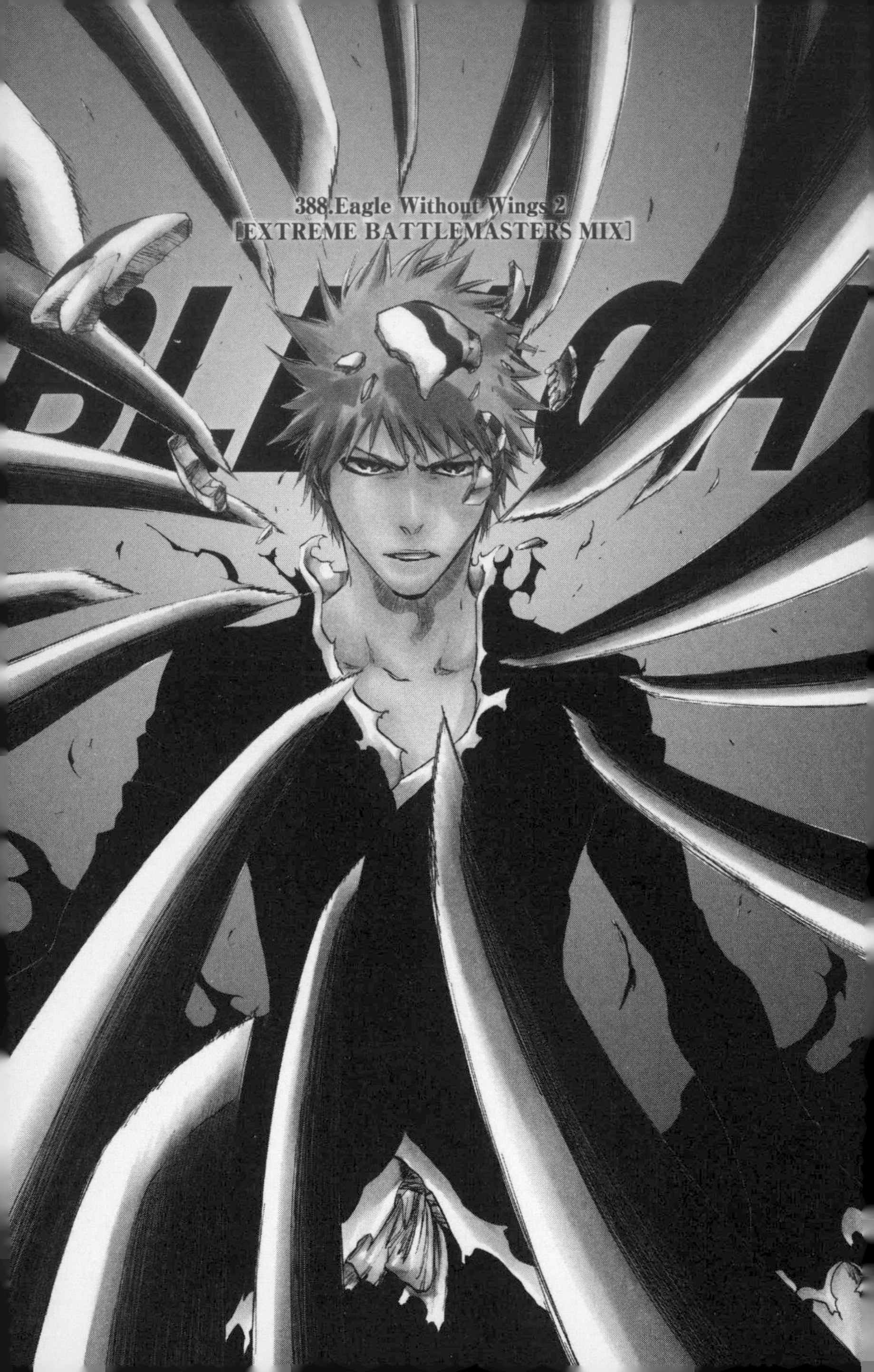
388.Eagle Without Wings 2
[EXTREME BATTLEMASTERS MIX]
BLEACH

BLEACH
ブリーチ

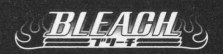

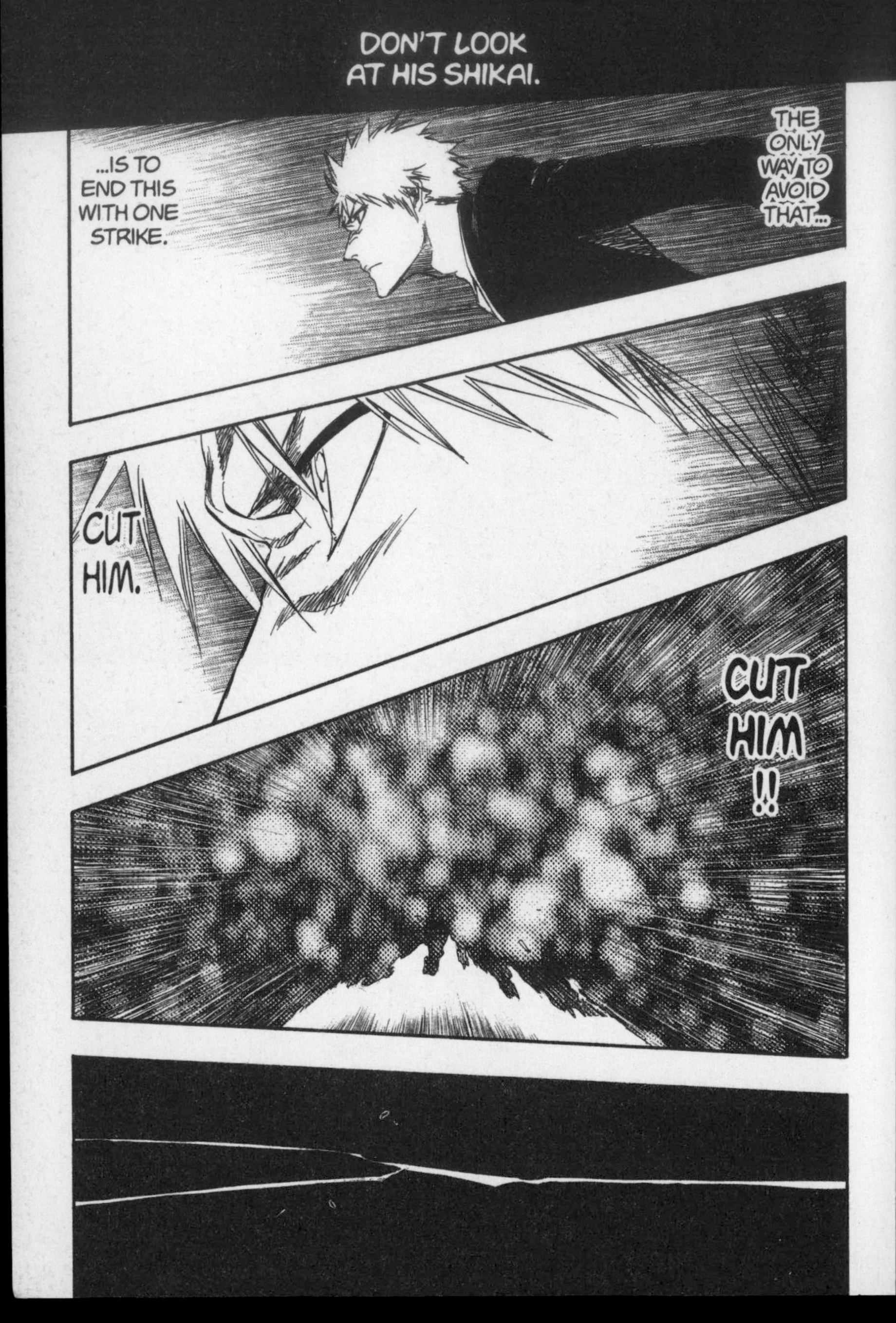
DON'T LOOK AT HIS SHIKAI.
THE ONLY WAY TO AVOID THAT...
...IS TO END THIS WITH ONE STRIKE.
CUT HIM.
CUT HIM !!

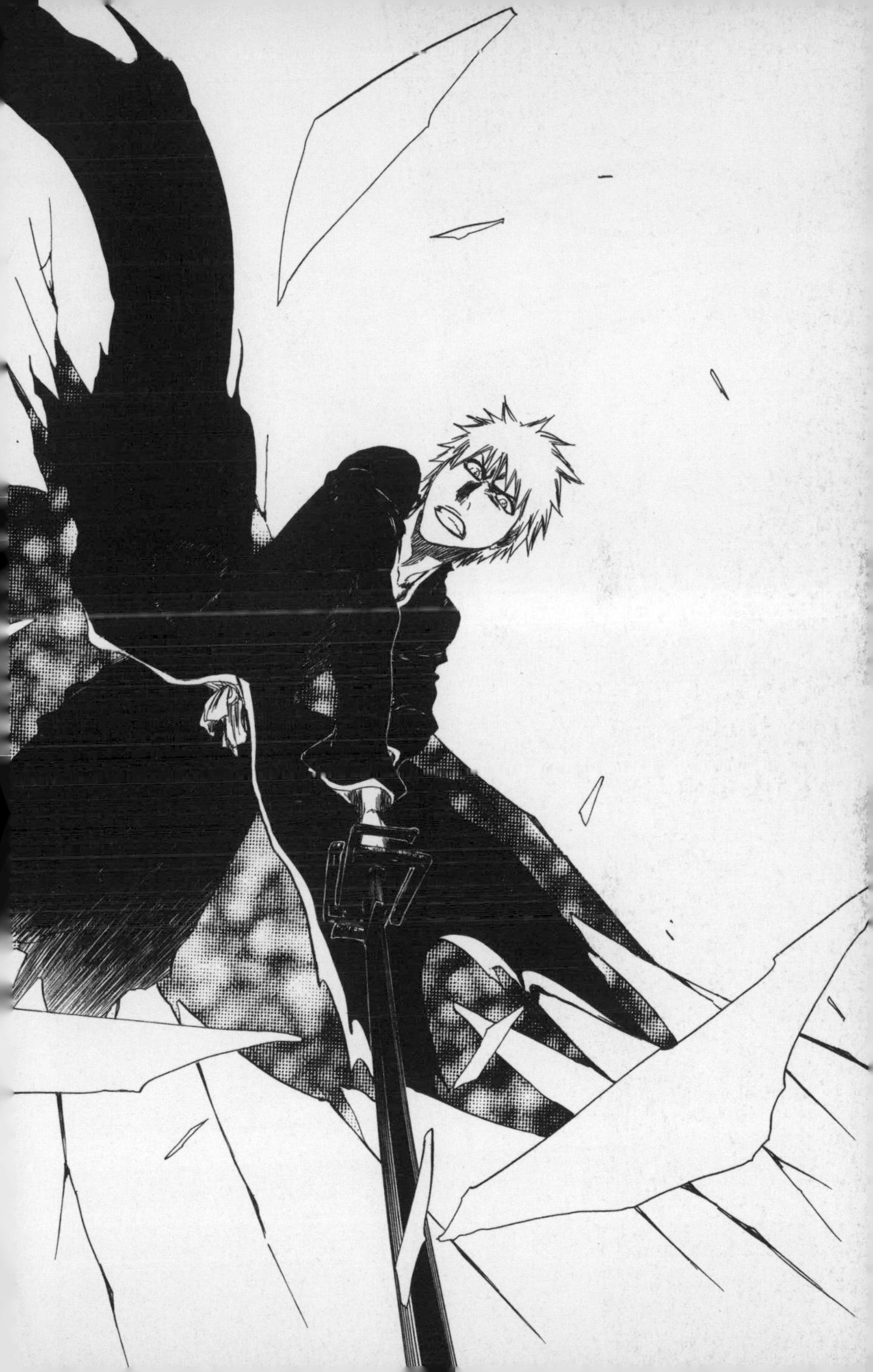

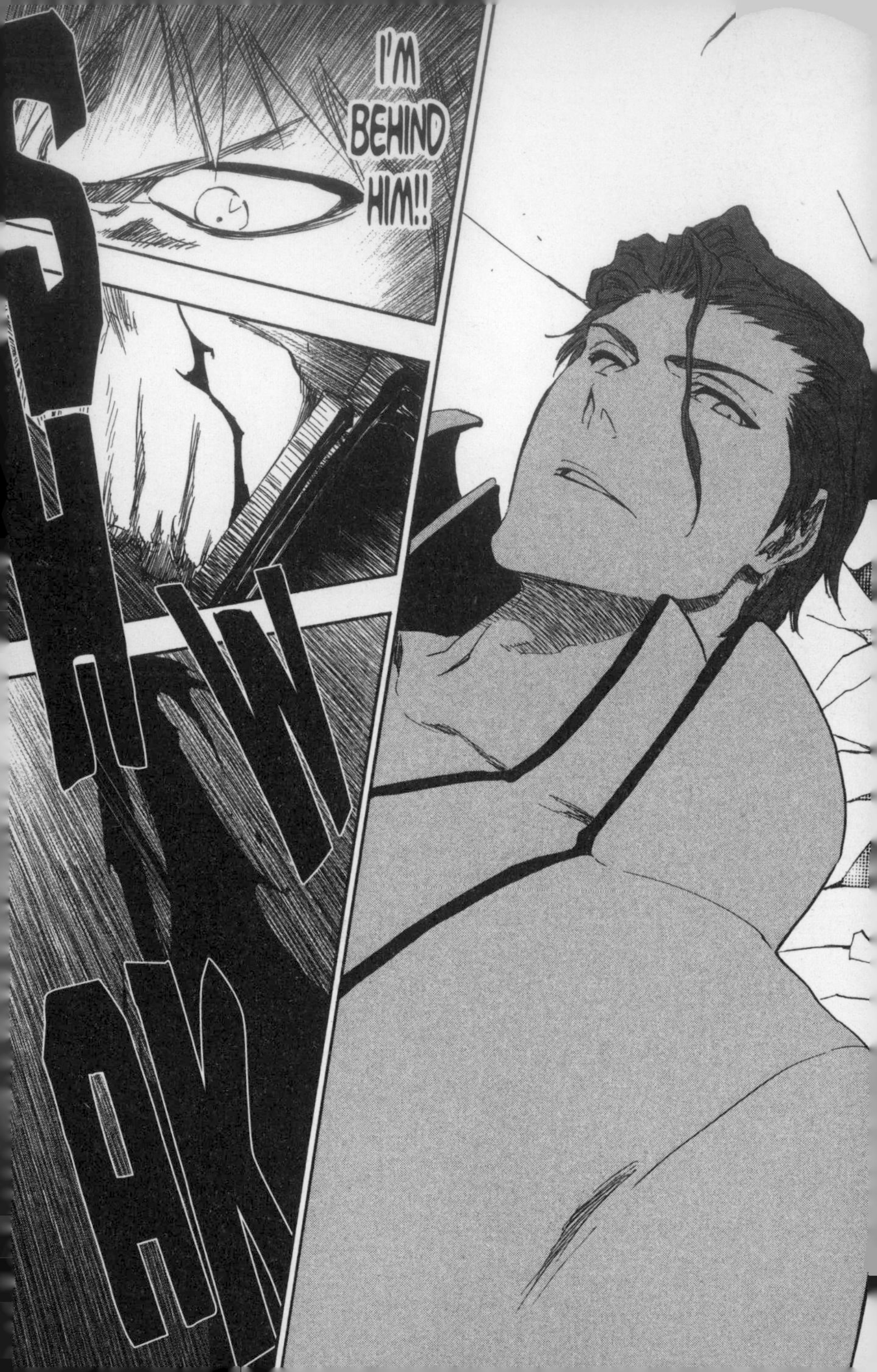
I'M BEHIND HIM!!

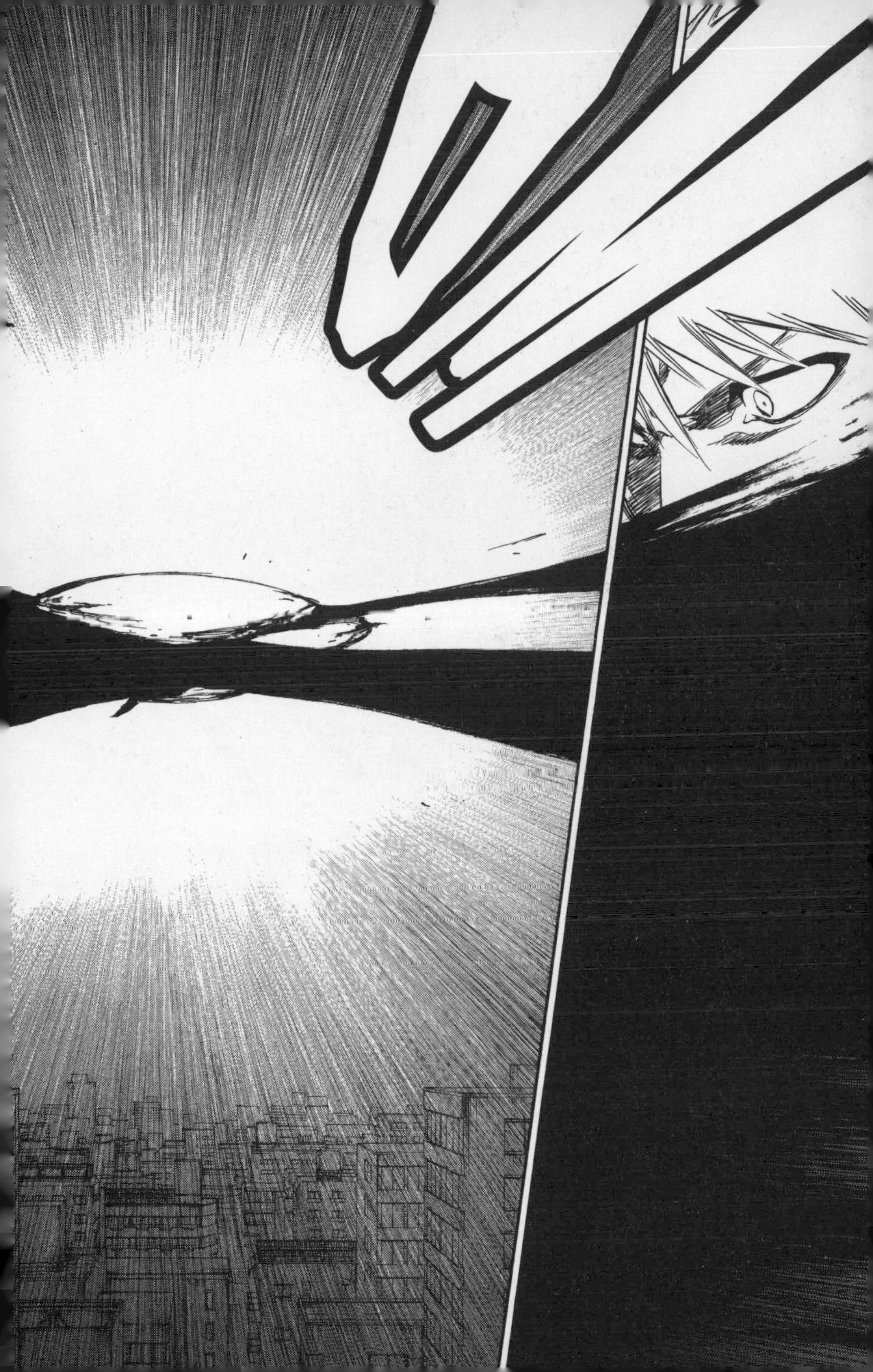

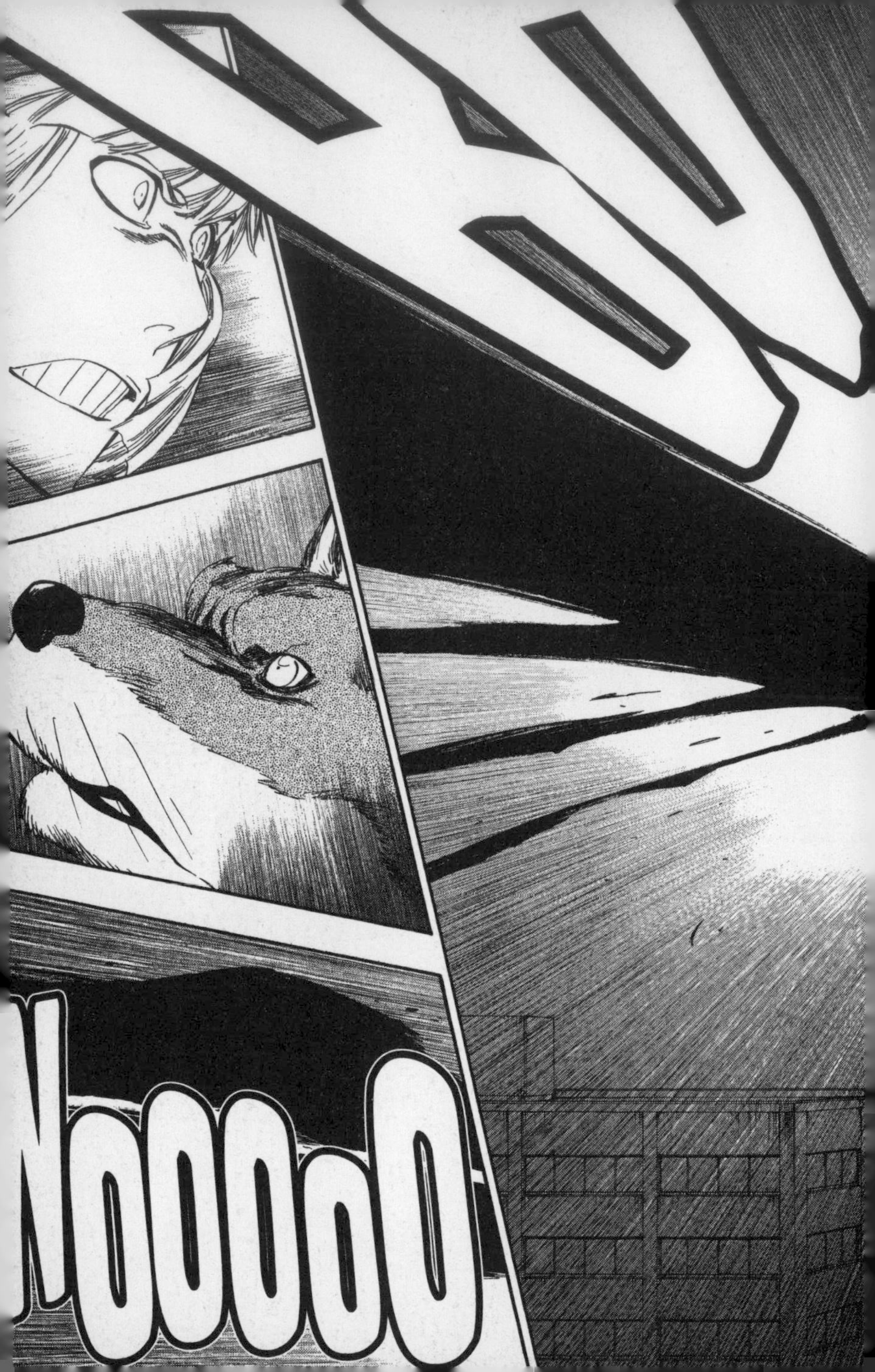
NOOOOO

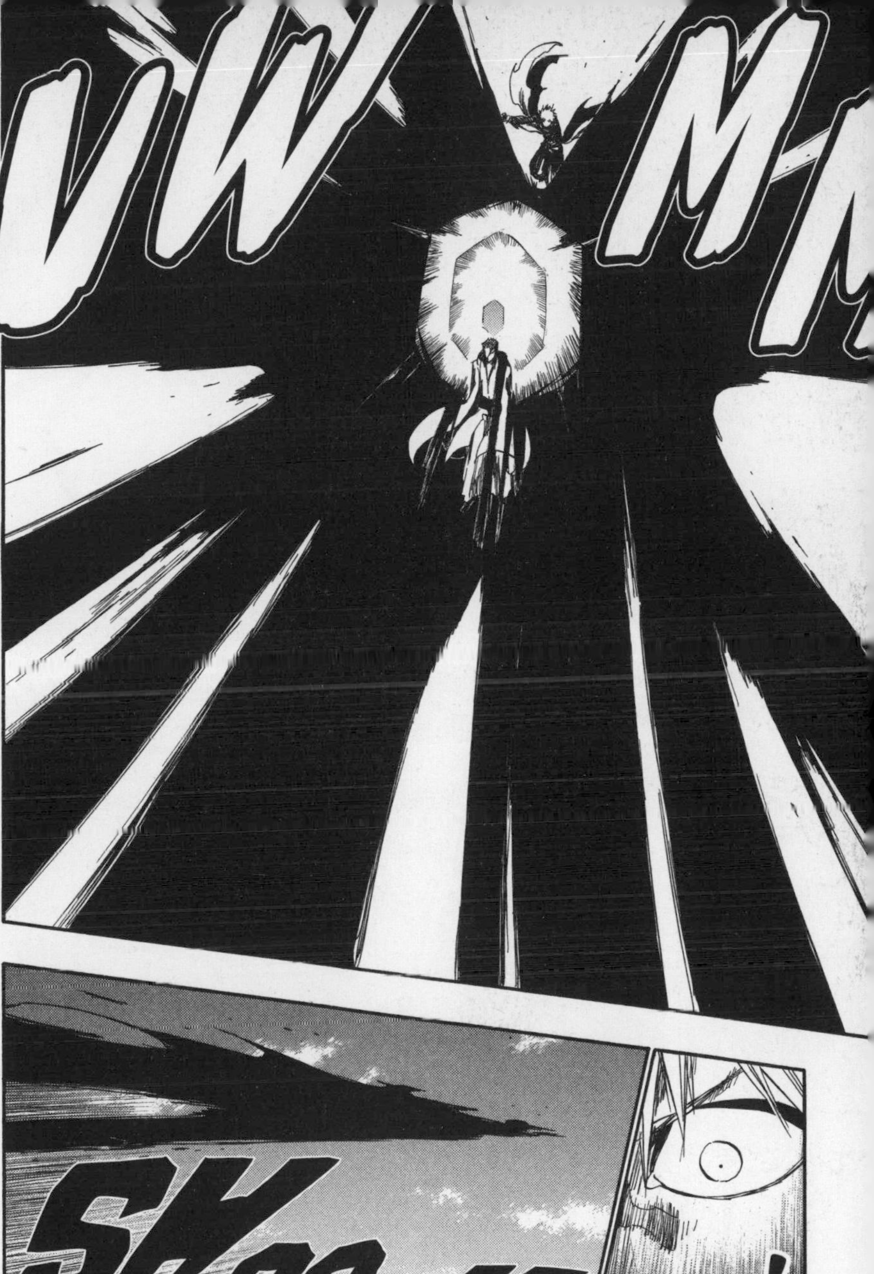
!
SHOOM

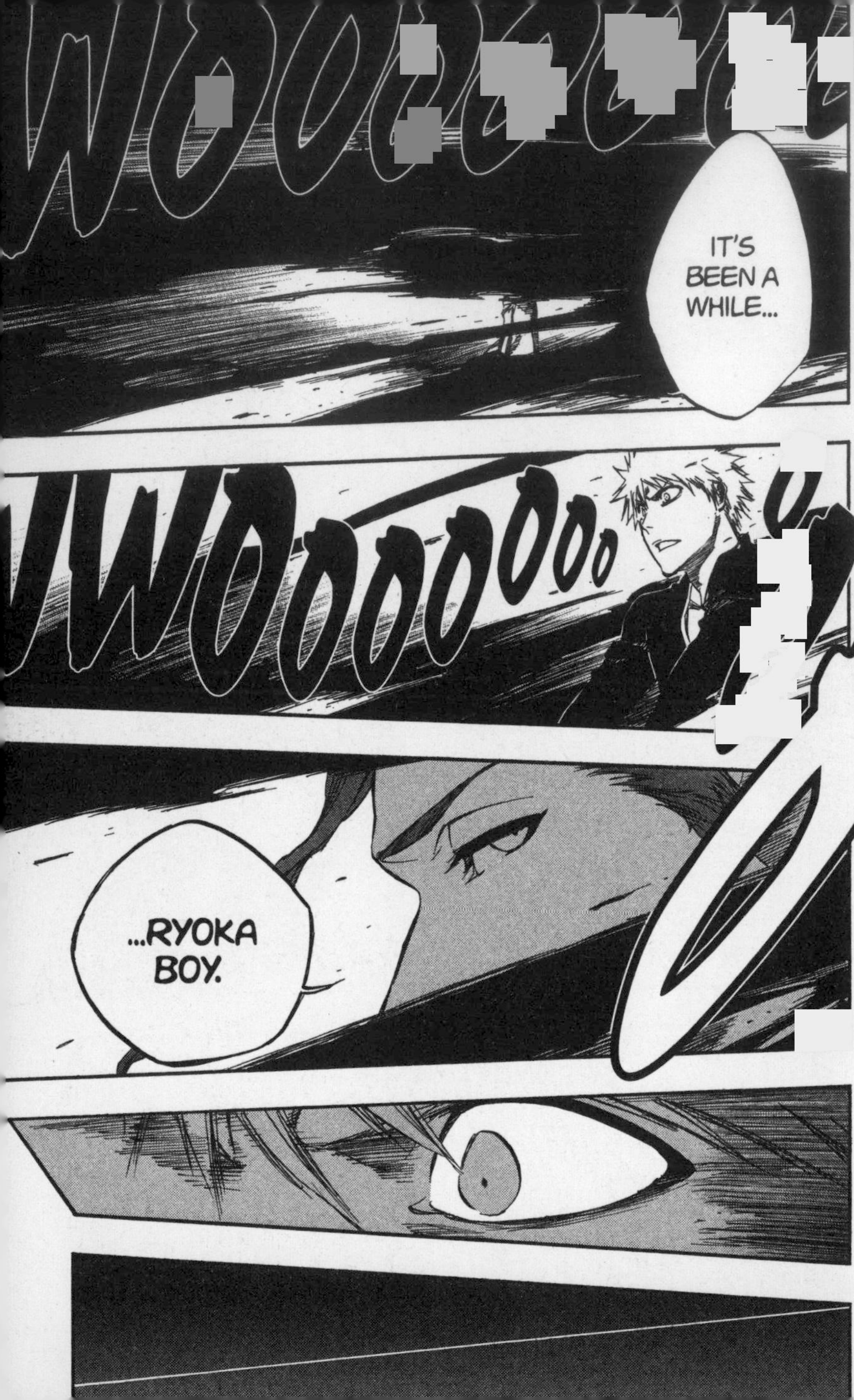
IT'S BEEN A WHILE...
...RYOKA BOY.

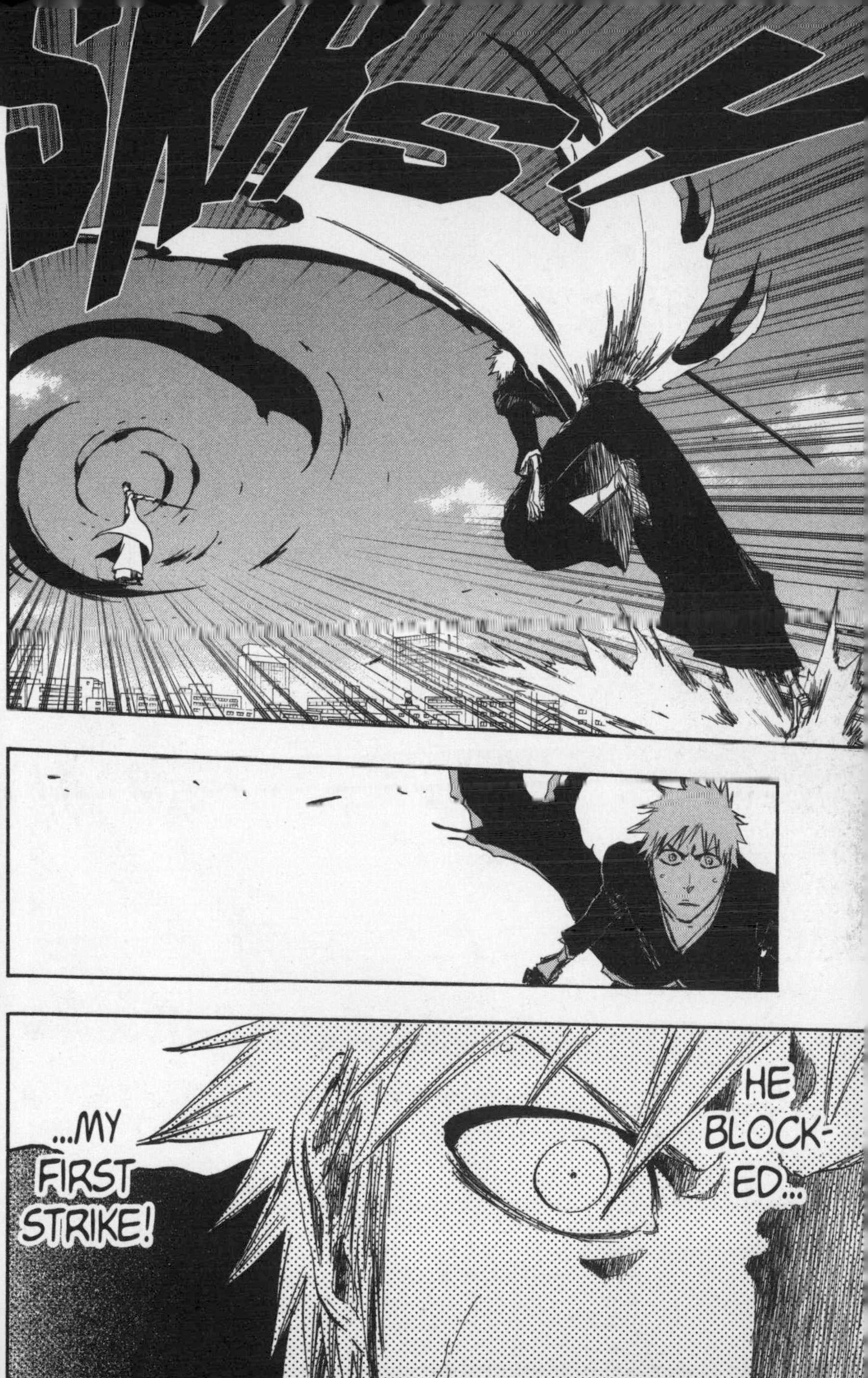
HE BLOCK-ED...
...MY FIRST STRIKE!

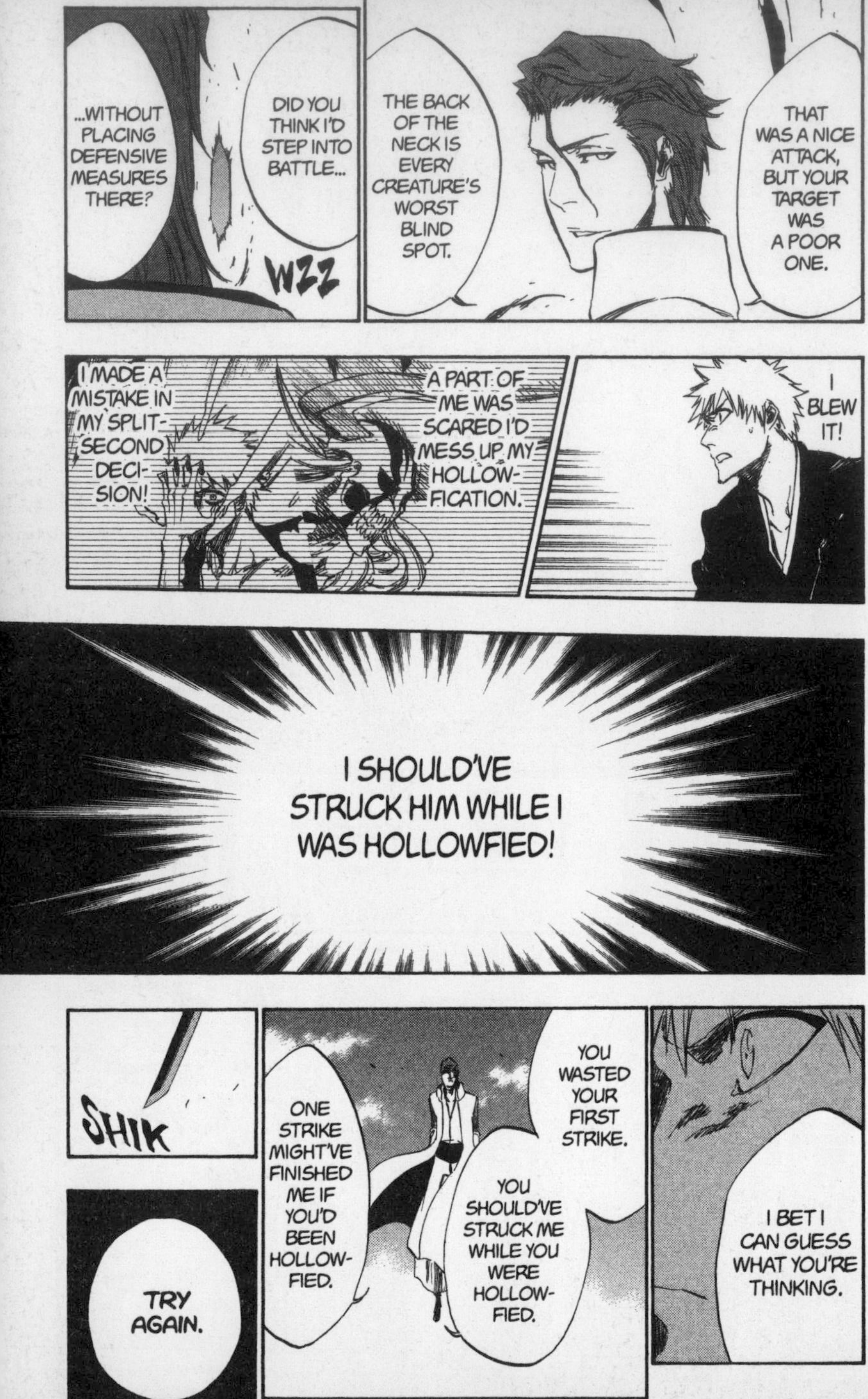
THAT WAS A NICE ATTACK, BUT YOUR TARGET WAS A POOR ONE.
THE BACK OF THE NECK IS EVERY CREATURE'S WORST BLIND SPOT.
DID YOU THINK I'D STEP INTO BATTLE...
...WITHOUT PLACING DEFENSIVE MEASURES THERE?
WZZ
I BLEW IT!
A PART OF ME WAS SCARED I'D MESS UP MY HOLLOWFICATION.
I MADE A MISTAKE IN MY SPLIT-SECOND DECISION!
I SHOULD'VE STRUCK HIM WHILE I WAS HOLLOWFIED!
I BET I CAN GUESS WHAT YOU'RE THINKING.
YOU WASTED YOUR FIRST STRIKE.
YOU SHOULD'VE STRUCK ME WHILE YOU WERE HOLLOWFIED.
ONE STRIKE MIGHT'VE FINISHED ME IF YOU'D BEEN HOLLOWFIED.
SHIK
TRY AGAIN.

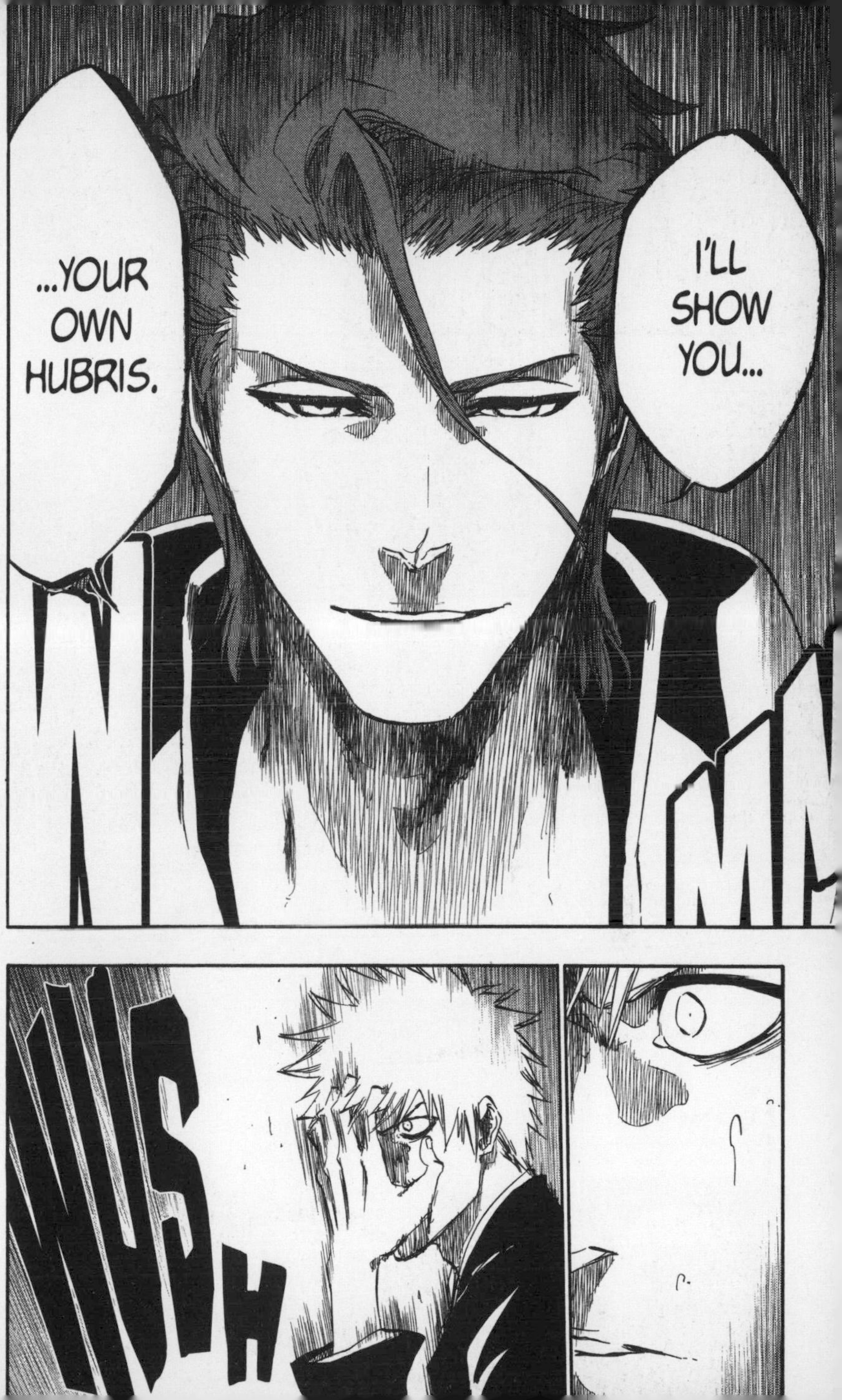
I'LL SHOW YOU...
...YOUR OWN HUBRIS.

READ THIS WAY

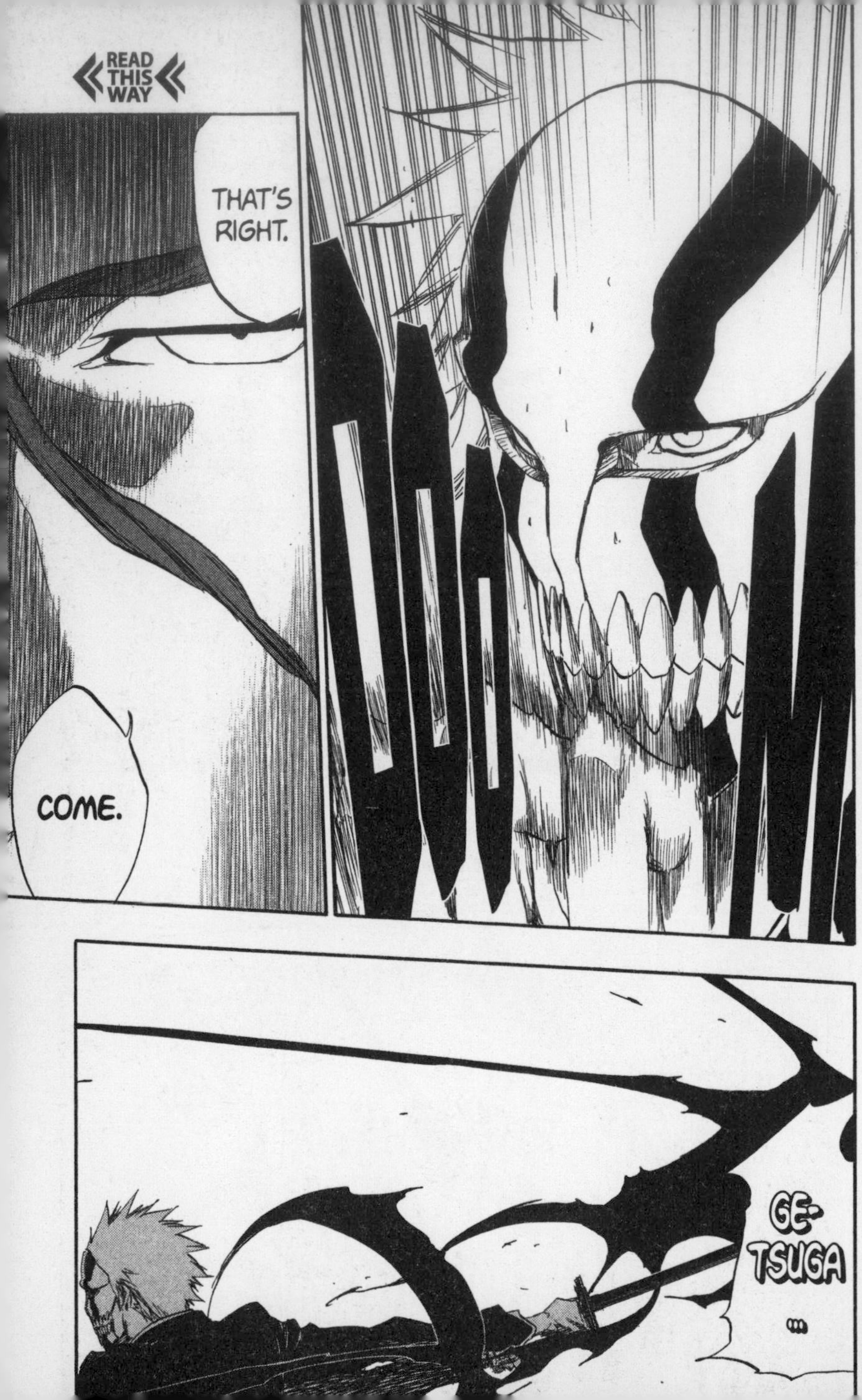
THAT'S RIGHT.
COME.
GE-TSUGA
...

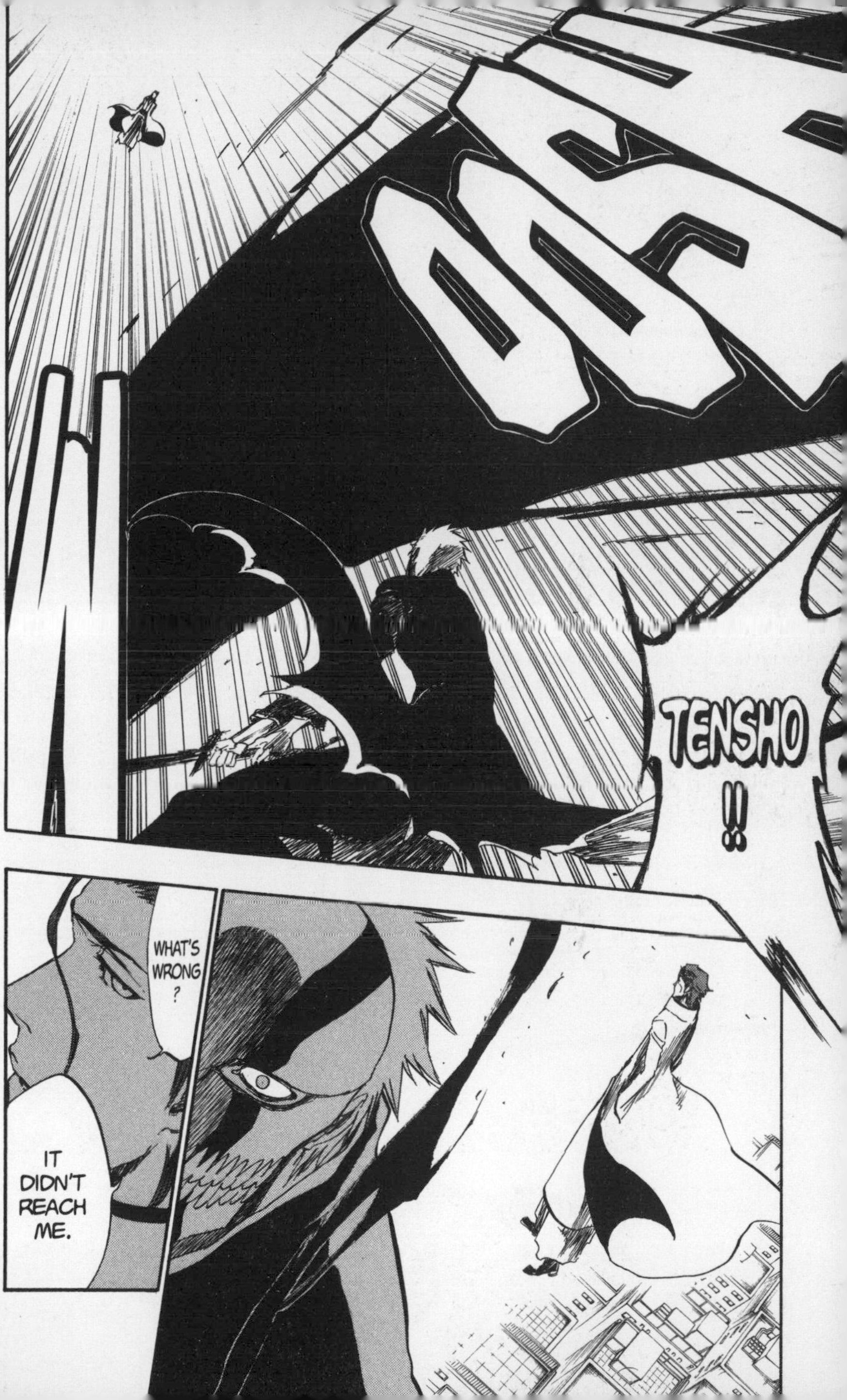
TENSHO !!
WHAT'S WRONG?
IT DIDN'T REACH ME.

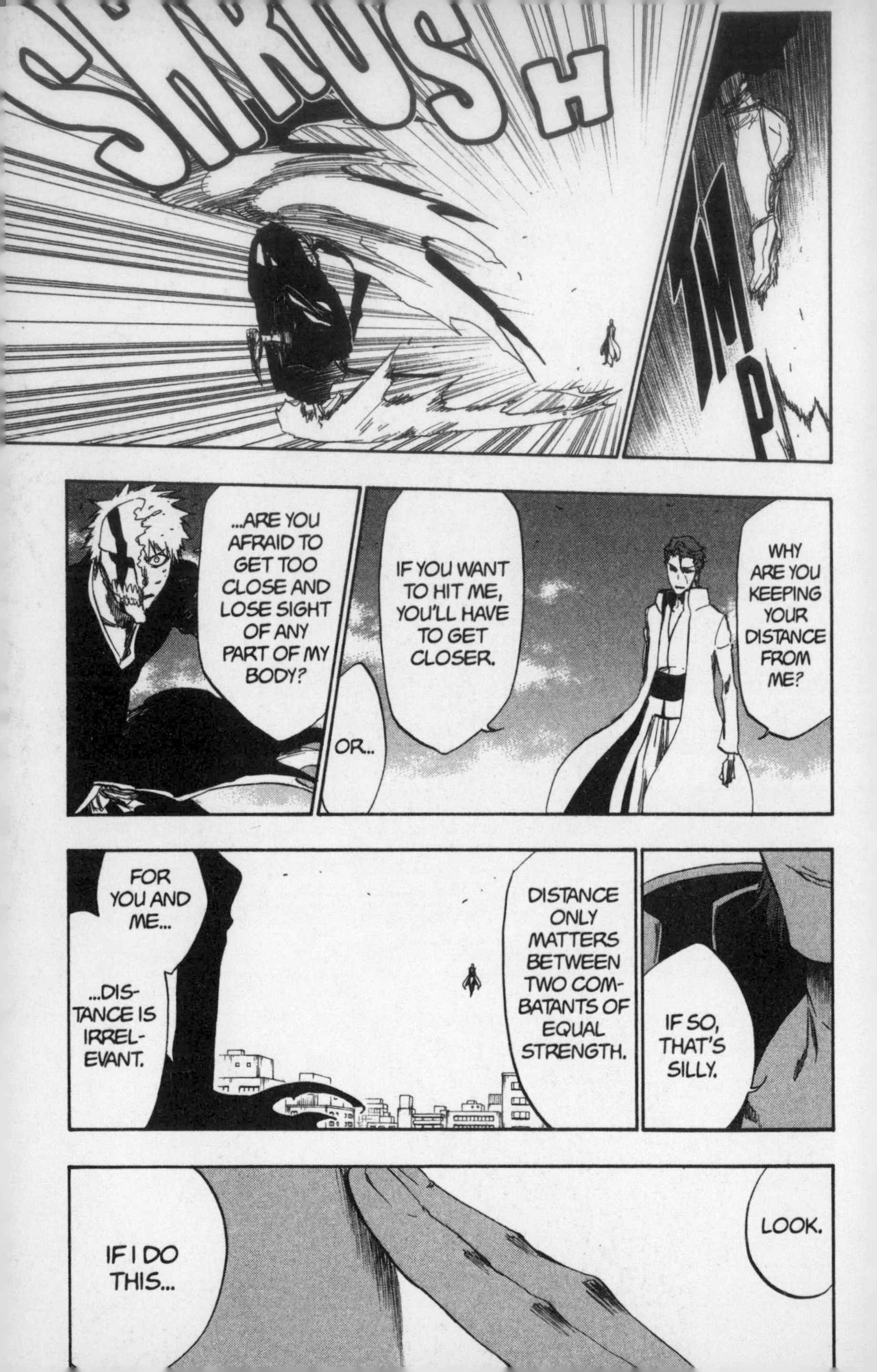
WHY ARE YOU KEEPING YOUR DISTANCE FROM ME?
IF YOU WANT TO HIT ME, YOU'LL HAVE TO GET CLOSER.
OR..
...ARE YOU AFRAID TO GET TOO CLOSE AND LOSE SIGHT OF ANY PART OF MY BODY?
IF SO, THAT'S SILLY.
DISTANCE ONLY MATTERS BETWEEN TWO COM-BATANTS OF EQUAL STRENGTH.
FOR YOU AND ME...
...DIS-TANCE IS IRREL-EVANT.
LOOK.
IF I DO THIS...

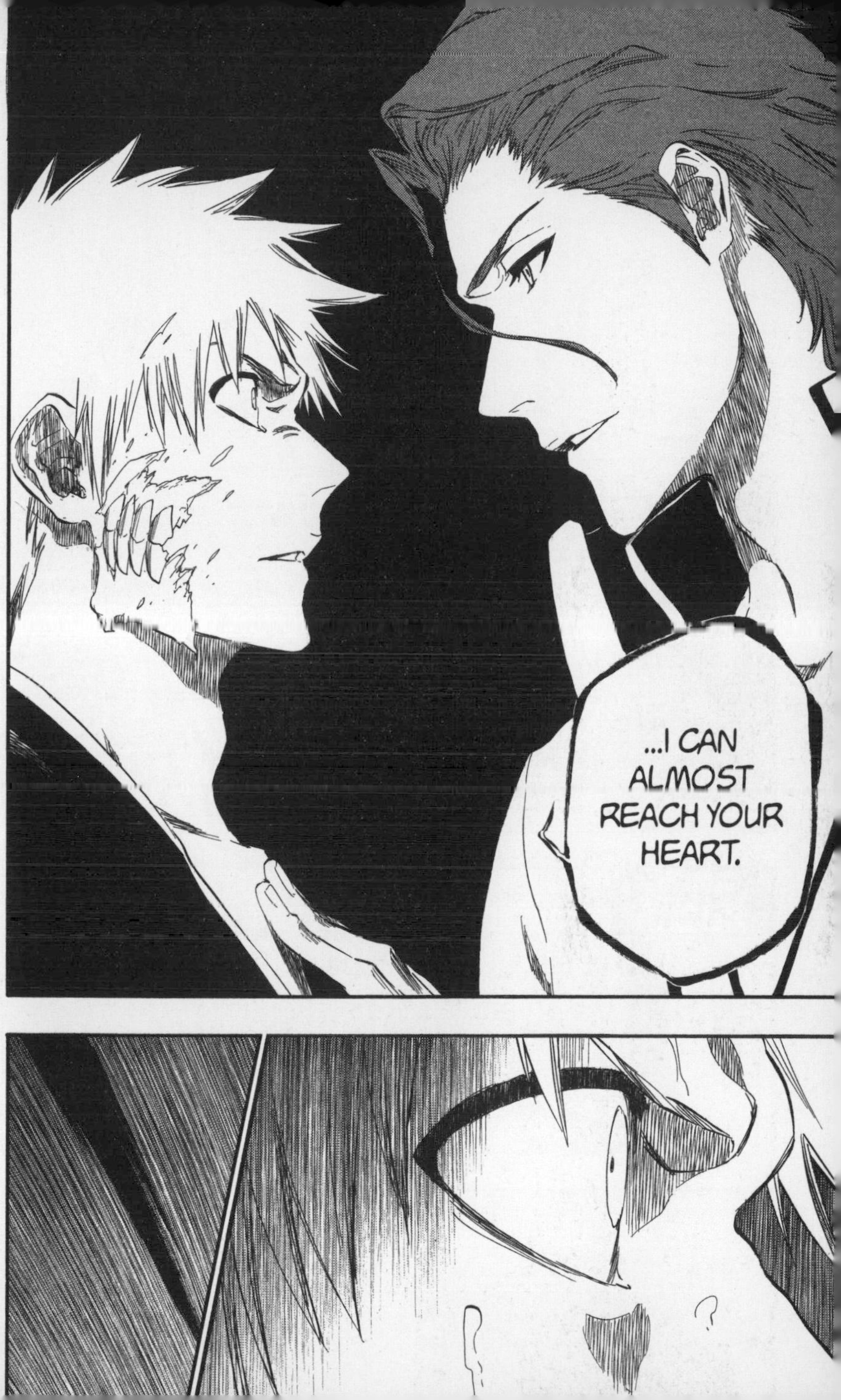
...I CAN ALMOST REACH YOUR HEART.

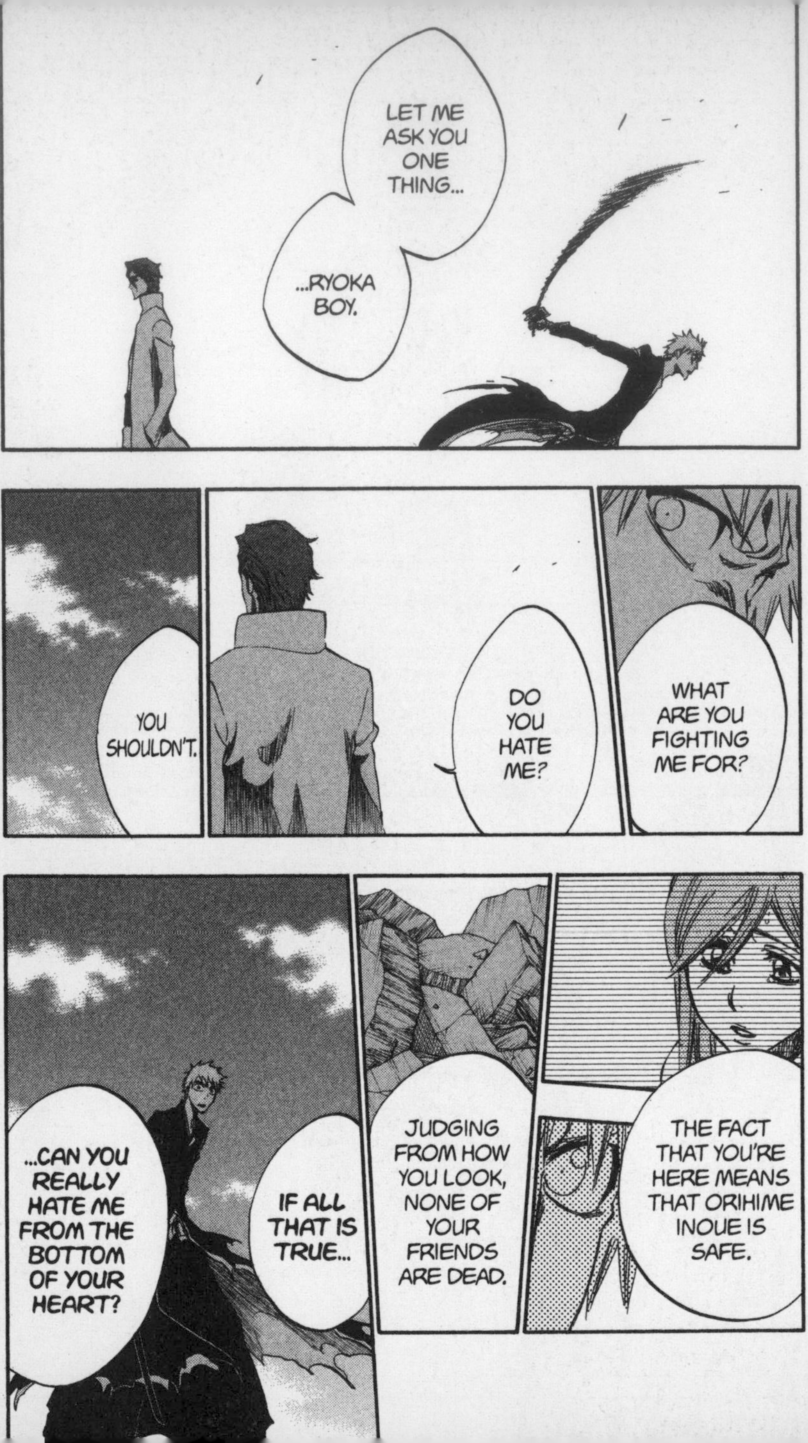
LET ME ASK YOU ONE THING...
...RYOKA BOY.
WHAT ARE YOU FIGHTING ME FOR?
DO YOU HATE ME?
YOU SHOULDN'T.
THE FACT THAT YOU'RE HERE MEANS THAT ORIHIME INOUE IS SAFE.
JUDGING FROM HOW YOU LOOK, NONE OF YOUR FRIENDS ARE DEAD.
IF ALL THAT IS TRUE...
...CAN YOU REALLY HATE ME FROM THE BOTTOM OF YOUR HEART?

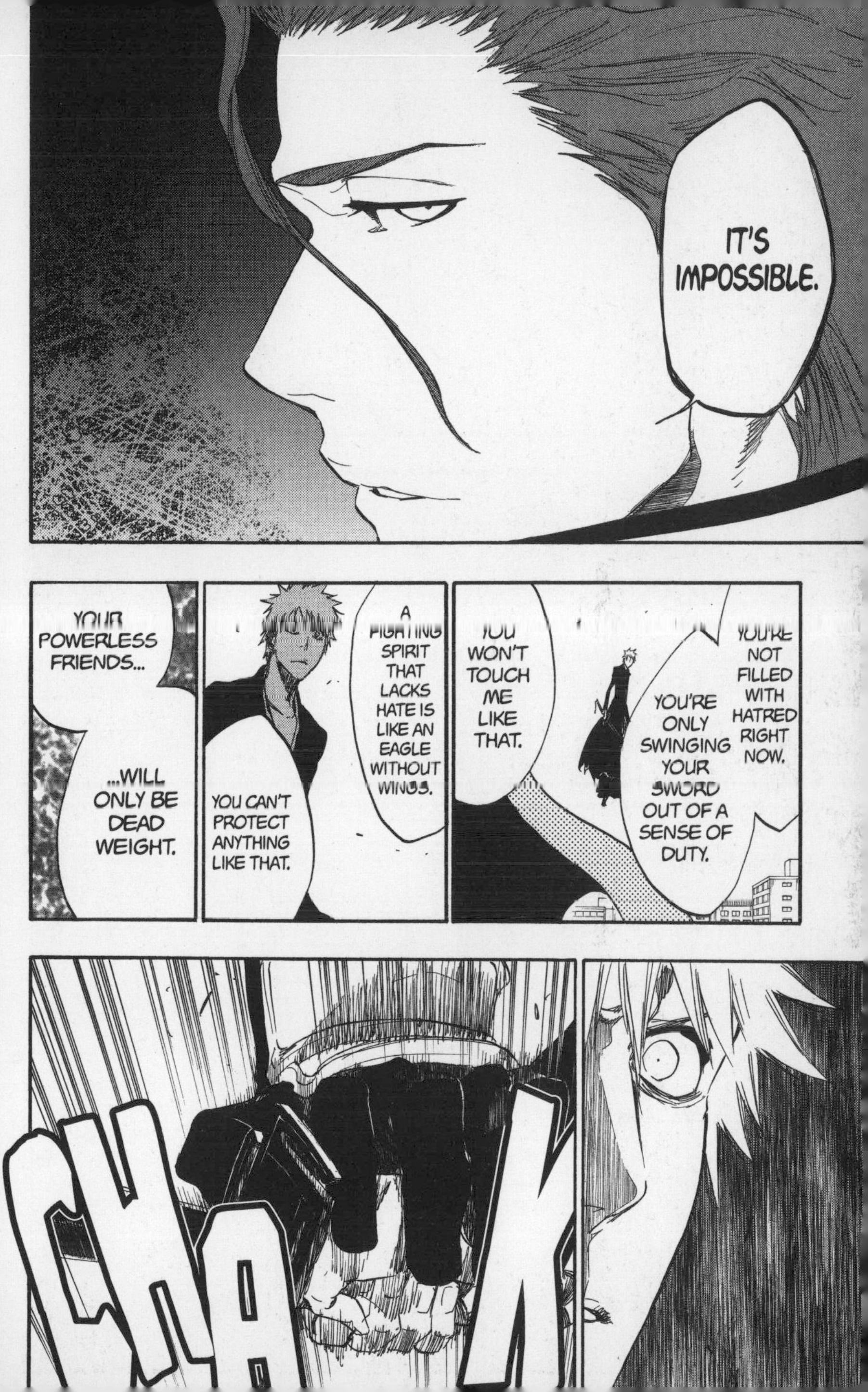
IT'S IMPOSSIBLE.
YOU'RE NOT FILLED WITH HATRED RIGHT NOW.
YOU'RE ONLY SWINGING YOUR SWORD OUT OF A SENSE OF DUTY.
YOU WON'T TOUCH ME LIKE THAT.
A FIGHTING SPIRIT THAT LACKS HATE IS LIKE AN EAGLE WITHOUT WINGS.
YOU CAN'T PROTECT ANYTHING LIKE THAT.
YOUR POWERLESS FRIENDS...
...WILL ONLY BE DEAD WEIGHT.
CHAK

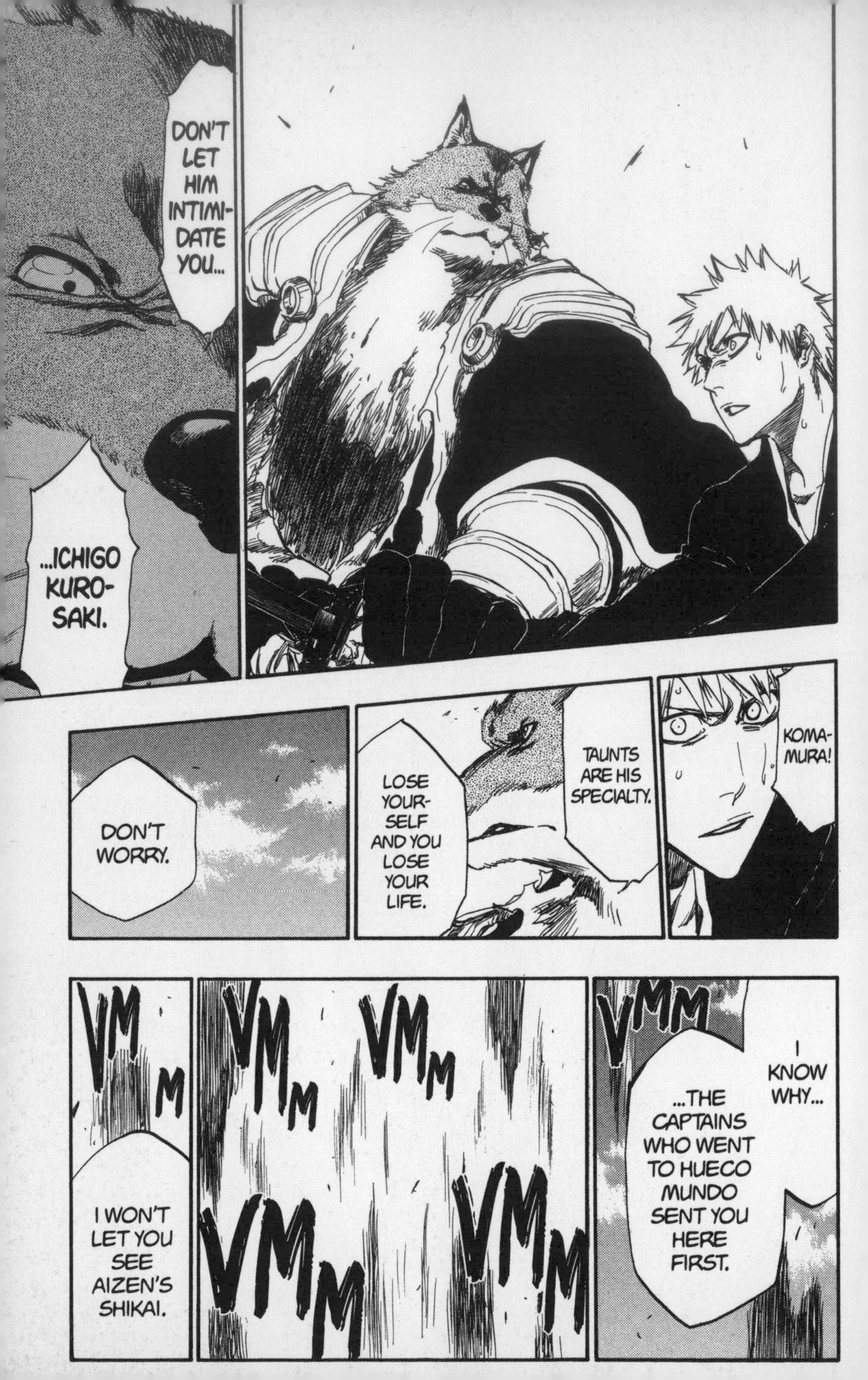
DON'T LET HIM INTIMIDATE YOU...
...ICHIGO KUROSAKI.
KOMAMURA!
TAUNTS ARE HIS SPECIALTY.
LOSE YOURSELF AND YOU LOSE YOUR LIFE.
DON'T WORRY.
VMM
I KNOW WHY...
...THE CAPTAINS WHO WENT TO HUECO MUNDO SENT YOU HERE FIRST.
VMM
VMM
VMM
VMM
VM M
I WON'T LET YOU SEE AIZEN'S SHIKAI.

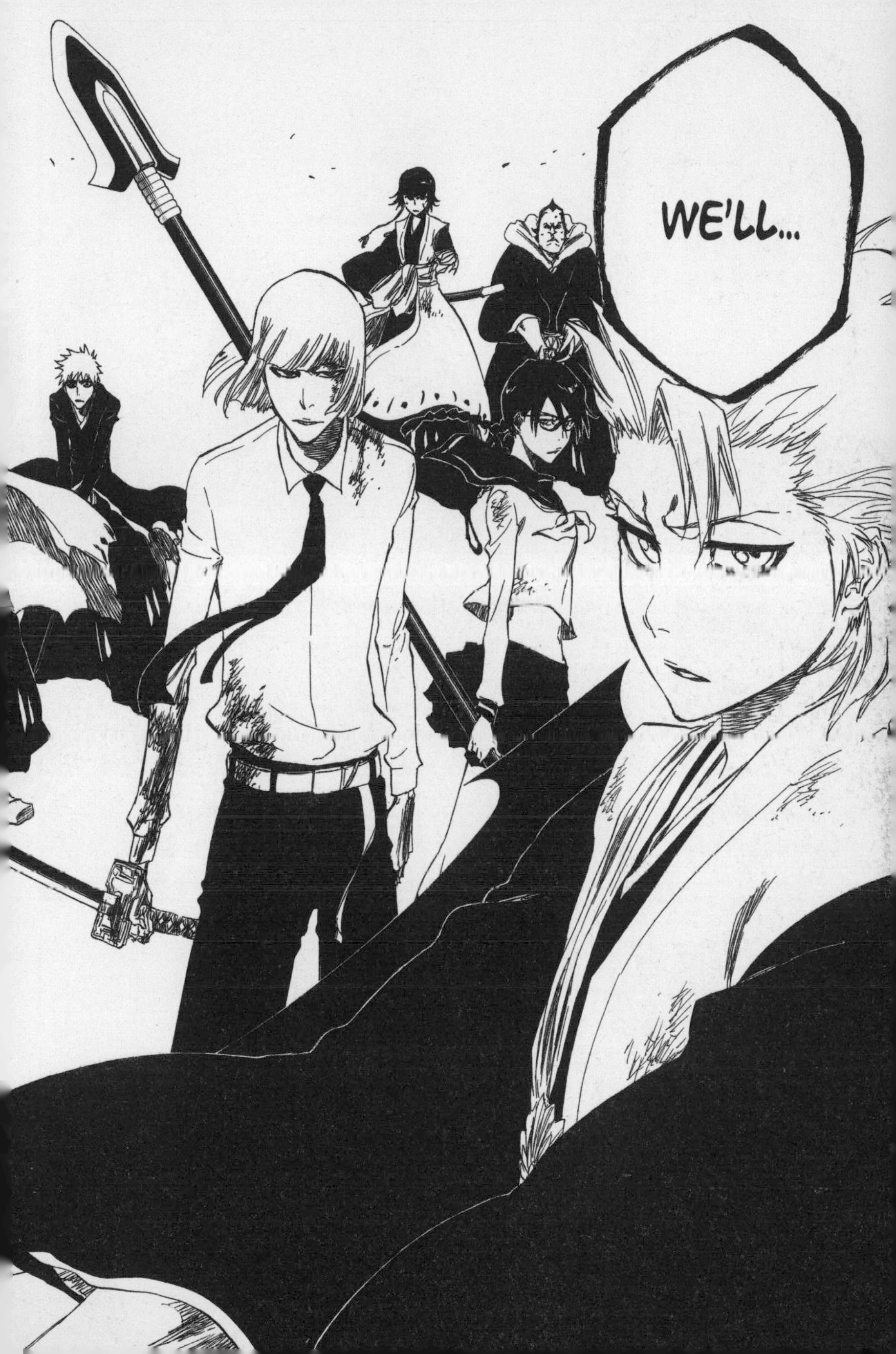
WE'LL...

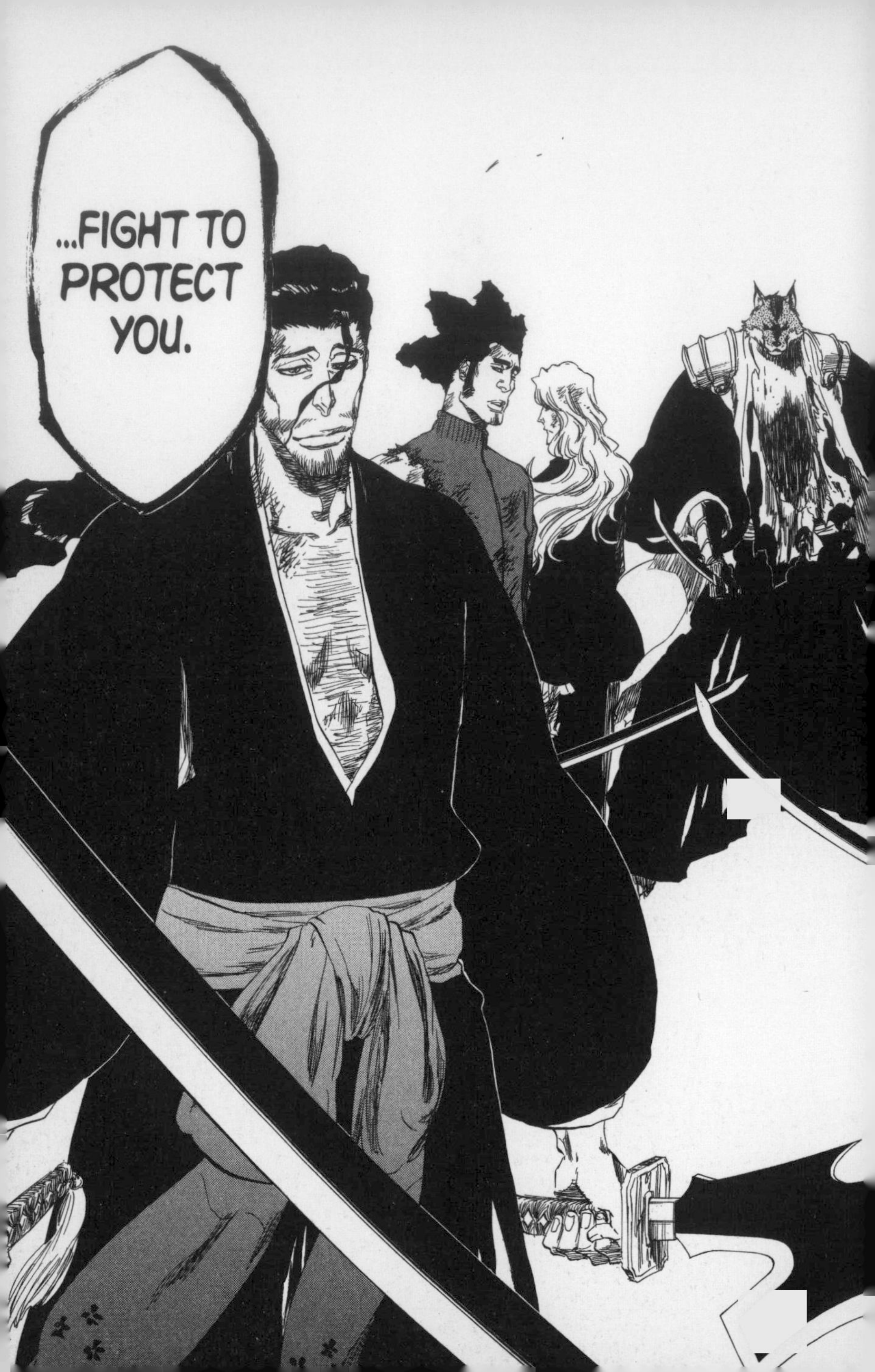
...FIGHT TO PROTECT YOU.

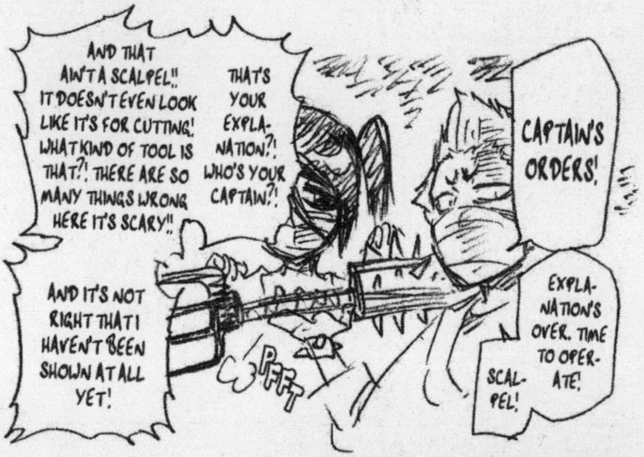
CAPTAIN'S ORDERS!
THAT'S YOUR EXPLANATION?! WHO'S YOUR CAPTAIN?!
AND THAT AIN'T A SCALPEL!! IT DOESN'T EVEN LOOK LIKE IT'S FOR CUTTING! WHAT KIND OF TOOL IS THAT?! THERE ARE SO MANY THINGS WRONG HERE IT'S SCARY!!
EXPLANATION'S OVER. TIME TO OPERATE!
SCALPEL!
PFFT
AND IT'S NOT RIGHT THAT I HAVEN'T BEEN SHOWN AT ALL YET!

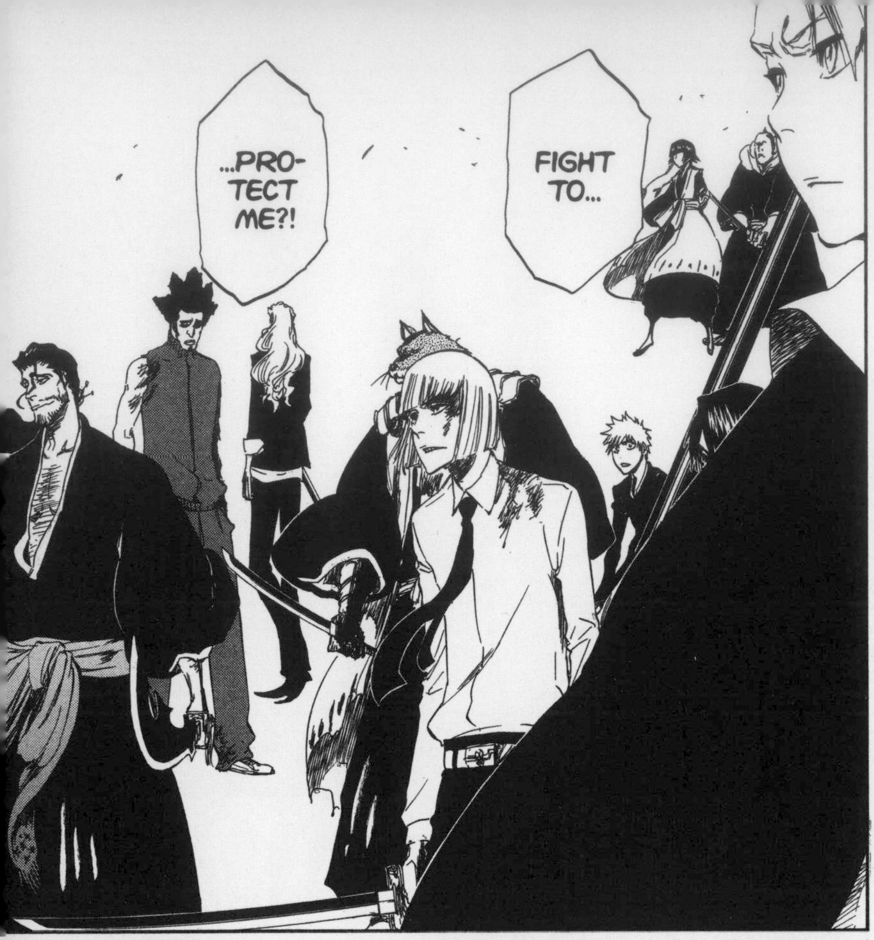
FIGHT TO...
...PRO-TECT ME?!

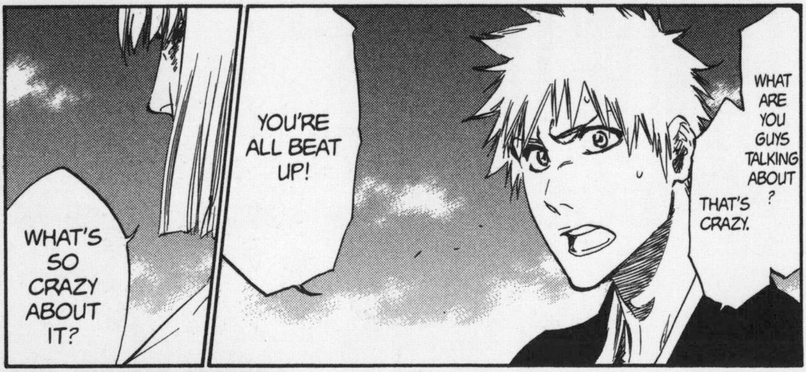
WHAT ARE YOU GUYS TALKING ABOUT?
THAT'S CRAZY.
YOU'RE ALL BEAT UP!
WHAT'S SO CRAZY ABOUT IT?

389. WINGED EAGLES 2

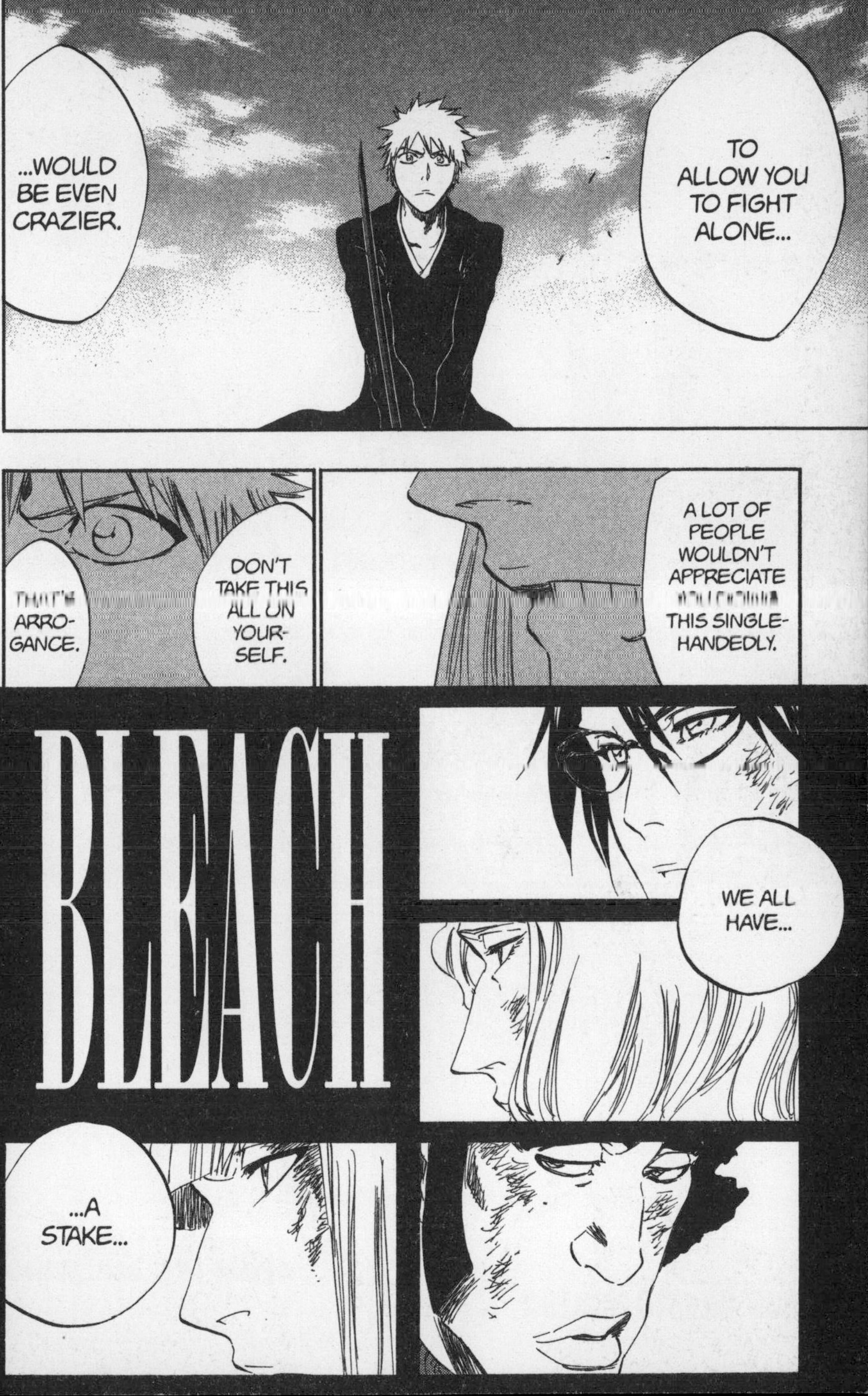
TO ALLOW YOU TO FIGHT ALONE...
...WOULD BE EVEN CRAZIER.
A LOT OF PEOPLE WOULDN'T APPRECIATE
THIS SINGLE-HANDEDLY.
DON'T TAKE THIS ALL ON YOURSELF.
THAT'S ARROGANCE.
BLEACH
WE ALL HAVE...
...A STAKE...

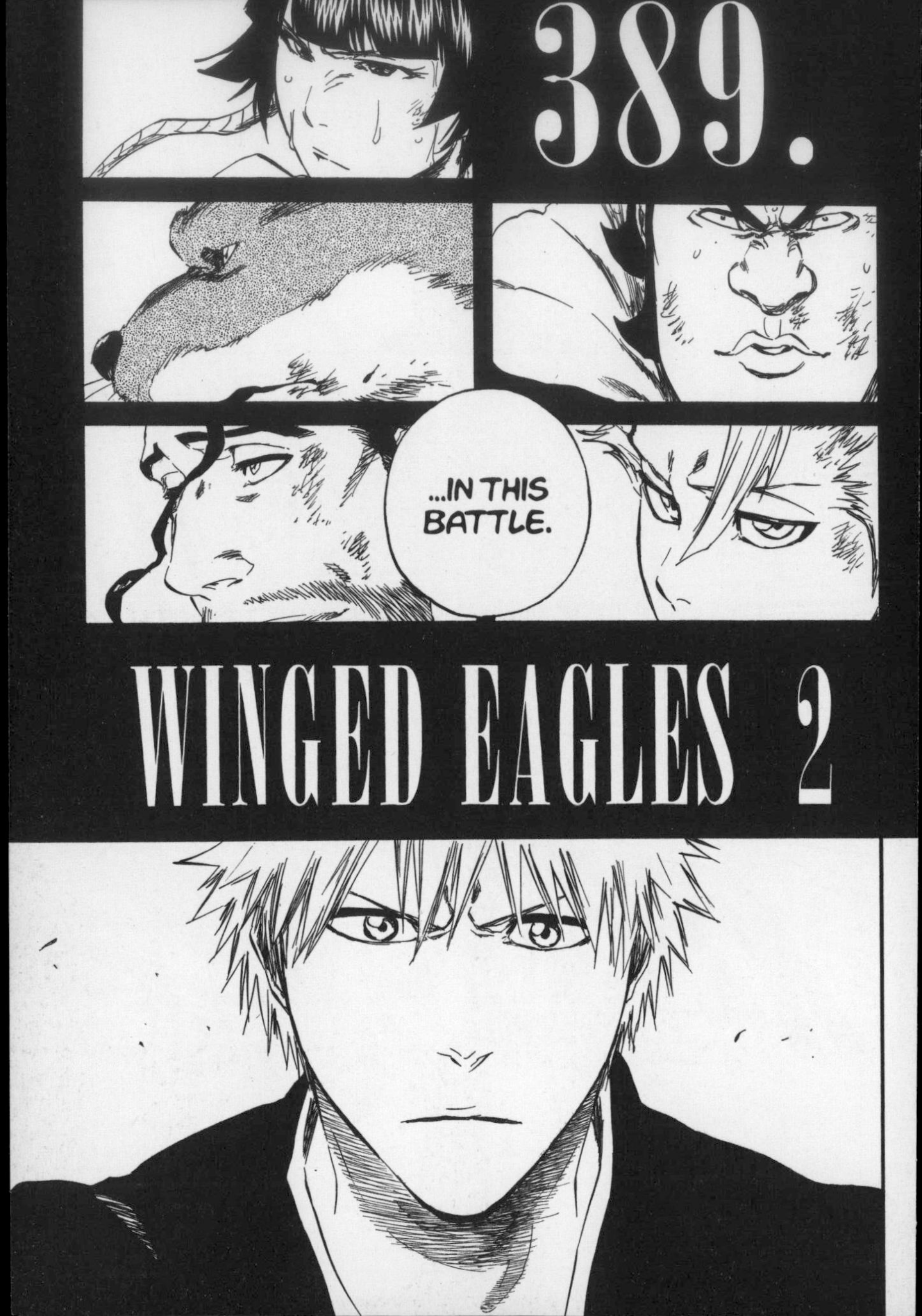
389.
...IN THIS BATTLE.
WINGED EAGLES 2

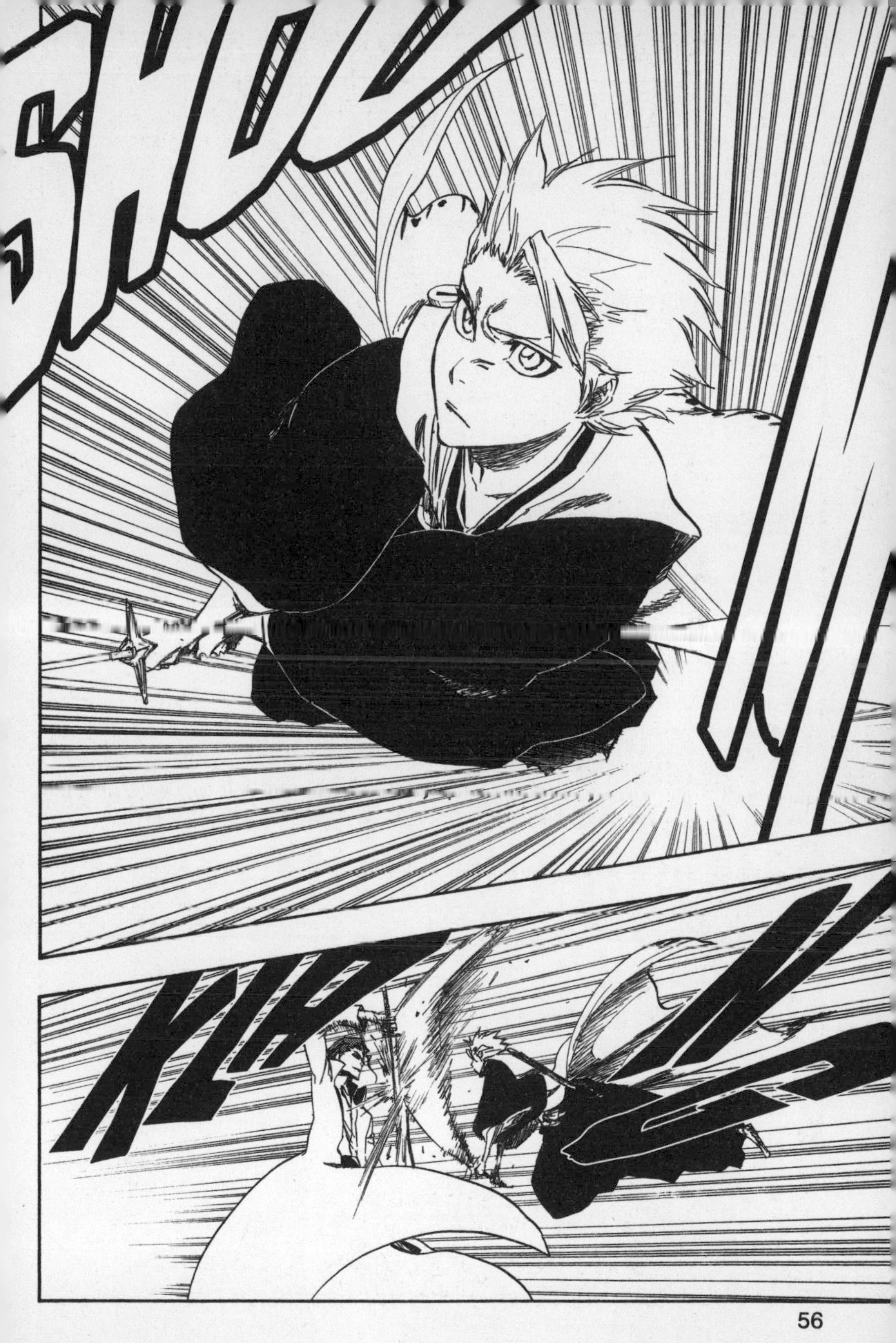

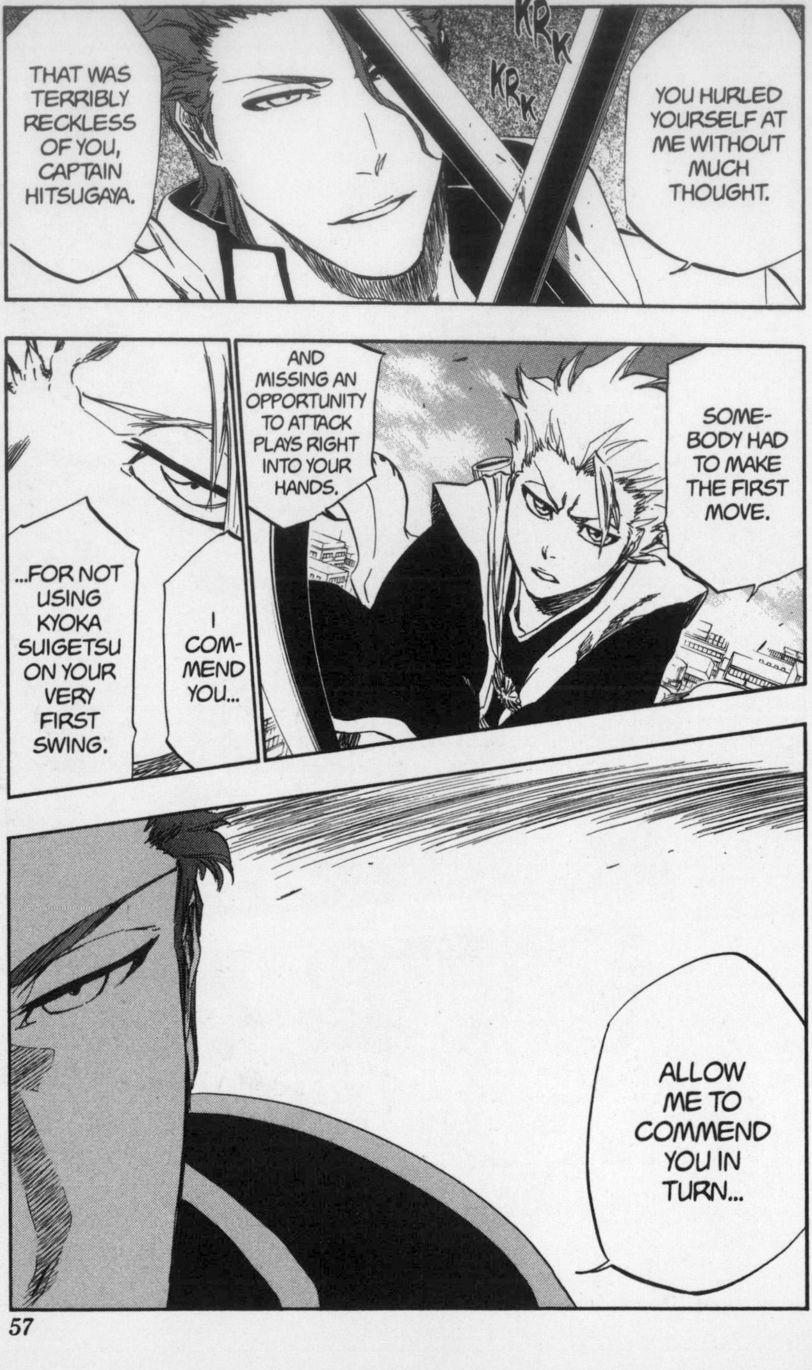
KRK KRK
YOU HURLED YOURSELF AT ME WITHOUT MUCH THOUGHT.
THAT WAS TERRIBLY RECKLESS OF YOU, CAPTAIN HITSUGAYA.
SOME-BODY HAD TO MAKE THE FIRST MOVE.
AND MISSING AN OPPORTUNITY TO ATTACK PLAYS RIGHT INTO YOUR HANDS.
I COM-MEND YOU...
...FOR NOT USING KYOKA SUIGETSU ON YOUR VERY FIRST SWING.
ALLOW ME TO COMMEND YOU IN TURN...

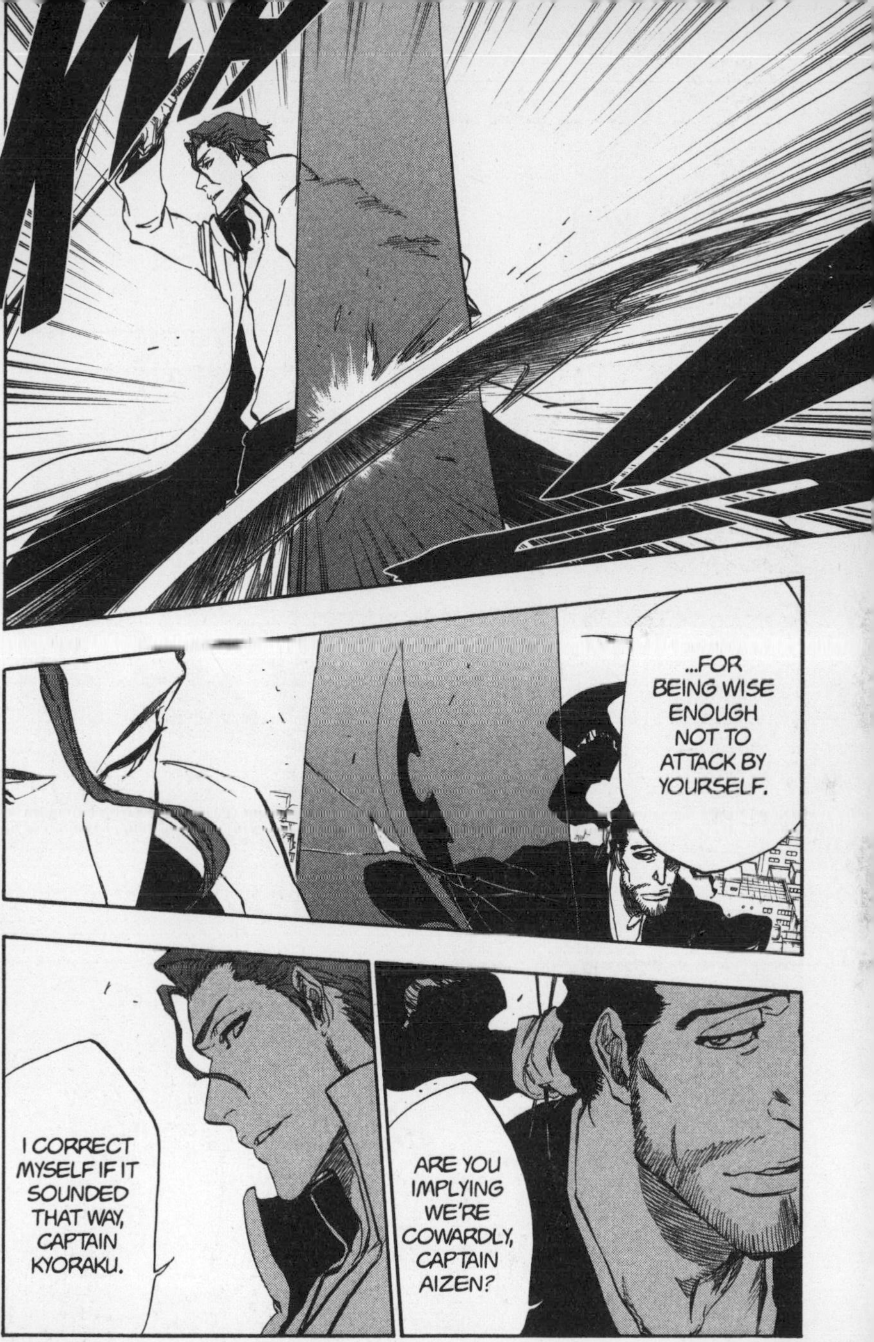
...FOR BEING WISE ENOUGH NOT TO ATTACK BY YOURSELF.
ARE YOU IMPLYING WE'RE COWARDLY, CAPTAIN AIZEN?
I CORRECT MYSELF IF IT SOUNDED THAT WAY, CAPTAIN KYORAKU.

READ THIS WAY

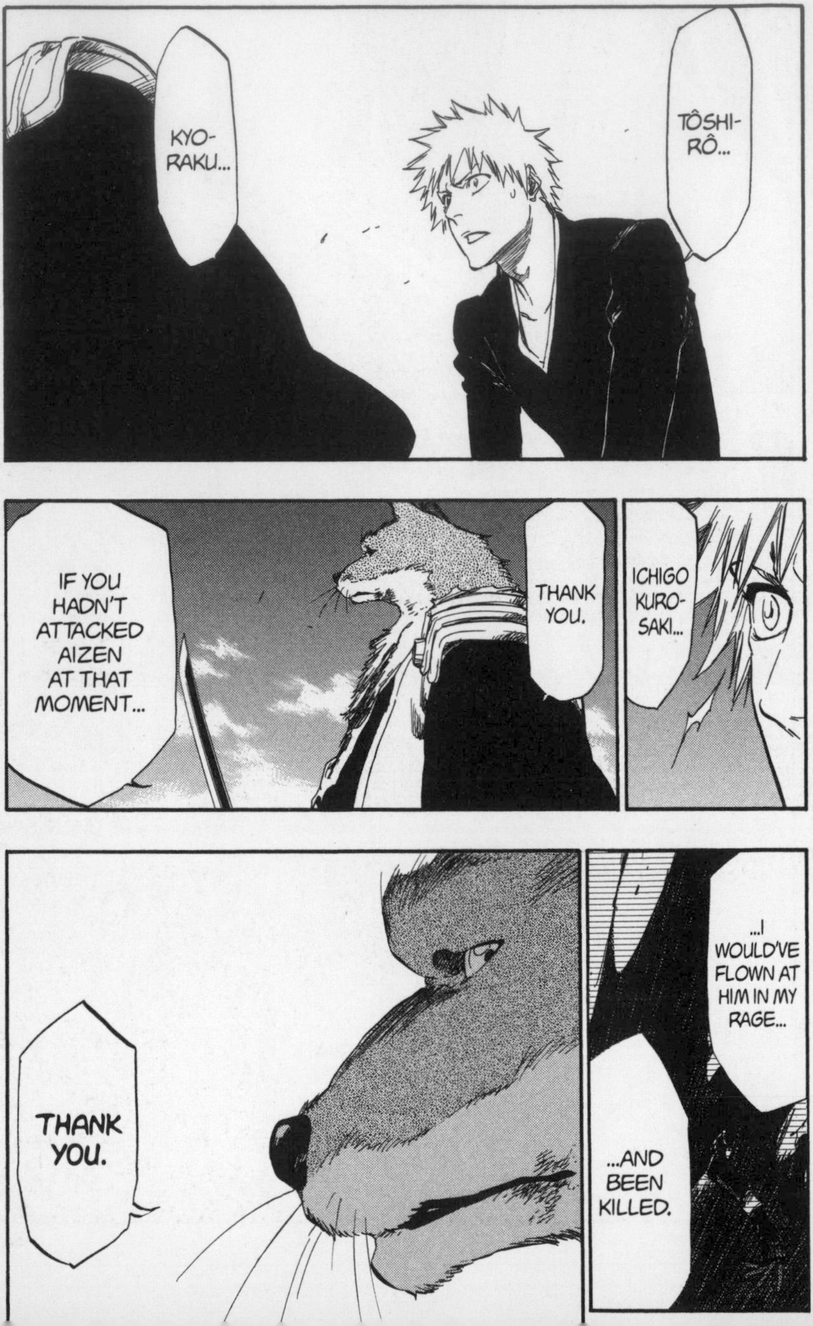
TÔSHI-RÔ...
KYO-RAKU...
ICHIGO KURO-SAKI...
THANK YOU.
IF YOU HADN'T ATTACKED AIZEN AT THAT MOMENT...
...I WOULD'VE FLOWN AT HIM IN MY RAGE...
...AND BEEN KILLED.
THANK YOU.

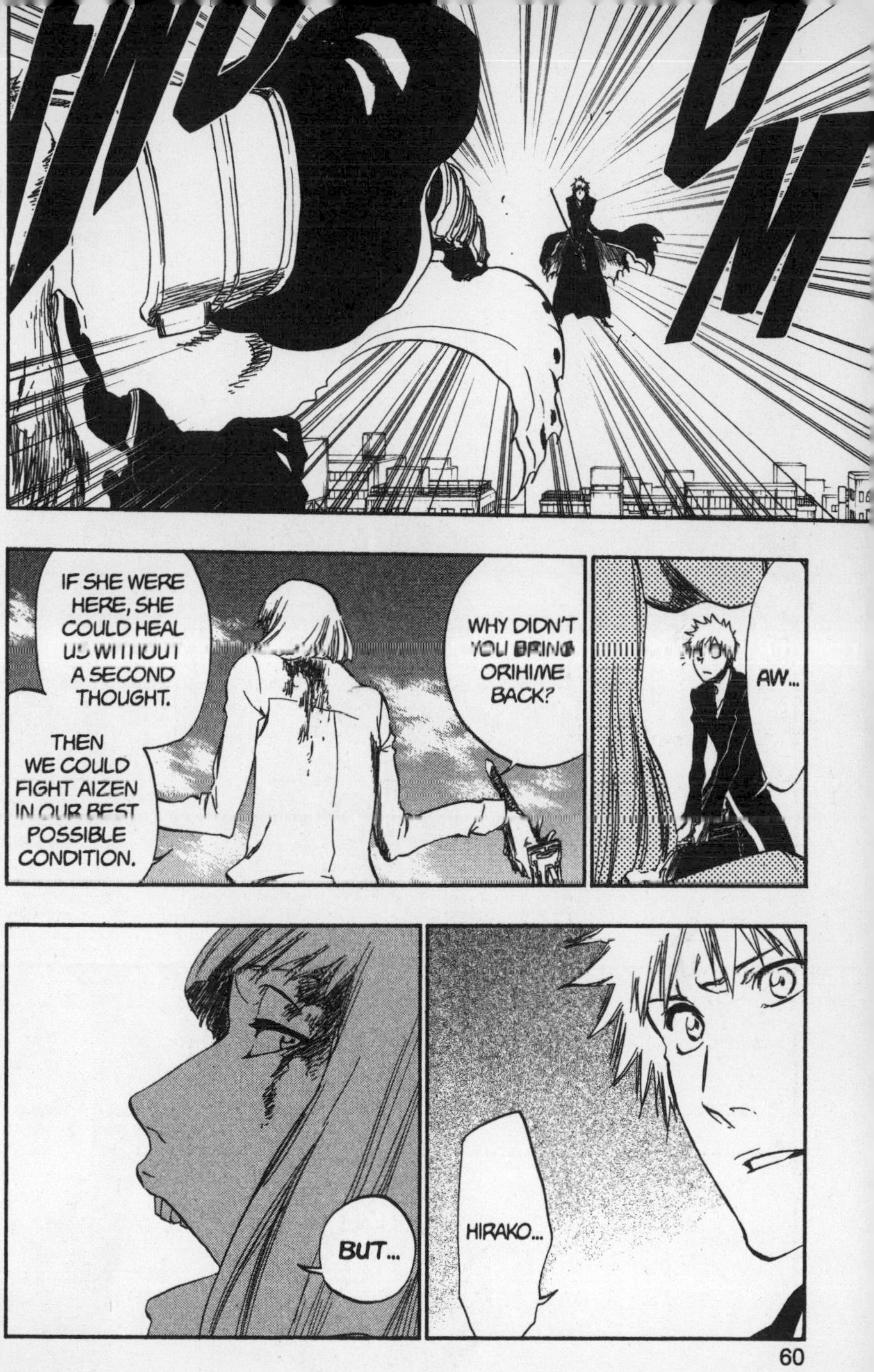
AW...
WHY DIDN'T YOU BRING ORIHIME BACK?
IF SHE WERE HERE, SHE COULD HEAL US WITHOUT A SECOND THOUGHT.
THEN WE COULD FIGHT AIZEN IN OUR BEST POSSIBLE CONDITION.
HIRAKO...
BUT...

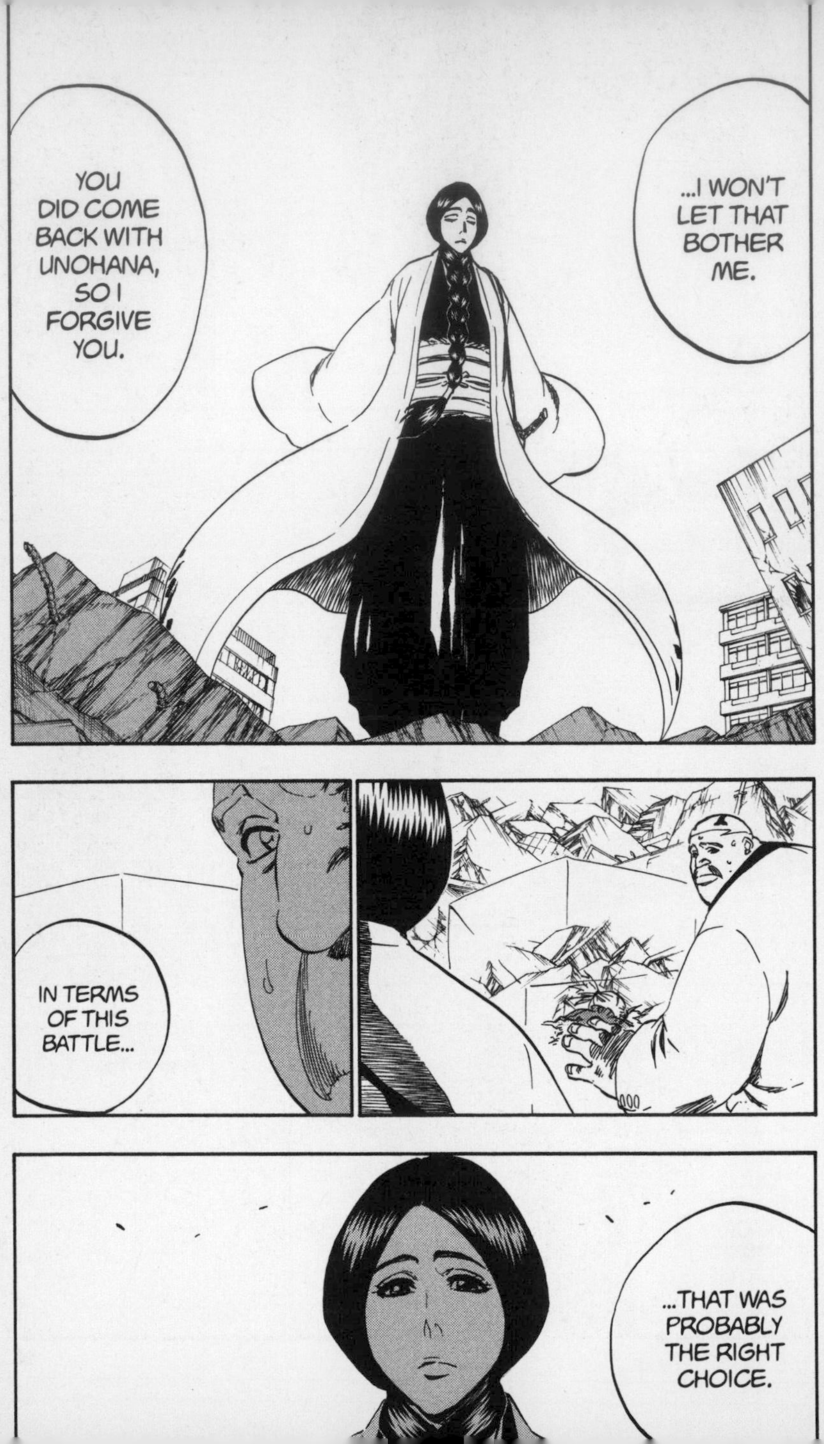
...I WON'T LET THAT BOTHER ME.
YOU DID COME BACK WITH UNOHANA, SO I FORGIVE YOU.
IN TERMS OF THIS BATTLE...
...THAT WAS PROBABLY THE RIGHT CHOICE.

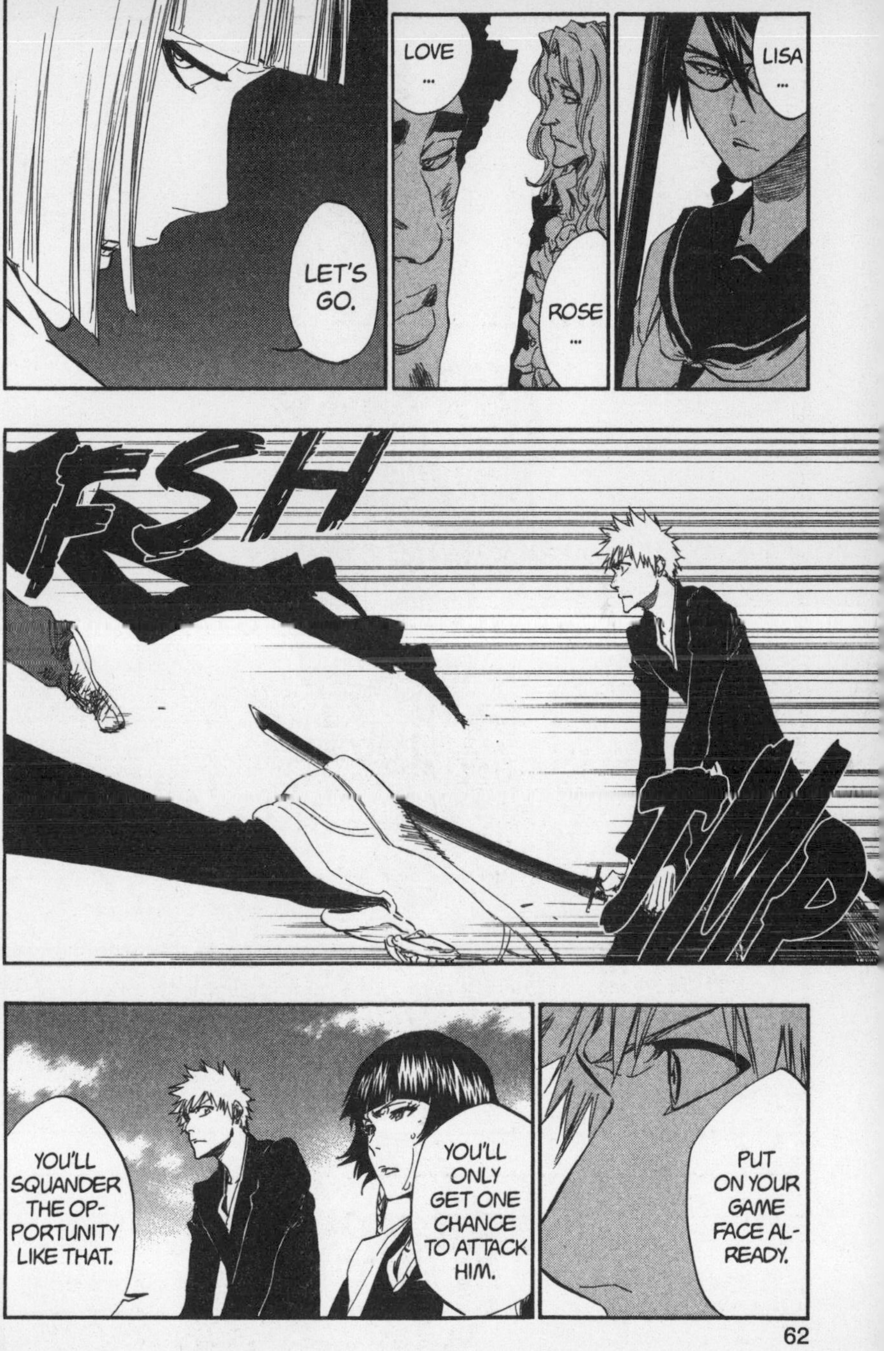
LISA ...
LOVE ...
ROSE ...
LET'S GO.
FSH
TMP
PUT ON YOUR GAME FACE ALREADY.
YOU'LL ONLY GET ONE CHANCE TO ATTACK HIM.
YOU'LL SQUANDER THE OPPORTUNITY LIKE THAT.

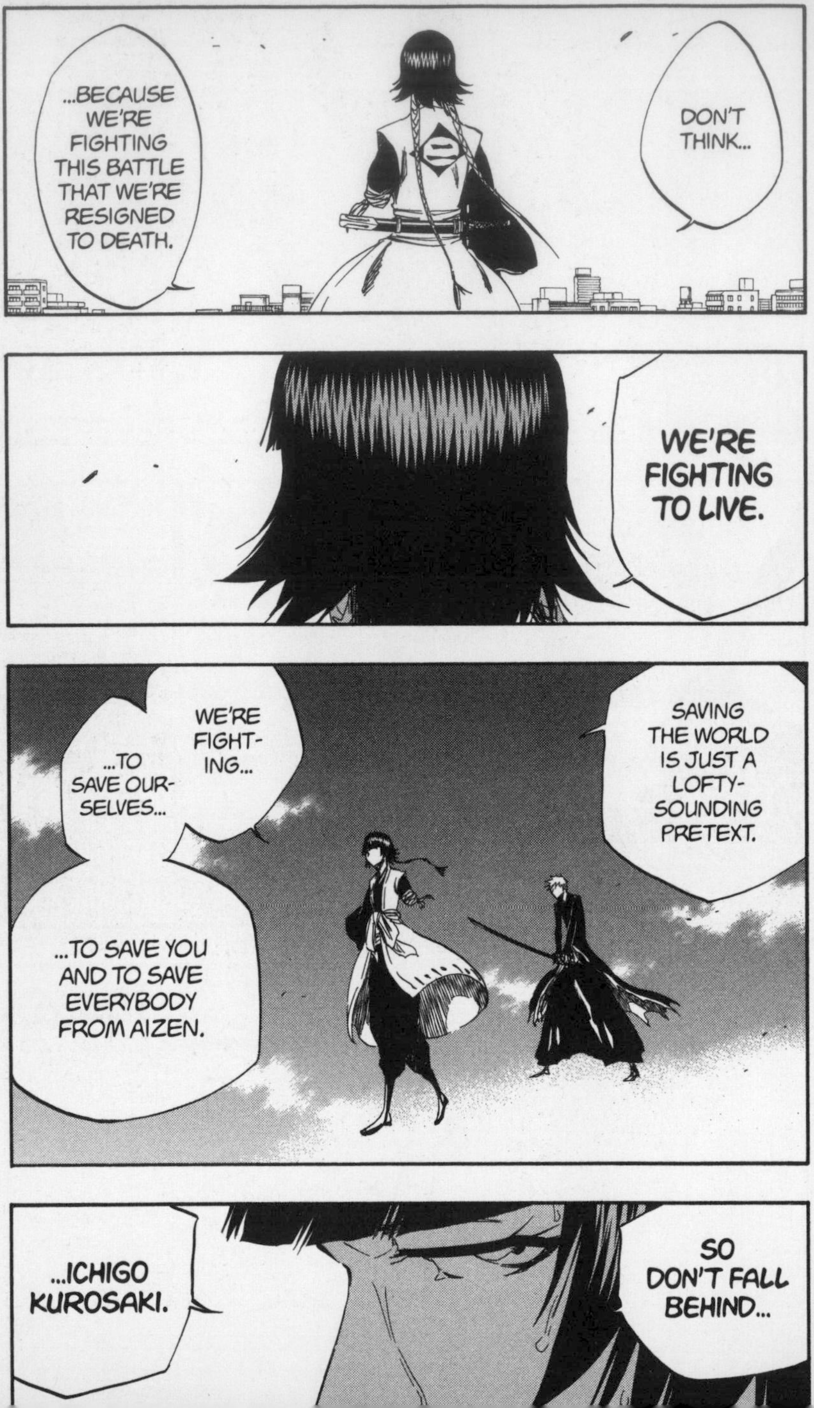
DON'T THINK...
...BECAUSE WE'RE FIGHTING THIS BATTLE THAT WE'RE RESIGNED TO DEATH.
WE'RE FIGHTING TO LIVE.
SAVING THE WORLD IS JUST A LOFTY-SOUNDING PRETEXT.
WE'RE FIGHT-ING...
...TO SAVE OUR-SELVES...
...TO SAVE YOU AND TO SAVE EVERYBODY FROM AIZEN.
SO DON'T FALL BEHIND...
...ICHIGO KUROSAKI.

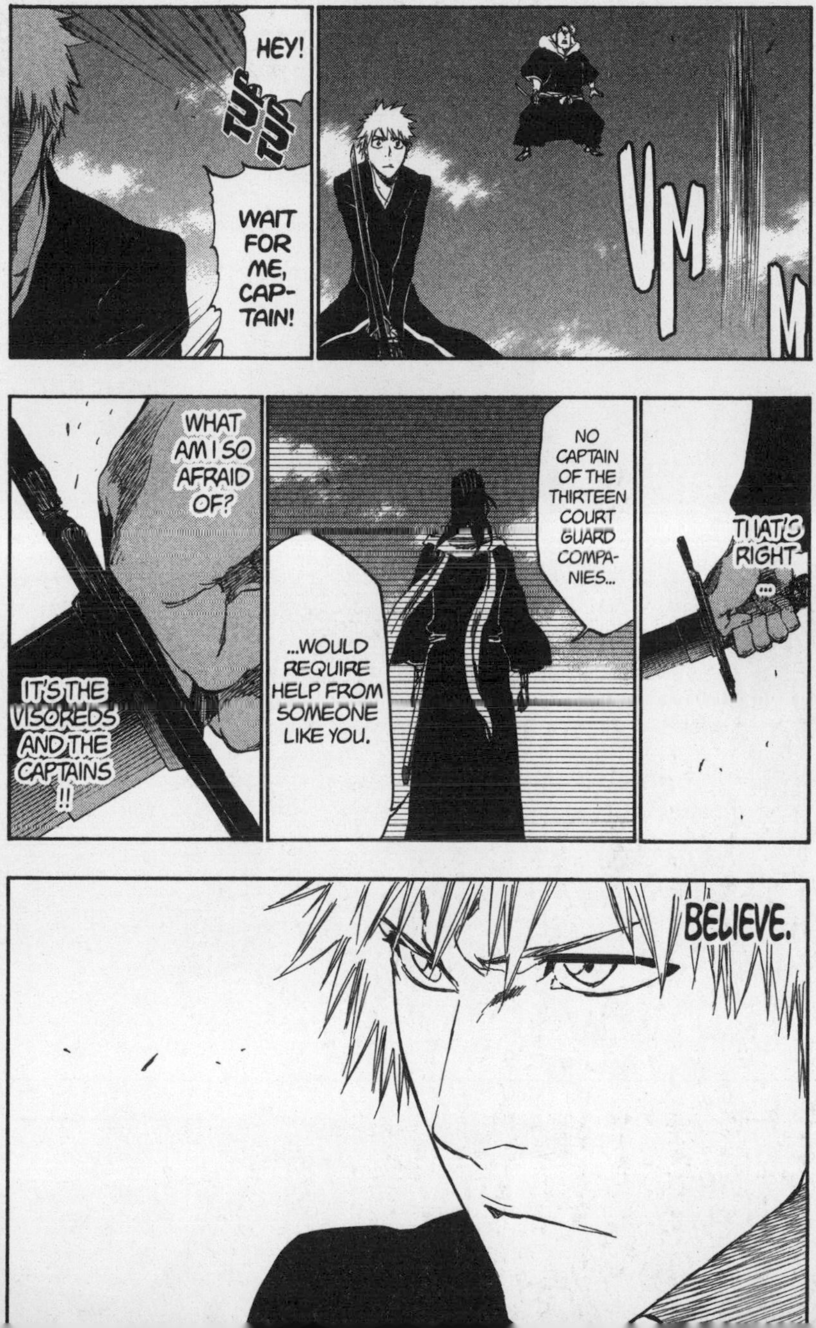
VMM
M
HEY!
TUP TUP
WAIT FOR ME, CAPTAIN!
THAT'S RIGHT...
NO CAPTAIN OF THE THIRTEEN COURT GUARD COMPANIES...
...WOULD REQUIRE HELP FROM SOMEONE LIKE YOU.
WHAT AM I SO AFRAID OF?
IT'S THE VISOREDS AND THE CAPTAINS!!
BELIEVE.

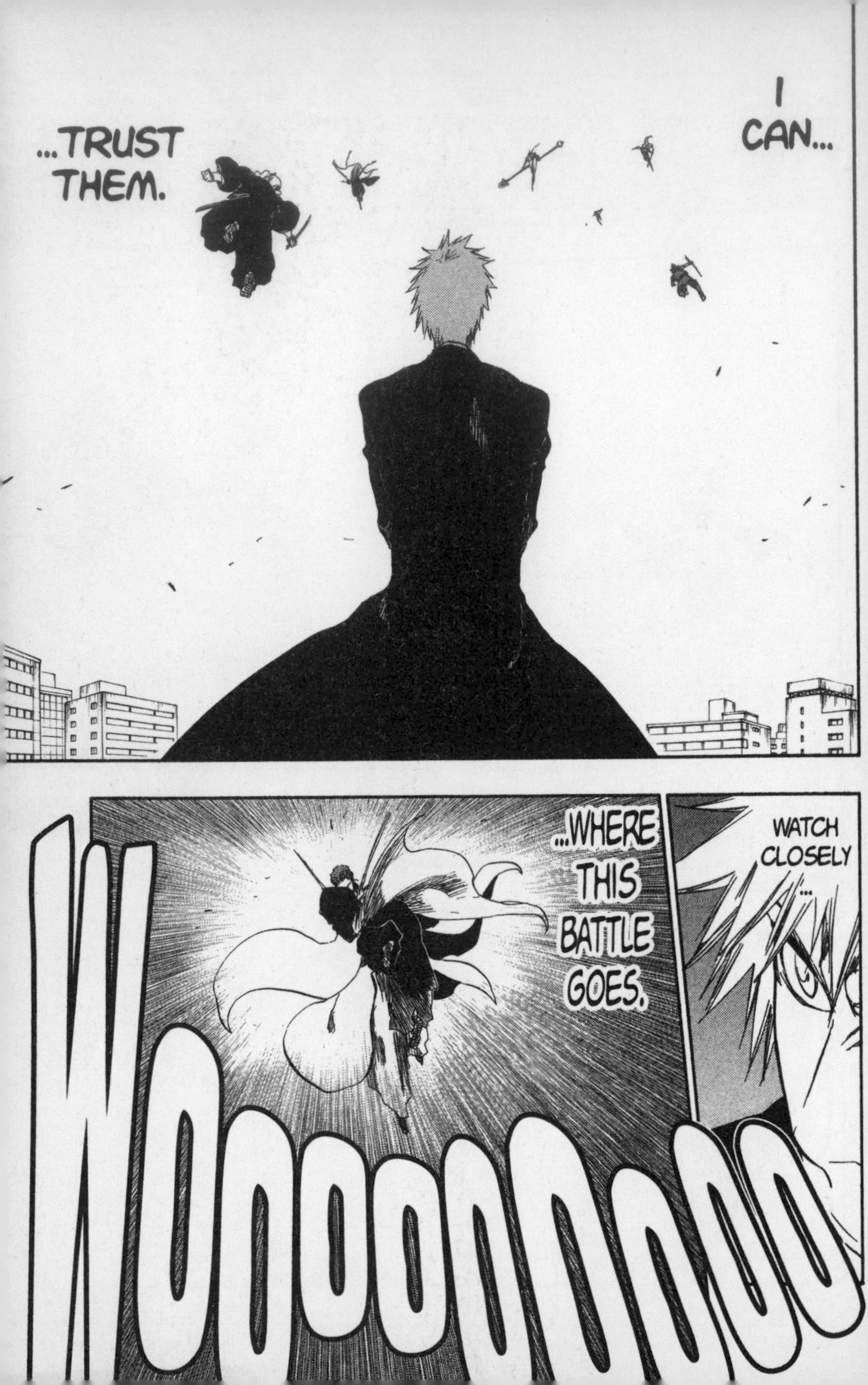
I CAN...
...TRUST THEM.
WATCH CLOSELY ...
...WHERE THIS BATTLE GOES.
WOOOONNNOO

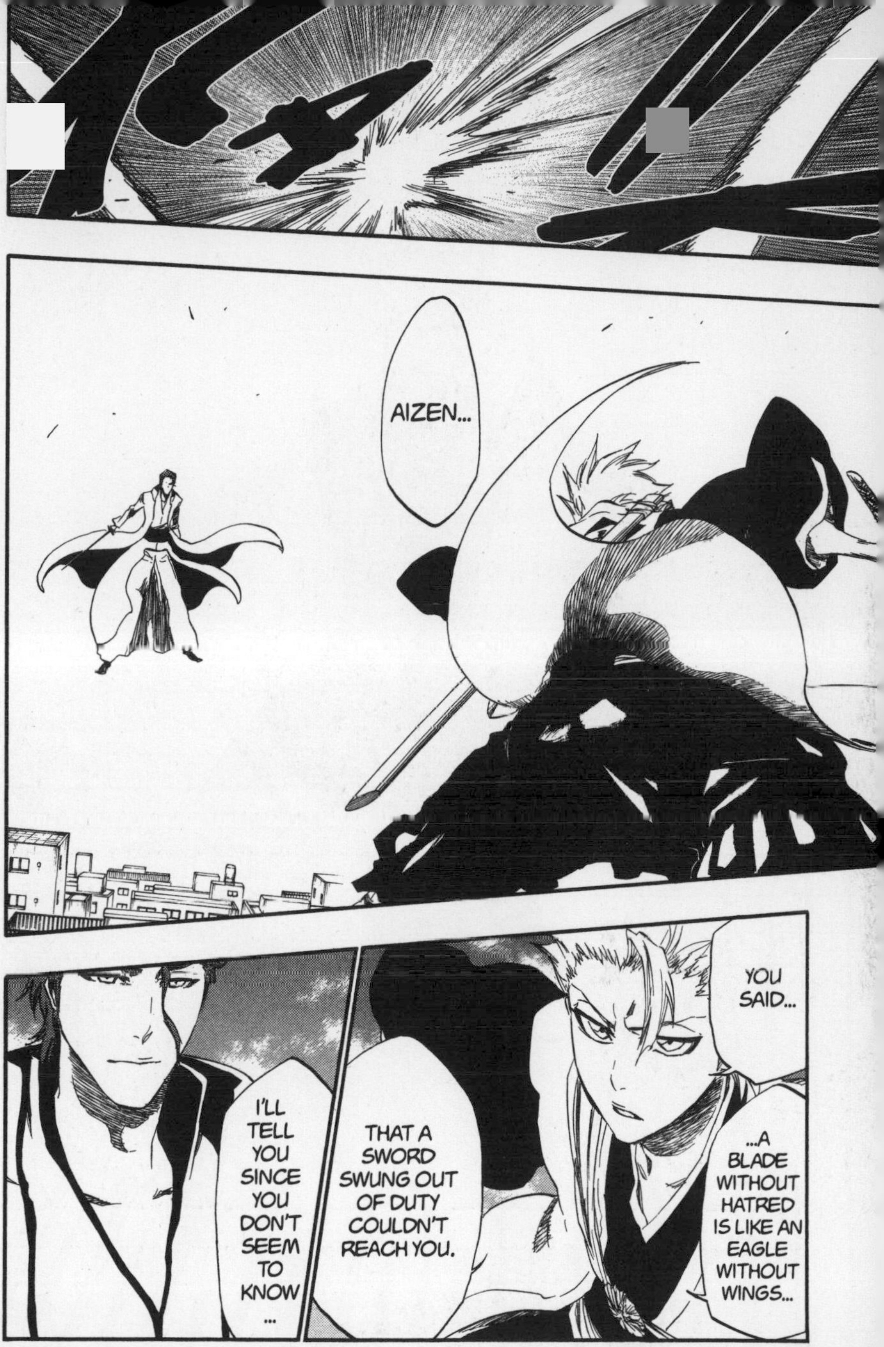
AIZEN...
YOU SAID...
...A BLADE WITHOUT HATRED IS LIKE AN EAGLE WITHOUT WINGS...
THAT A SWORD SWUNG OUT OF DUTY COULDN'T REACH YOU.
I'LL TELL YOU SINCE YOU DON'T SEEM TO KNOW...

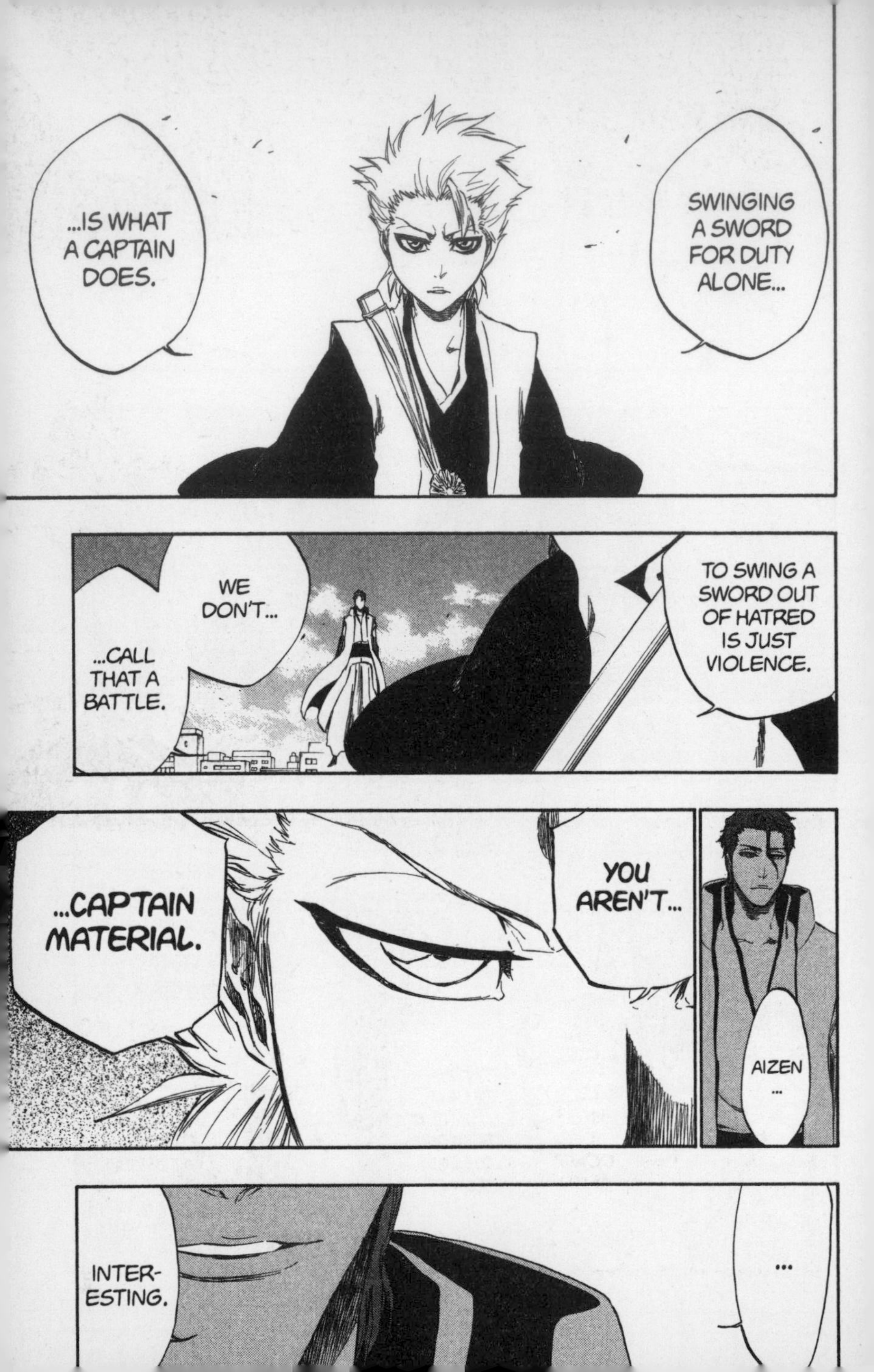
SWINGING A SWORD FOR DUTY ALONE...
...IS WHAT A CAPTAIN DOES.
TO SWING A SWORD OUT OF HATRED IS JUST VIOLENCE.
WE DON'T...
...CALL THAT A BATTLE.
AIZEN ...
YOU AREN'T...
...CAPTAIN MATERIAL.
...
INTER-ESTING.

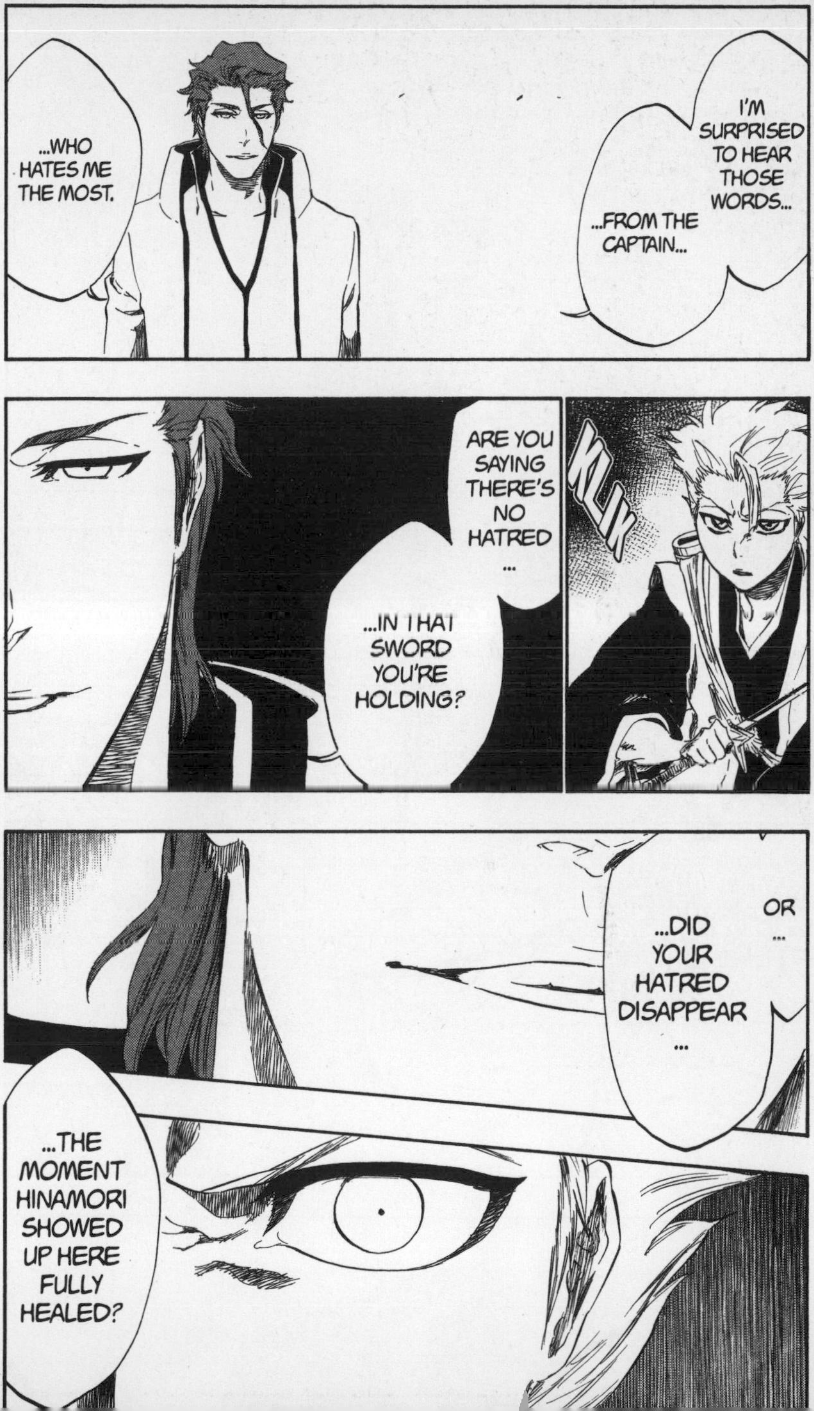
I'M SURPRISED TO HEAR THOSE WORDS...
...FROM THE CAPTAIN...
...WHO HATES ME THE MOST.
KLIK
ARE YOU SAYING THERE'S NO HATRED ...
...IN THAT SWORD YOU'RE HOLDING?
OR ...
...DID YOUR HATRED DISAPPEAR ...
...THE MOMENT HINAMORI SHOWED UP HERE FULLY HEALED?

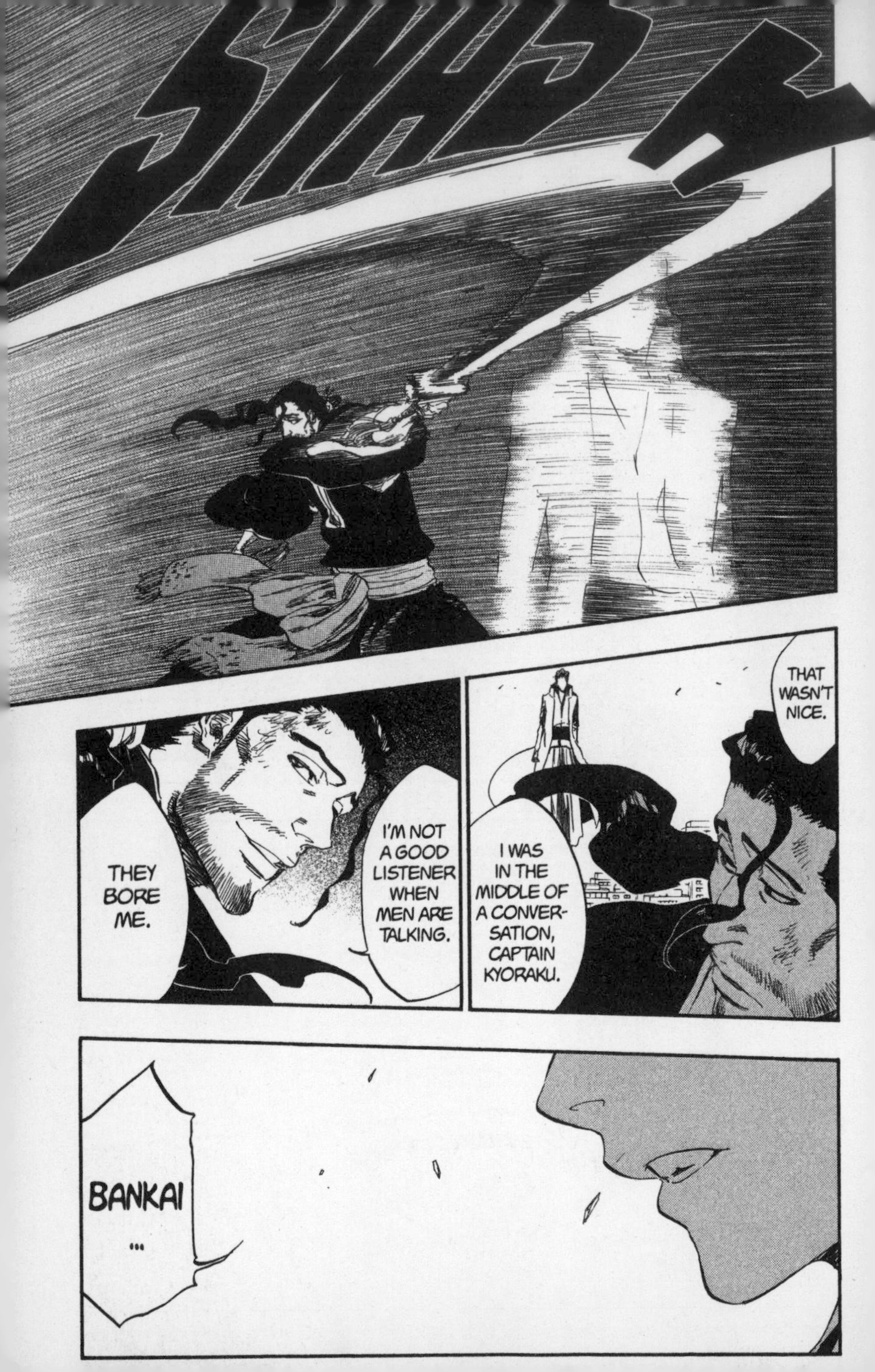
THAT WASN'T NICE.
I WAS IN THE MIDDLE OF A CONVER-SATION, CAPTAIN KYORAKU.
I'M NOT A GOOD LISTENER WHEN MEN ARE TALKING.
THEY BORE ME.
BANKAI ...

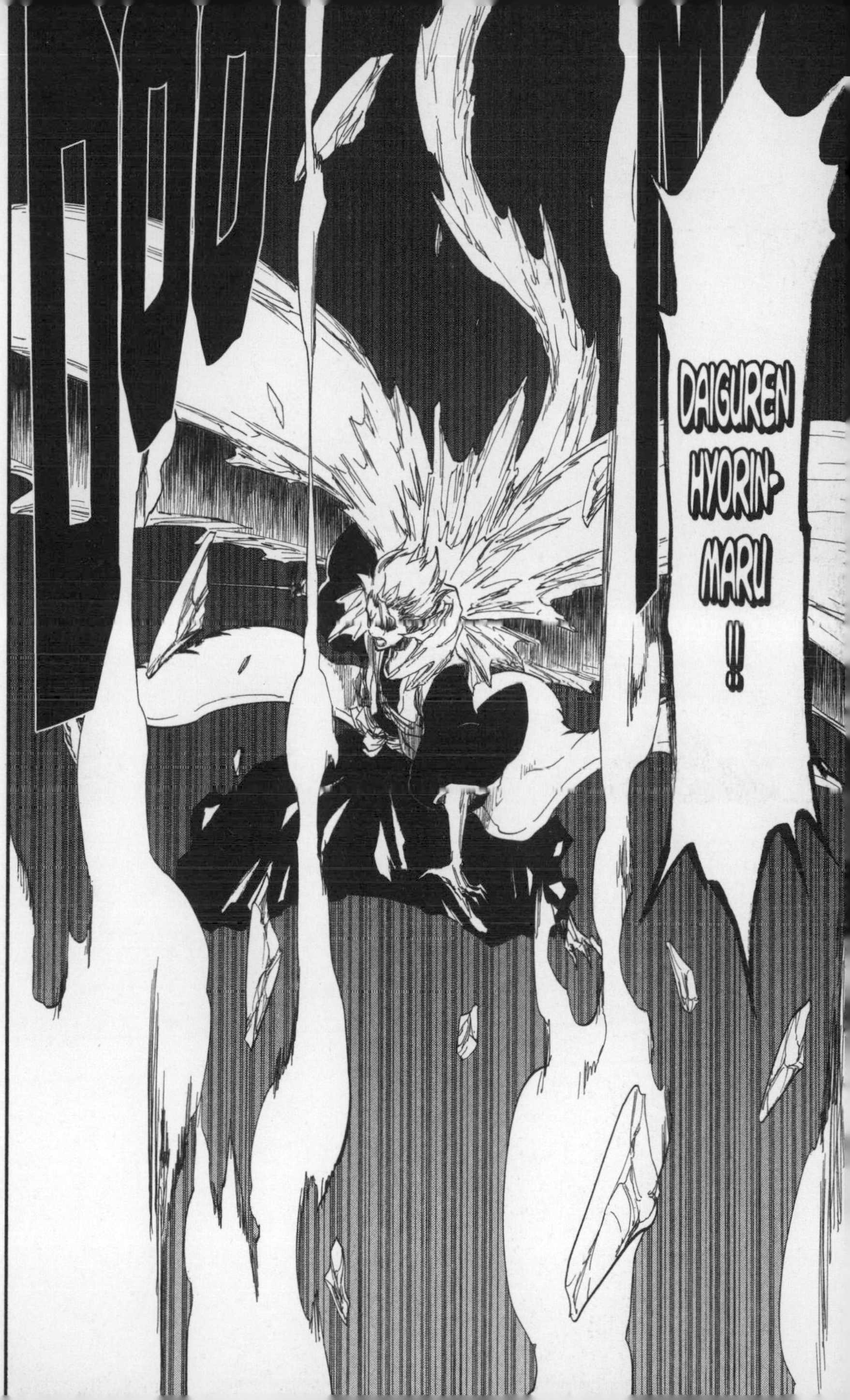
DAIGUREN HYORIN-MARU !!

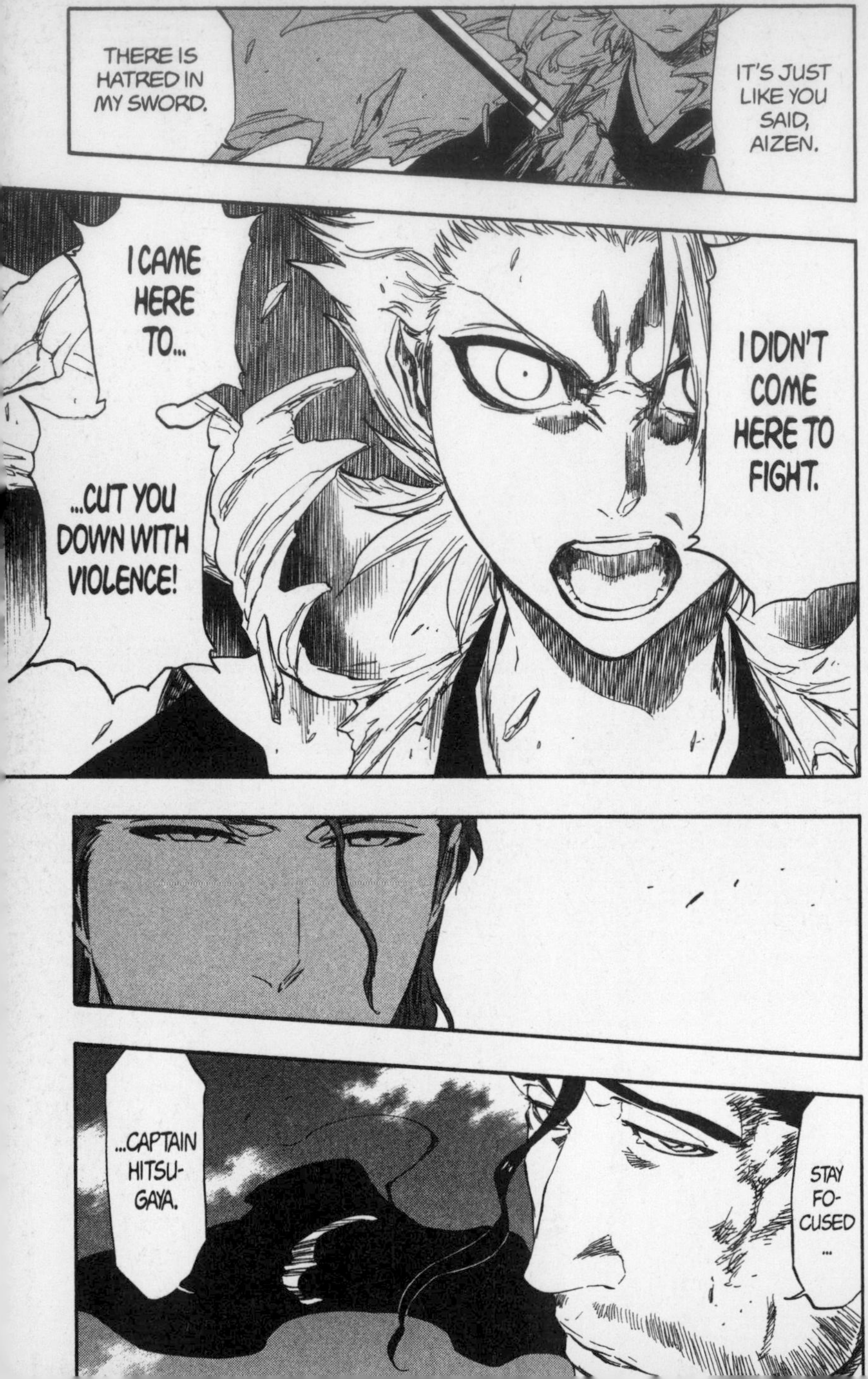
IT'S JUST LIKE YOU SAID, AIZEN.
THERE IS HATRED IN MY SWORD.
I DIDN'T COME HERE TO FIGHT.
I CAME HERE TO...
...CUT YOU DOWN WITH VIOLENCE!
STAY FO-CUSED ...
...CAPTAIN HITSU-GAYA.

TUP
TUP
HOLD ON! YOU'RE SERIOUSLY GONNA OPERATE ON ME?! WHAT FOR?!
TUP
INFORMED CONSENT, PLEASE!!
GASP!! I'M BEING SHOWN!! Y-YES!!
HEH HEH HEH...
YOU SEEM TO BE IN SOME TROUBLE, KON.
TUP

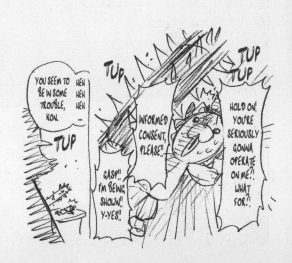

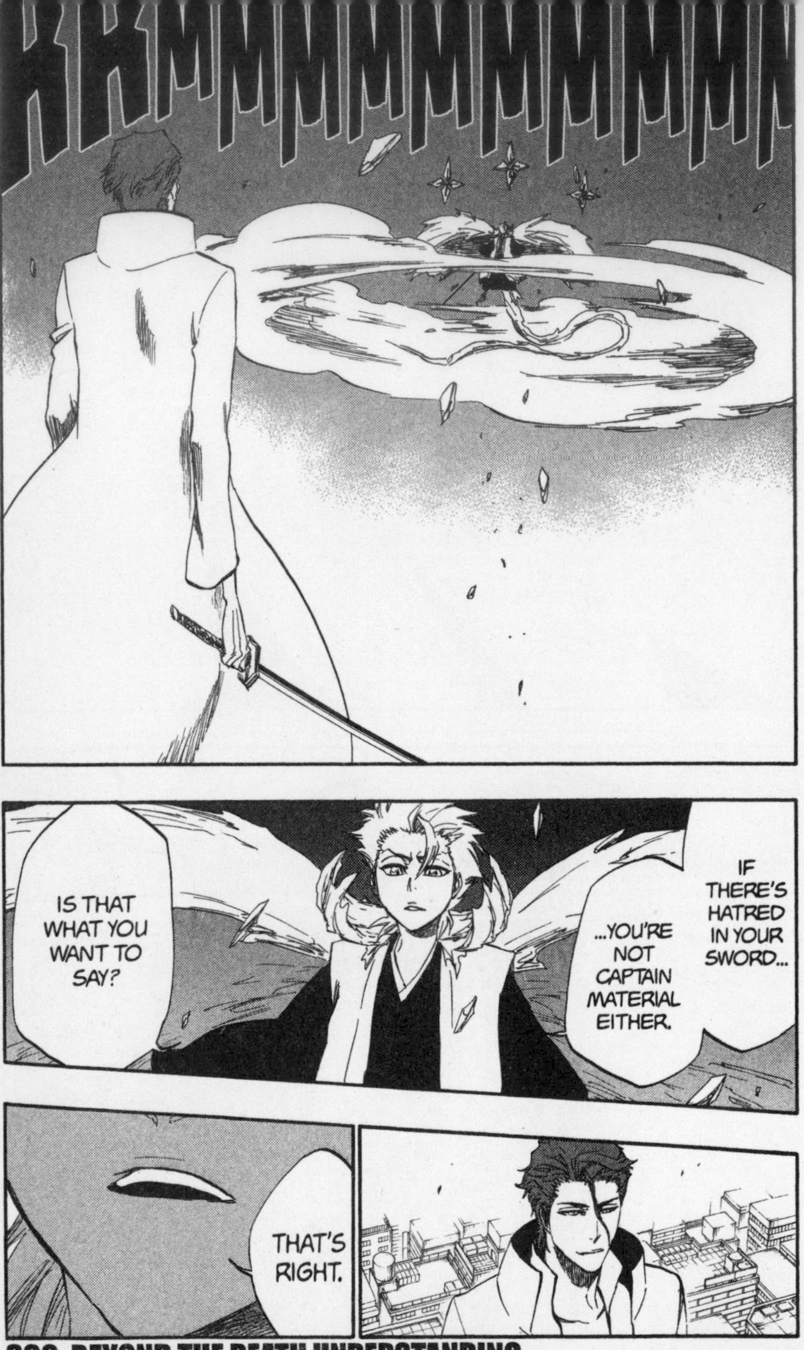
KRMMMMMMMMMMMN
IF THERE'S HATRED IN YOUR SWORD...
...YOU'RE NOT CAPTAIN MATERIAL EITHER.
IS THAT WHAT YOU WANT TO SAY?
THAT'S RIGHT.

390. BEYOND THE DEATH UNDERSTANDING

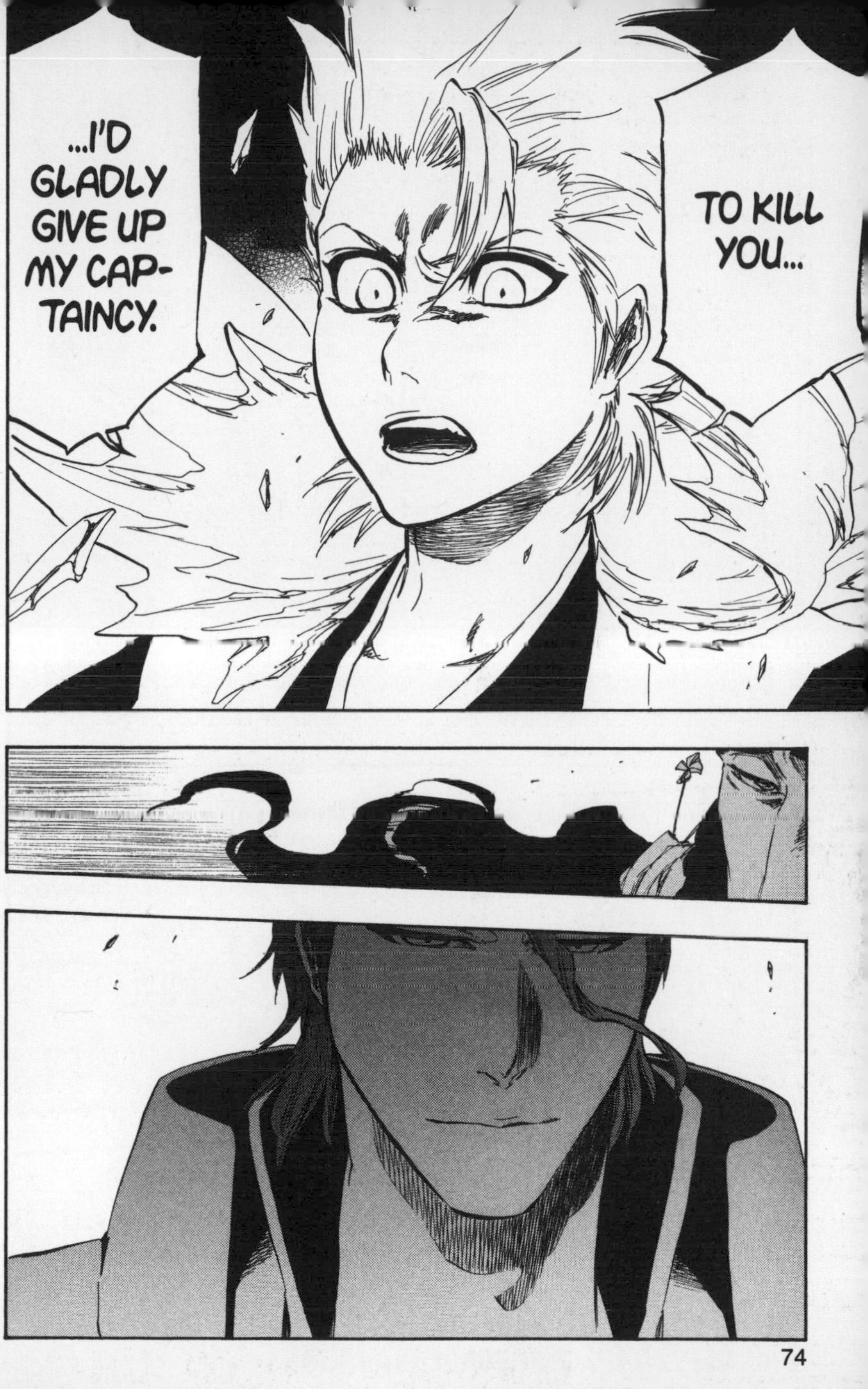
TO KILL YOU...
...I'D GLADLY GIVE UP MY CAP-TAINCY.

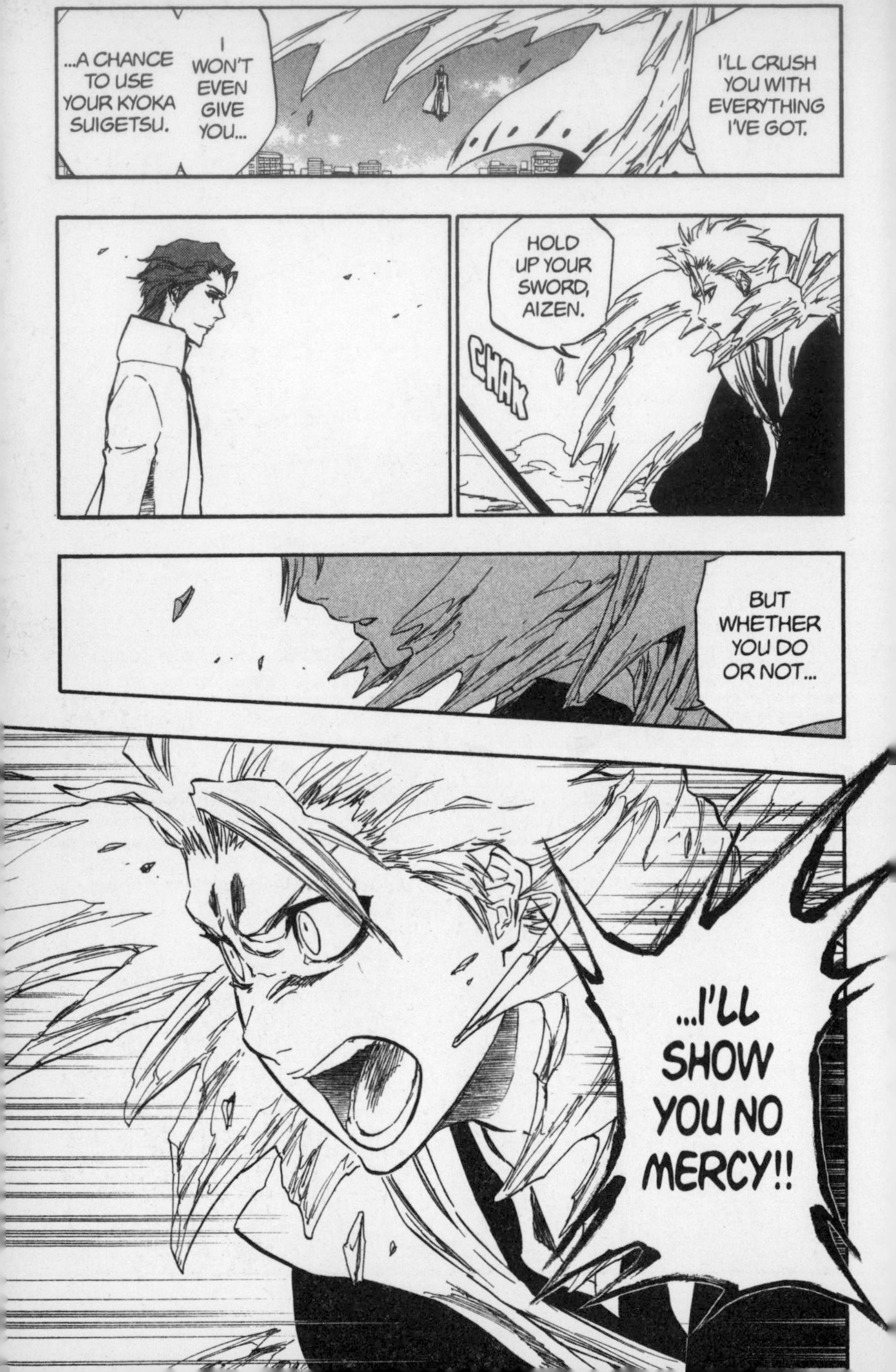
I'LL CRUSH YOU WITH EVERYTHING I'VE GOT.
I WON'T EVEN GIVE YOU...
...A CHANCE TO USE YOUR KYOKA SUIGETSU.
HOLD UP YOUR SWORD, AIZEN.
CHAK
BUT WHETHER YOU DO OR NOT...
...I'LL SHOW YOU NO MERCY!!

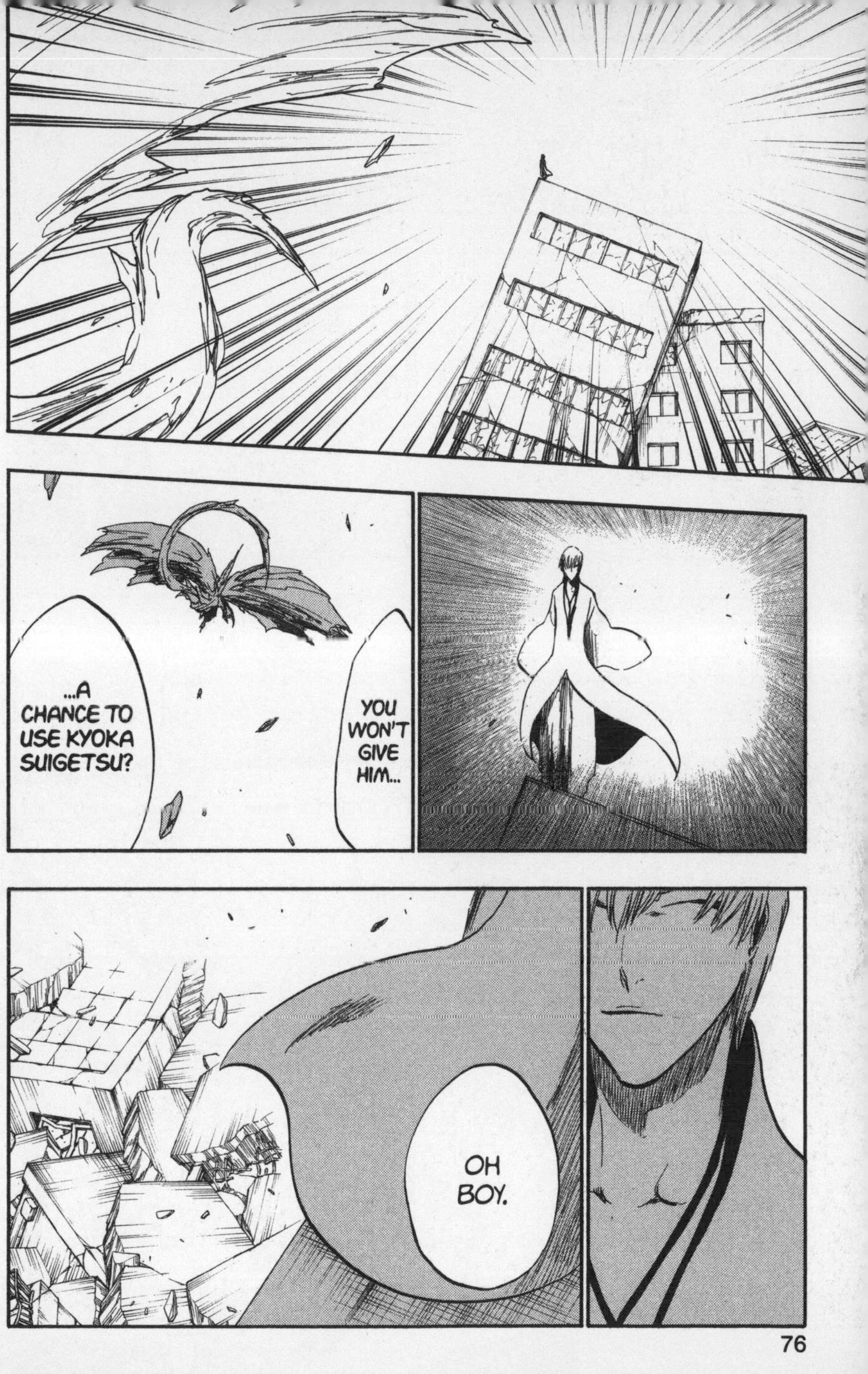
YOU WON'T GIVE HIM...
...A CHANCE TO USE KYOKA SUIGETSU?
OH BOY.

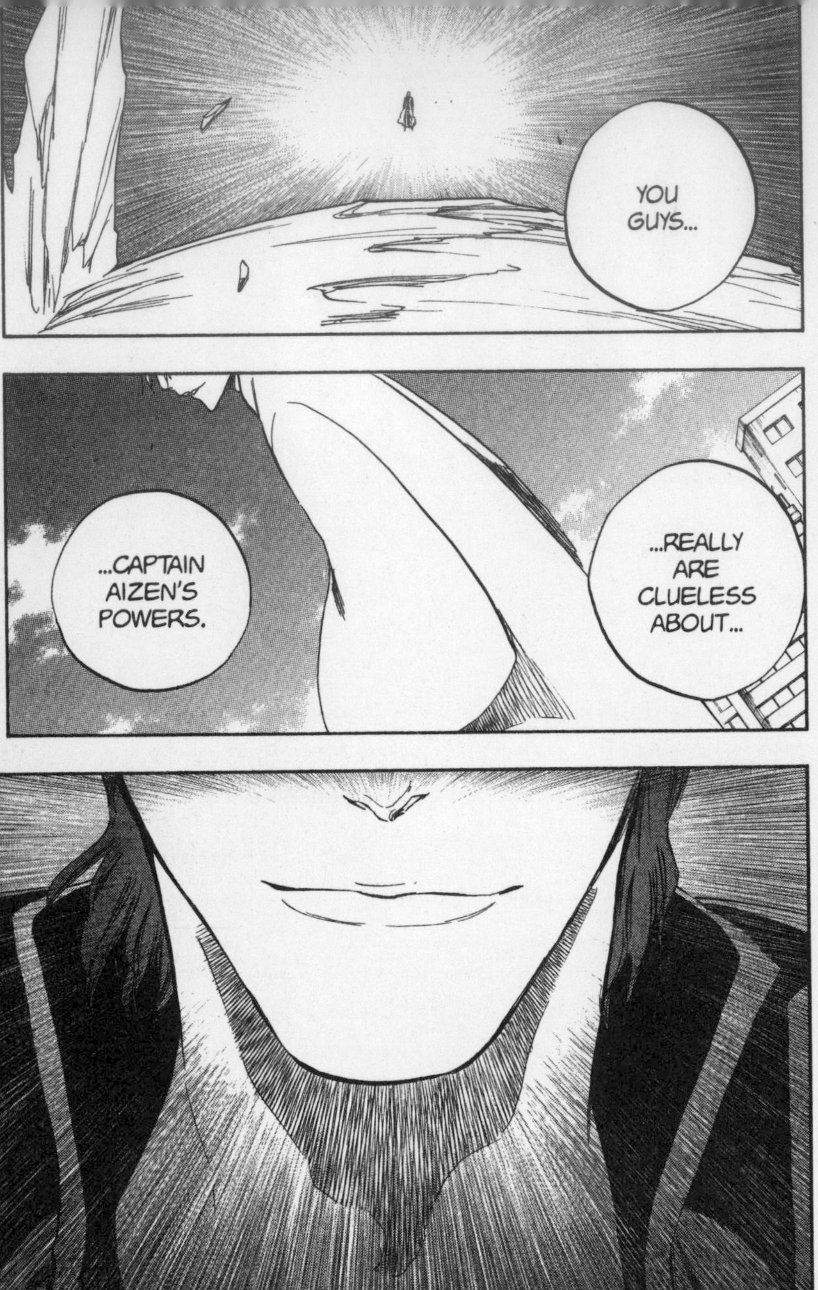
YOU GUYS...
...REALLY ARE CLUELESS ABOUT...
...CAPTAIN AIZEN'S POWERS.

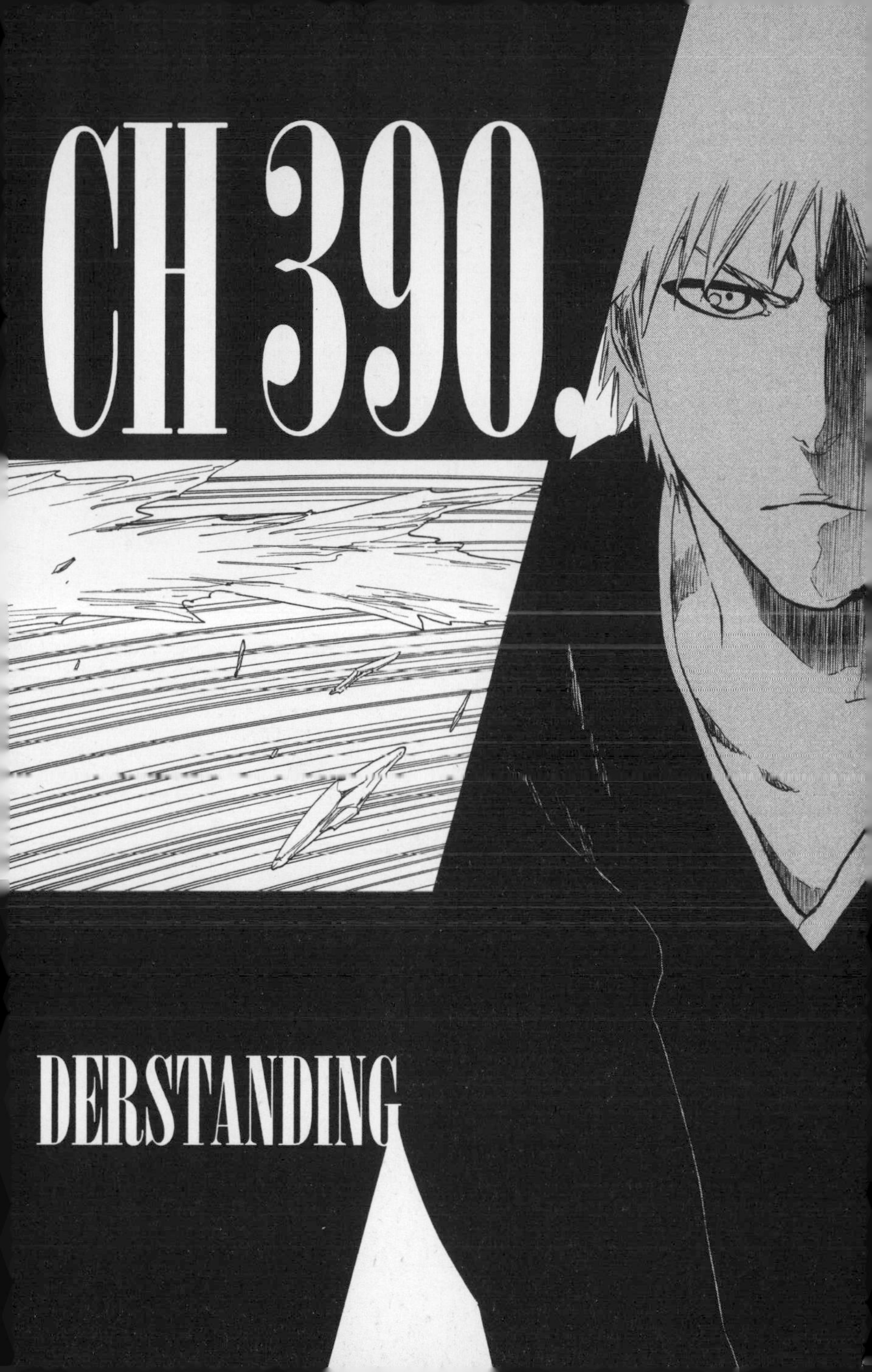
CH 390.
DERSTANDING

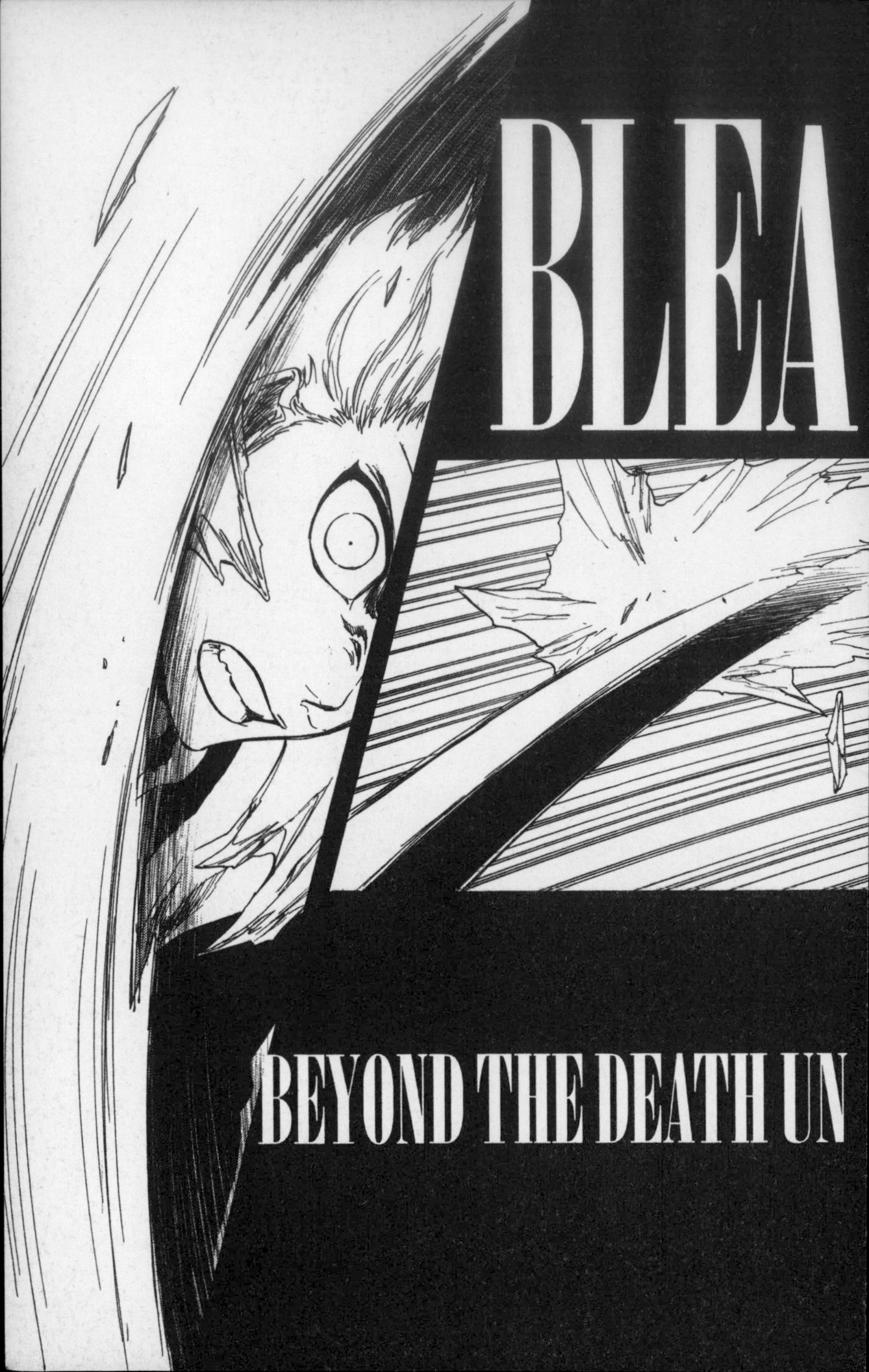
BLEA
BEYOND THE DEATH UN

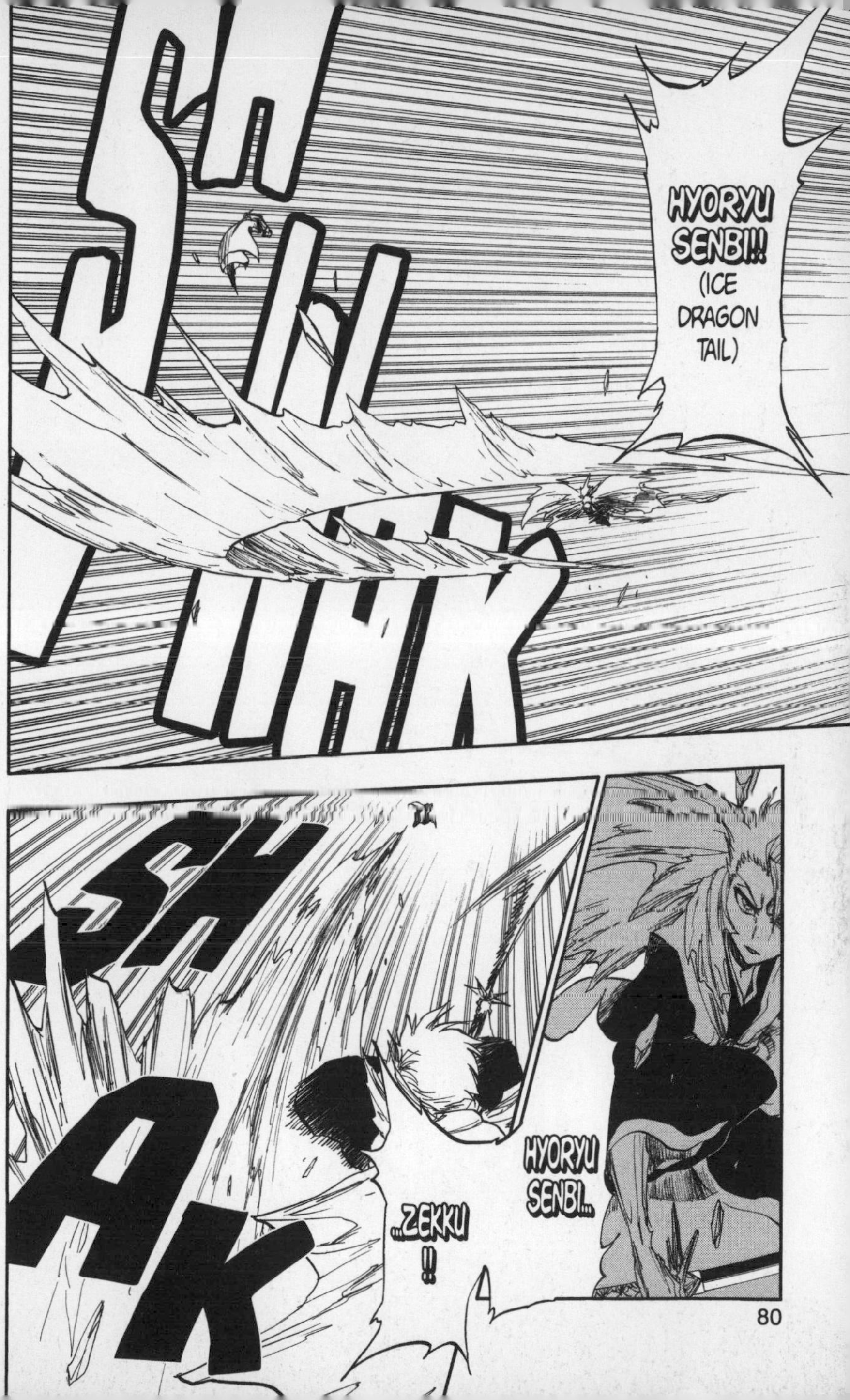
HYORYU SENBI!!! (ICE DRAGON TAIL)
HYORYU SENBI...
...ZEKKU!!

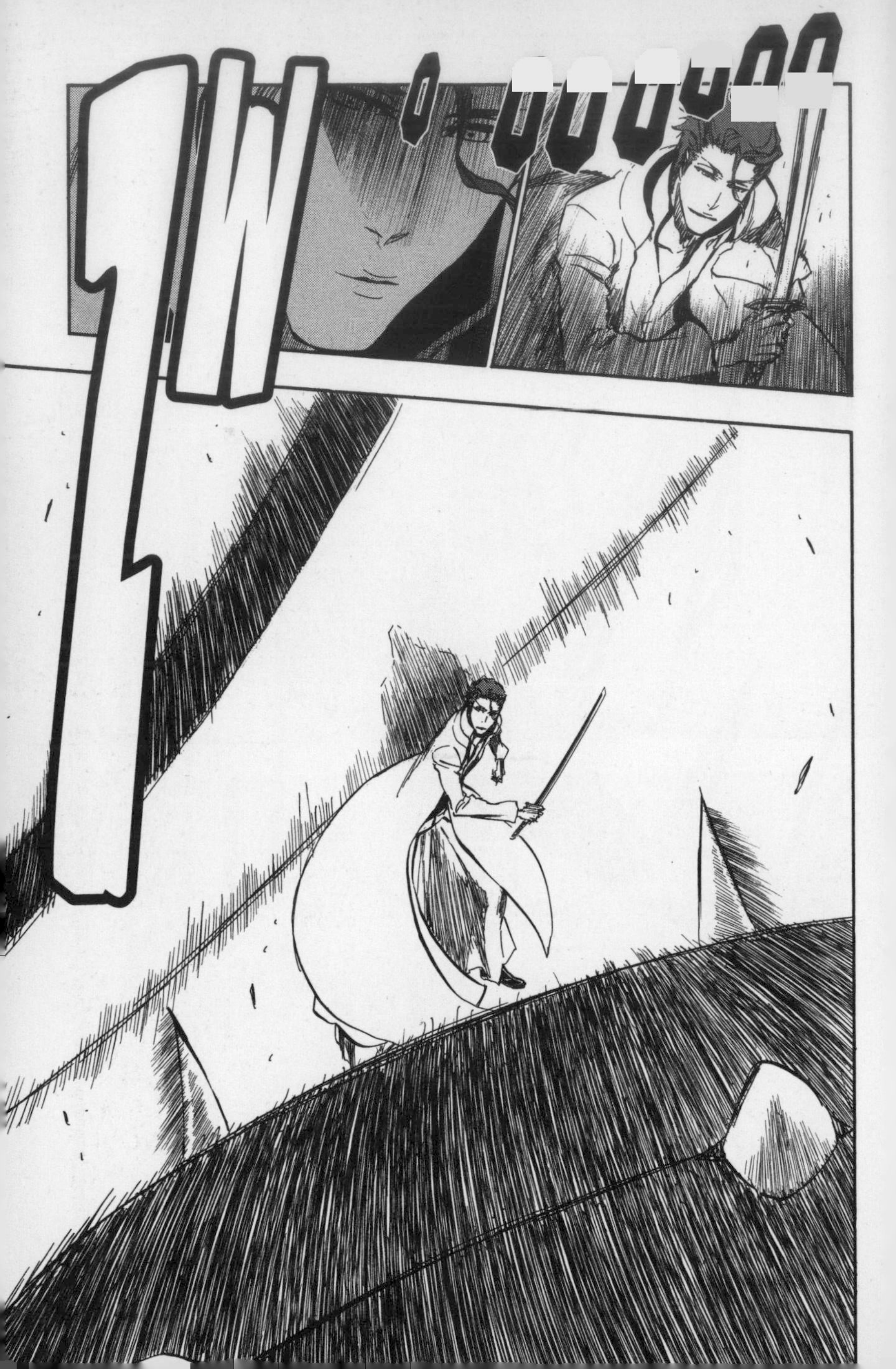

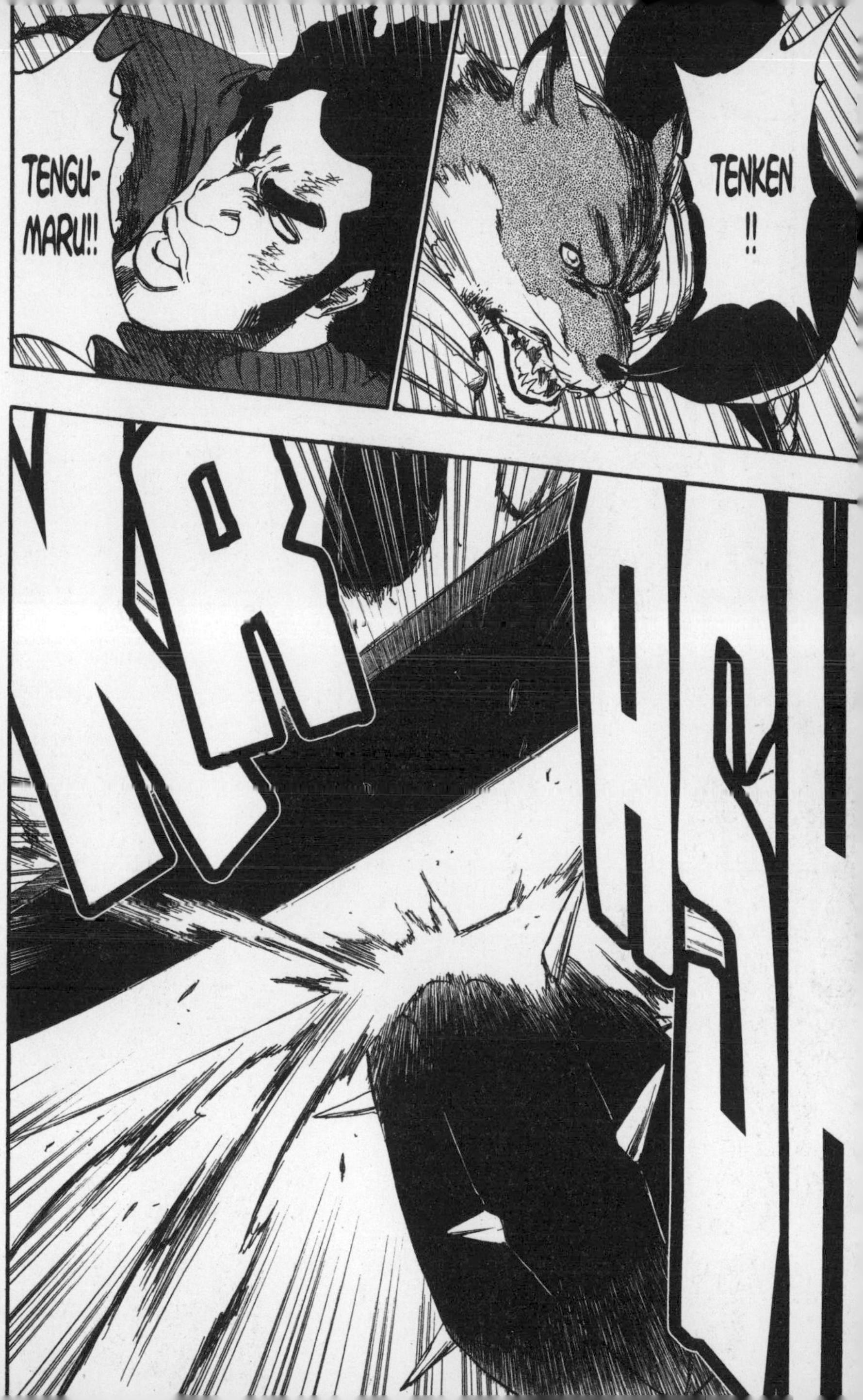
TENKEN !!
TENGU-MARU!!
KRAASH

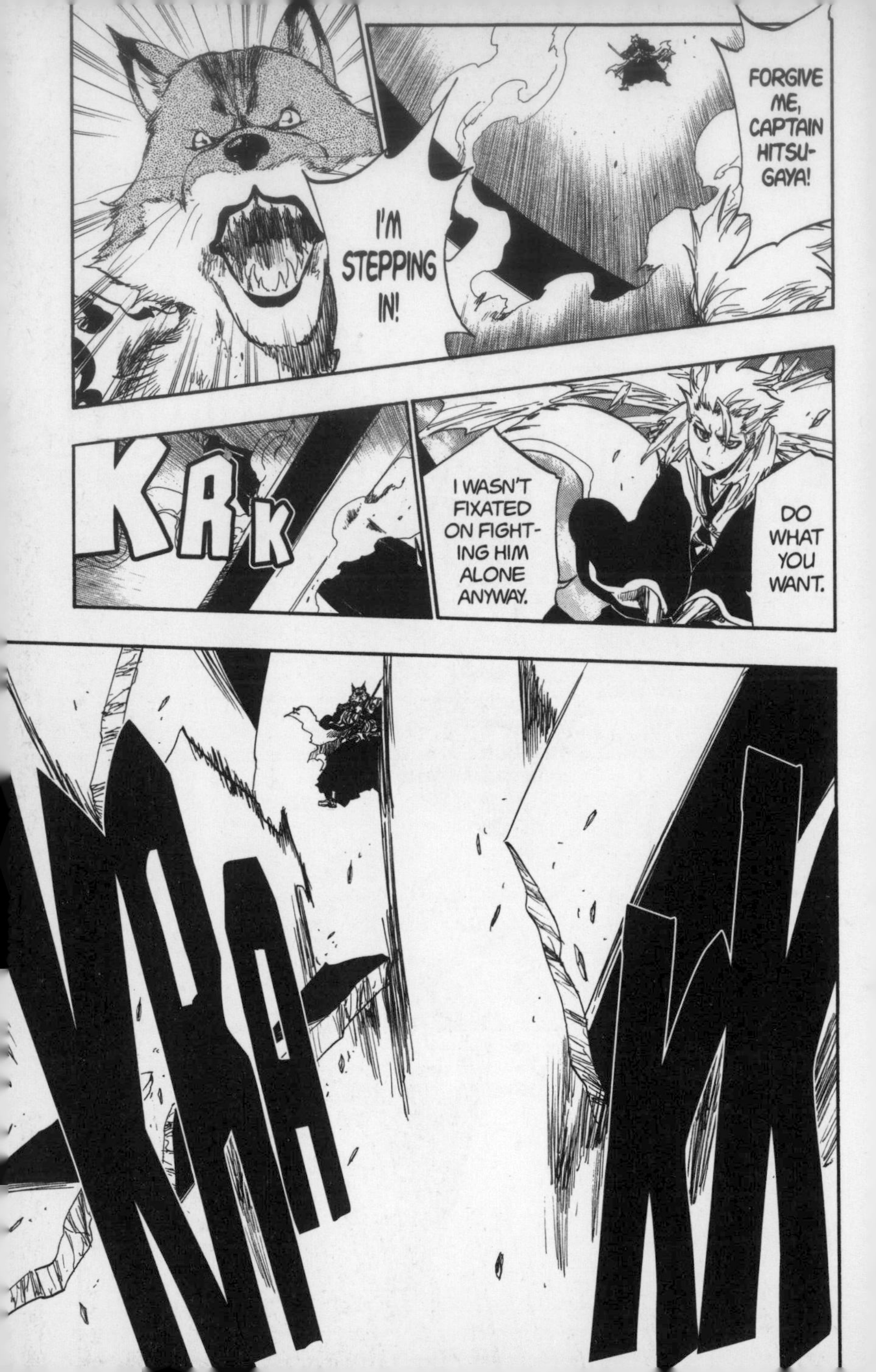
FORGIVE ME, CAPTAIN HITSU-GAYA!
I'M STEPPING IN!
DO WHAT YOU WANT.
I WASN'T FIXATED ON FIGHT-ING HIM ALONE ANYWAY.
KRAK

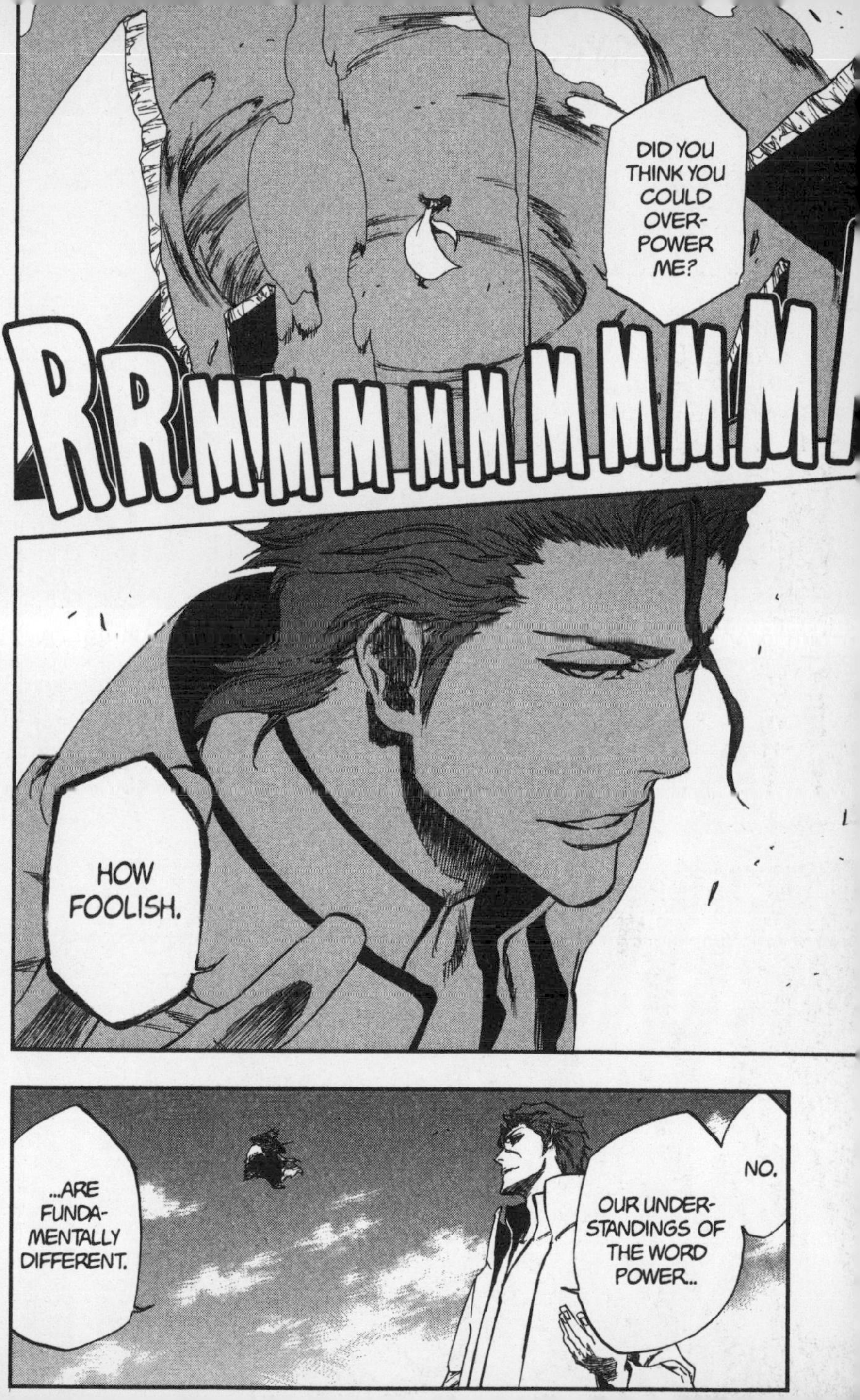
DID YOU THINK YOU COULD OVER-POWER ME?
RRMMMMMMMMMMM
HOW FOOLISH.
NO.
OUR UNDER-STANDINGS OF THE WORD POWER...
...ARE FUNDA-MENTALLY DIFFERENT.

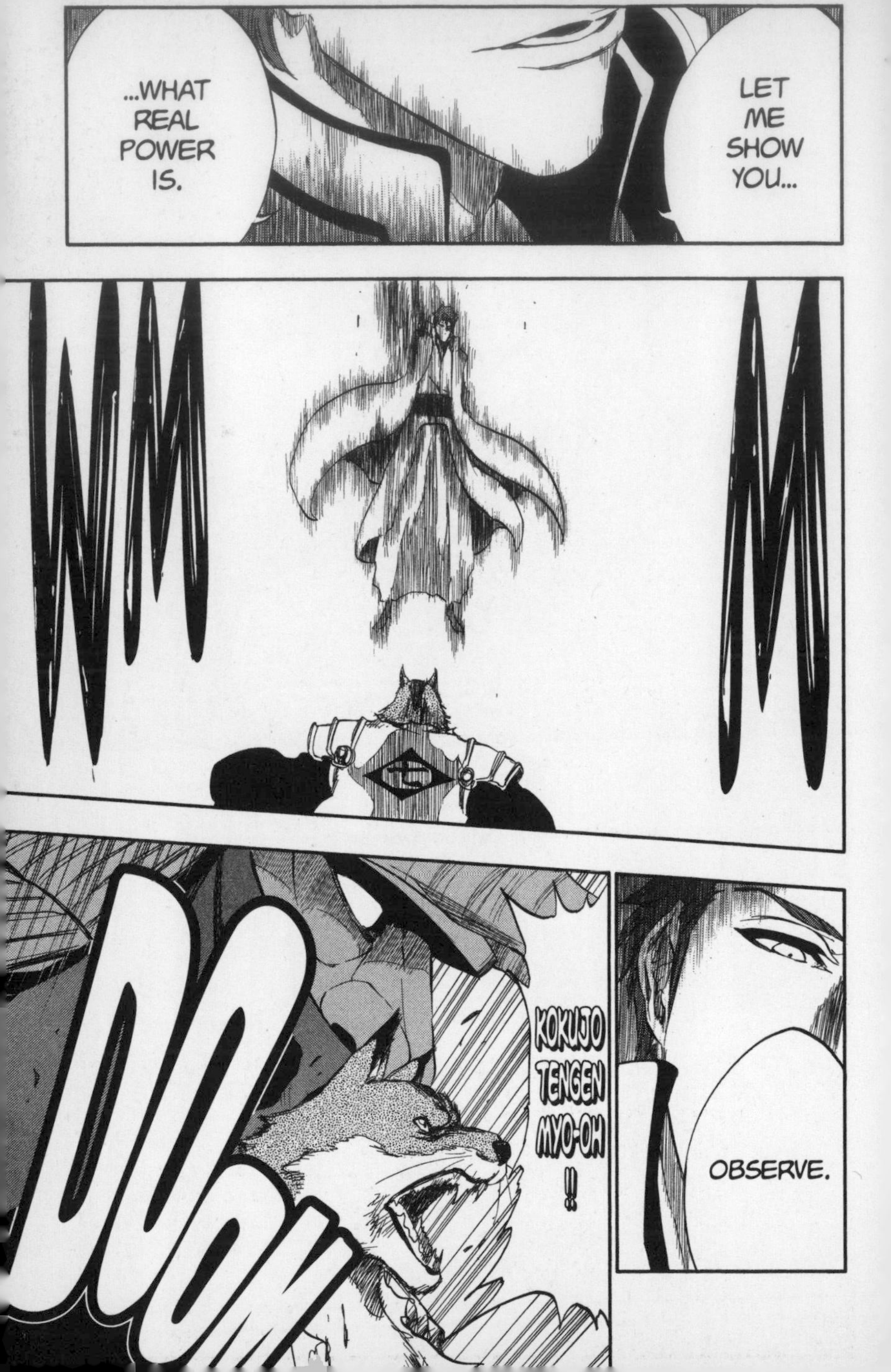
LET ME SHOW YOU...
...WHAT REAL POWER IS.
OBSERVE.
KOKUJO TENGEN MYO-OH!!

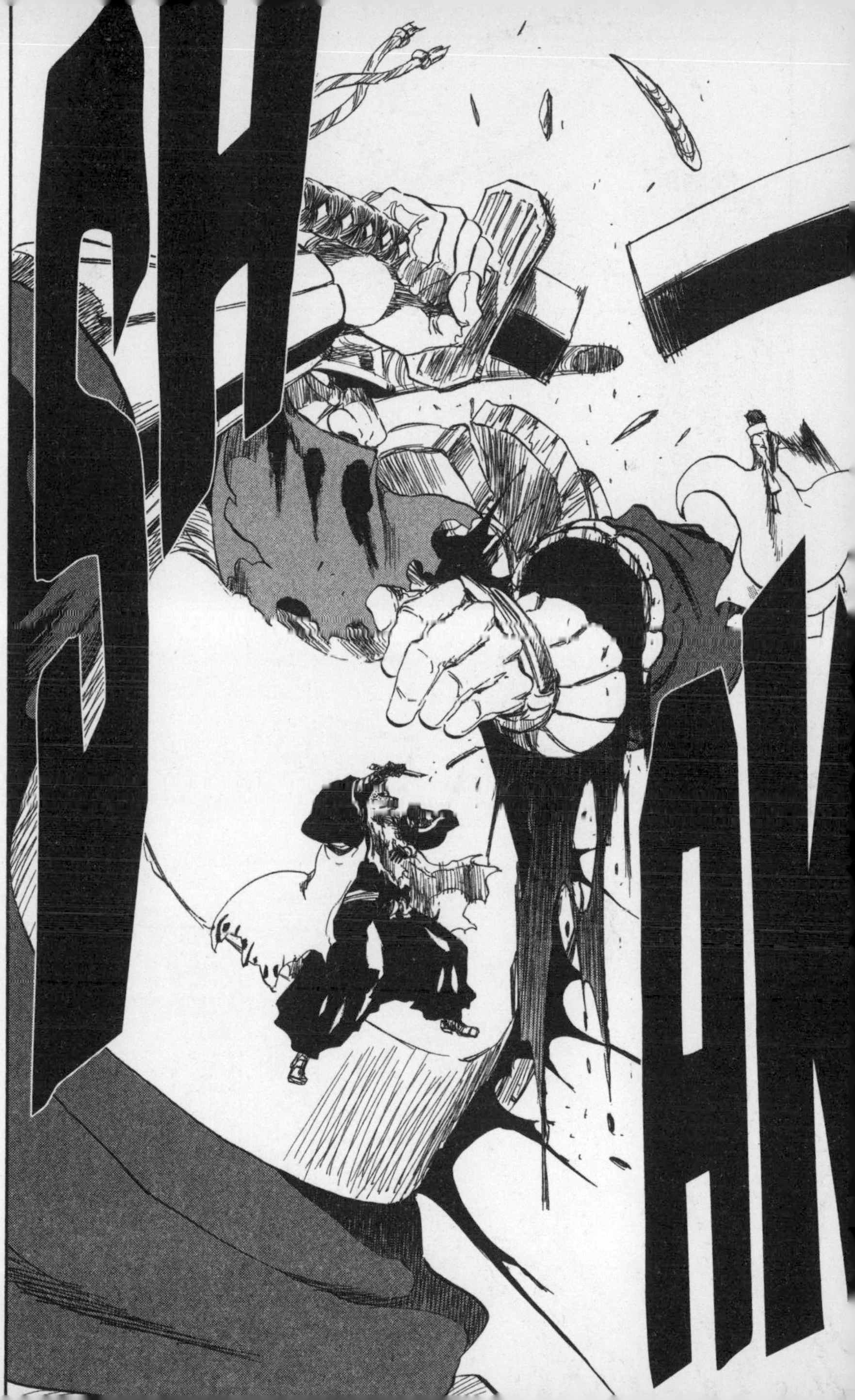

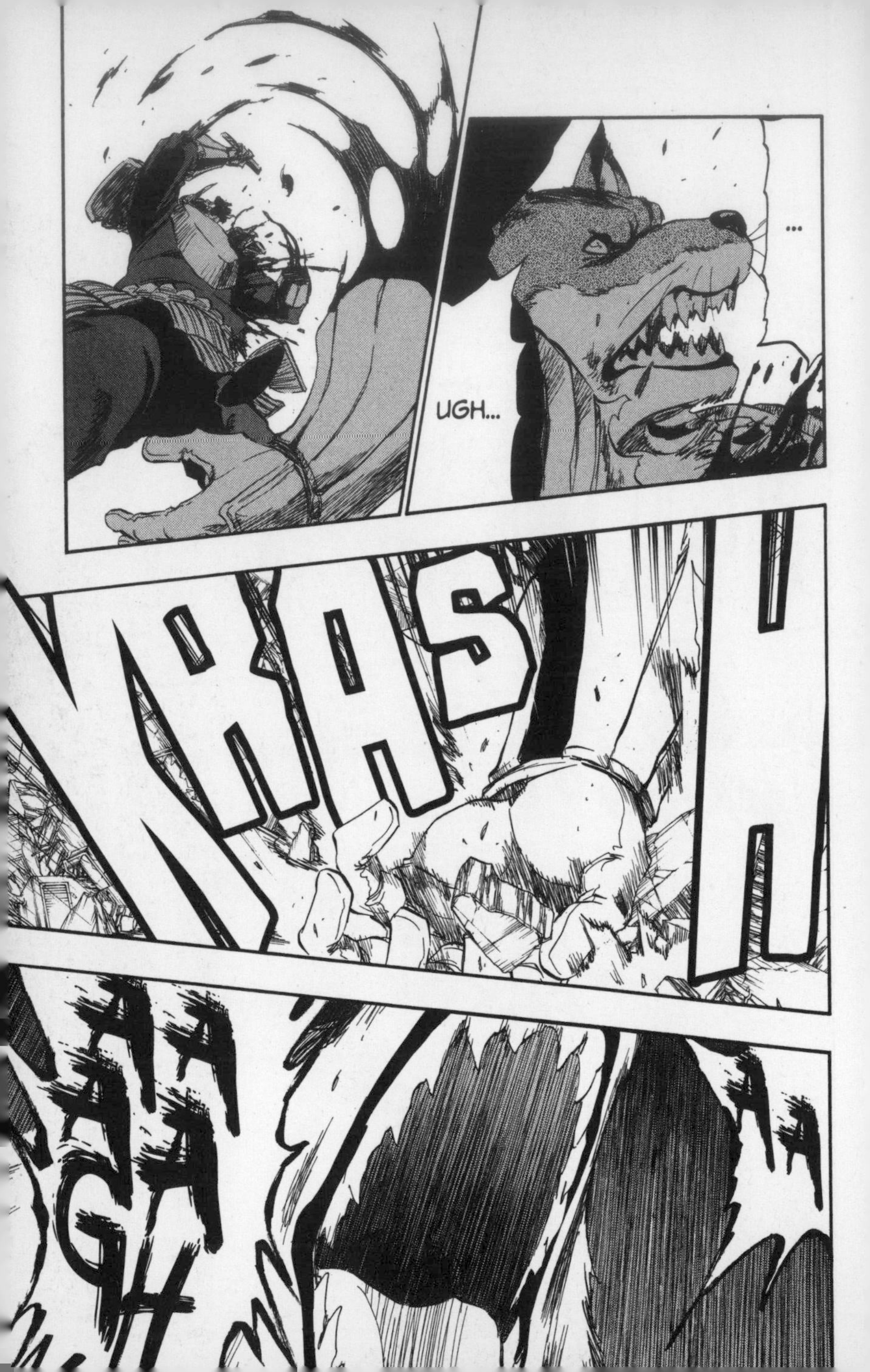
...
UGH...
KRASH
AAA
AAAAGH

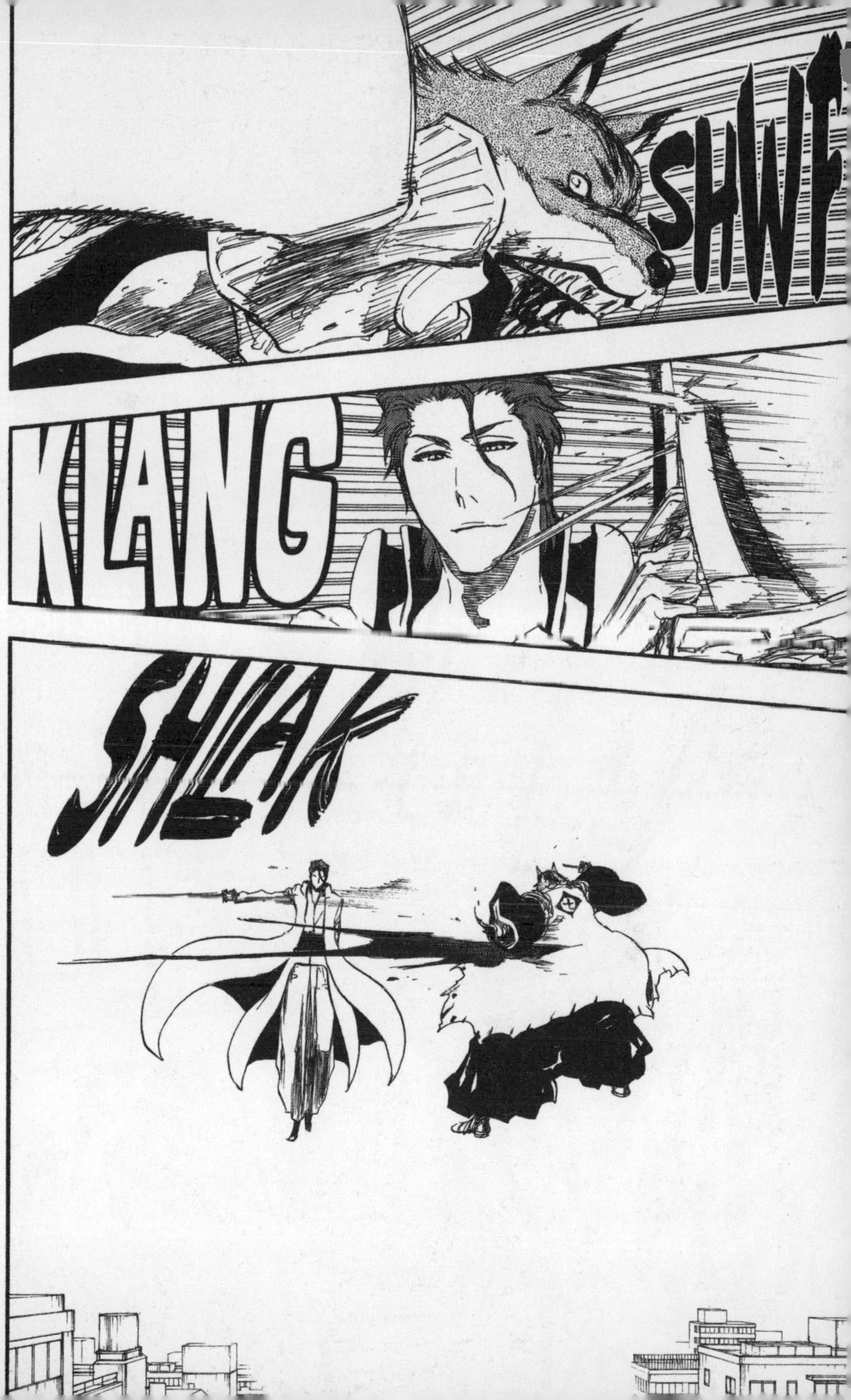
SHWF
KLANG
SHLAK

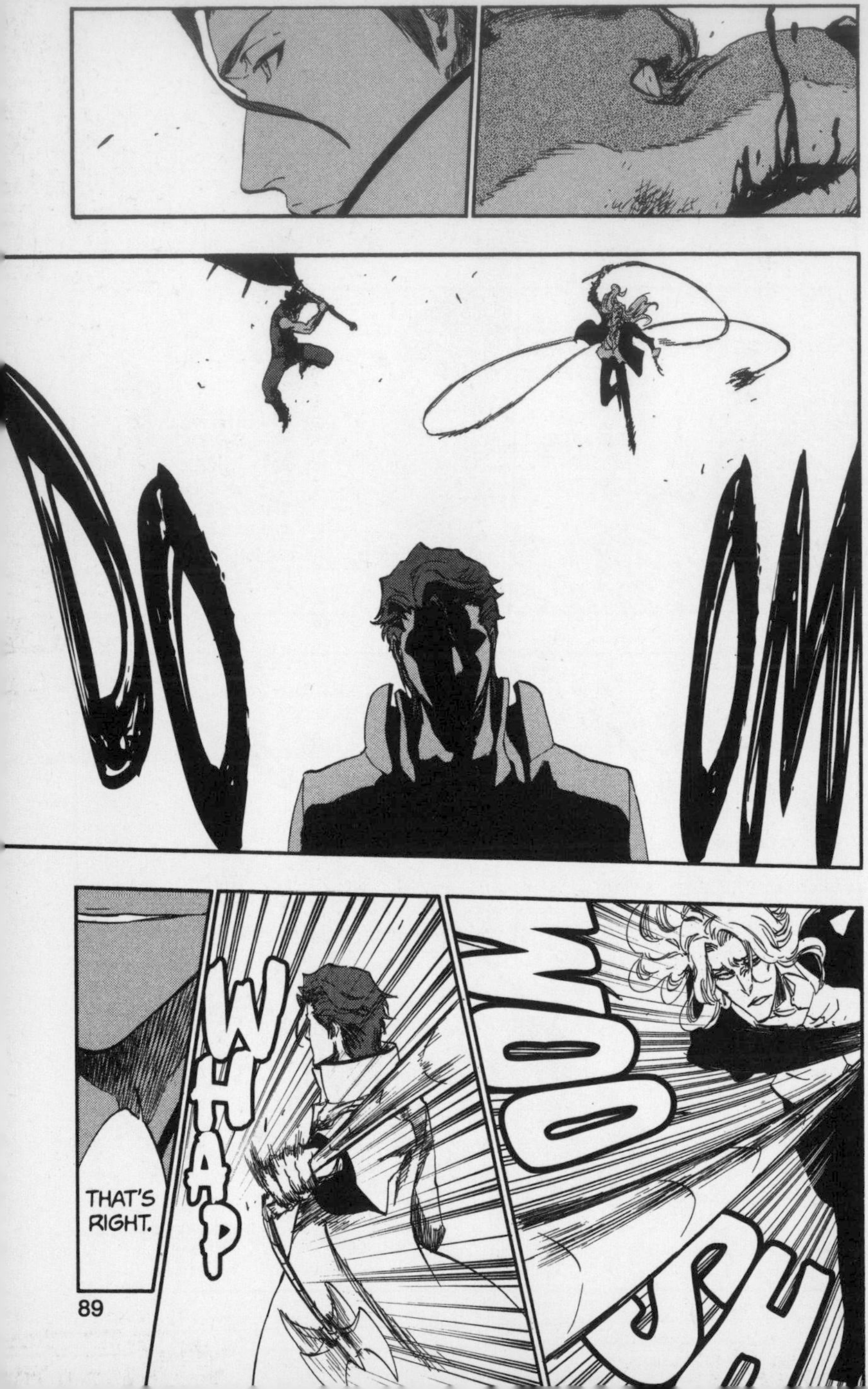
DOOM
WOOSH
WHAP
THAT'S RIGHT.

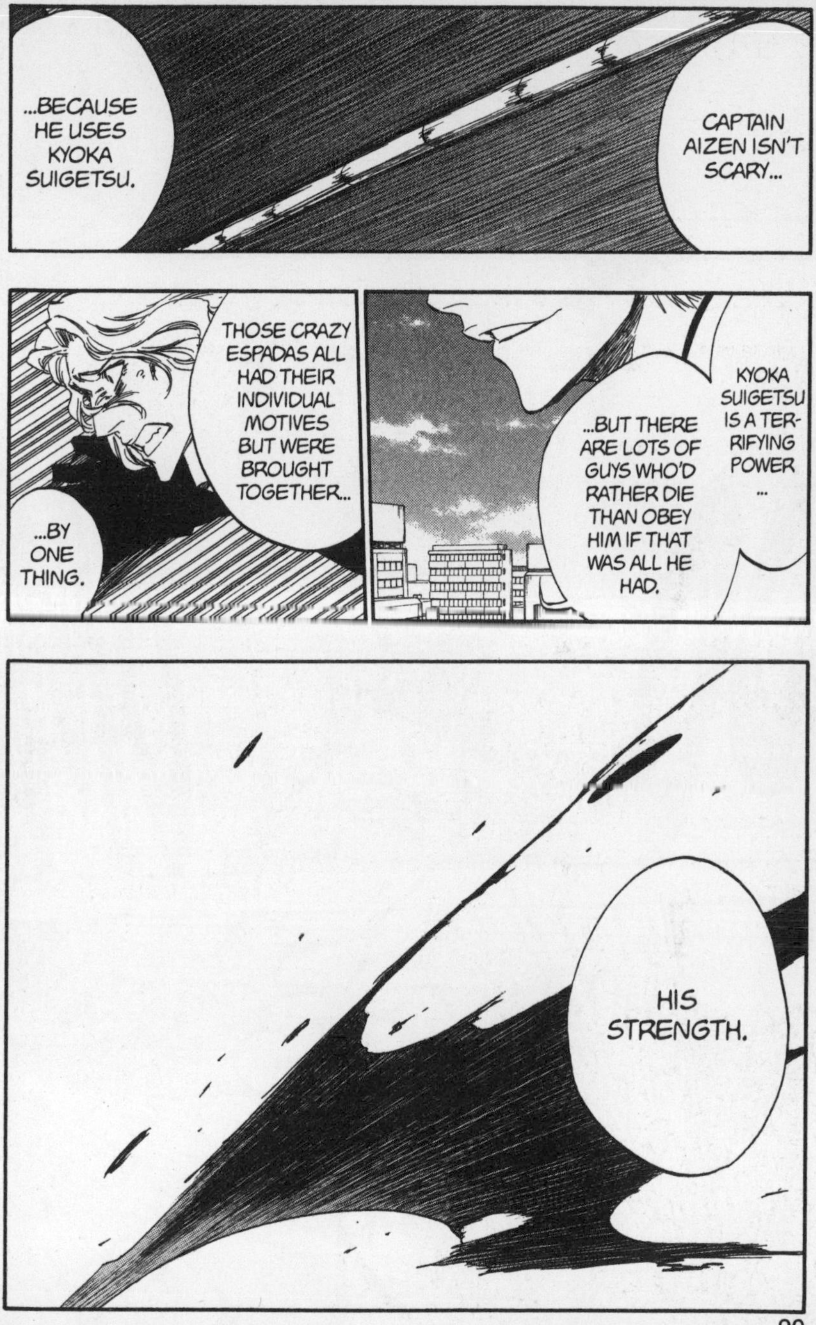
CAPTAIN AIZEN ISN'T SCARY...
...BECAUSE HE USES KYOKA SUIGETSU.
KYOKA SUIGETSU IS A TER-RIFYING POWER ...
...BUT THERE ARE LOTS OF GUYS WHO'D RATHER DIE THAN OBEY HIM IF THAT WAS ALL HE HAD.
THOSE CRAZY ESPADAS ALL HAD THEIR INDIVIDUAL MOTIVES BUT WERE BROUGHT TOGETHER...
...BY ONE THING.
HIS STRENGTH.

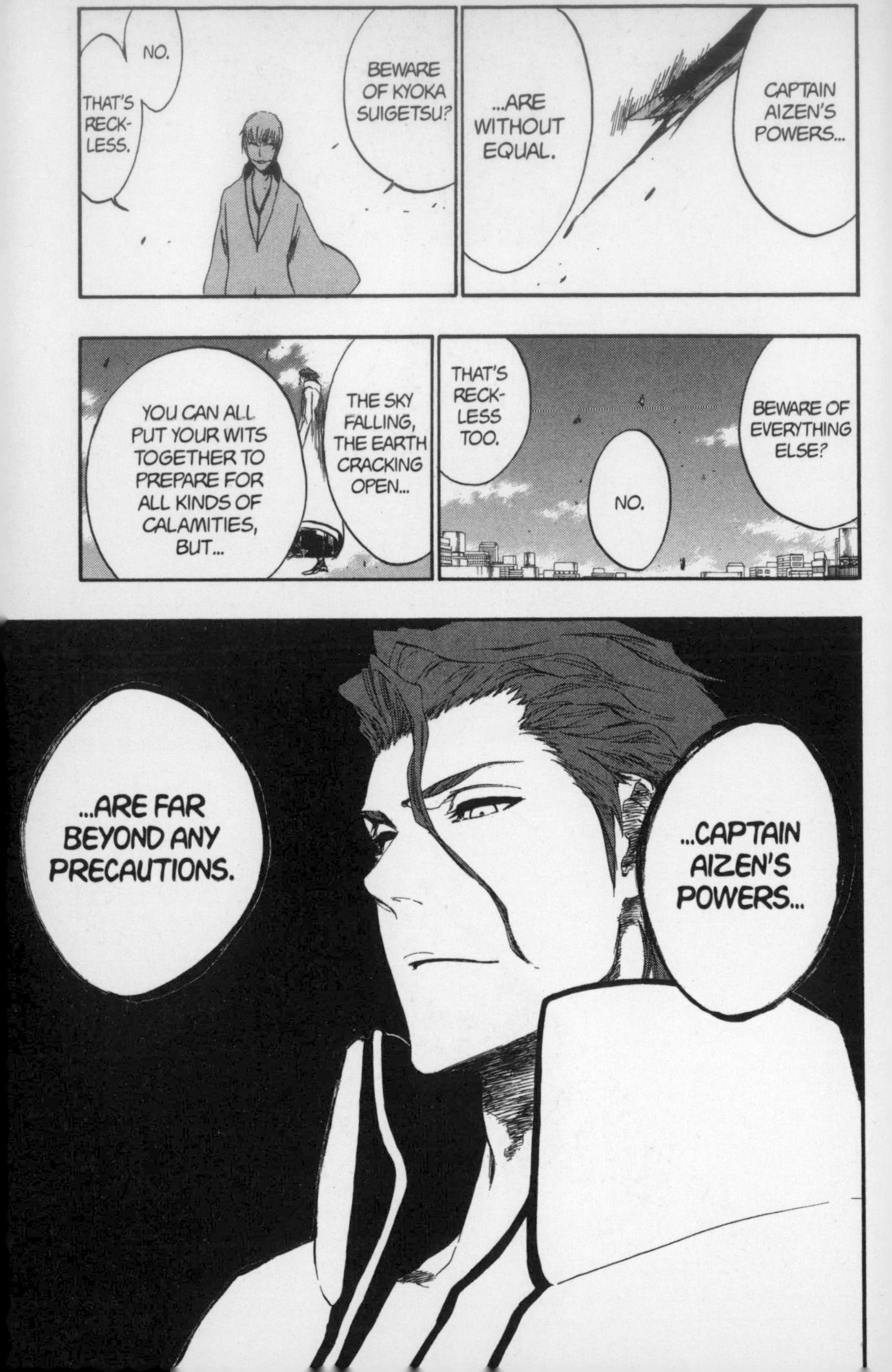
CAPTAIN AIZEN'S POWERS...
...ARE WITHOUT EQUAL.
BEWARE OF KYOKA SUIGETSU?
NO.
THAT'S RECK-LESS.
BEWARE OF EVERYTHING ELSE?
NO.
THAT'S RECK-LESS TOO.
THE SKY FALLING, THE EARTH CRACKING OPEN...
YOU CAN ALL PUT YOUR WITS TOGETHER TO PREPARE FOR ALL KINDS OF CALAMITIES, BUT...
...CAPTAIN AIZEN'S POWERS...
...ARE FAR BEYOND ANY PRECAUTIONS.

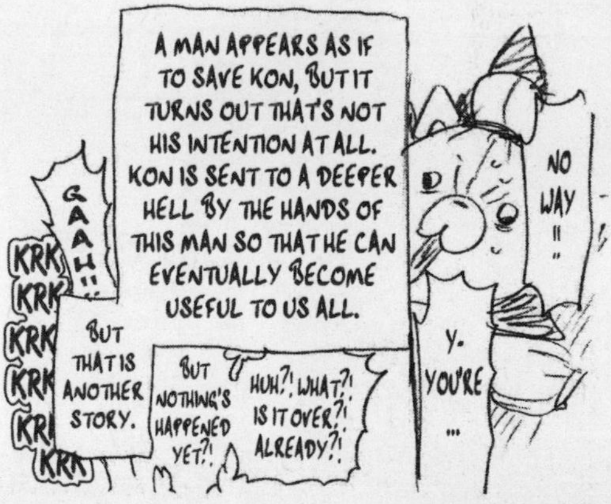
NO WAY!!
A MAN APPEARS AS IF TO SAVE KON, BUT IT TURNS OUT THAT'S NOT HIS INTENTION AT ALL. KON IS SENT TO A DEEPER HELL BY THE HANDS OF THIS MAN SO THAT HE CAN EVENTUALLY BECOME USEFUL TO US ALL.
Y. YOU'RE ...
HUH?! WHAT?! IS IT OVER?! ALREADY?!
BUT NOTHING'S HAPPENED YET?!
GAAAH!!
BUT THAT IS ANOTHER STORY.
KRK KRK KRK KRK KRK KRK

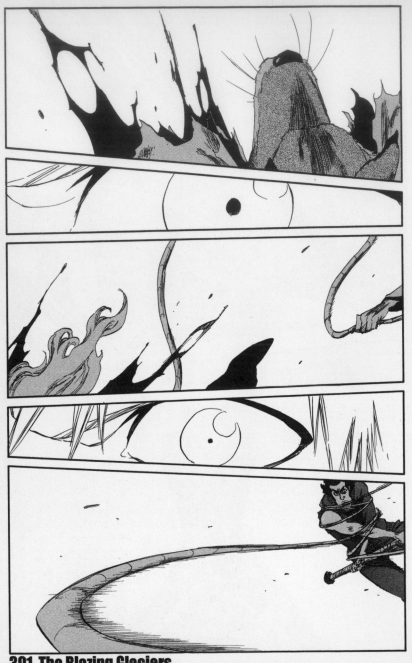

391. The Blazing Glaciers

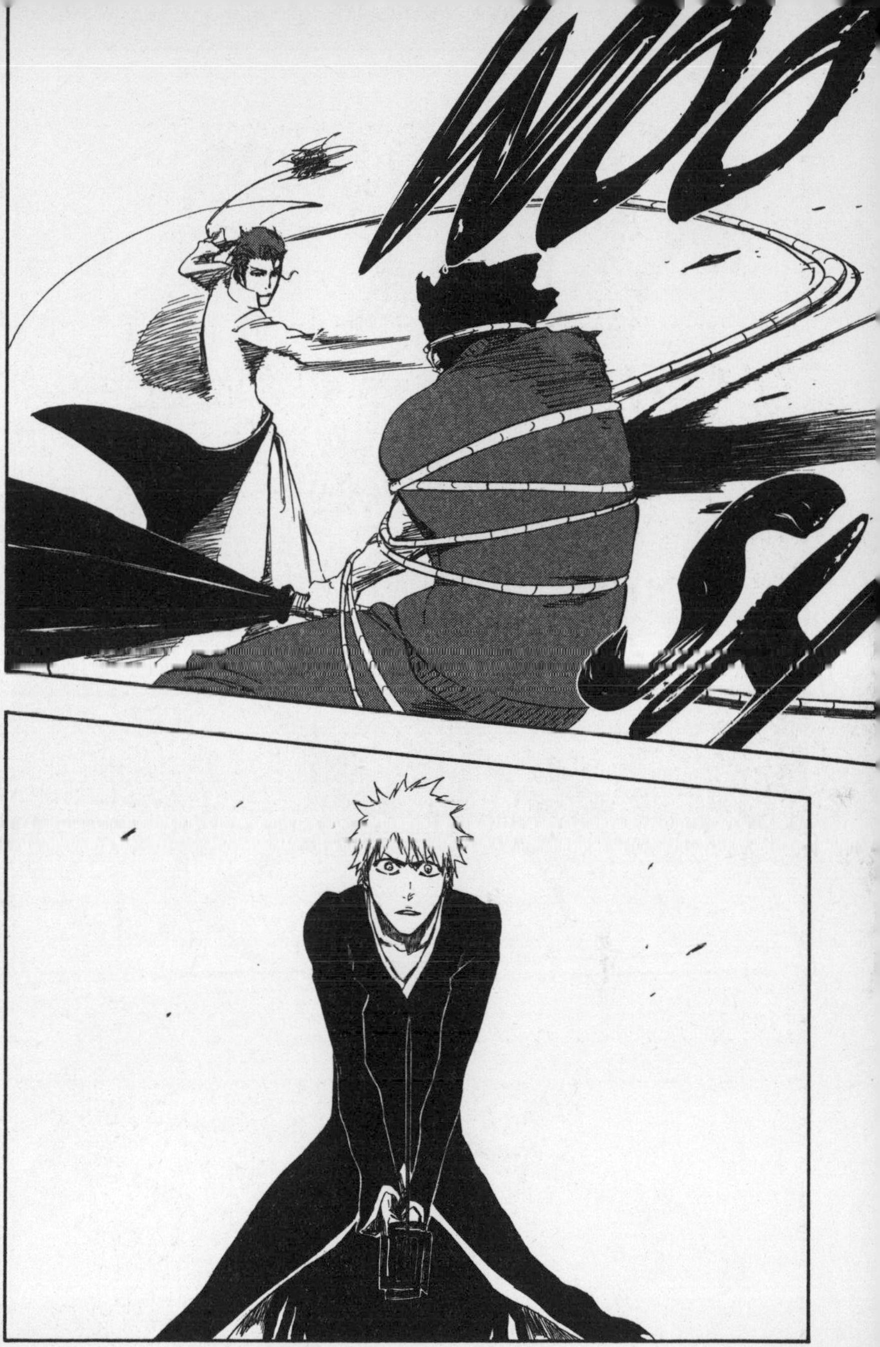
WOOSH

READ THIS WAY

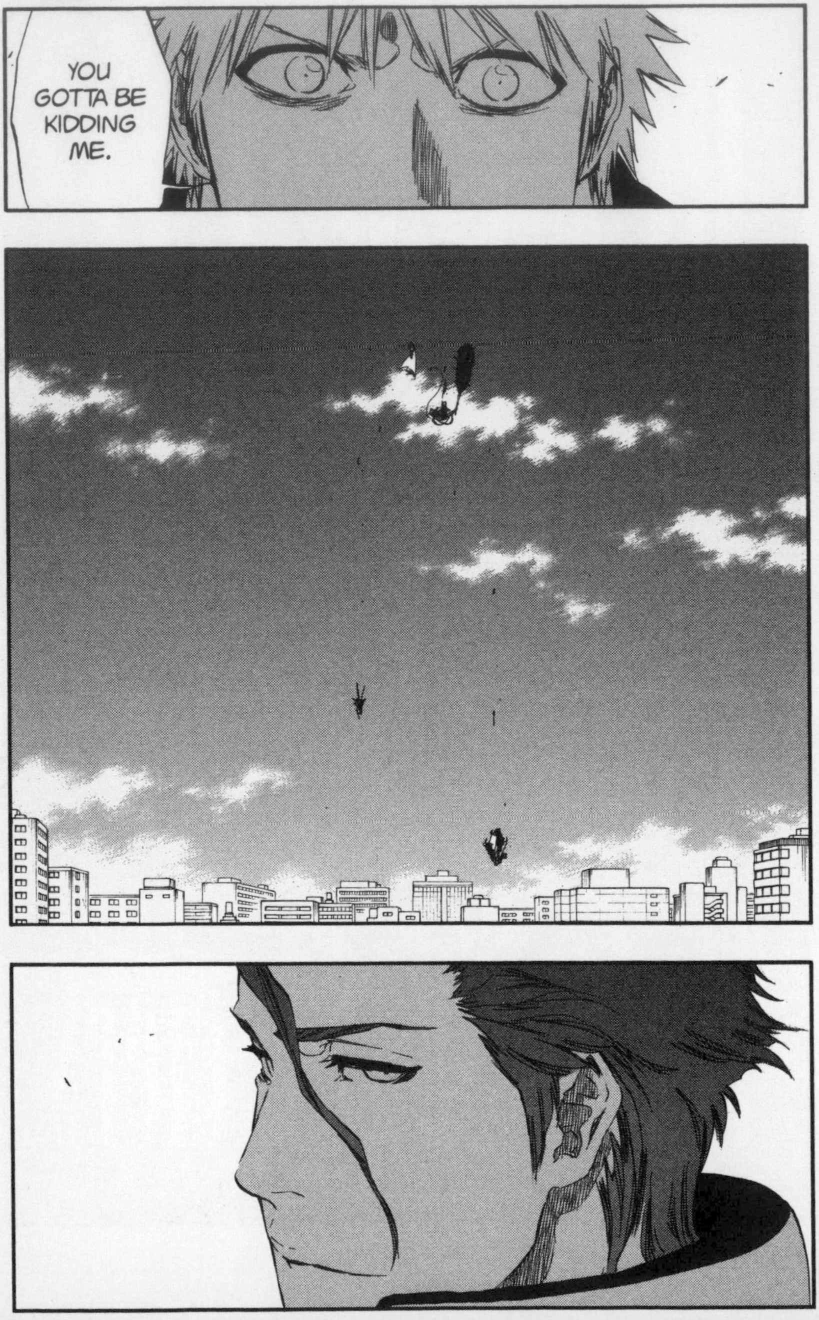
YOU GOTTA BE KIDDING ME.

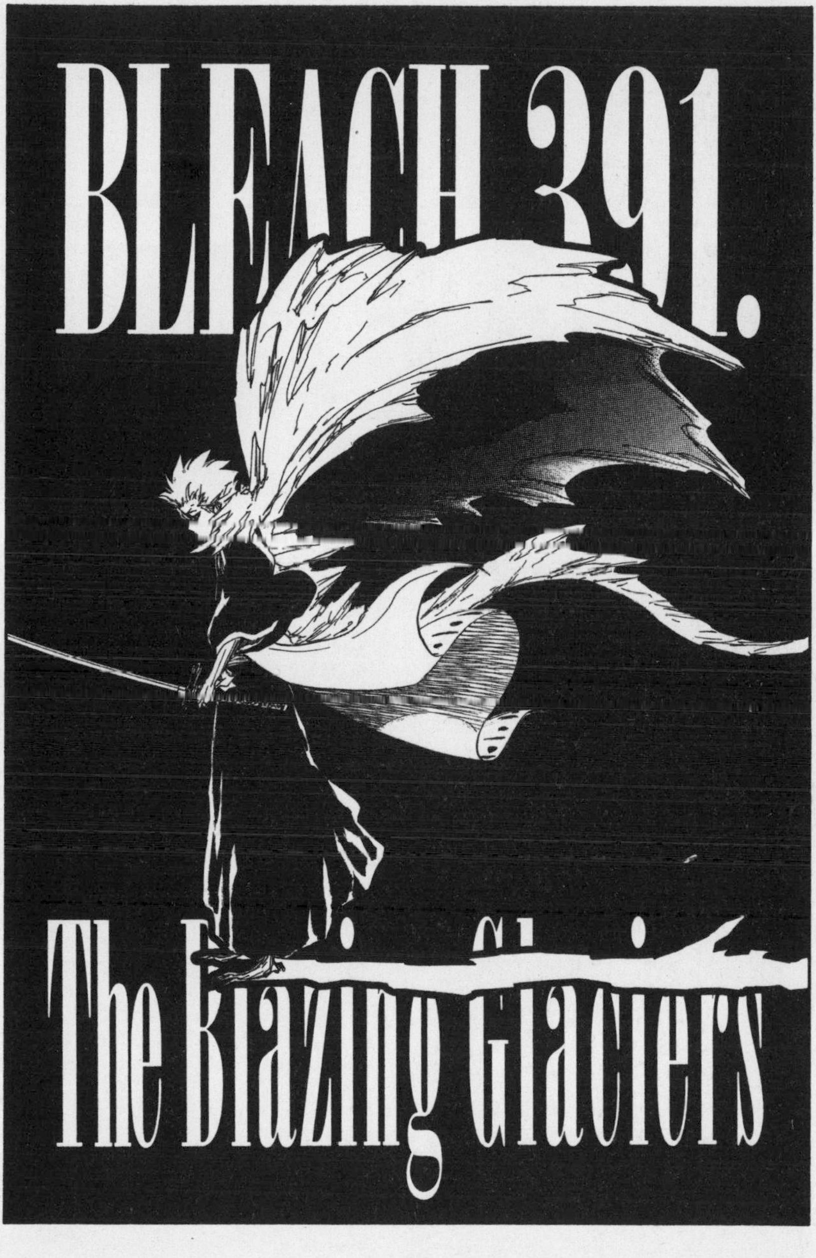
BLEACH 391.
The Blazing Glaciers

READ THIS WAY

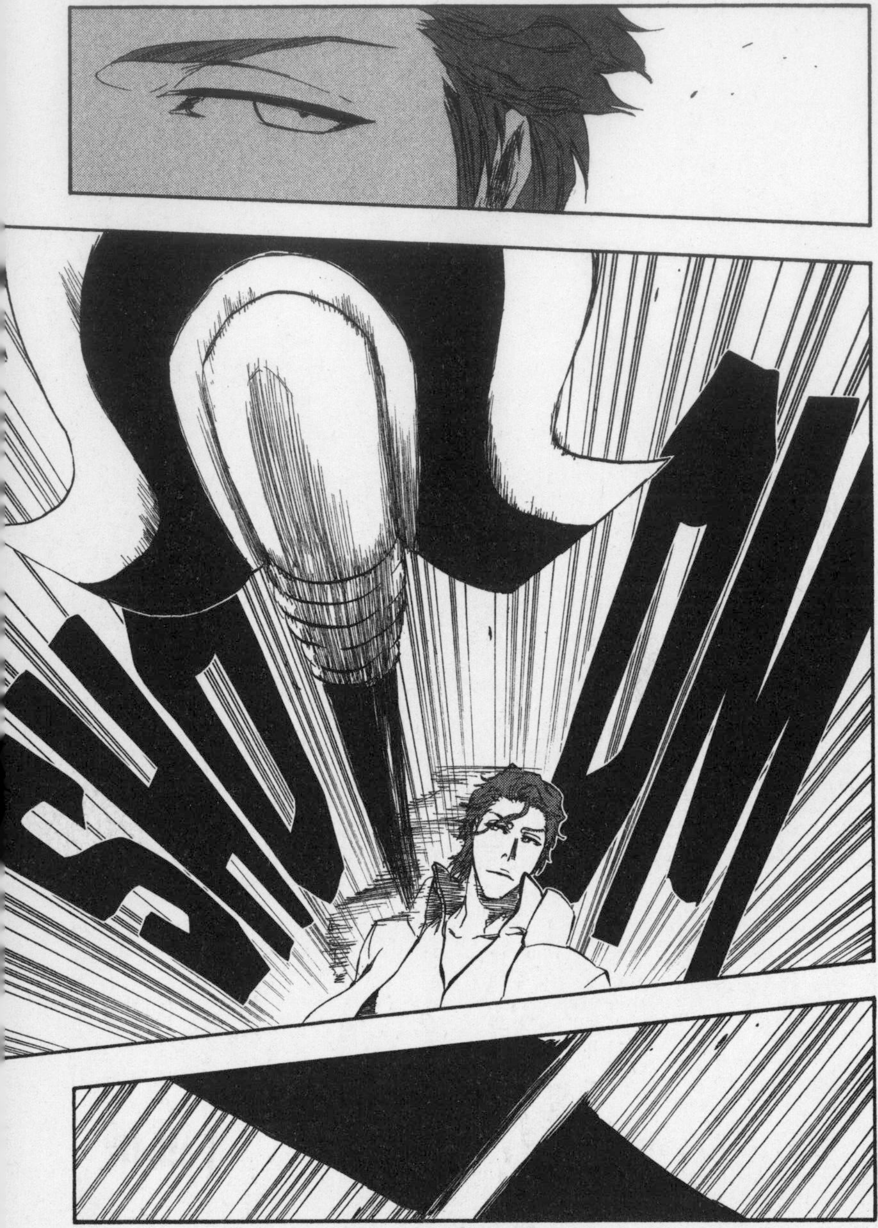

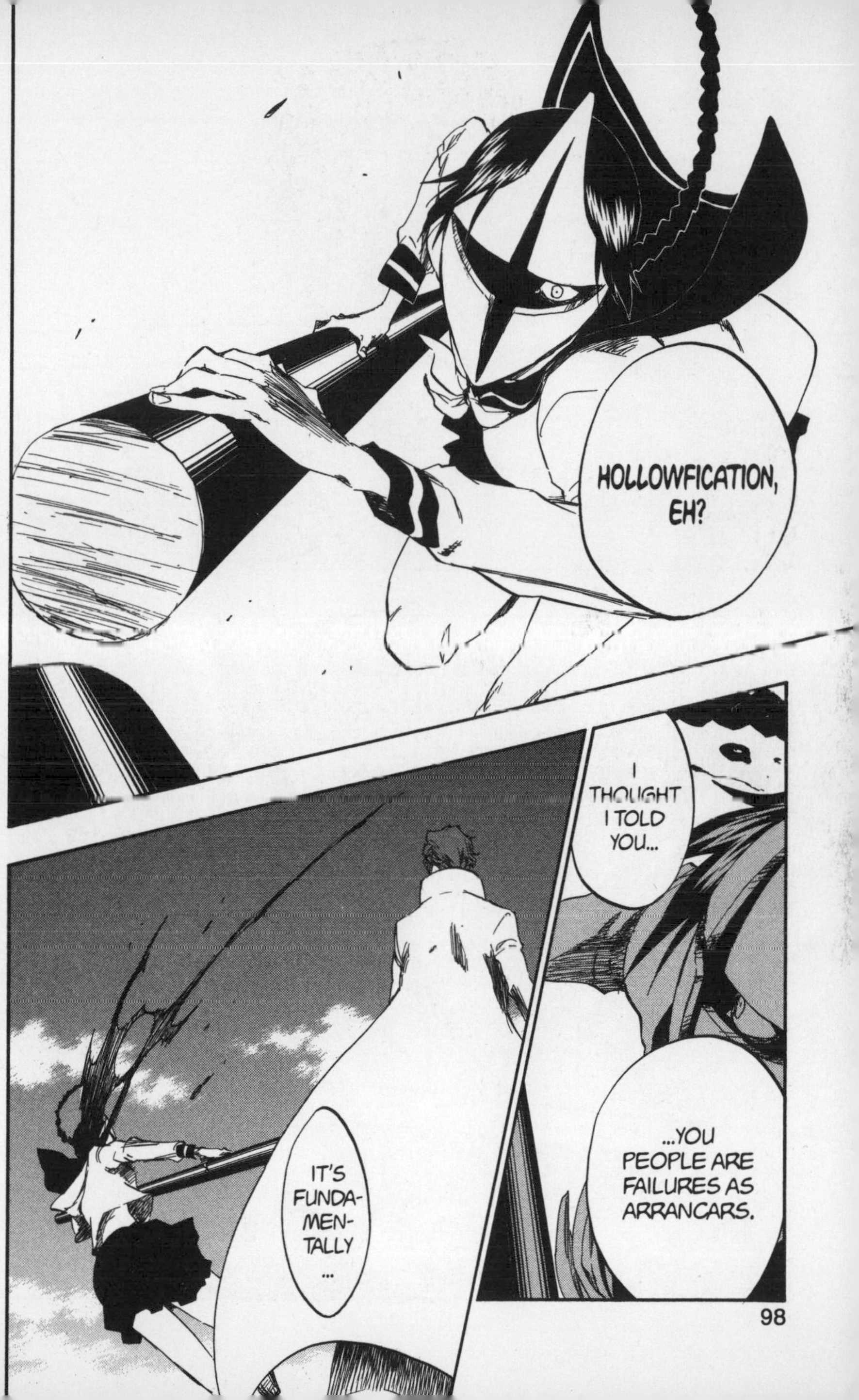
HOLLOWFICATION, EH?
I THOUGHT I TOLD YOU...
...YOU PEOPLE ARE FAILURES AS ARRANCARS.
IT'S FUNDAMENTALLY ...

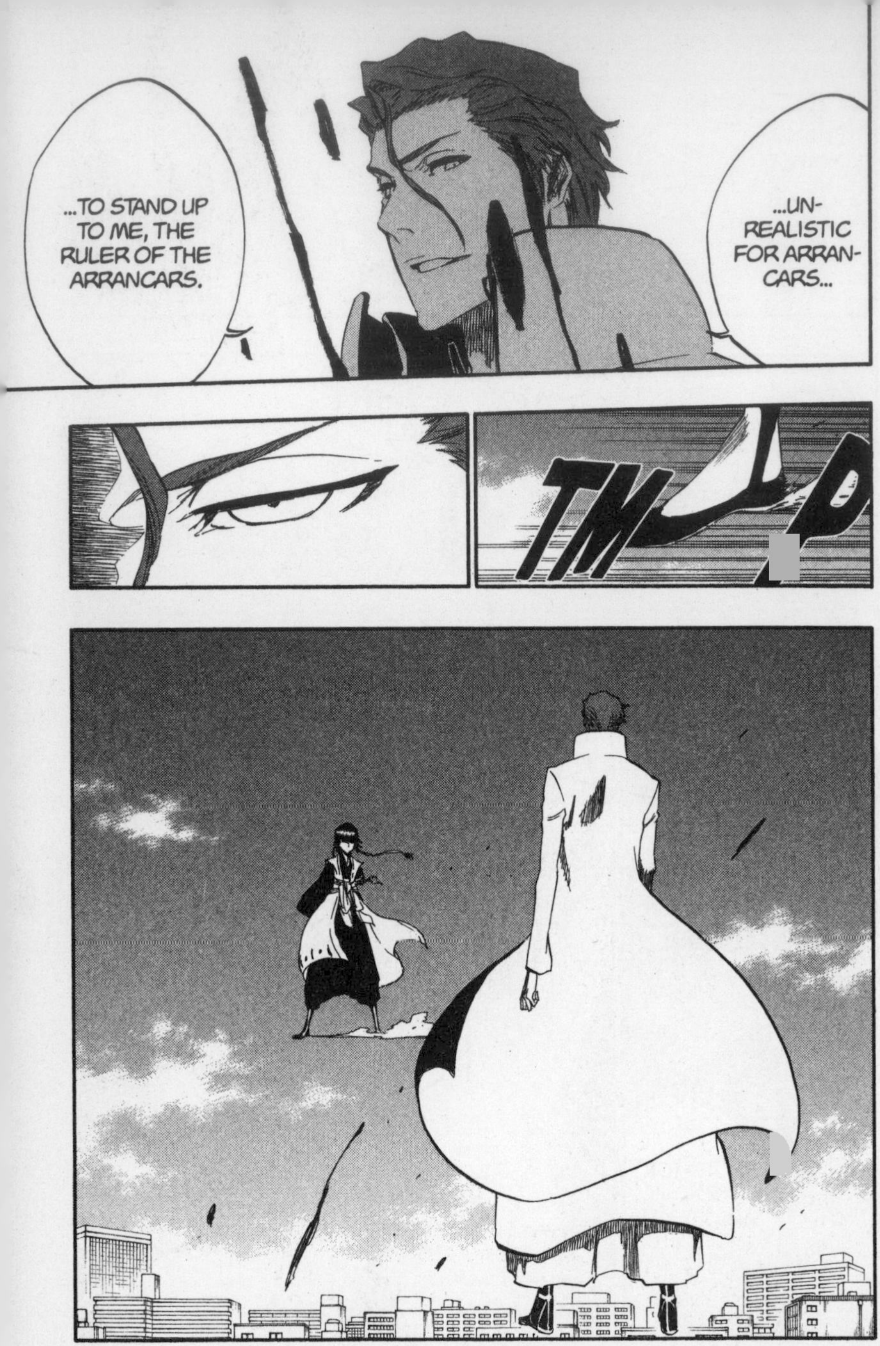
...UN-REALISTIC FOR ARRAN-CARS...
...TO STAND UP TO ME, THE RULER OF THE ARRANCARS.
TMP

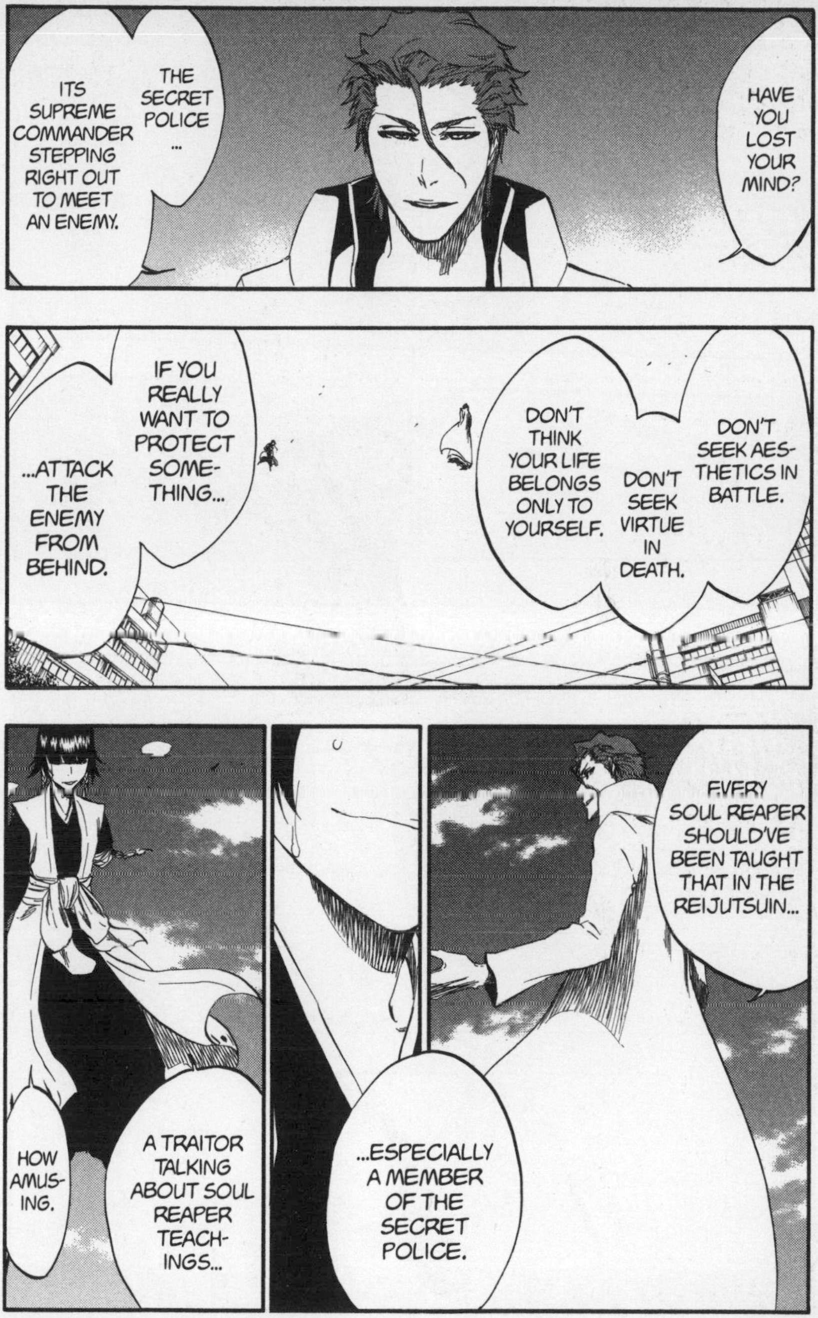
HAVE YOU LOST YOUR MIND?
THE SECRET POLICE...
ITS SUPREME COMMANDER STEPPING RIGHT OUT TO MEET AN ENEMY.
DON'T SEEK AES-THETICS IN BATTLE.
DON'T SEEK VIRTUE IN DEATH.
DON'T THINK YOUR LIFE BELONGS ONLY TO YOURSELF.
IF YOU REALLY WANT TO PROTECT SOME-THING...
...ATTACK THE ENEMY FROM BEHIND.
EVERY SOUL REAPER SHOULD'VE BEEN TAUGHT THAT IN THE REIJUTSUIN...
...ESPECIALLY A MEMBER OF THE SECRET POLICE.
A TRAITOR TALKING ABOUT SOUL REAPER TEACH-INGS...
HOW AMUS-ING.

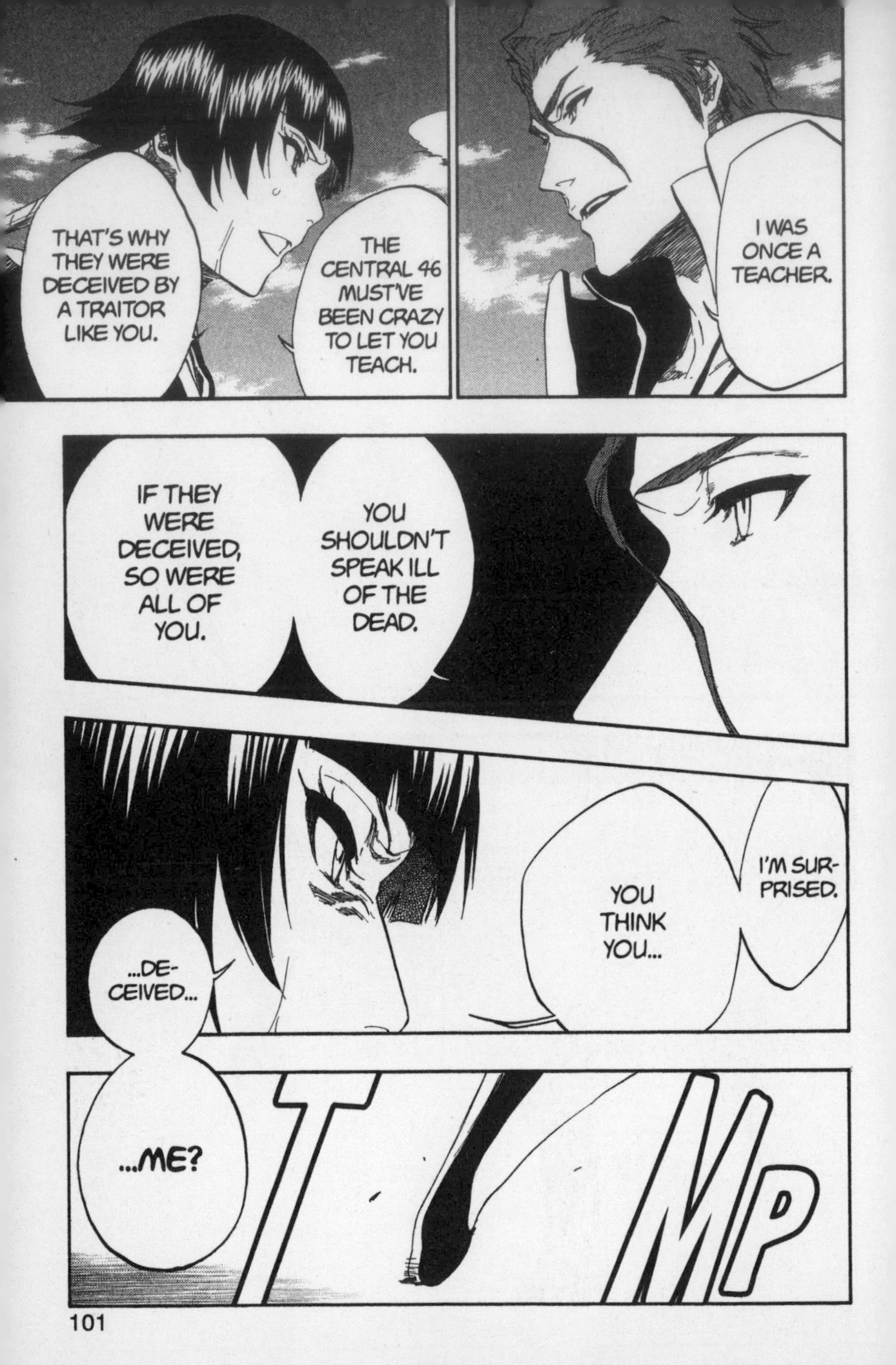
I WAS ONCE A TEACHER.
THE CENTRAL 46 MUST'VE BEEN CRAZY TO LET YOU TEACH.
THAT'S WHY THEY WERE DECEIVED BY A TRAITOR LIKE YOU.
YOU SHOULDN'T SPEAK ILL OF THE DEAD.
IF THEY WERE DECEIVED, SO WERE ALL OF YOU.
I'M SUR-PRISED.
YOU THINK YOU...
...DE-CEIVED...
...ME?
TMP

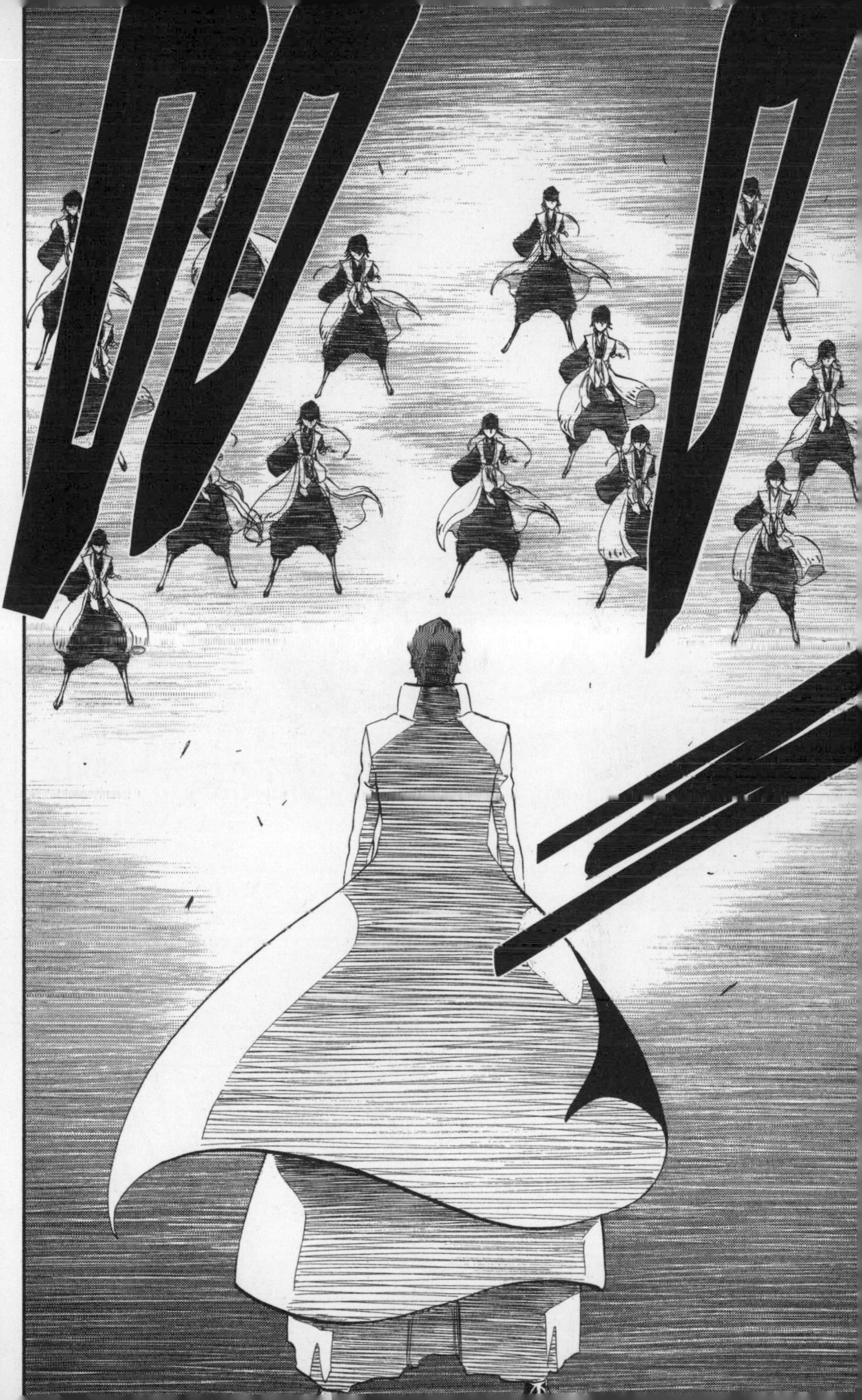

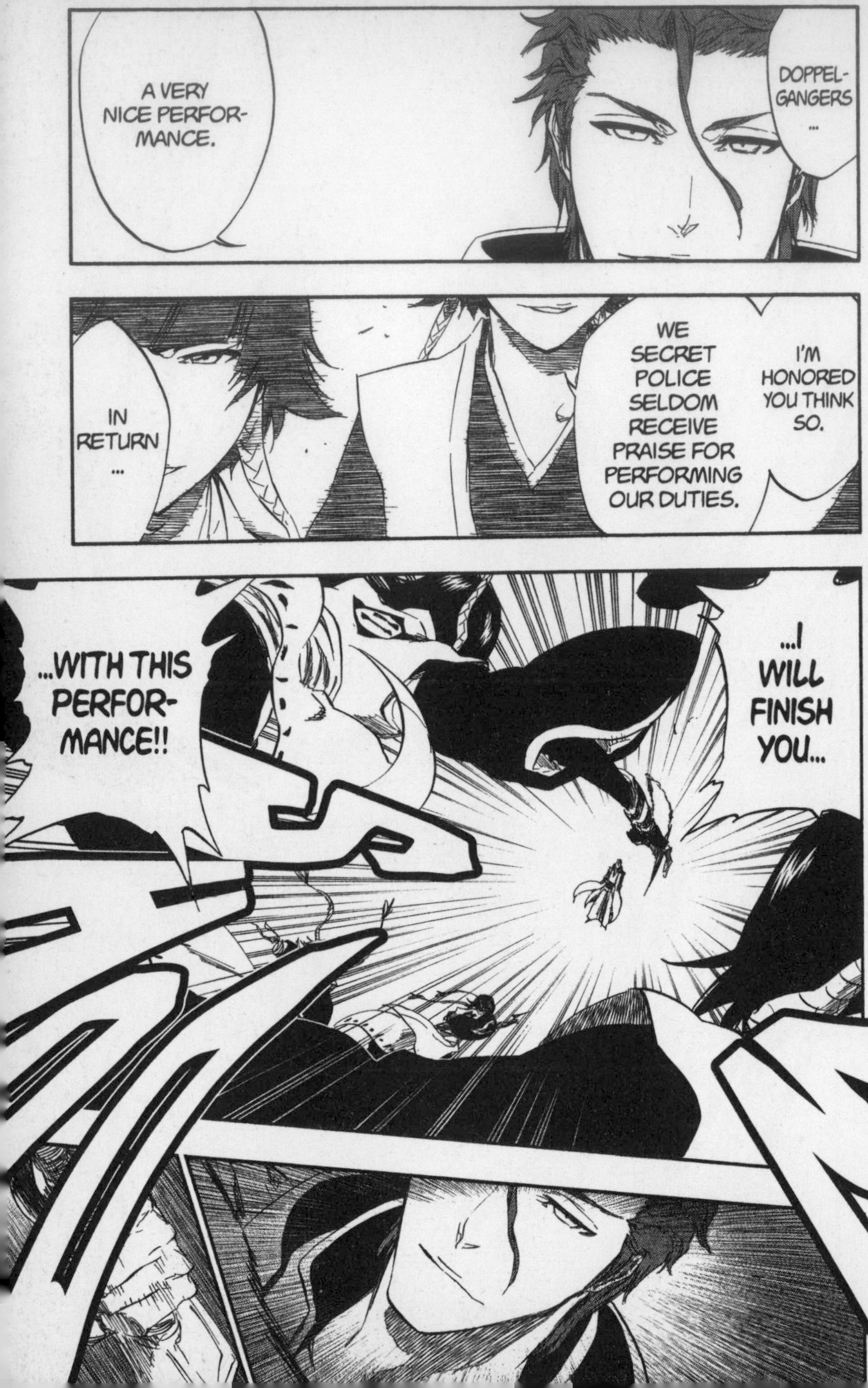
DOPPEL-GANGERS ...
A VERY NICE PERFORMANCE.
I'M HONORED YOU THINK SO.
WE SECRET POLICE SELDOM RECEIVE PRAISE FOR PERFORMING OUR DUTIES.
IN RETURN ...
...I WILL FINISH YOU...
...WITH THIS PERFORMANCE!!

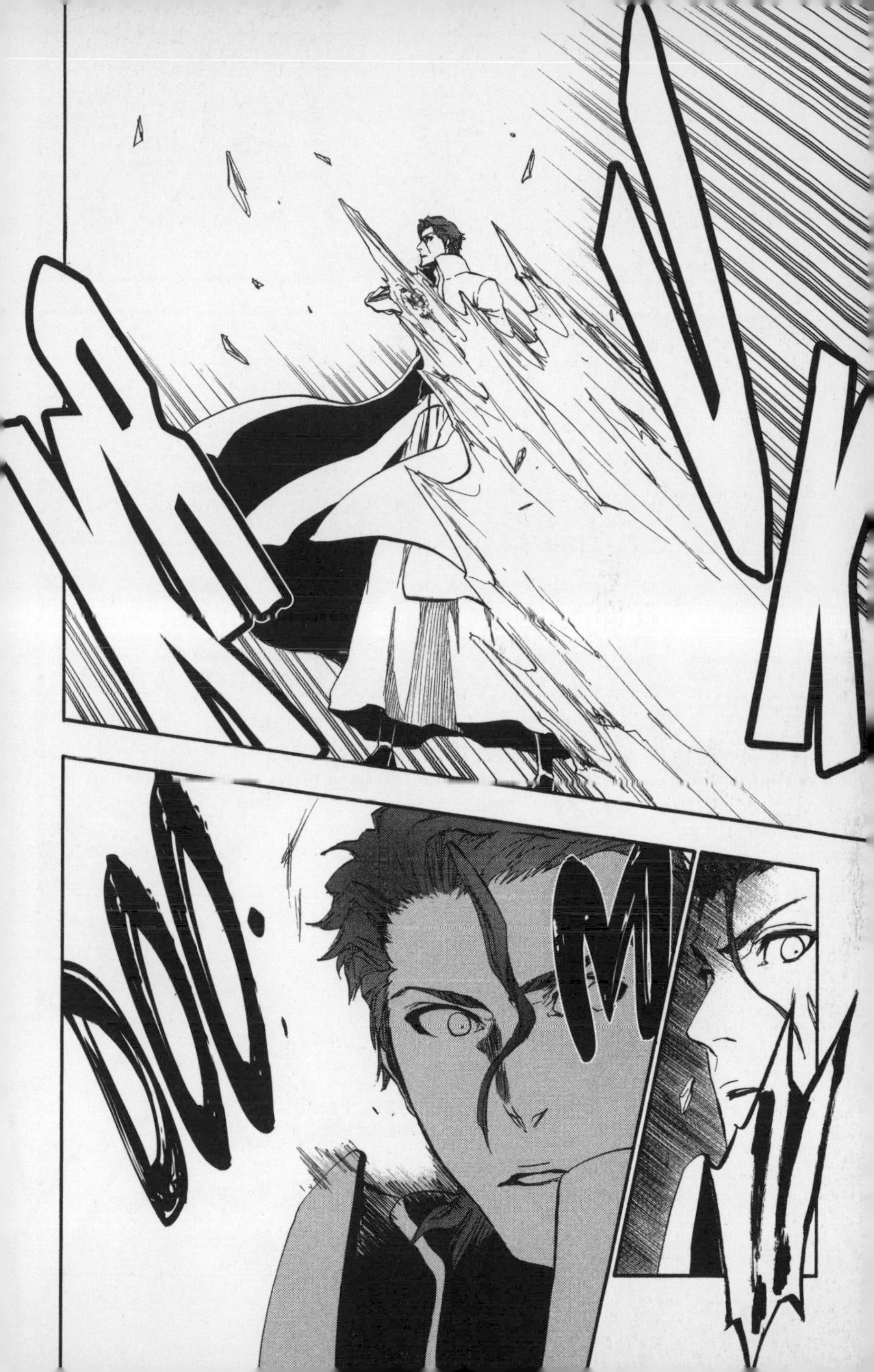

READ THIS WAY

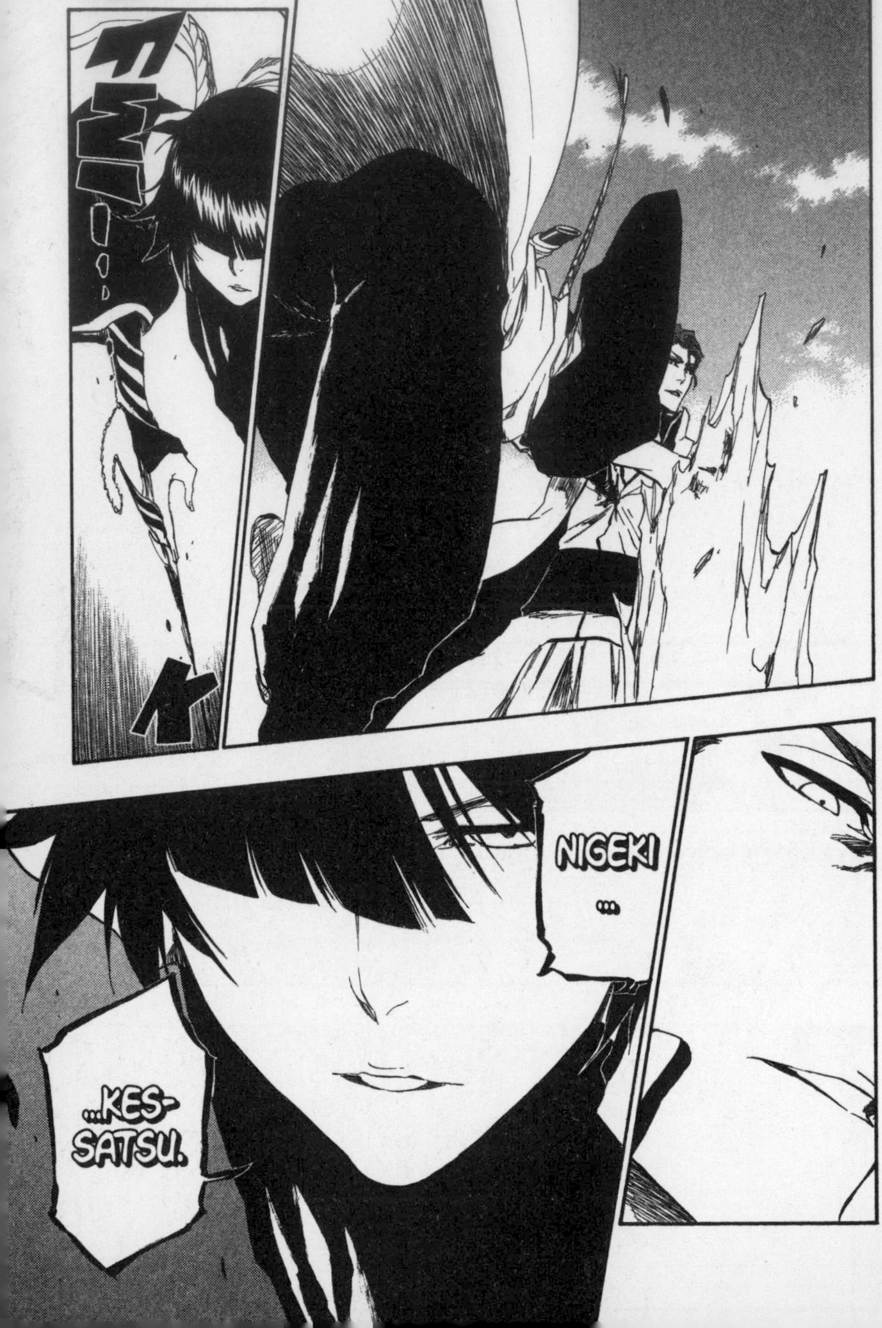
NIGEKI
...
...KES-
SATSU.

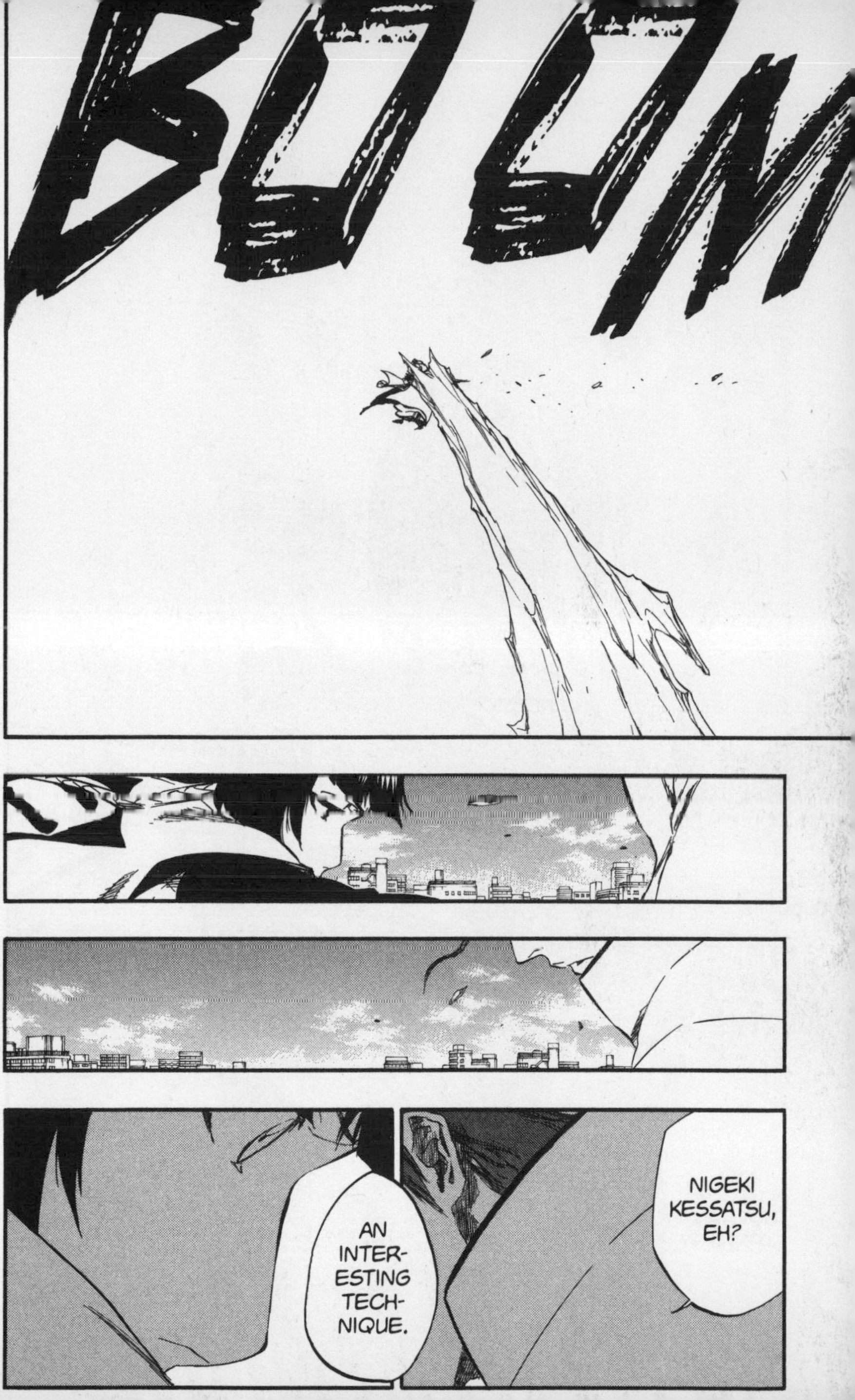
BOOM
NIGEKI KESSATSU, EH?
AN INTER-ESTING TECH-NIQUE.

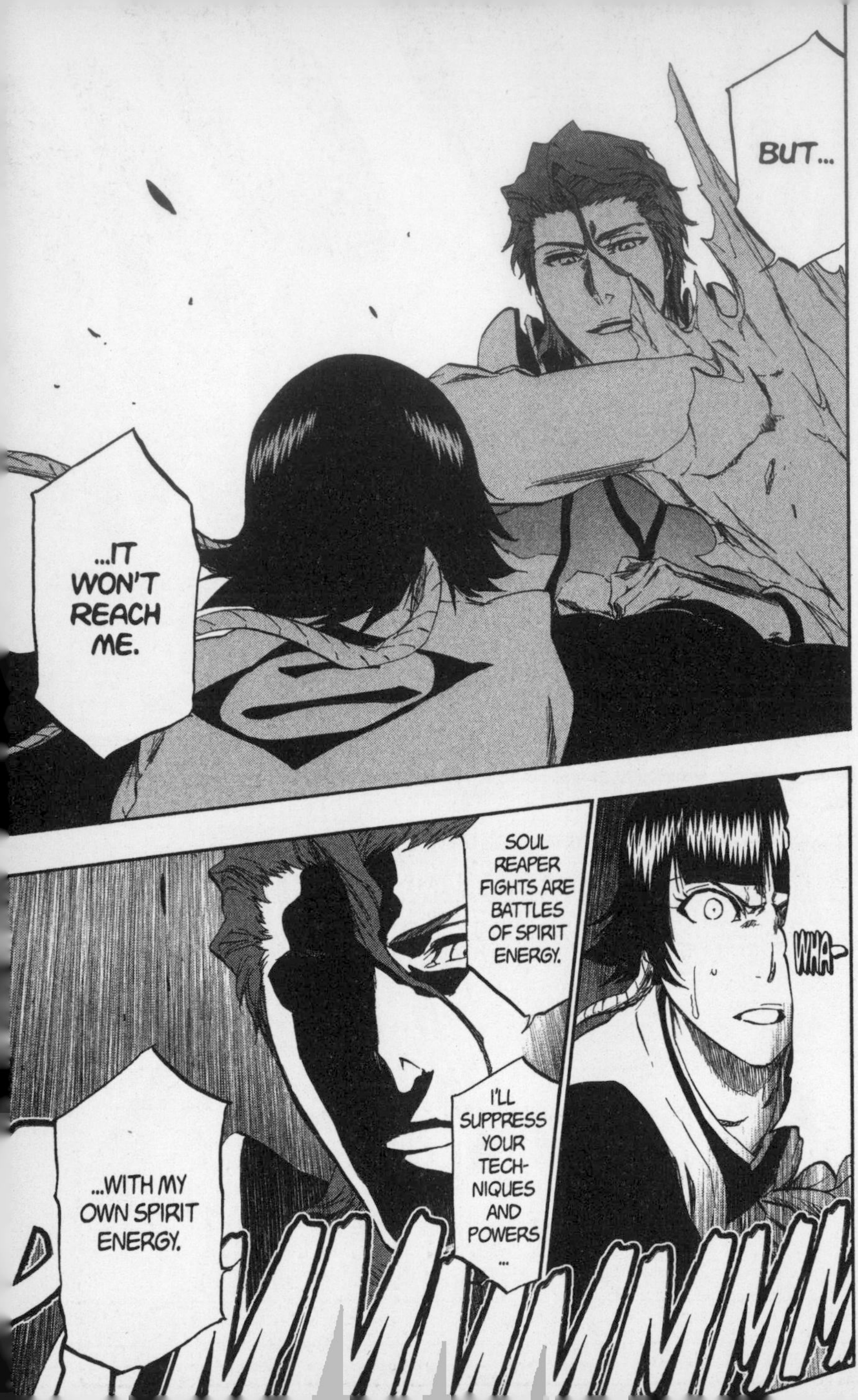
BUT...
...IT WON'T REACH ME.
SOUL REAPER FIGHTS ARE BATTLES OF SPIRIT ENERGY.
WHA-
I'LL SUPPRESS YOUR TECH-NIQUES AND POWERS...
...WITH MY OWN SPIRIT ENERGY.

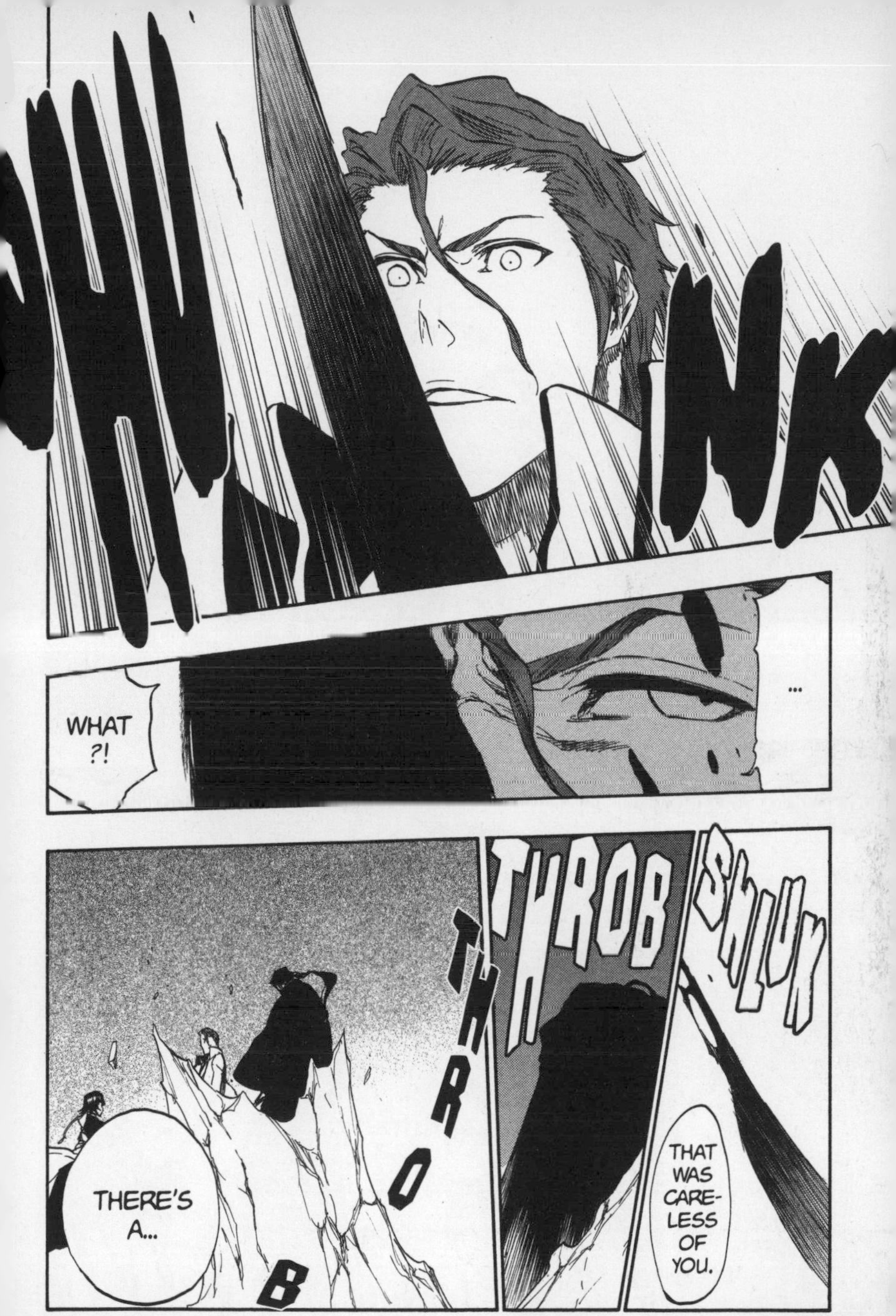
SHHINK
...
WHAT ?!
SHLUK
THAT WAS CARELESS OF YOU.
THROB
THROB
THERE'S A...

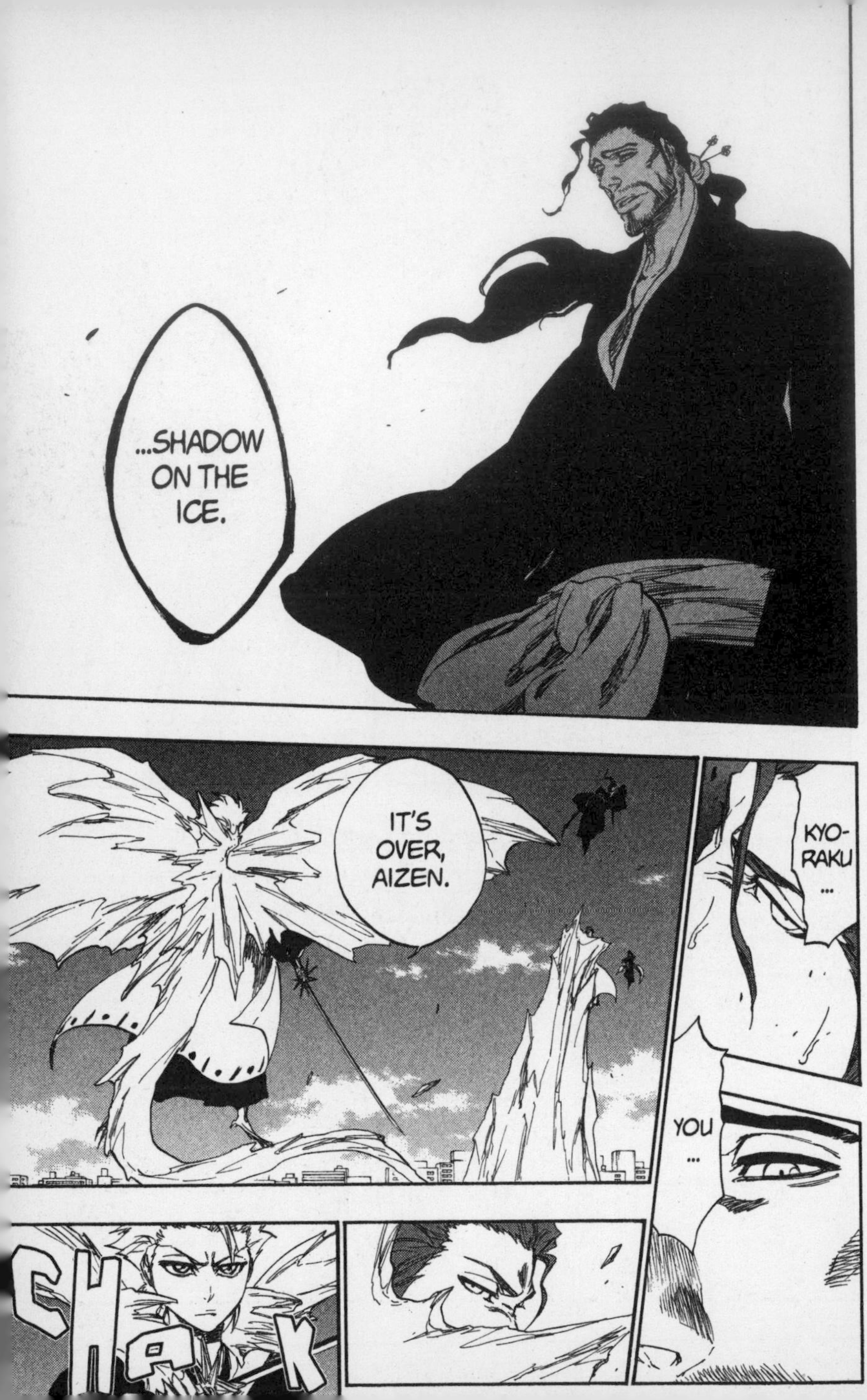
...SHADOW ON THE ICE.
KYO-RAKU ...
YOU ...
IT'S OVER, AIZEN.
CHAK

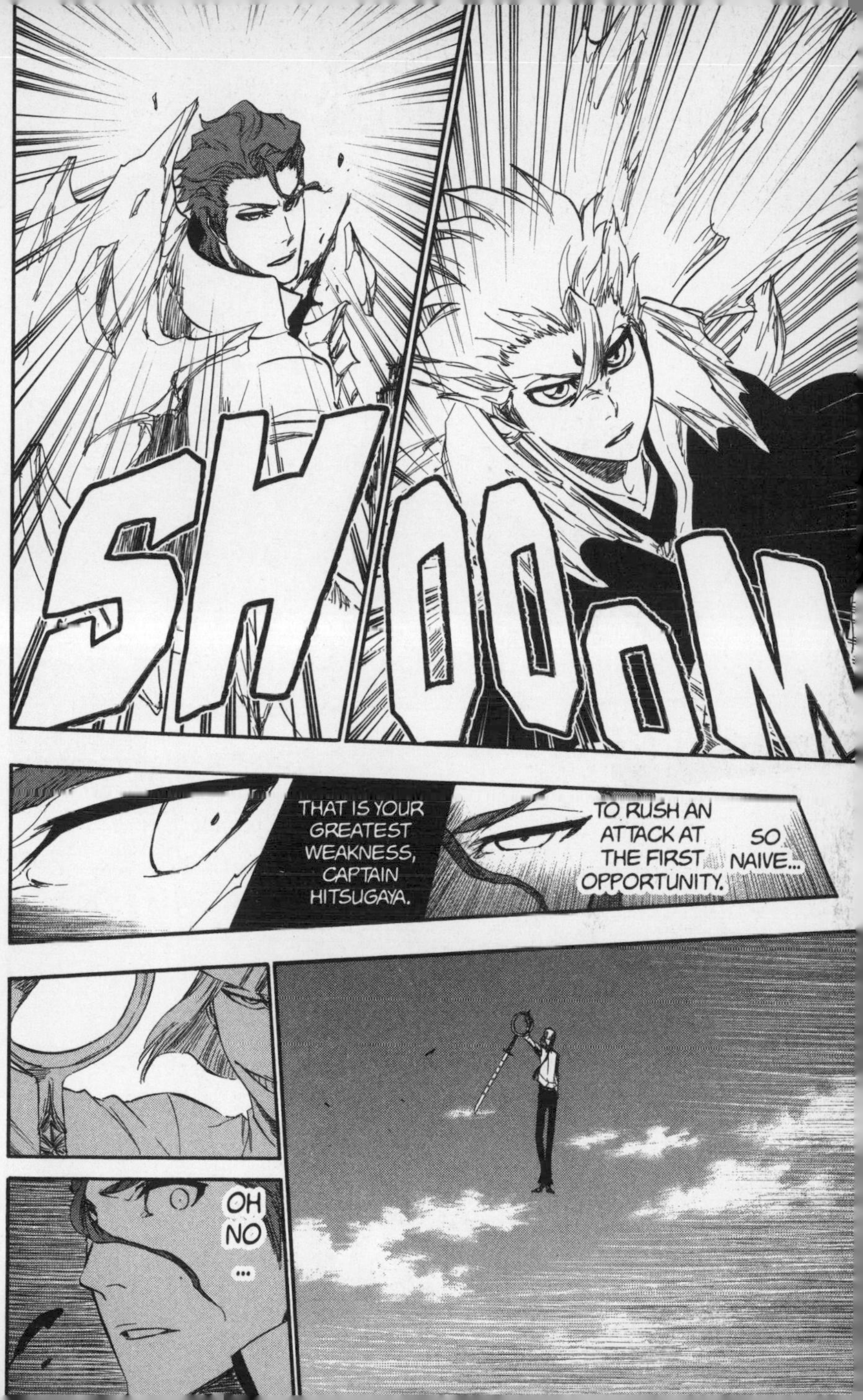
SHOOOM
SO NAIVE...
TO RUSH AN ATTACK AT THE FIRST OPPORTUNITY.
THAT IS YOUR GREATEST WEAKNESS, CAPTAIN HITSUGAYA.
OH NO ...

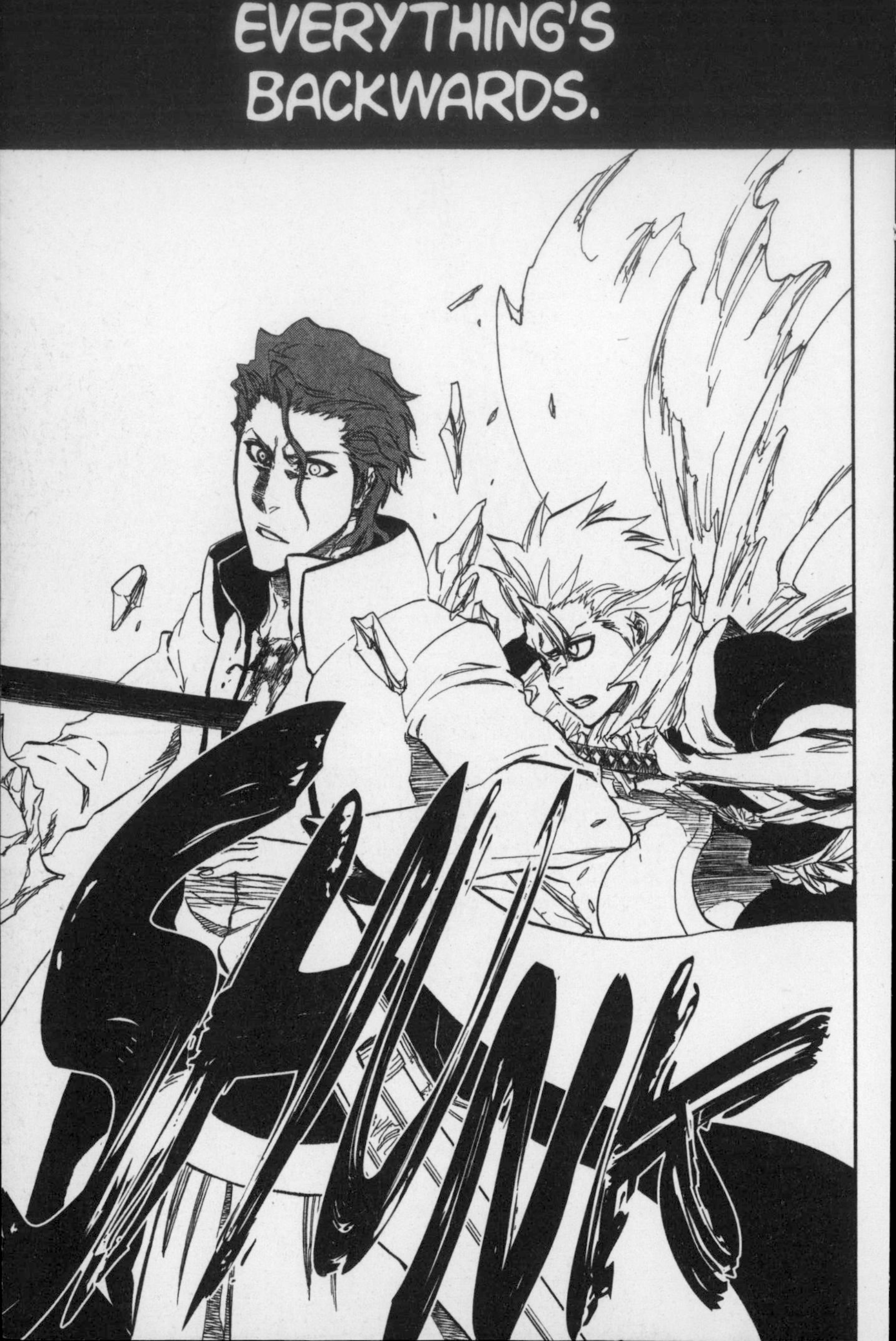
EVERYTHING'S BACKWARDS.
SHUNK

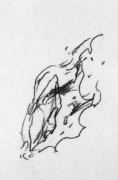

BLEACH 392.

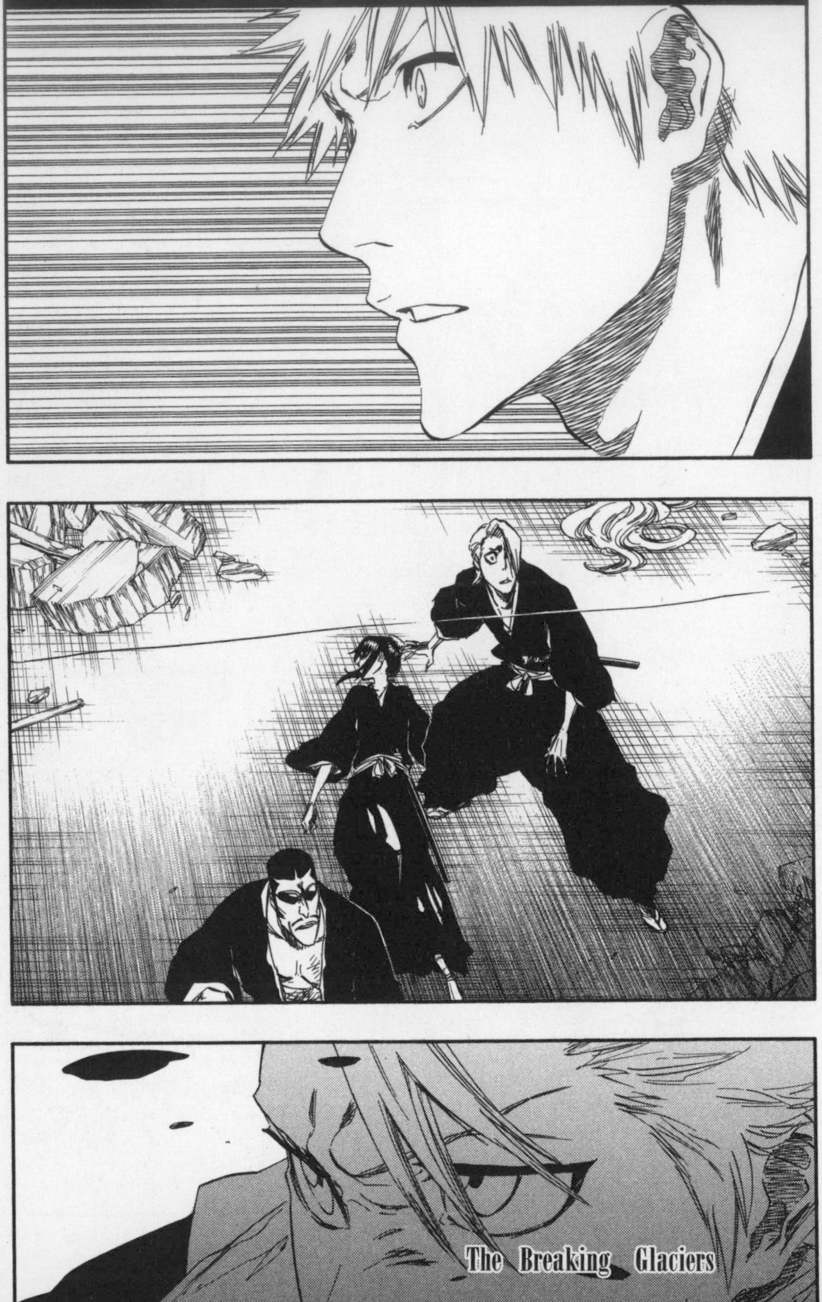
The Breaking Glaciers

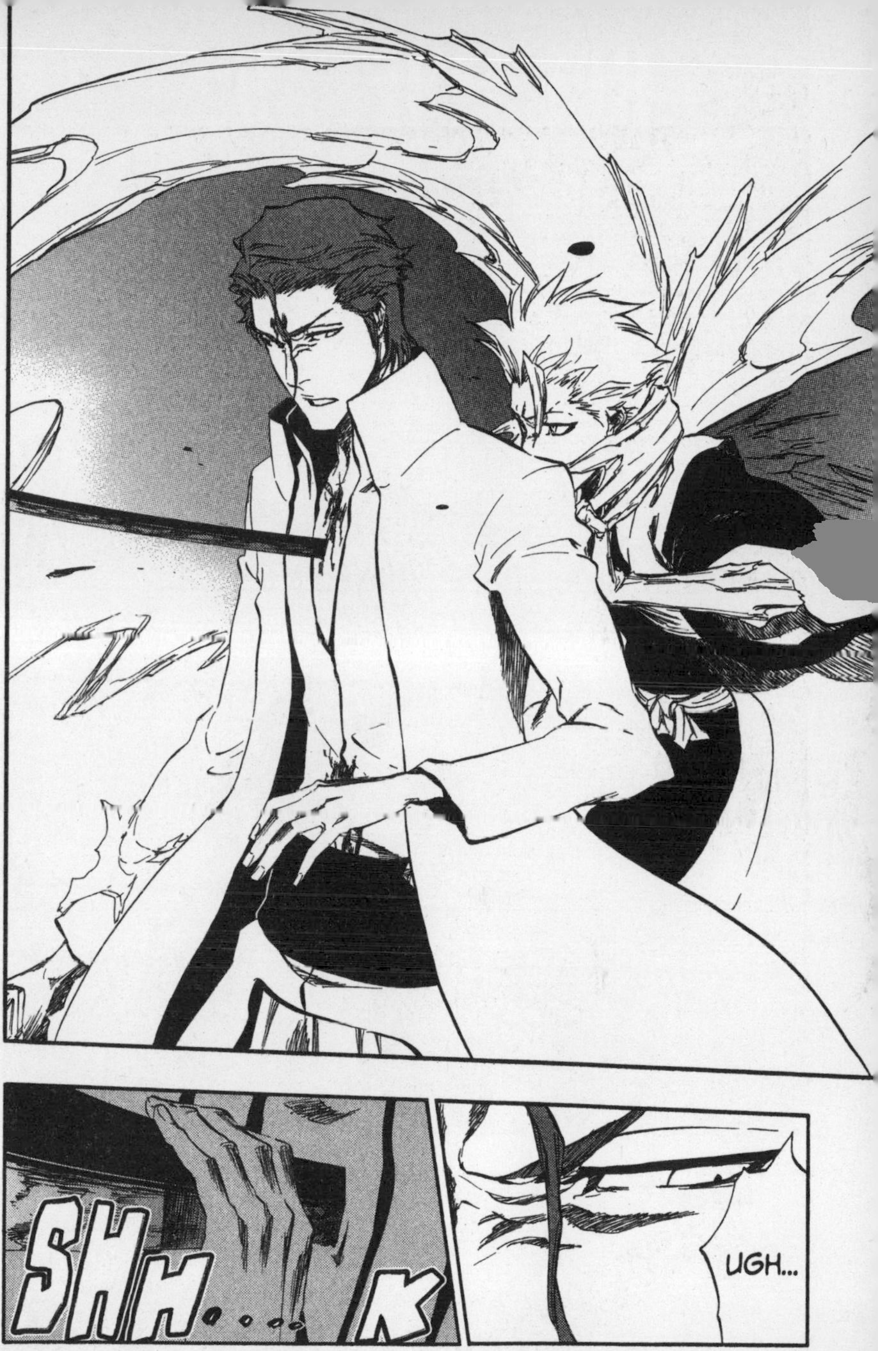
UGH...
SHH...K

READ THIS WAY

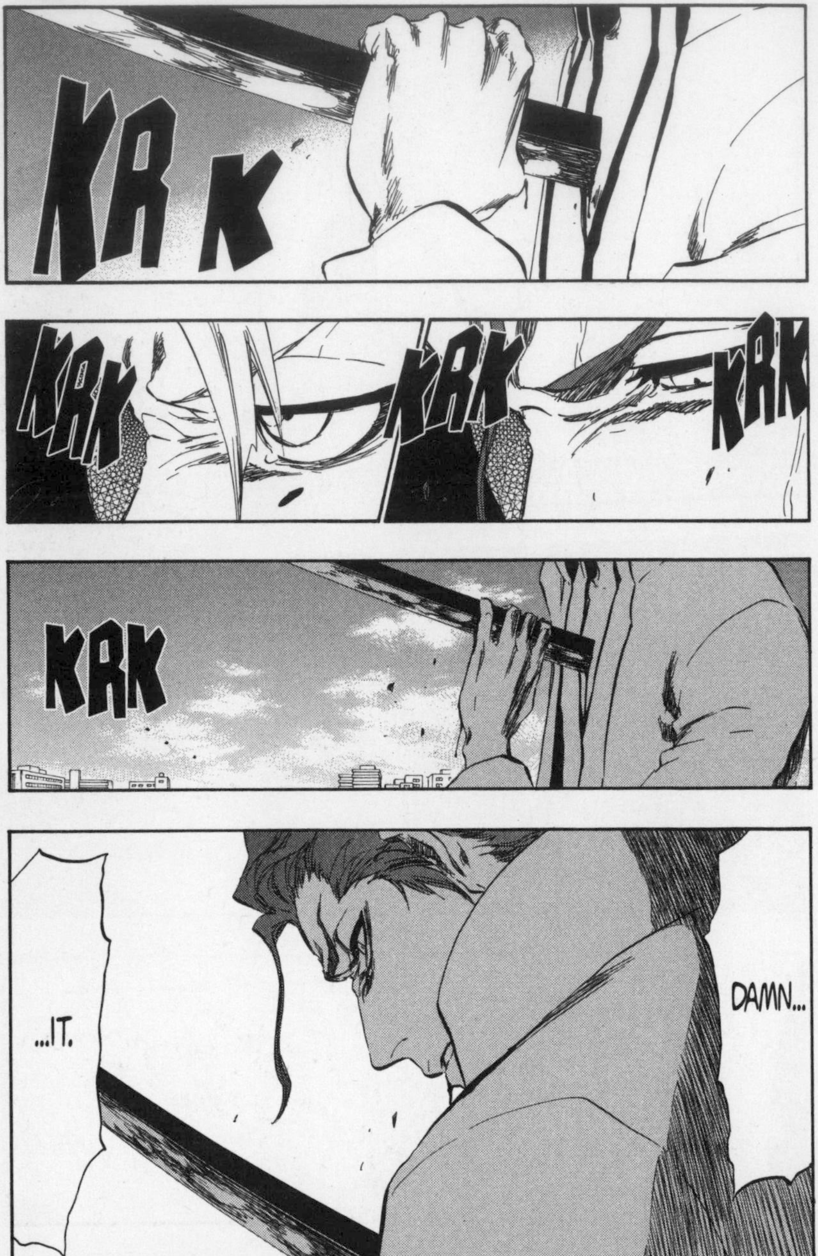
KR K
KRK
KRK
KRK
KRK
DAMN...
...IT.

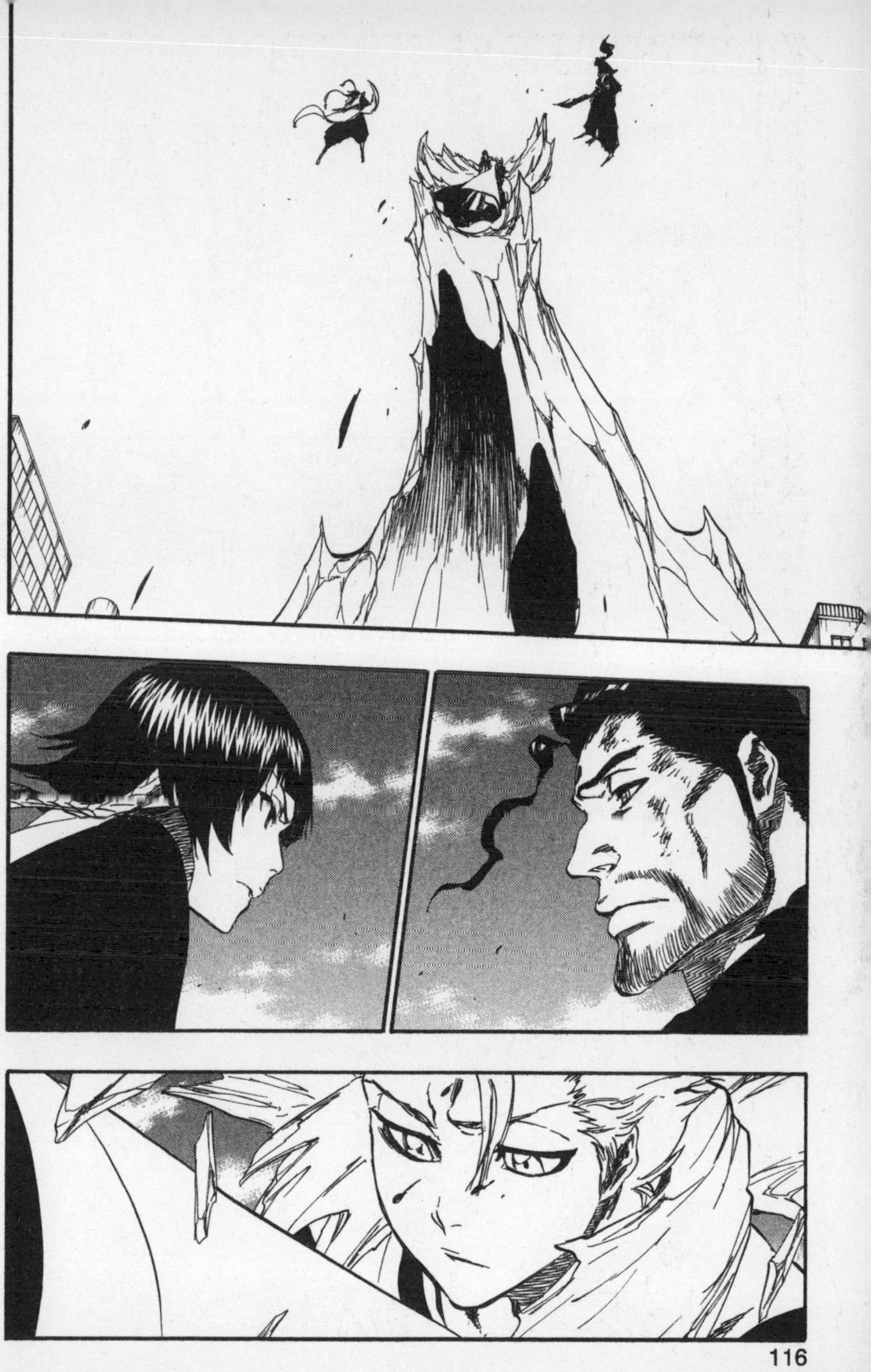

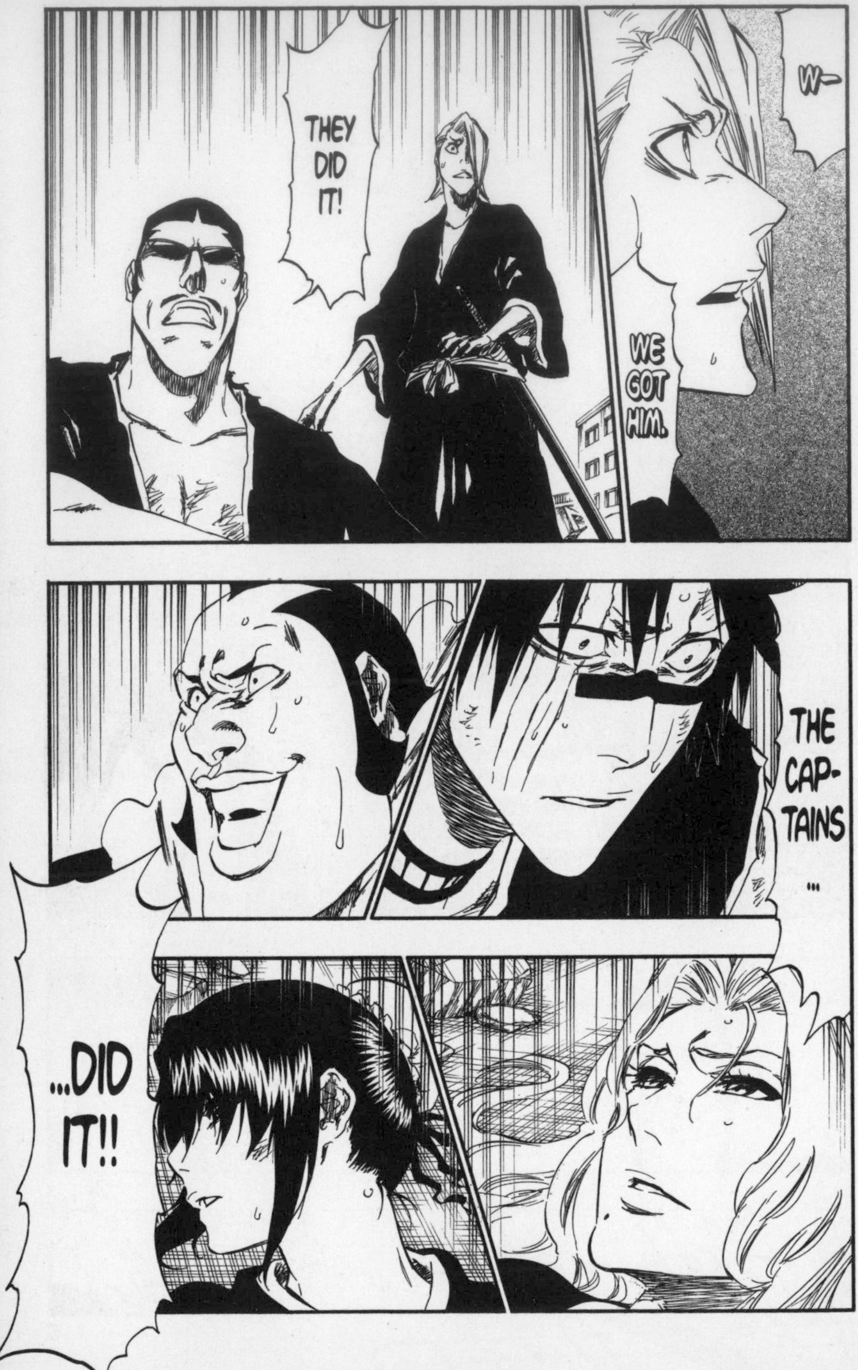
W-
WE GOT HIM.
THEY DID IT!
THE CAP-TAINS...
...DID IT!!

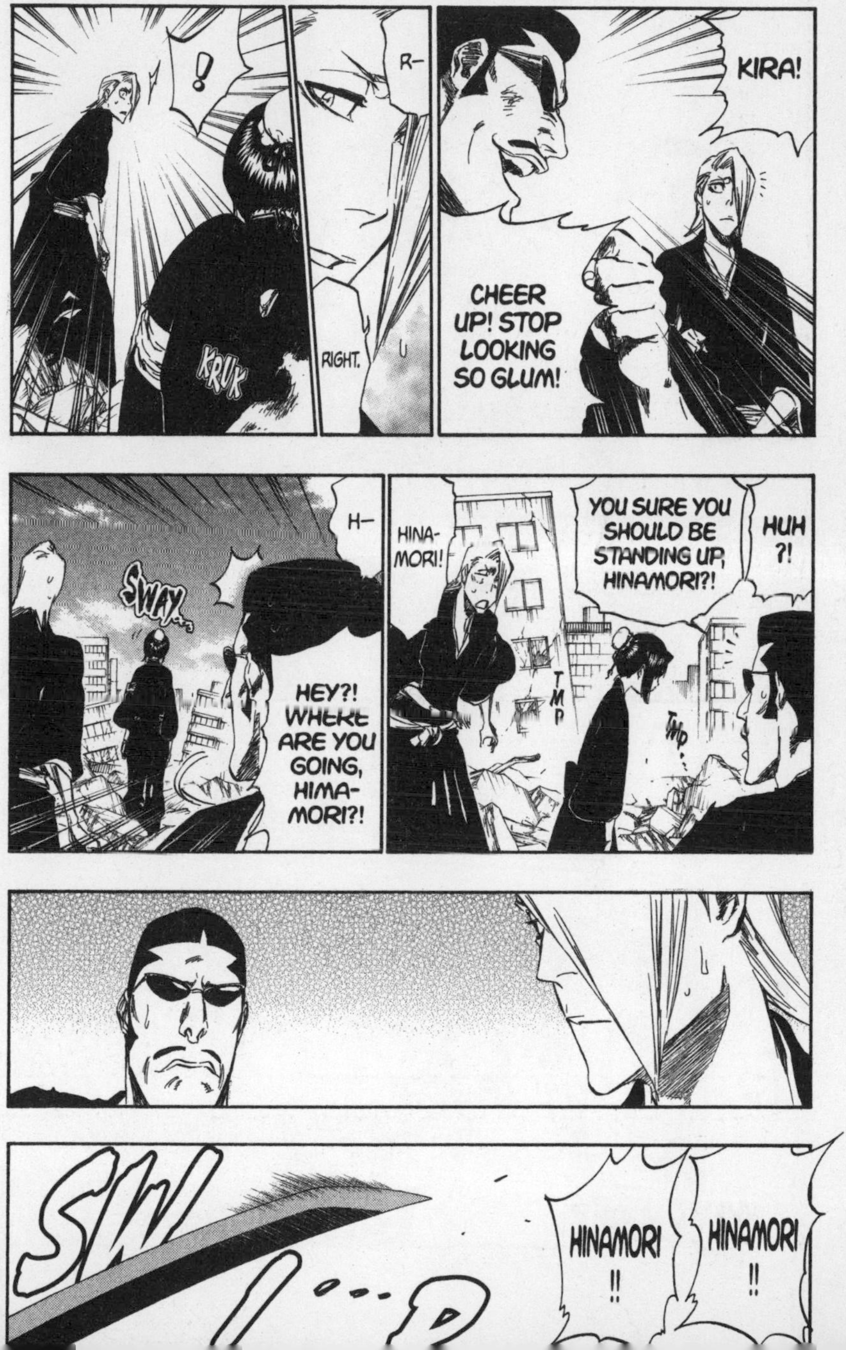
KIRA!
CHEER UP! STOP LOOKING SO GLUM!
R–
RIGHT.
!
KRUK
HUH ?!
YOU SURE YOU SHOULD BE STANDING UP, HINAMORI?!
HINA-MORI!
TMP
TMP...
H–
HEY?! WHERE ARE YOU GOING, HIMA-MORI?!
SWAY...
HINAMORI !!
HINAMORI !!
SW

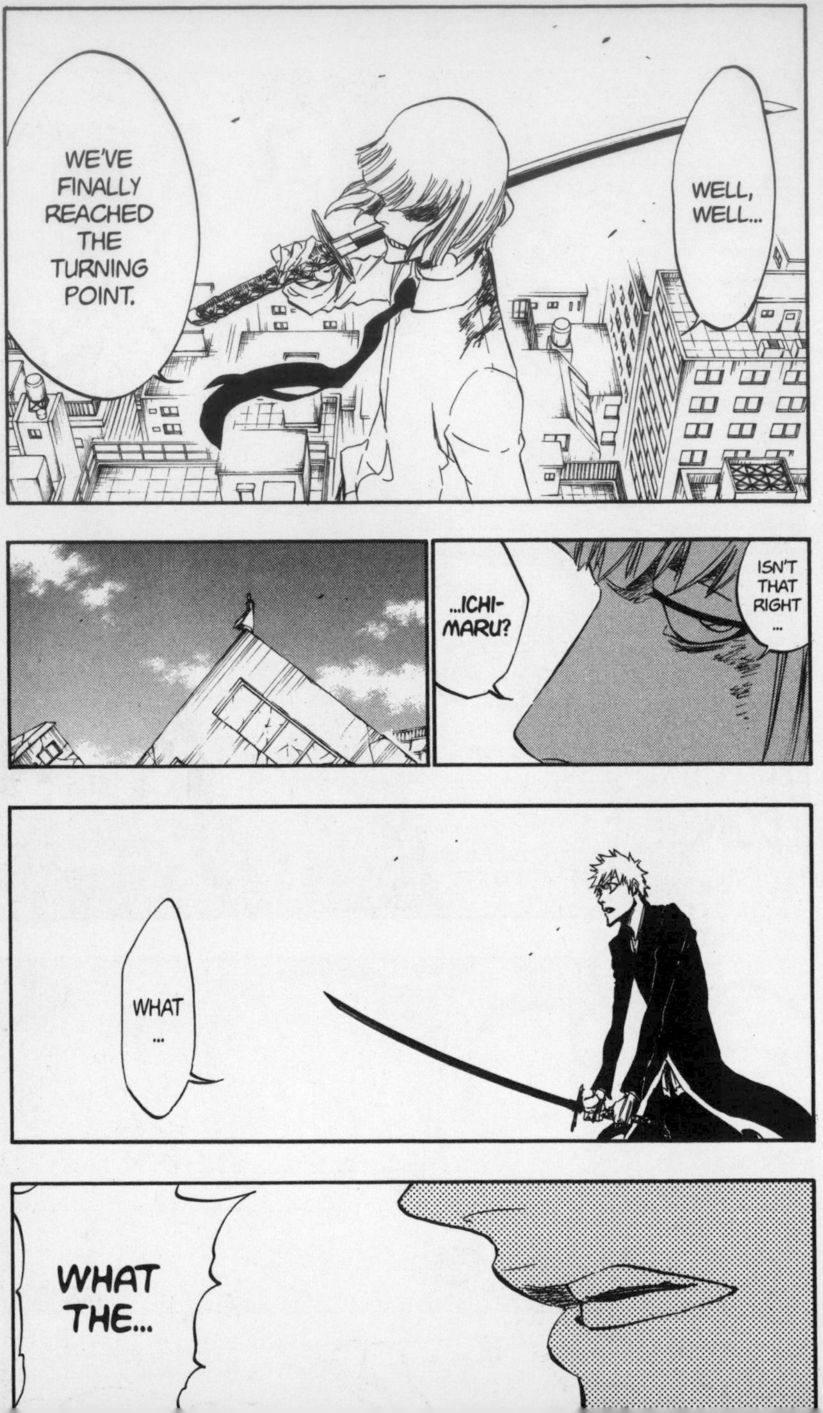
WELL, WELL...
WE'VE FINALLY REACHED THE TURNING POINT.
ISN'T THAT RIGHT ...
...ICHI-MARU?
WHAT ...
WHAT THE...

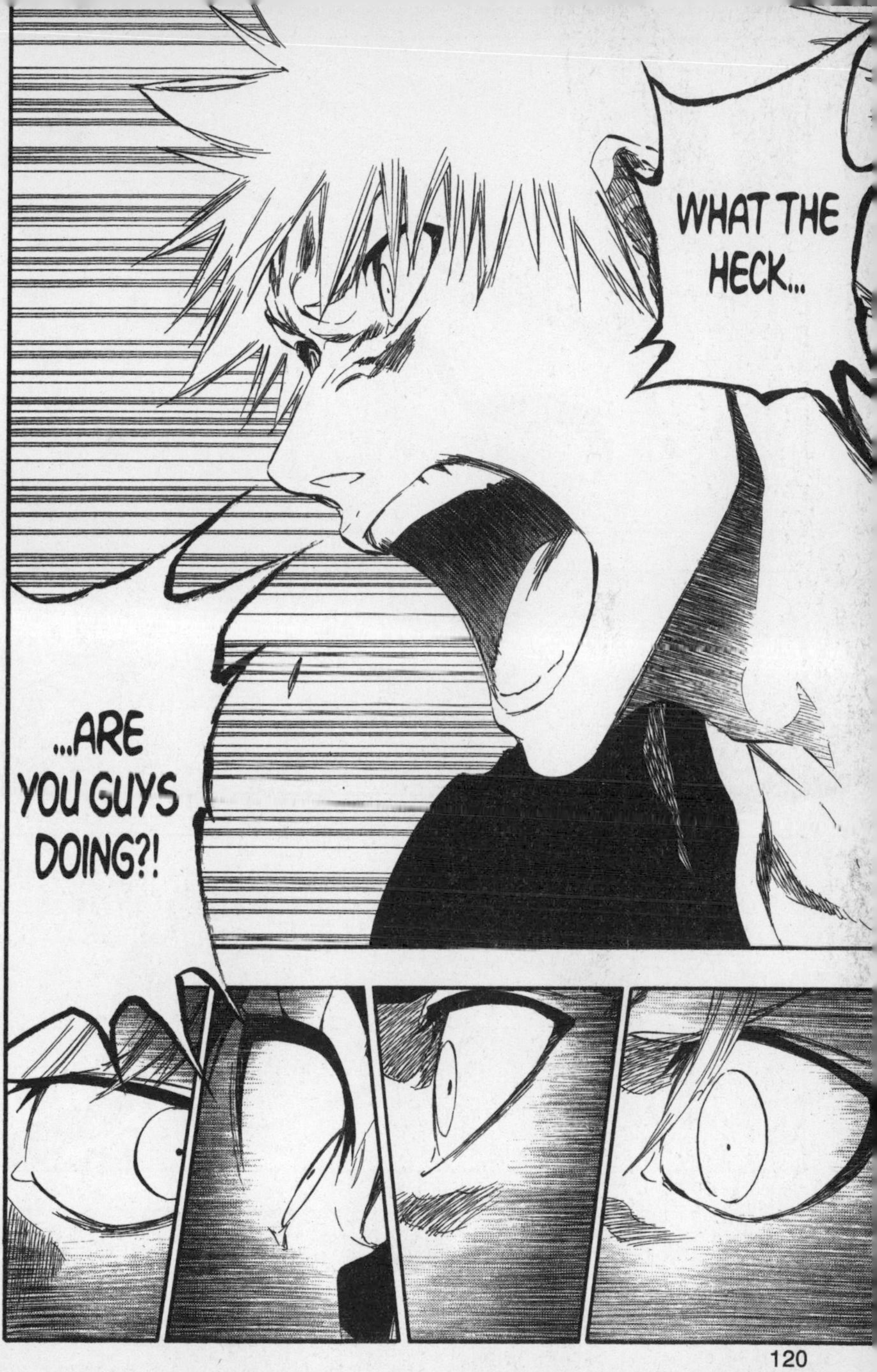
WHAT THE HECK...
...ARE YOU GUYS DOING?!

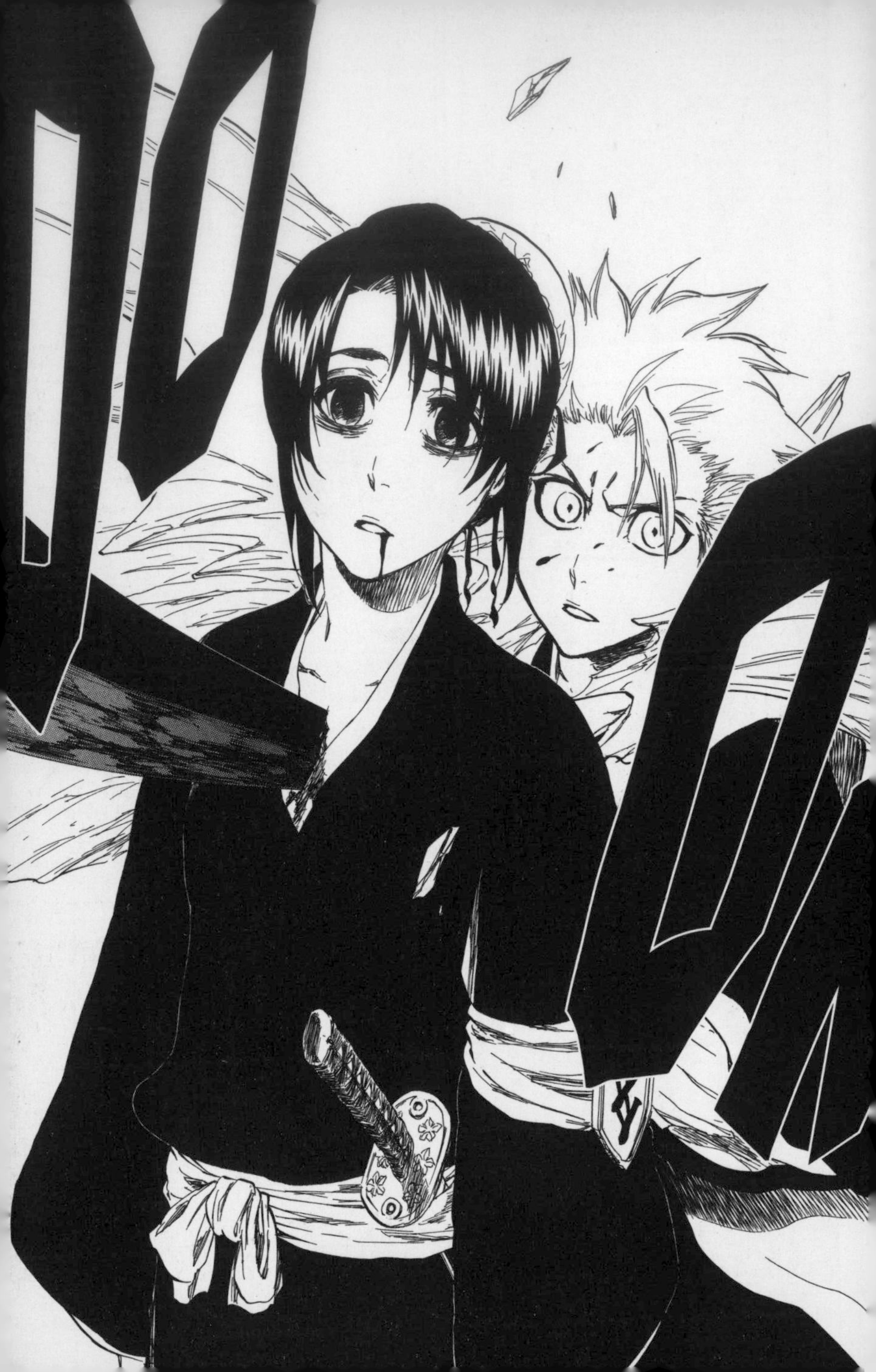

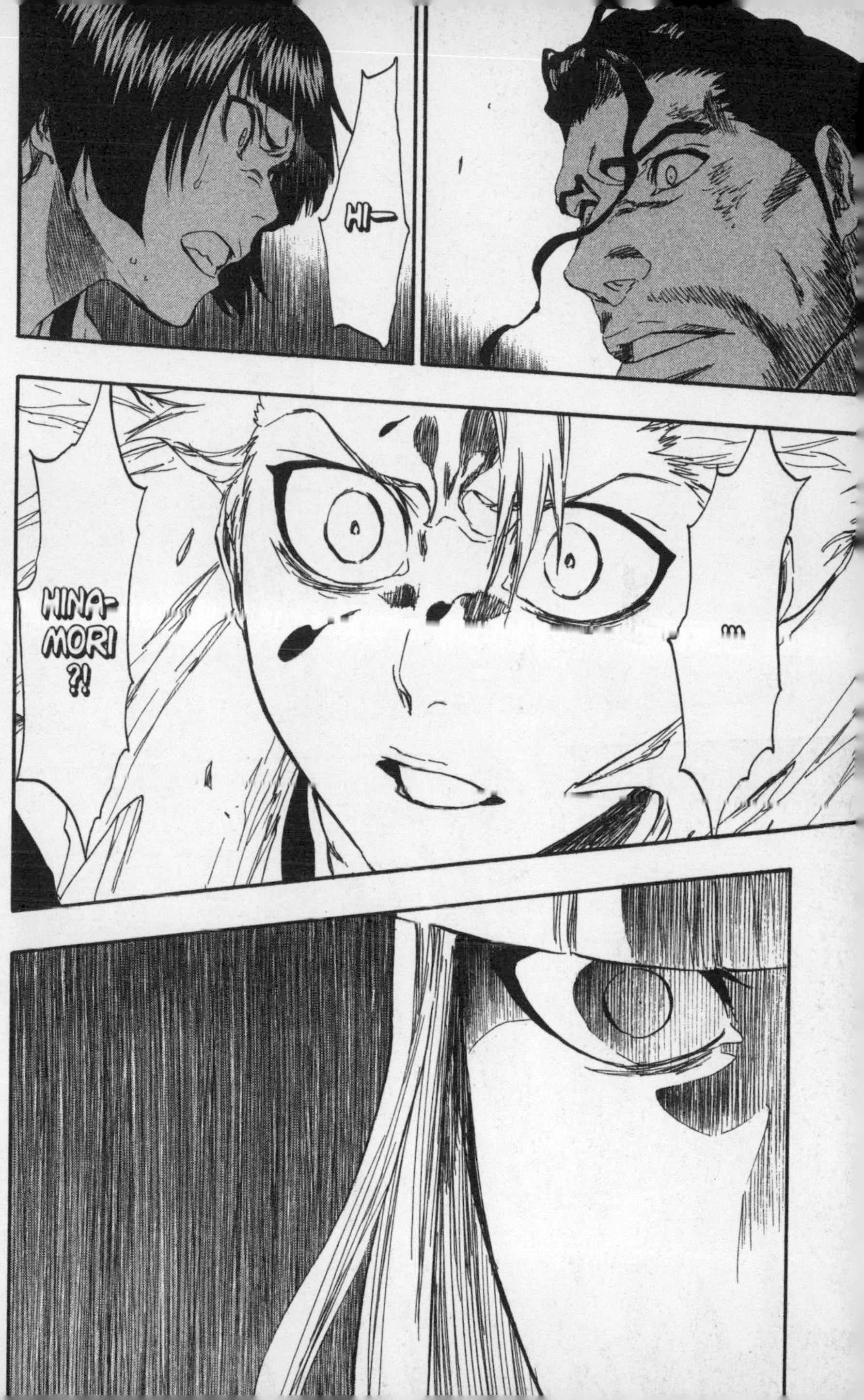
HI-
!!!
HINA-
MORI
?!

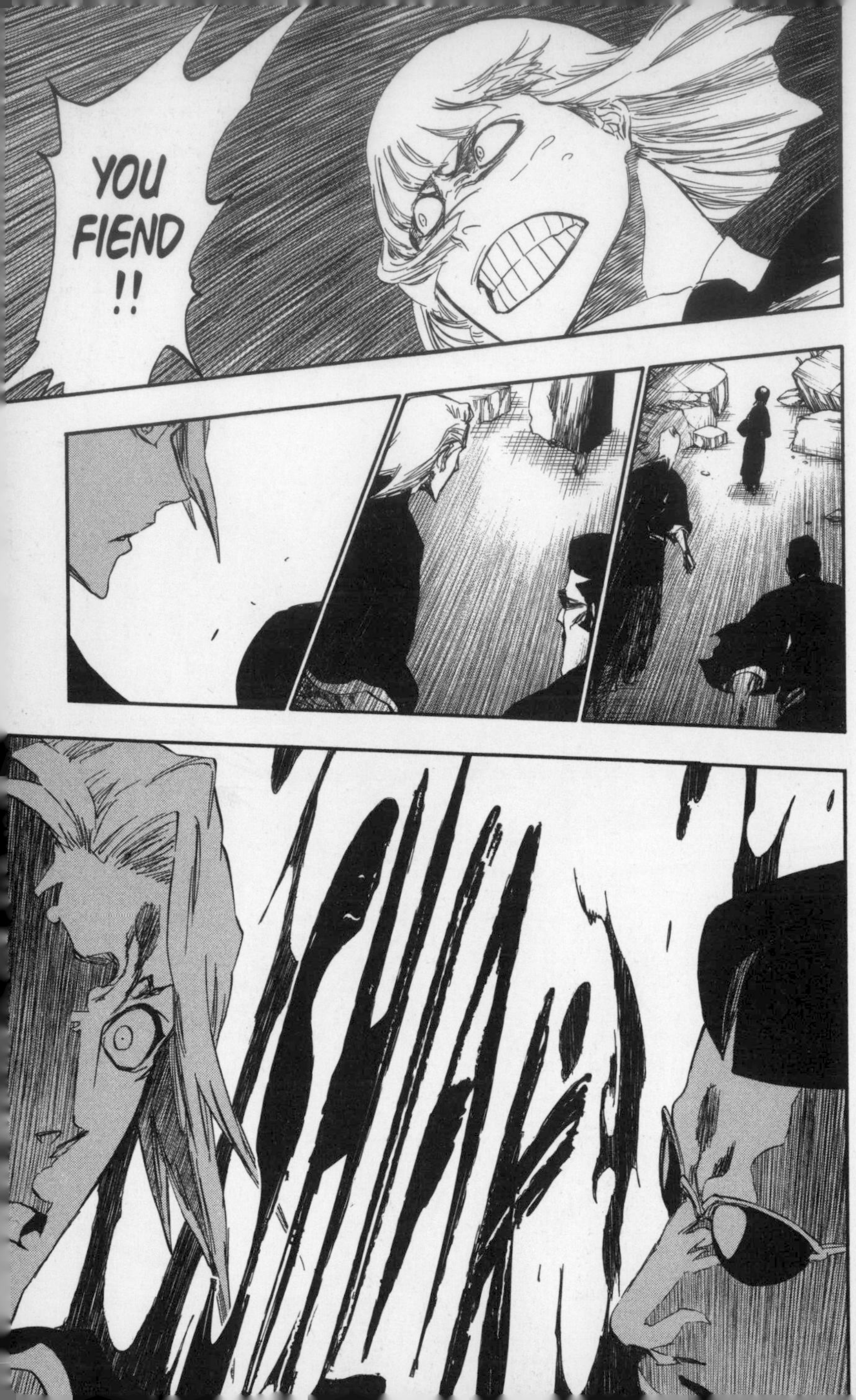
YOU FIEND !!

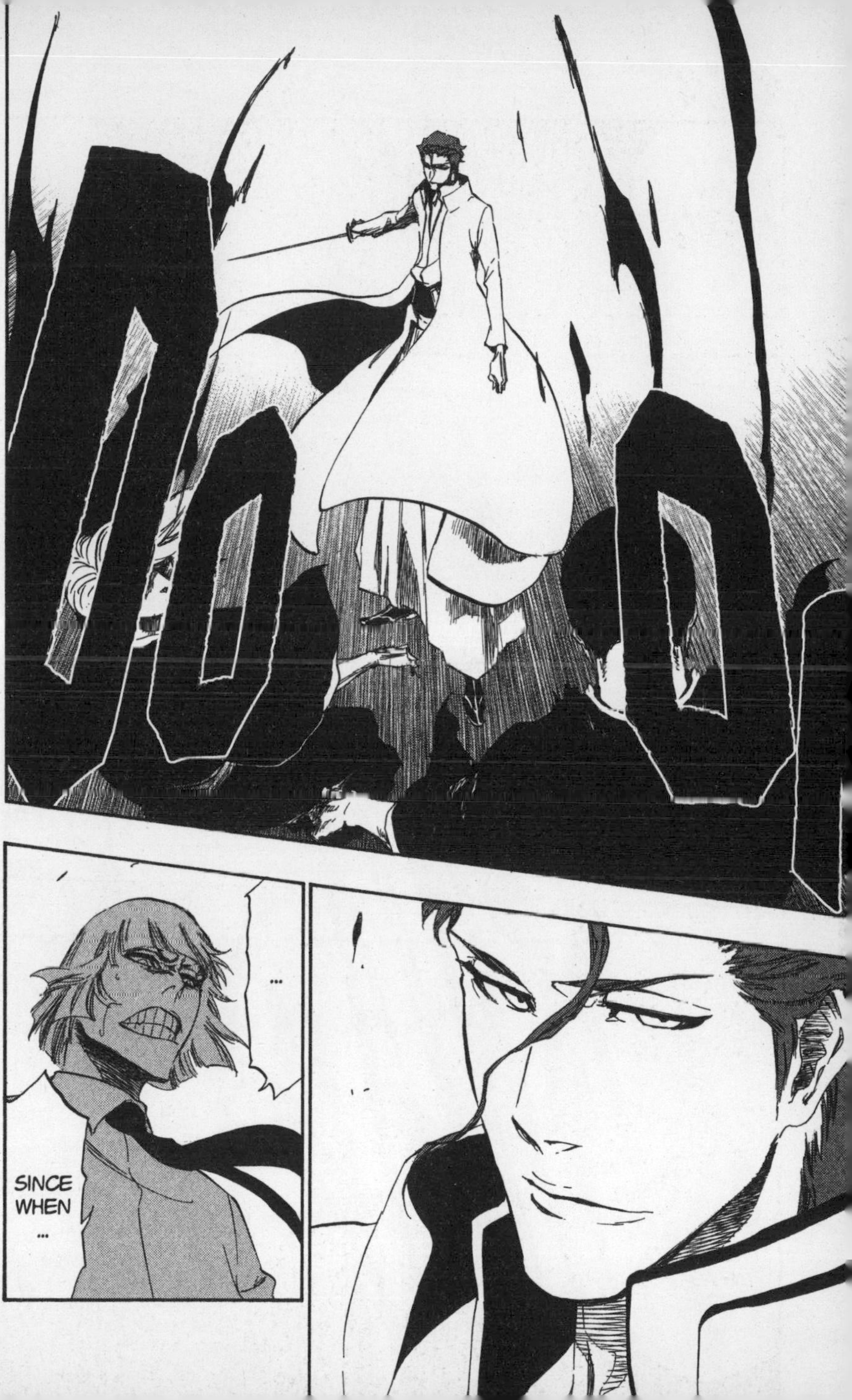
...
SINCE WHEN
...

READ THIS WAY

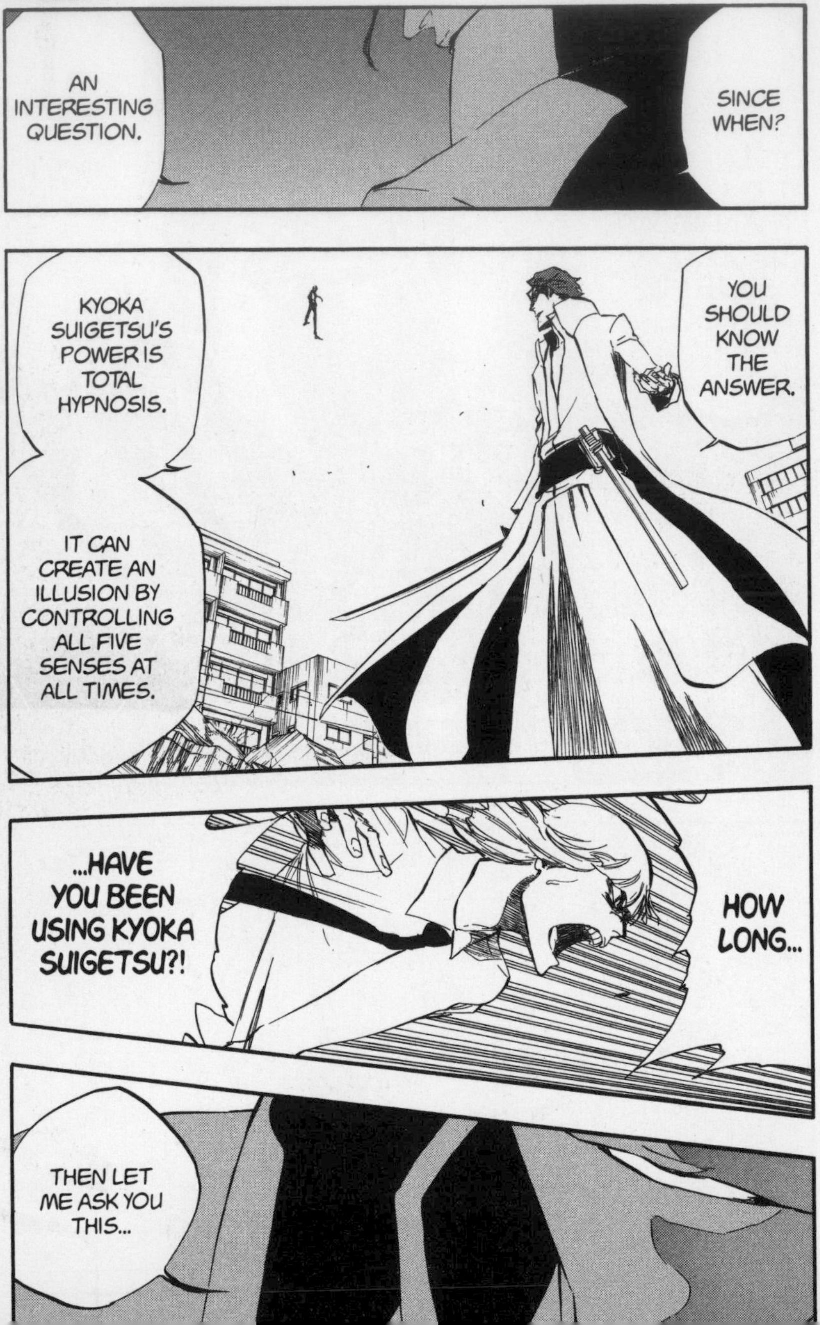
SINCE WHEN?
AN INTERESTING QUESTION.
YOU SHOULD KNOW THE ANSWER.
KYOKA SUIGETSU'S POWER IS TOTAL HYPNOSIS.
IT CAN CREATE AN ILLUSION BY CONTROLLING ALL FIVE SENSES AT ALL TIMES.
HOW LONG...
...HAVE YOU BEEN USING KYOKA SUIGETSU?!
THEN LET ME ASK YOU THIS...

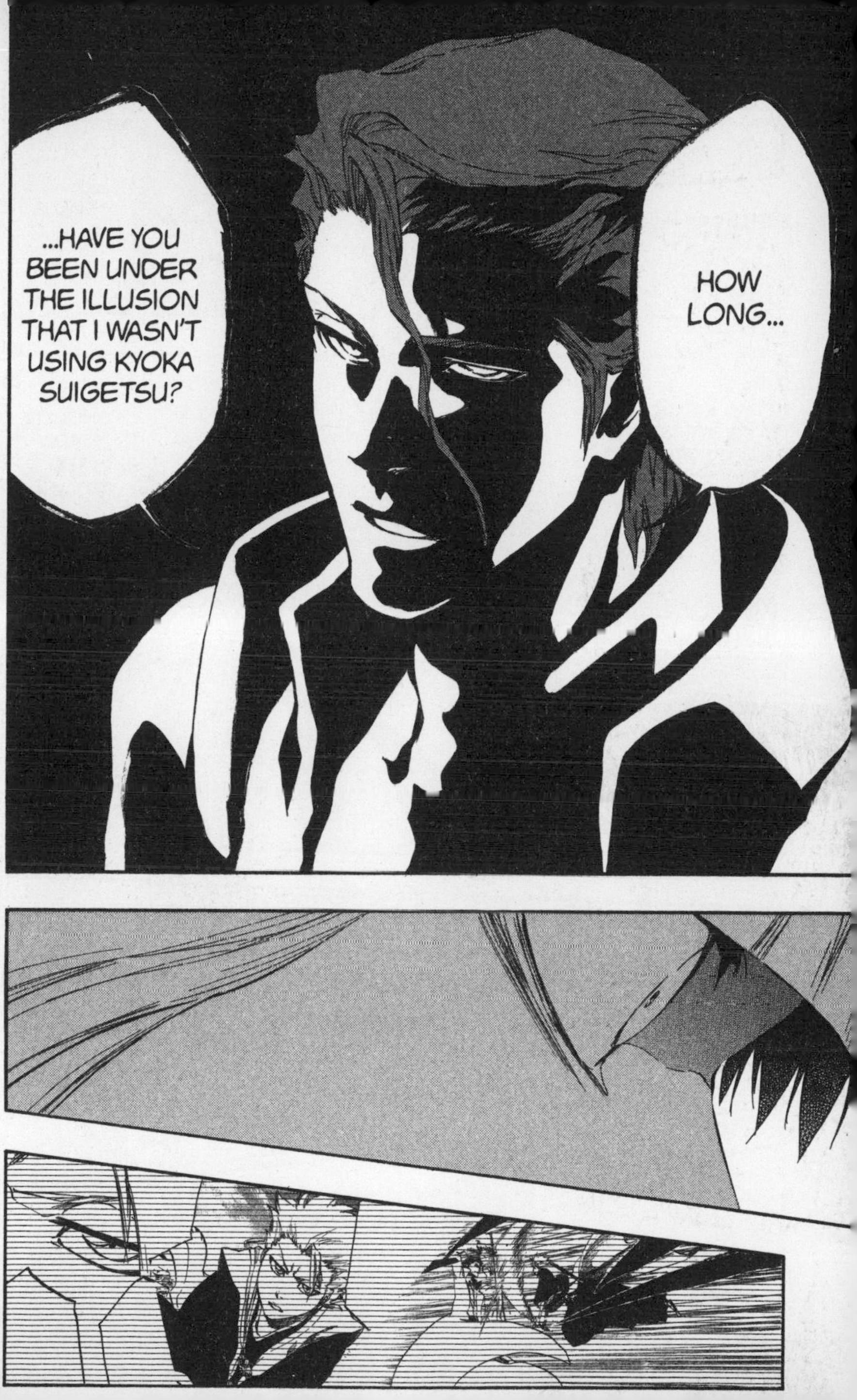
HOW LONG...
...HAVE YOU BEEN UNDER THE ILLUSION THAT I WASN'T USING KYOKA SUIGETSU?

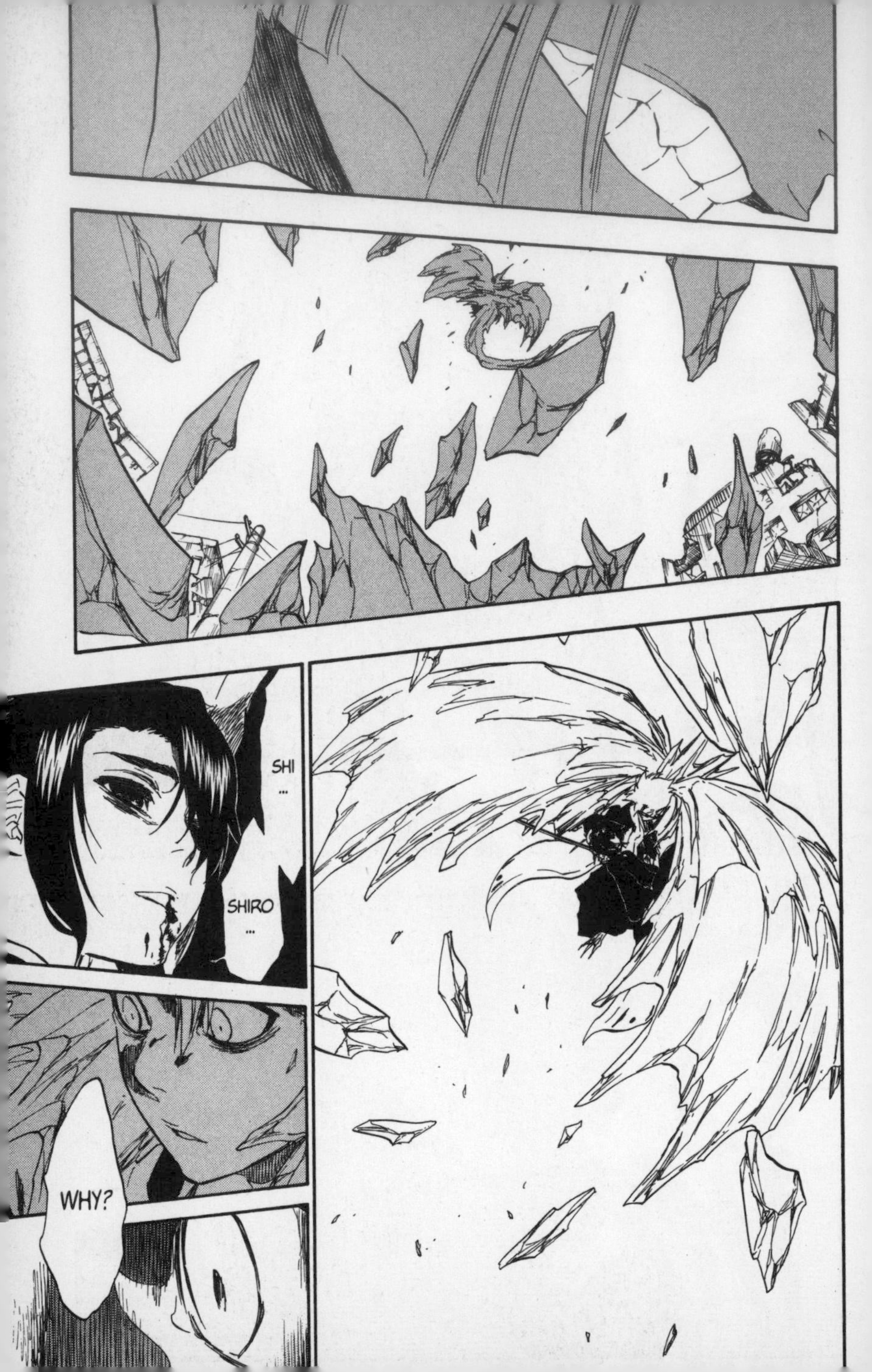
SHI
...
SHIRO
...
WHY?

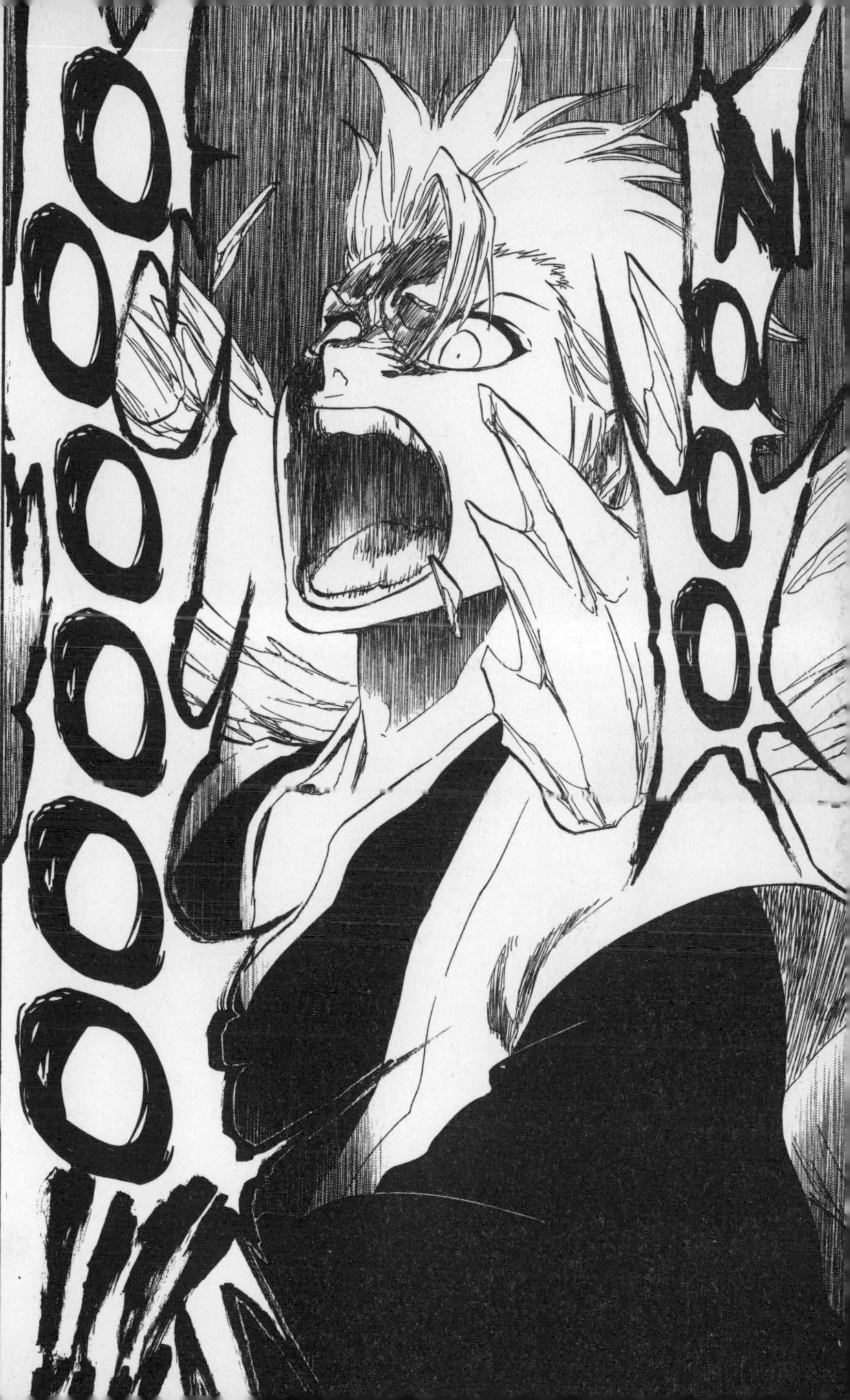
NOOOO
OOOOOOOH

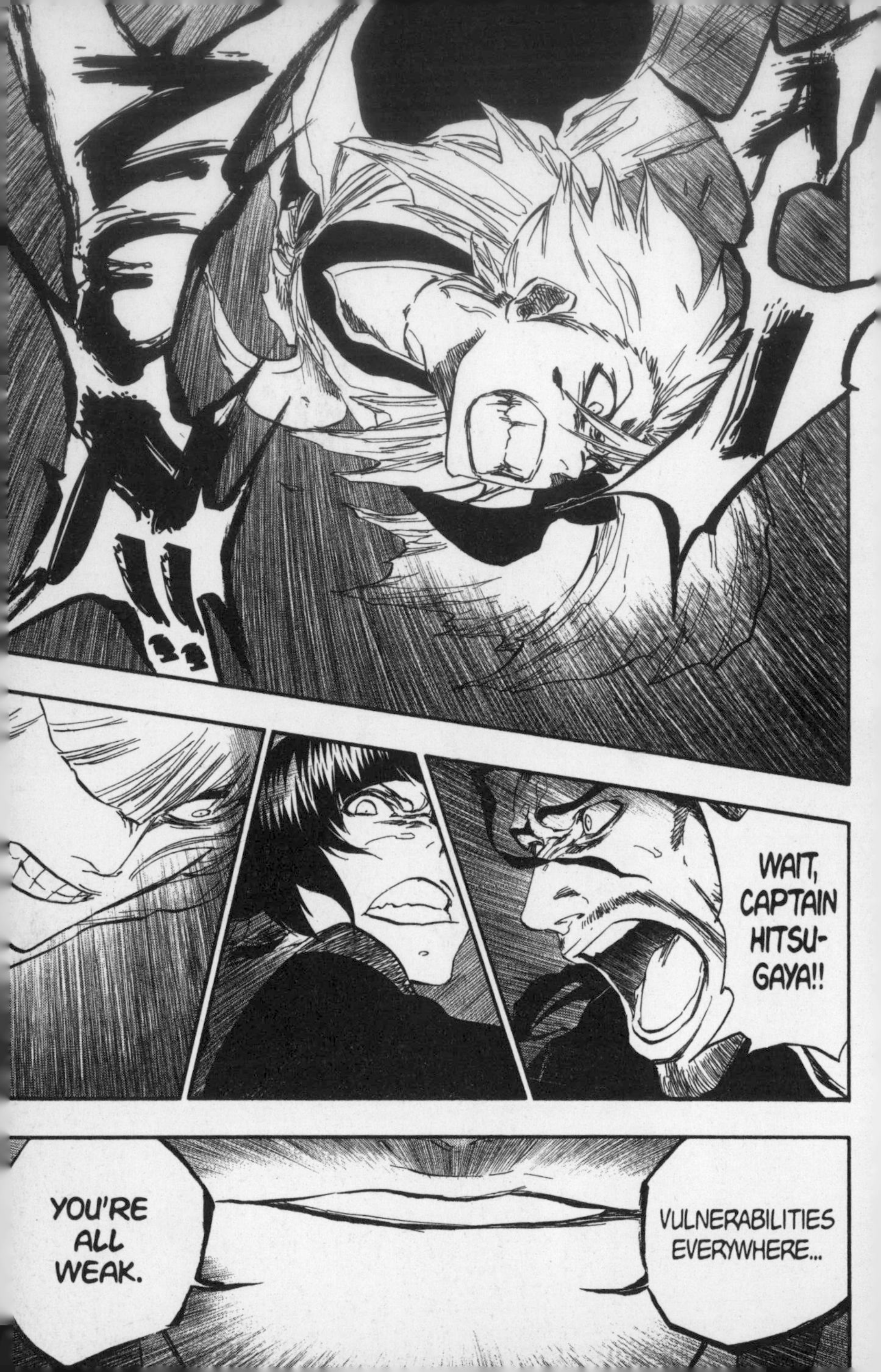
WAIT, CAPTAIN HITSU-GAYA!!
VULNERABILITIES EVERYWHERE...
YOU'RE ALL WEAK.

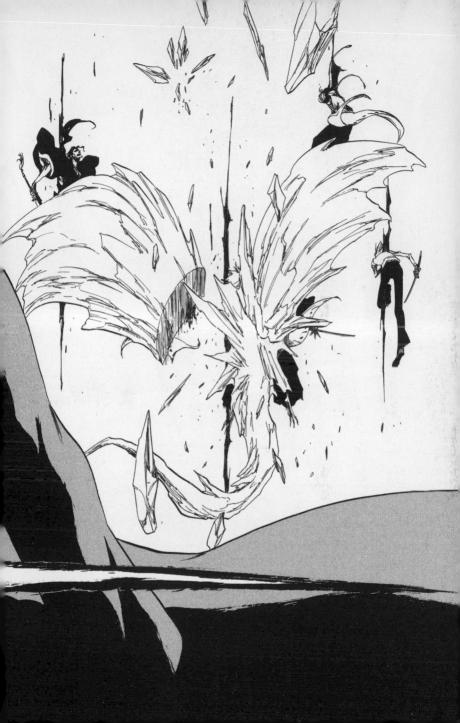

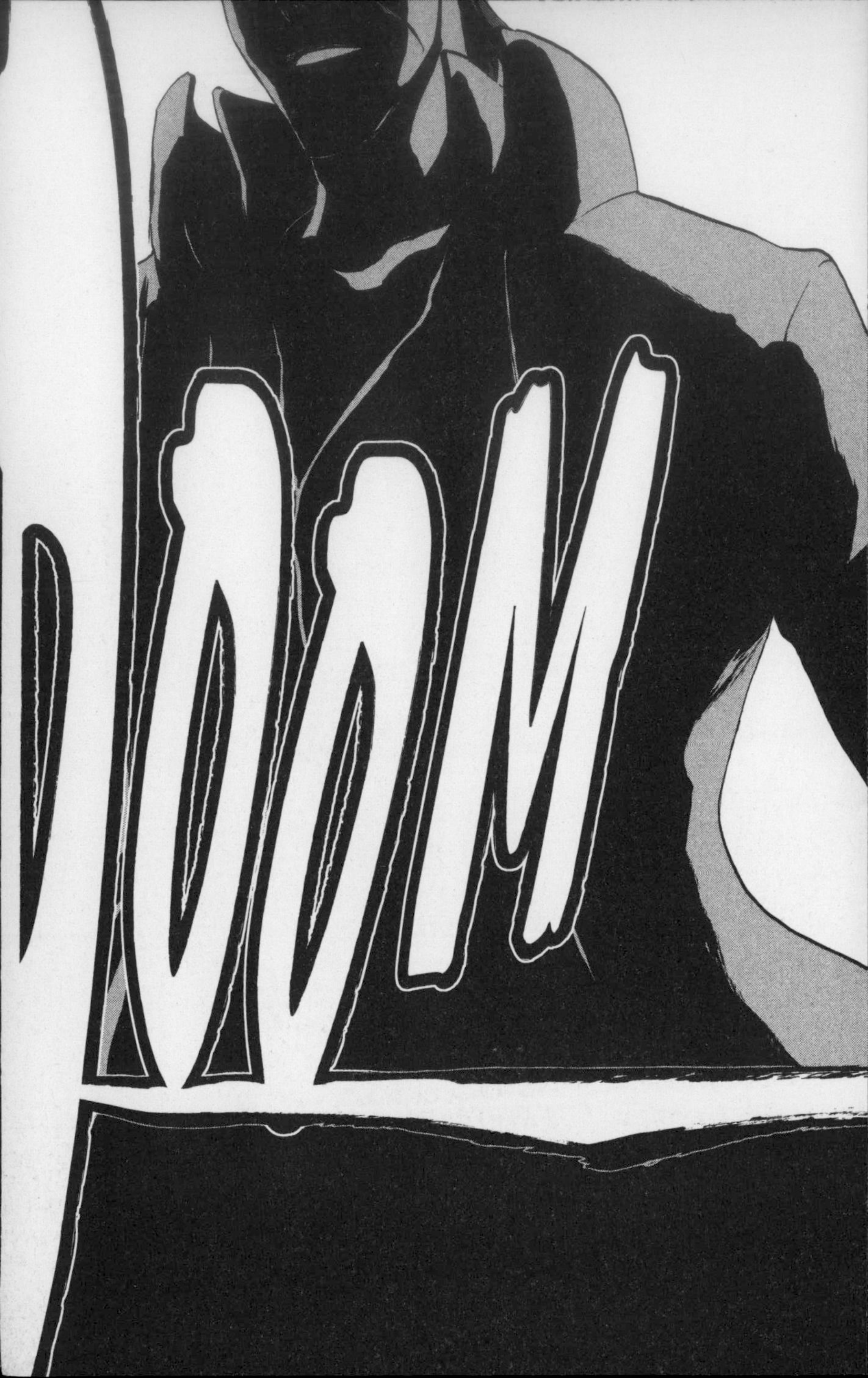

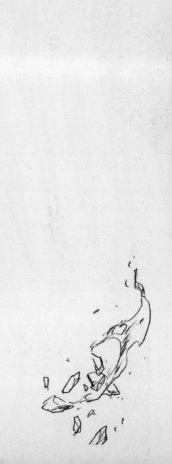

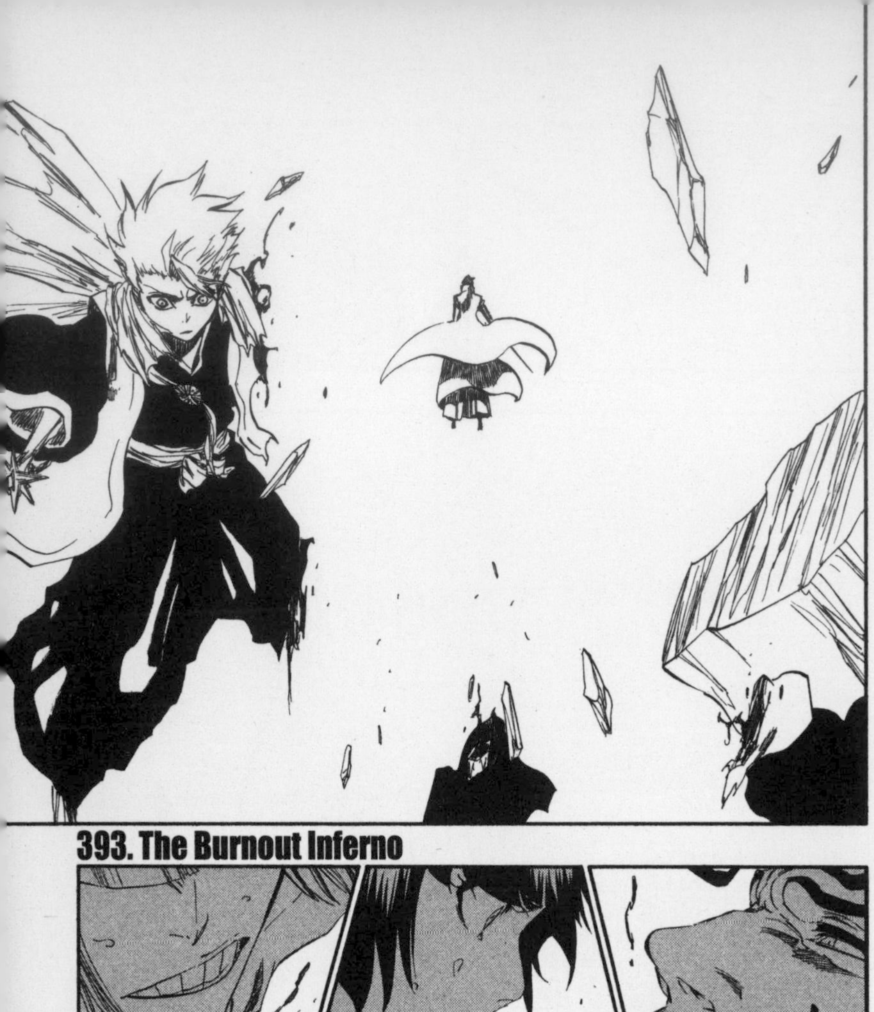

393. The Burnout Inferno

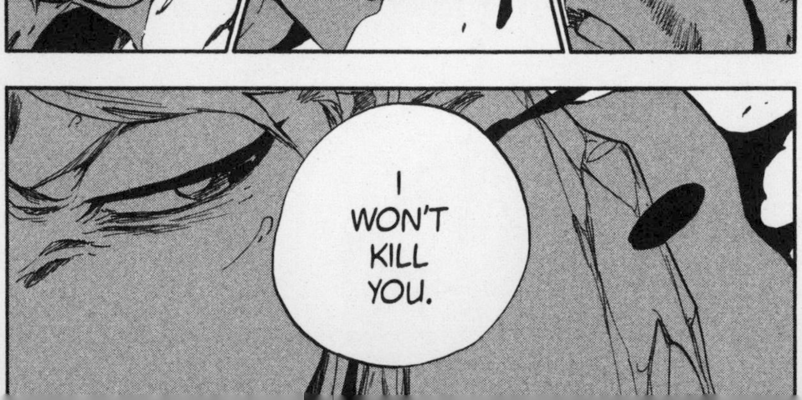
I WON'T KILL YOU.

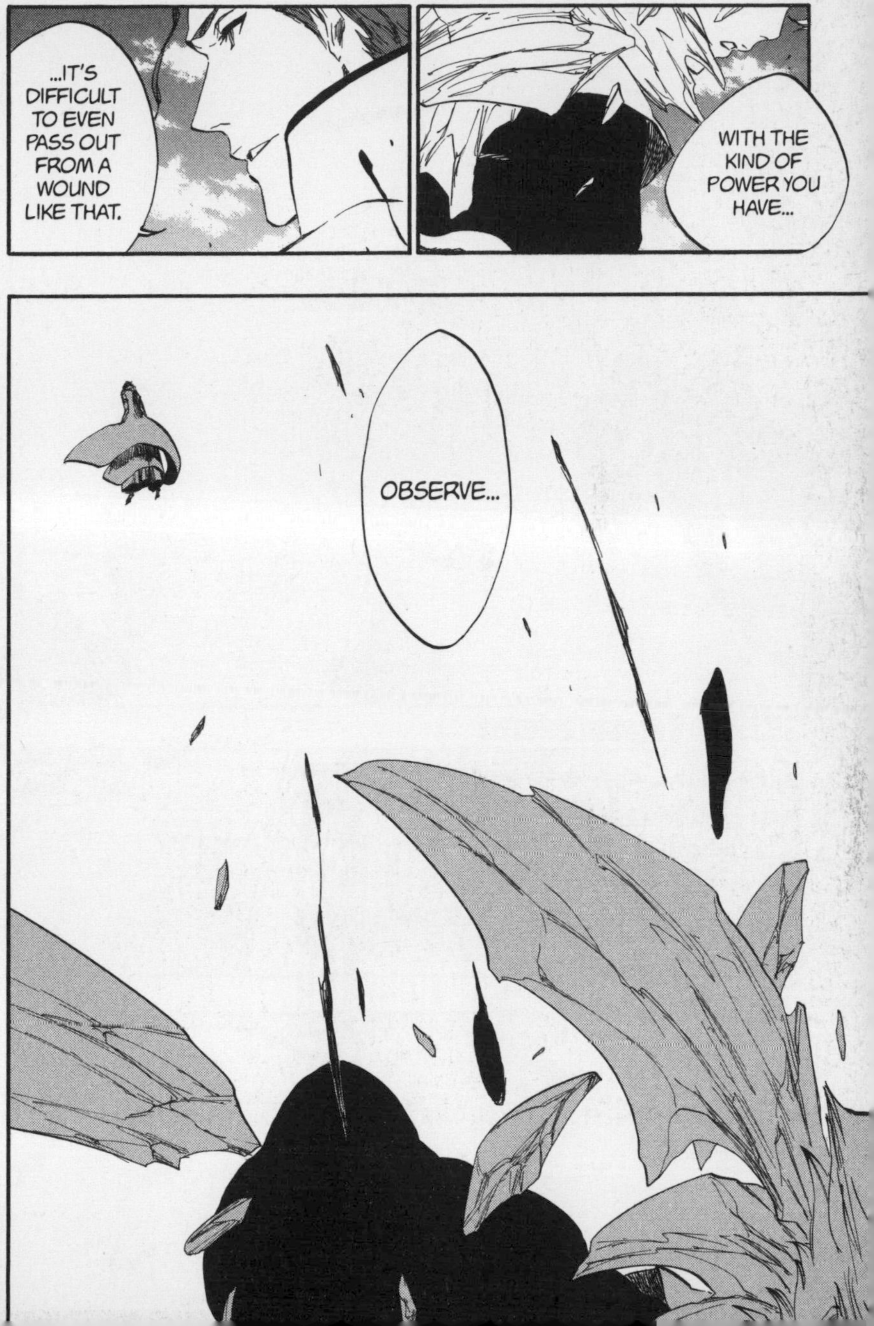
WITH THE KIND OF POWER YOU HAVE...
...IT'S DIFFICULT TO EVEN PASS OUT FROM A WOUND LIKE THAT.
OBSERVE...

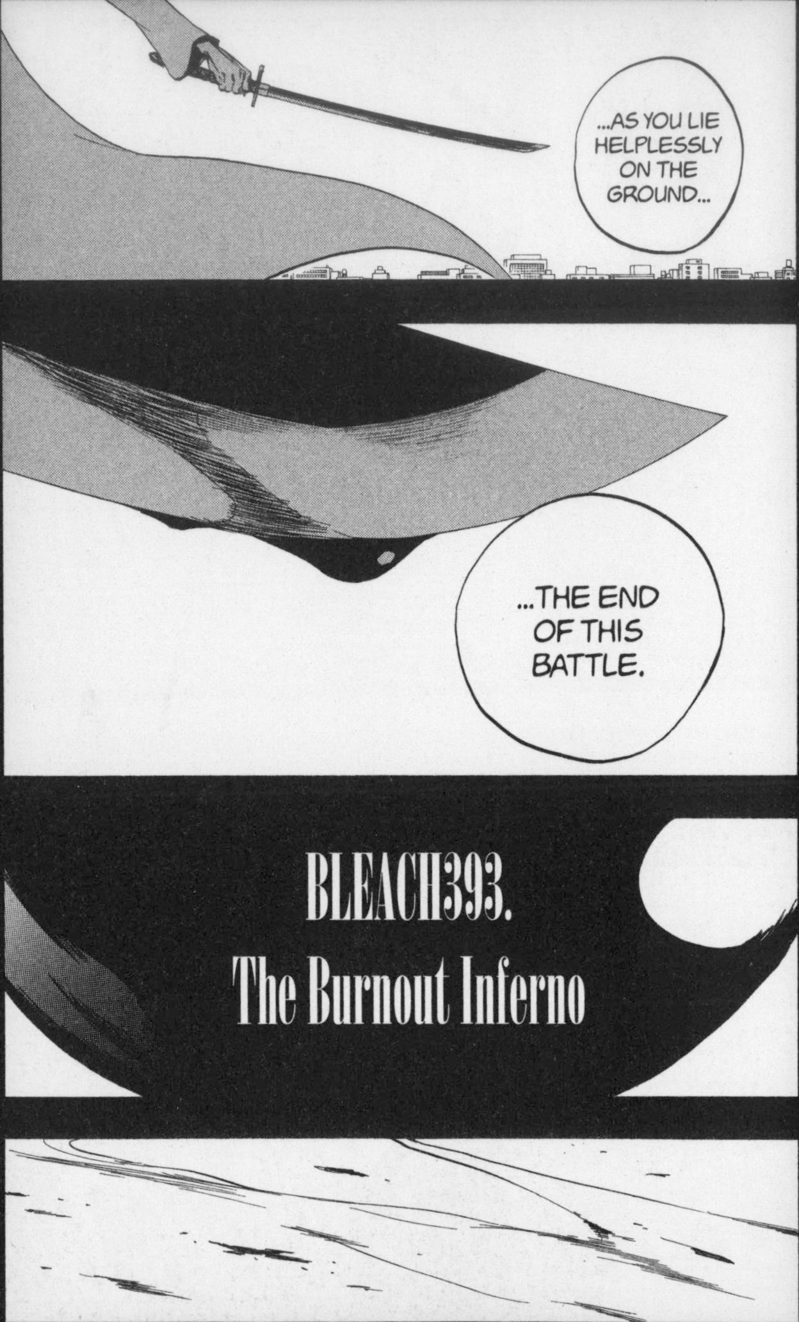
...AS YOU LIE HELPLESSLY ON THE GROUND...
...THE END OF THIS BATTLE.
BLEACH393.
The Burnout Inferno

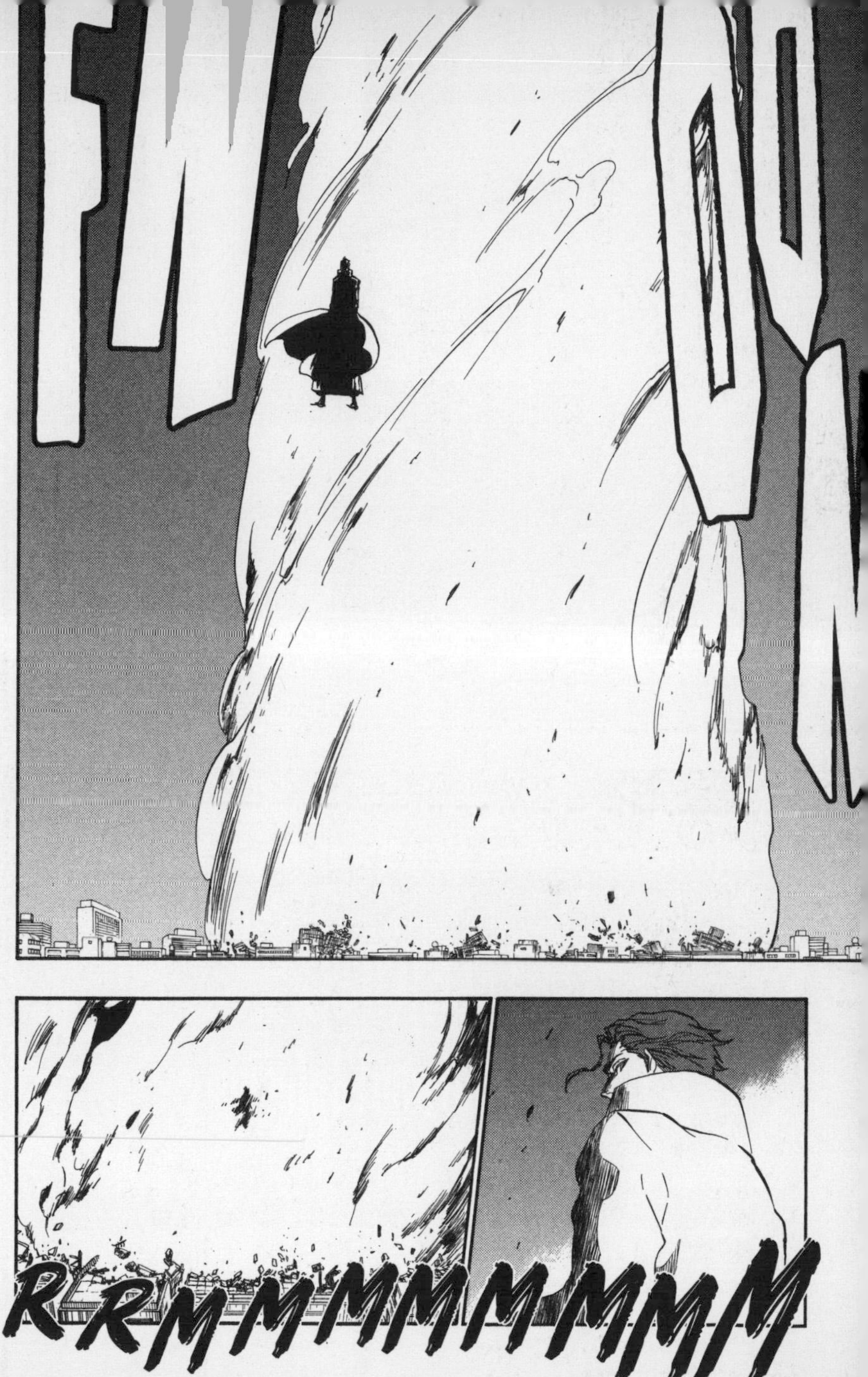
RRMMMMMMMM

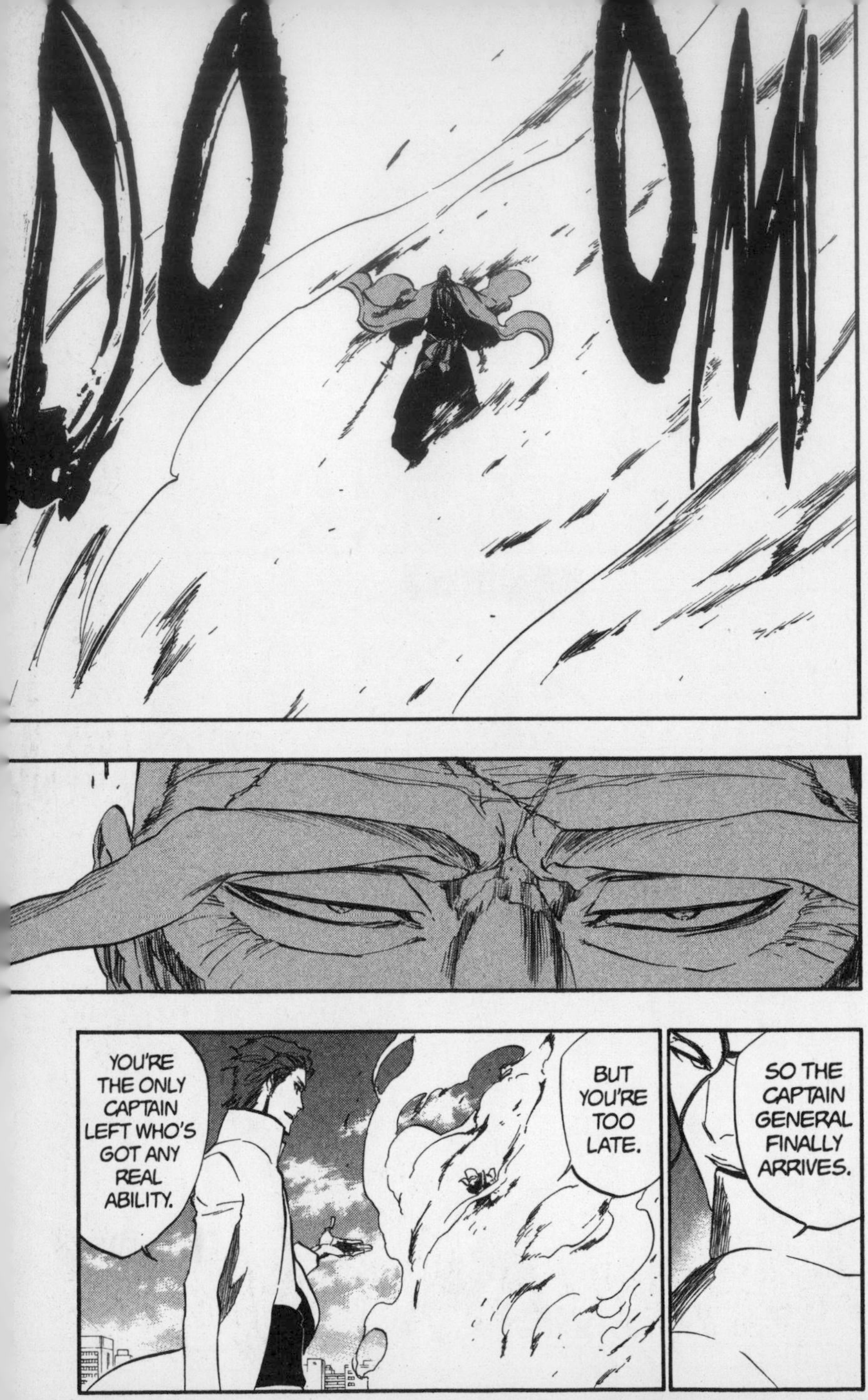
DOOM
SO THE CAPTAIN GENERAL FINALLY ARRIVES.
BUT YOU'RE TOO LATE.
YOU'RE THE ONLY CAPTAIN LEFT WHO'S GOT ANY REAL ABILITY.

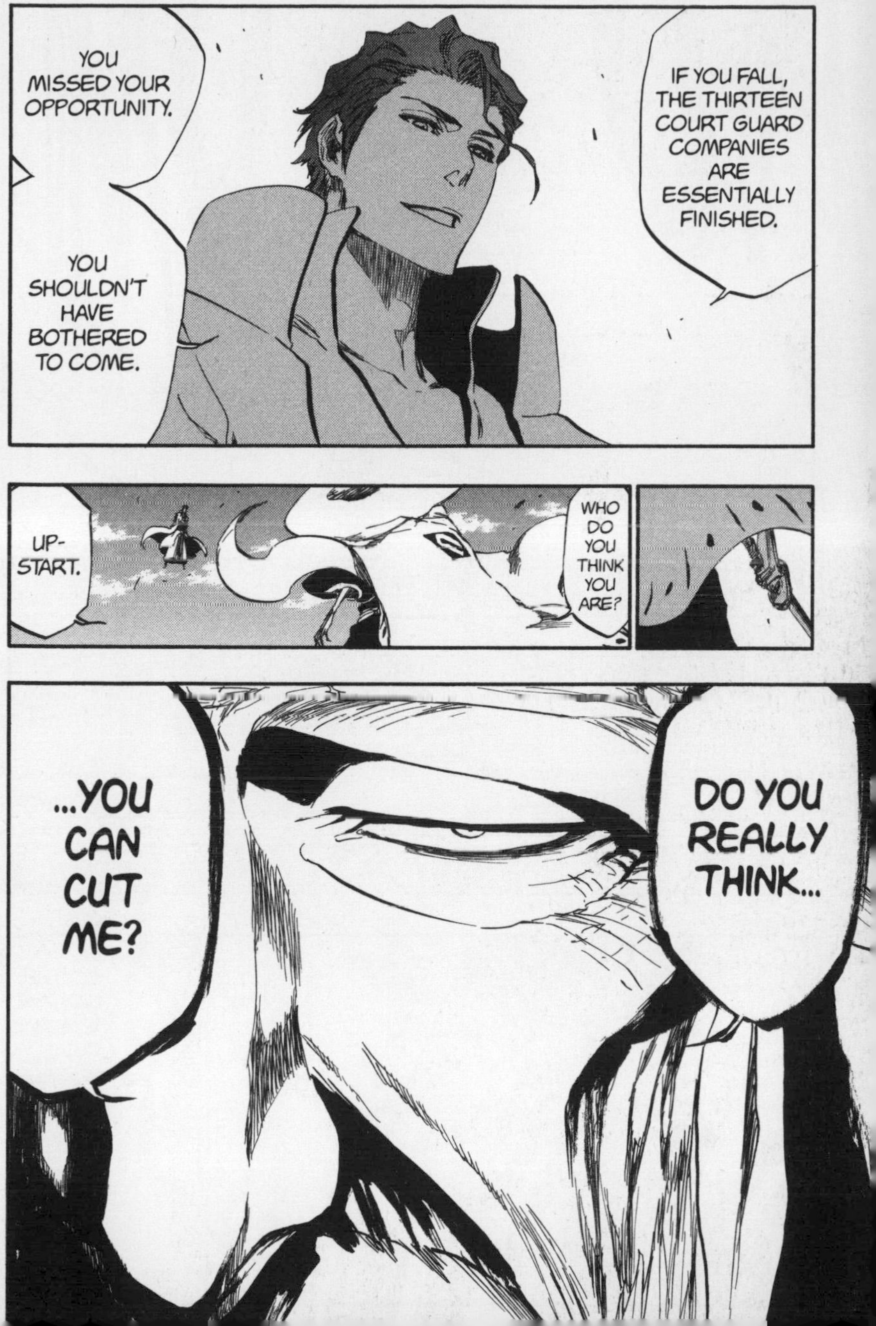
IF YOU FALL, THE THIRTEEN COURT GUARD COMPANIES ARE ESSENTIALLY FINISHED.
YOU MISSED YOUR OPPORTUNITY.
YOU SHOULDN'T HAVE BOTHERED TO COME.
WHO DO YOU THINK YOU ARE?
UP-START.
DO YOU REALLY THINK...
...YOU CAN CUT ME?

READ THIS WAY

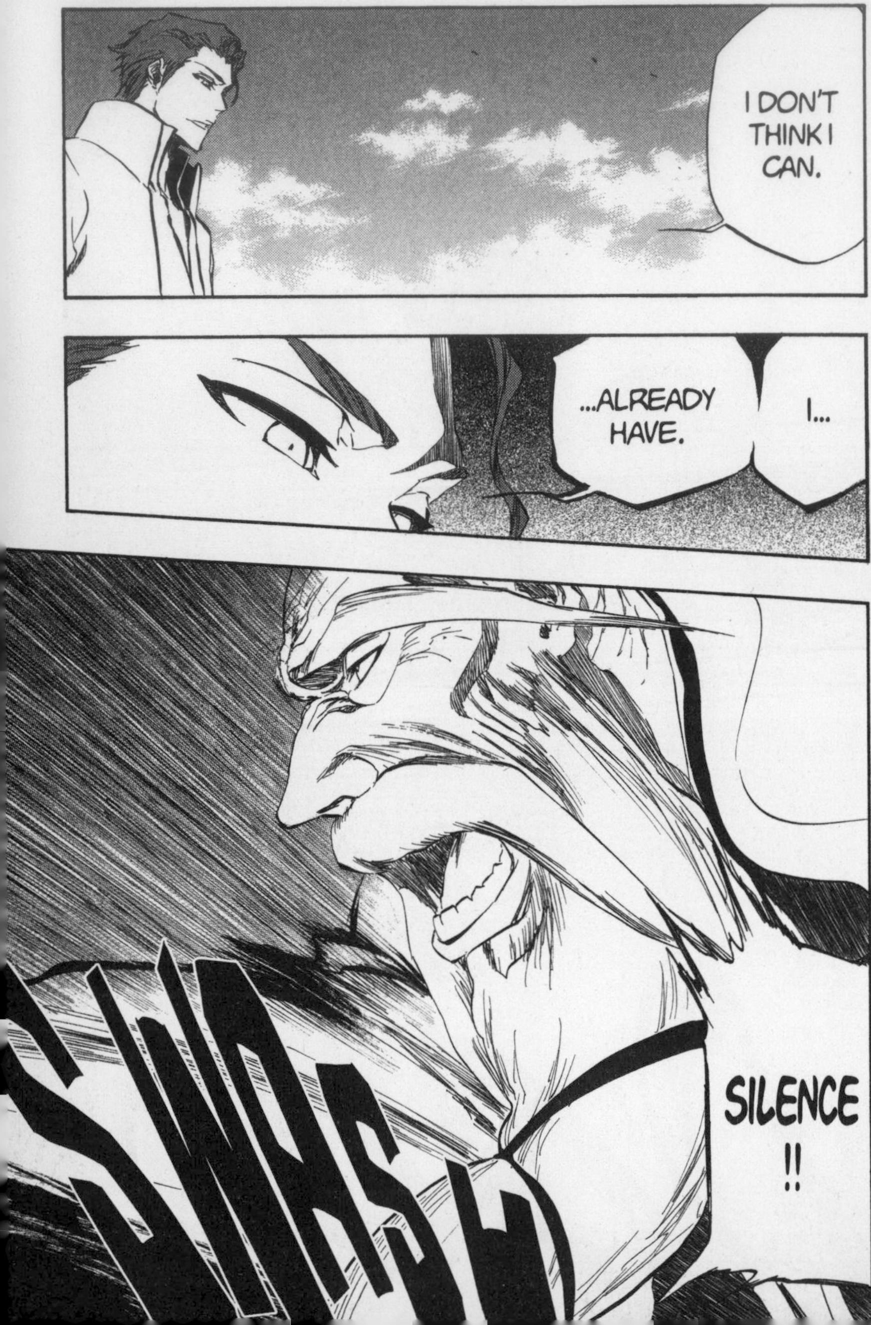
I DON'T THINK I CAN.
I...
...ALREADY HAVE.
SILENCE !!

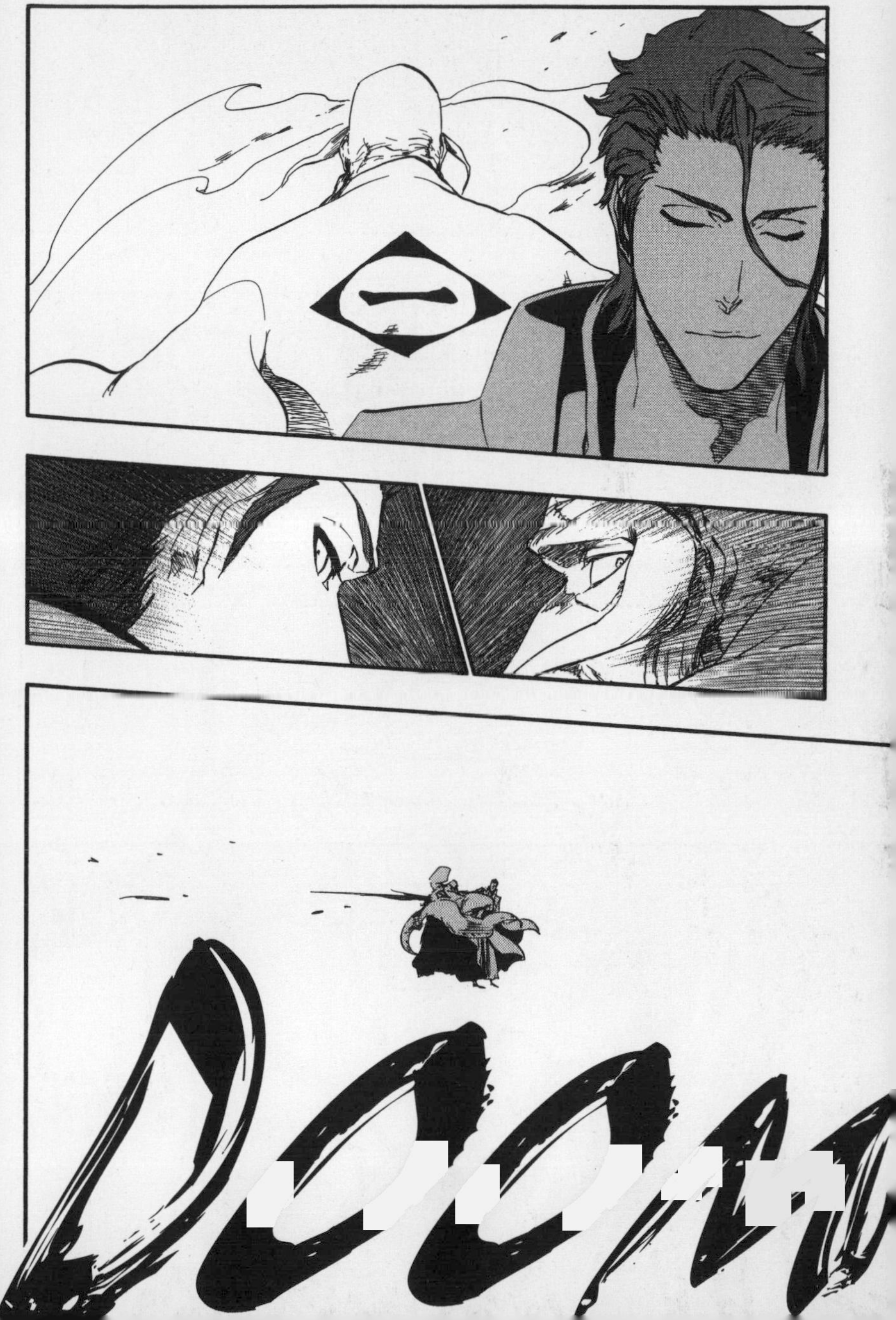

READ THIS WAY

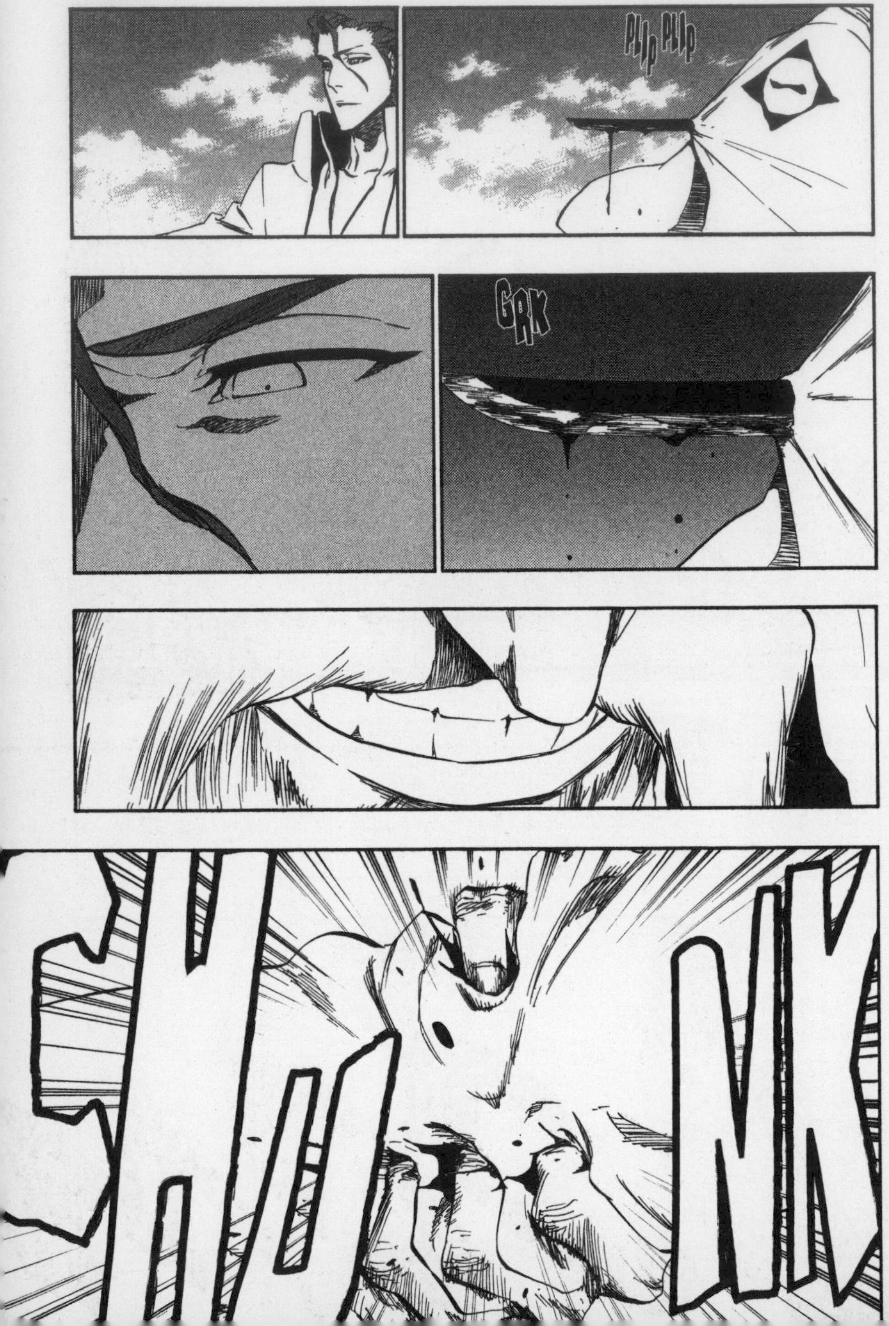
PLIP PLIP
GRK

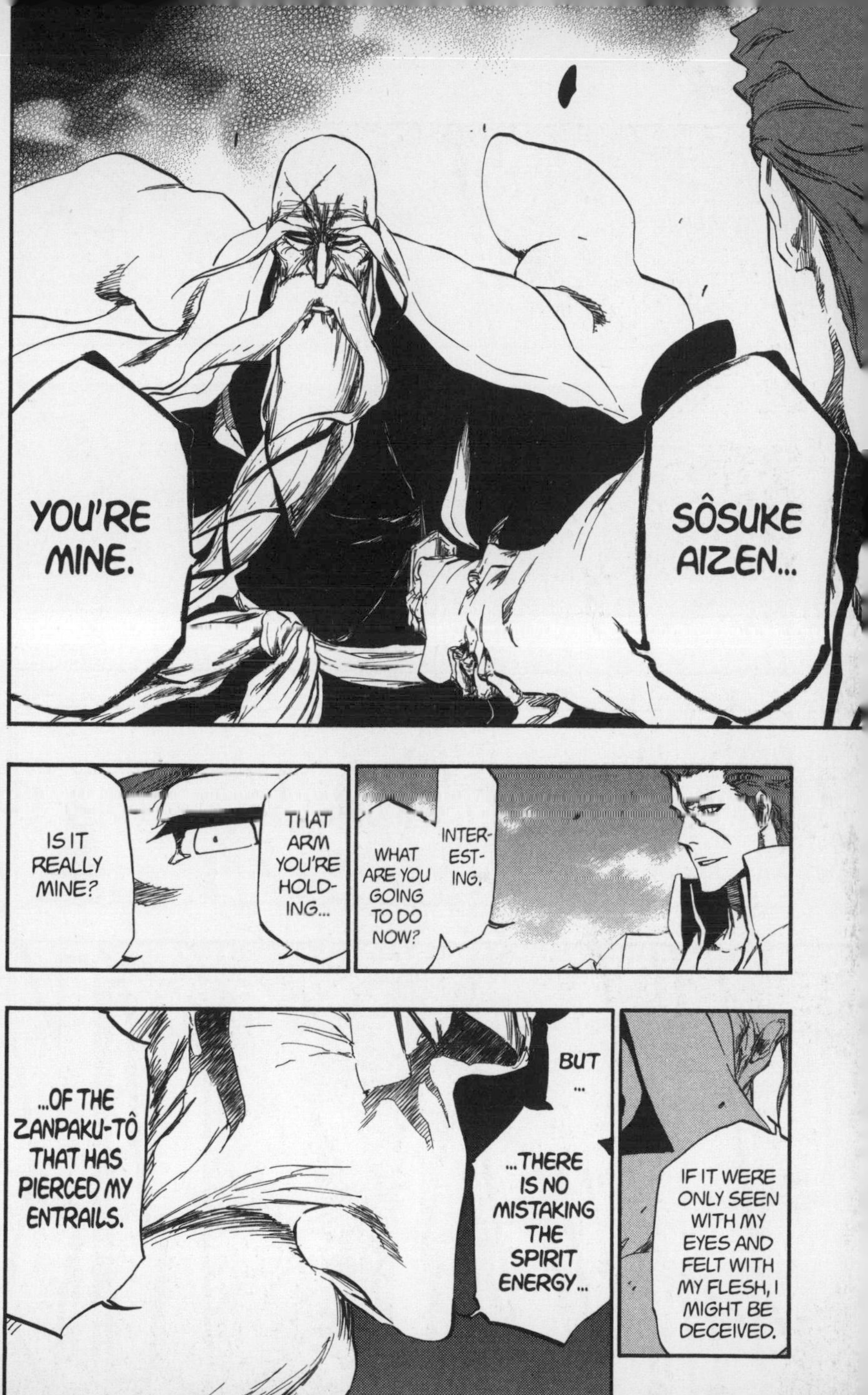
SÔSUKE AIZEN...
YOU'RE MINE.
INTEREST-ING.
WHAT ARE YOU GOING TO DO NOW?
THAT ARM YOU'RE HOLDING...
IS IT REALLY MINE?
IF IT WERE ONLY SEEN WITH MY EYES AND FELT WITH MY FLESH, I MIGHT BE DECEIVED.
BUT...
...THERE IS NO MISTAKING THE SPIRIT ENERGY...
...OF THE ZANPAKU-TÔ THAT HAS PIERCED MY ENTRAILS.

READ THIS WAY

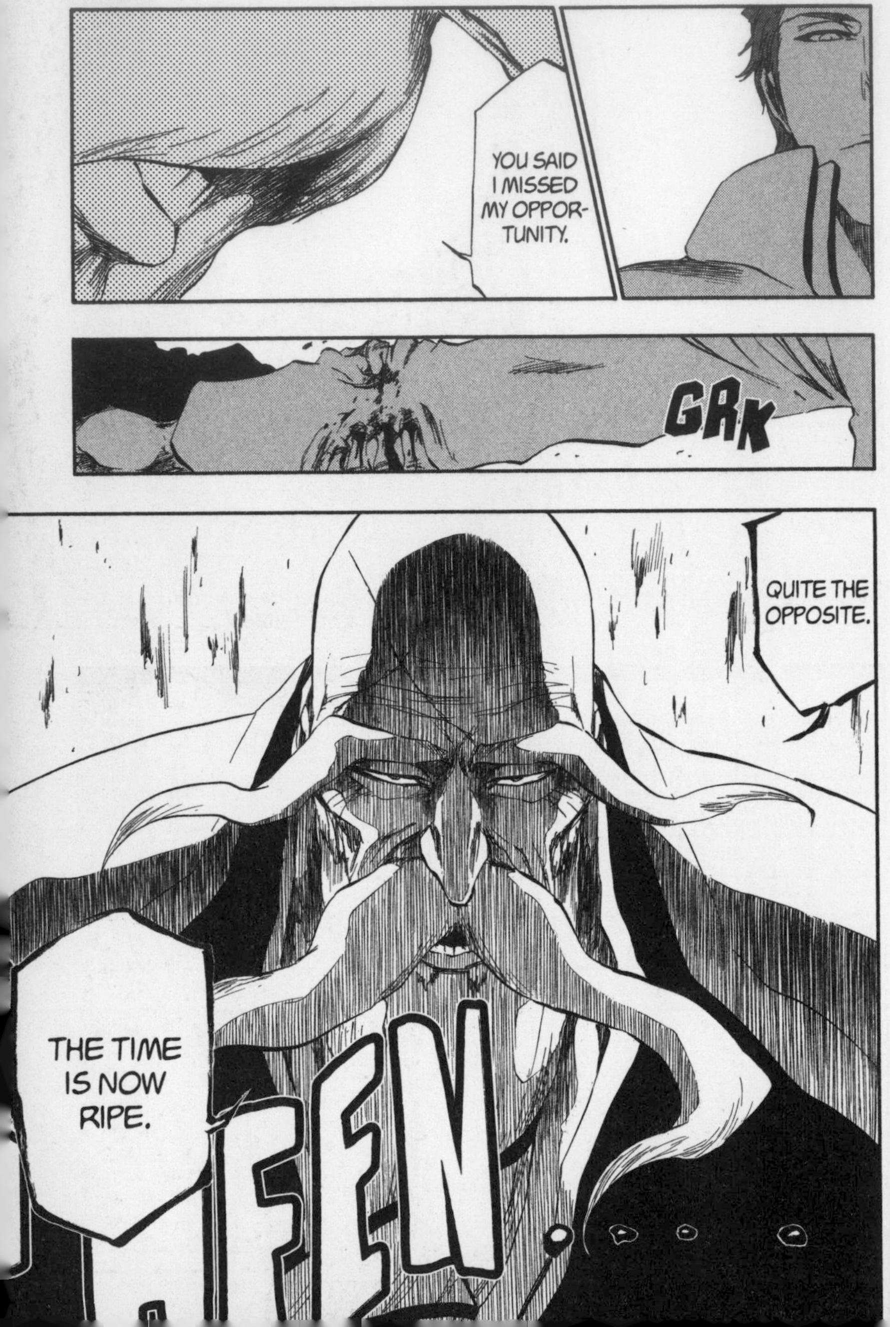

YOU SAID I MISSED MY OPPORTUNITY.
GRK
QUITE THE OPPOSITE.
THE TIME IS NOW RIPE.
FEN...

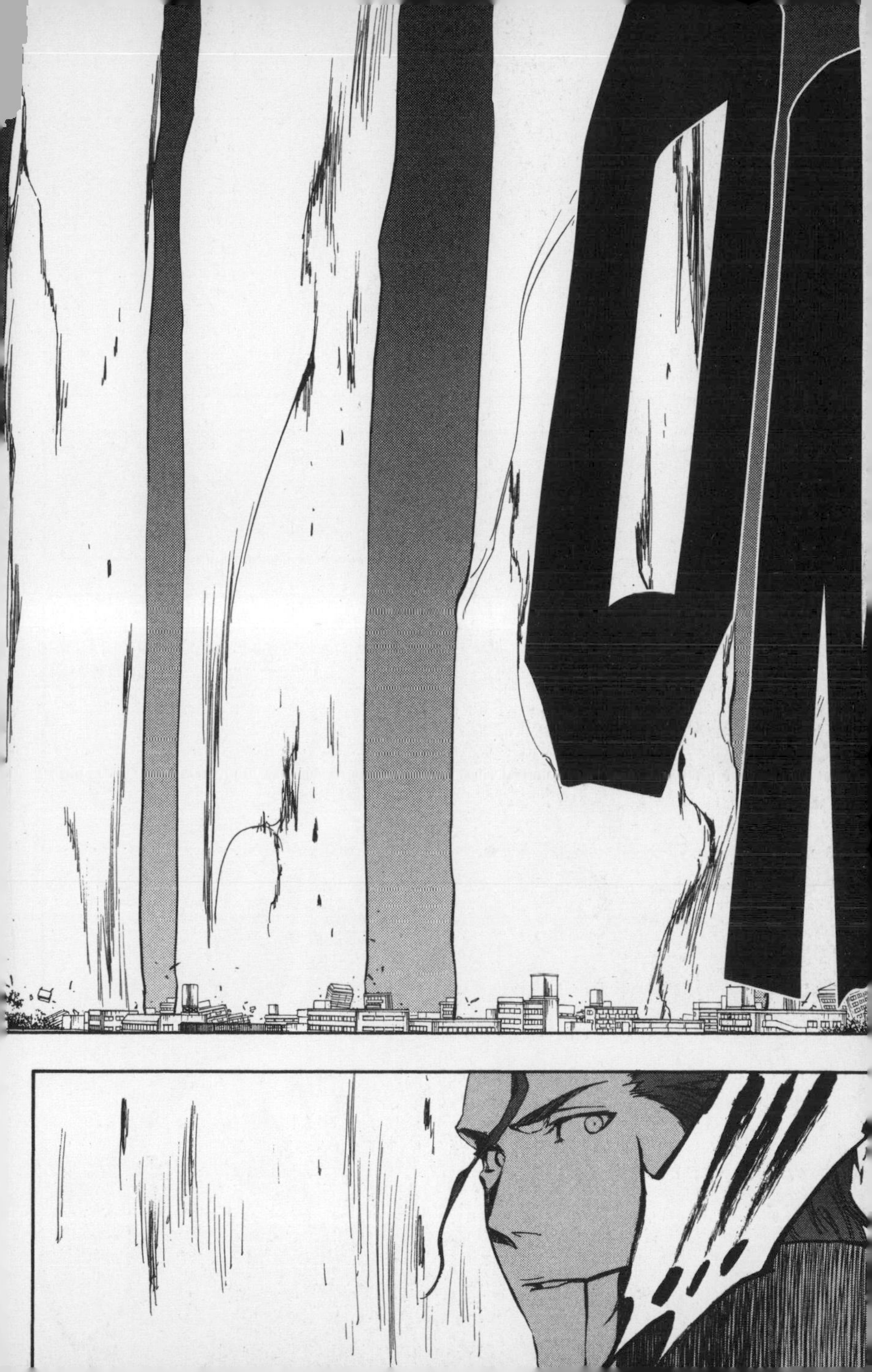

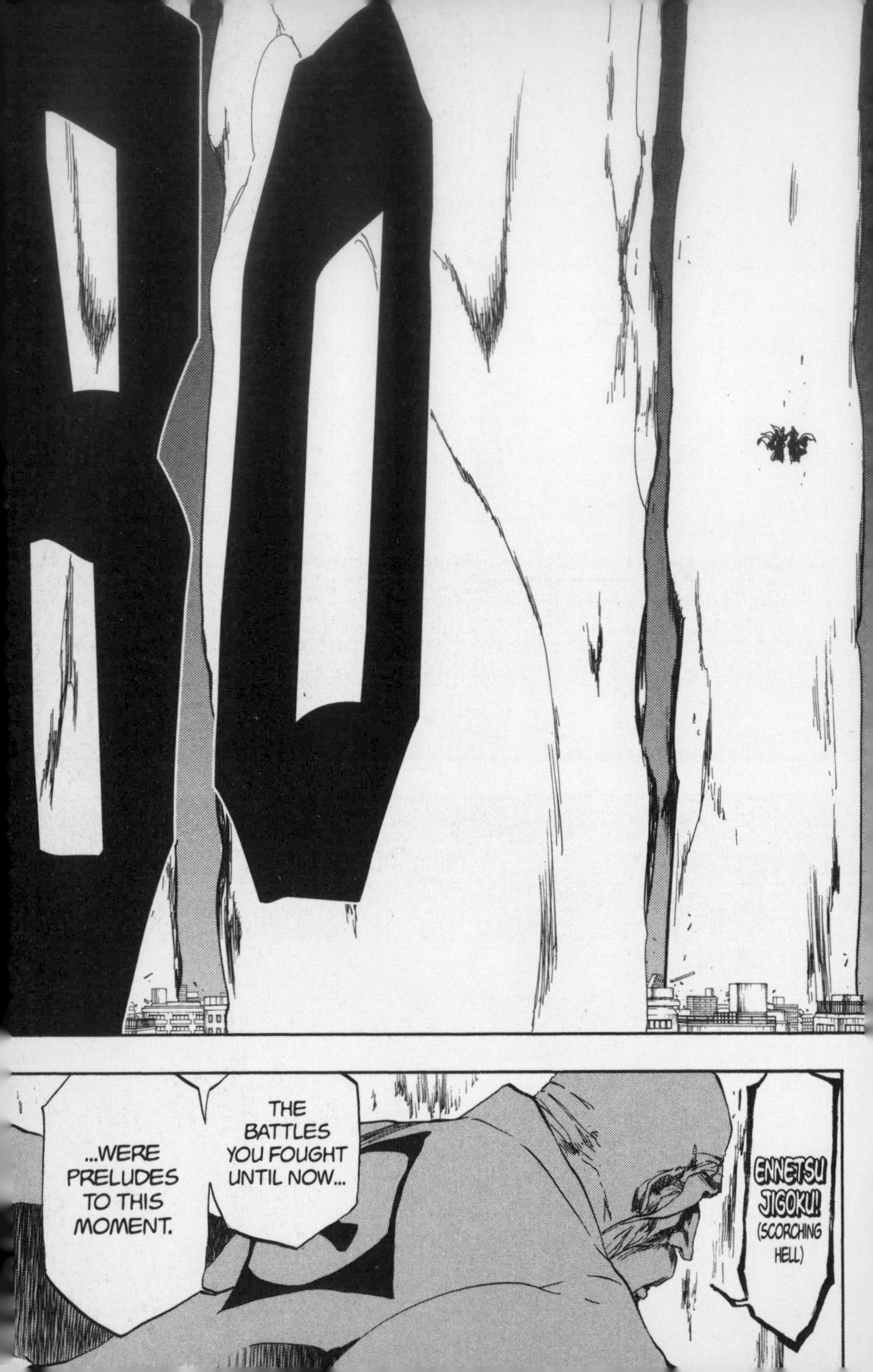
ENNETSU JIGOKU!! (SCORCHING HELL)
THE BATTLES YOU FOUGHT UNTIL NOW...
...WERE PRELUDES TO THIS MOMENT.

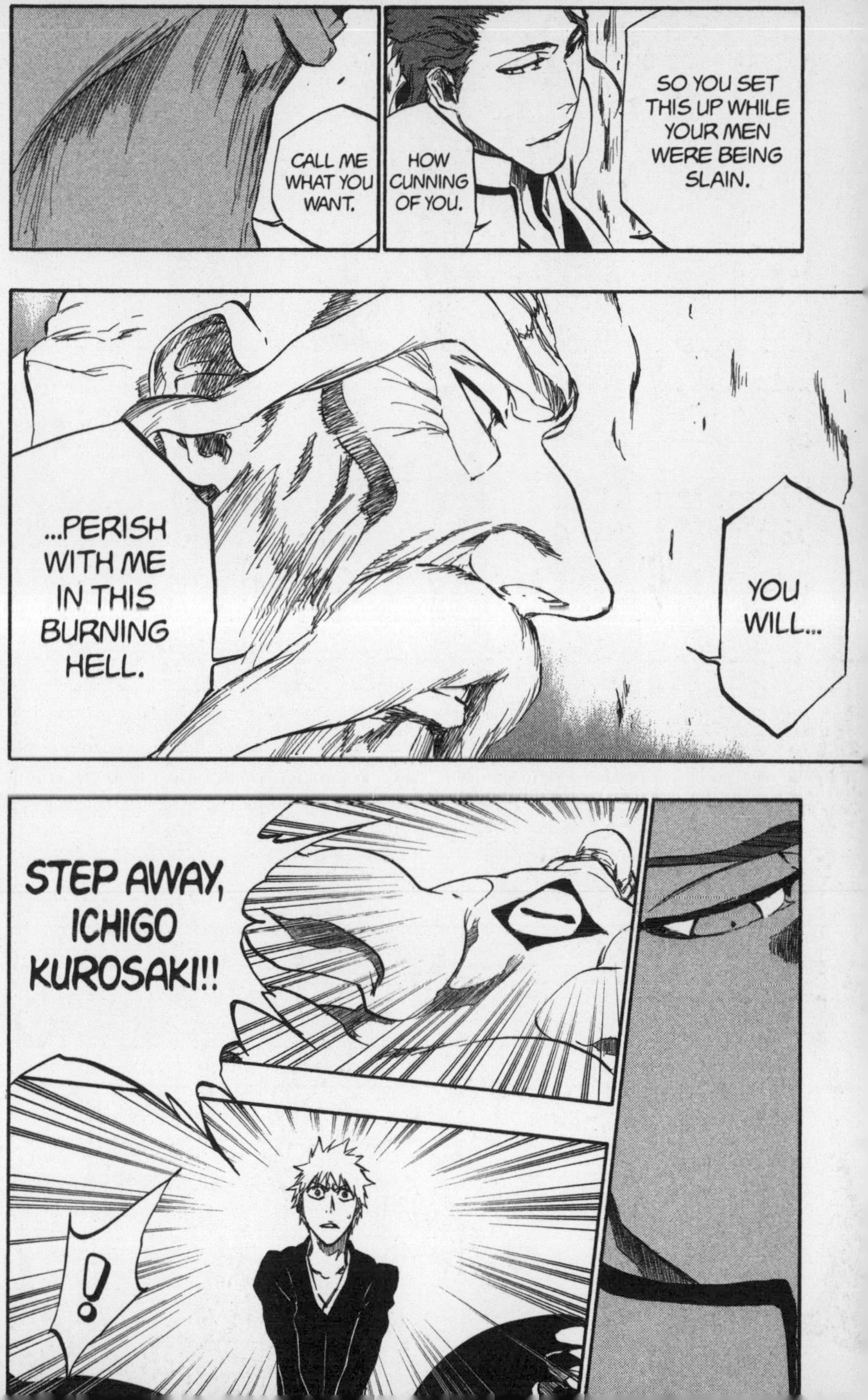
SO YOU SET THIS UP WHILE YOUR MEN WERE BEING SLAIN.
HOW CUNNING OF YOU.
CALL ME WHAT YOU WANT.
YOU WILL...
...PERISH WITH ME IN THIS BURNING HELL.
STEP AWAY, ICHIGO KUROSAKI!!
!

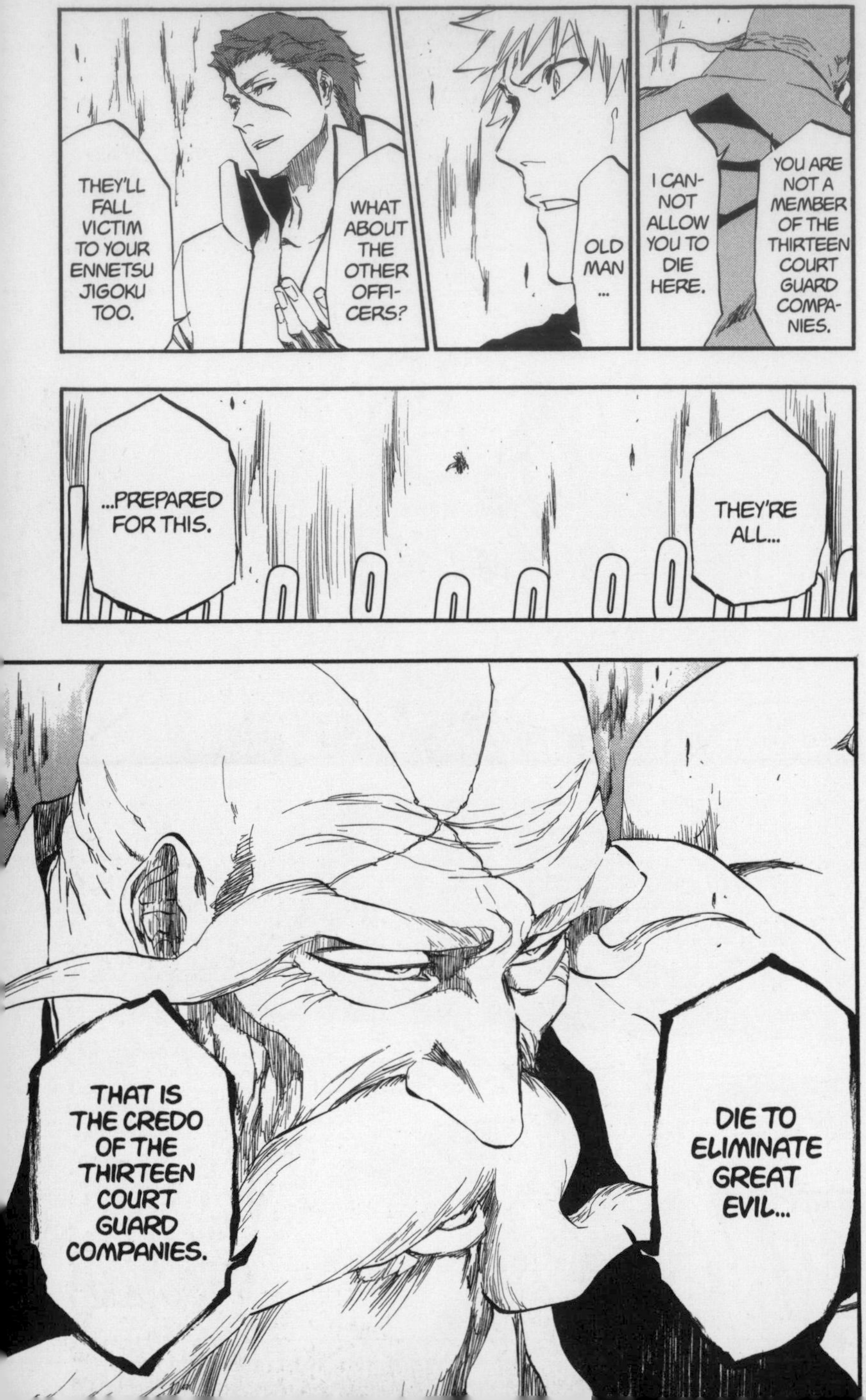
YOU ARE NOT A MEMBER OF THE THIRTEEN COURT GUARD COMPANIES.
I CANNOT ALLOW YOU TO DIE HERE.
OLD MAN...
WHAT ABOUT THE OTHER OFFICERS?
THEY'LL FALL VICTIM TO YOUR ENNETSU JIGOKU TOO.
THEY'RE ALL...
...PREPARED FOR THIS.
DIE TO ELIMINATE GREAT EVIL...
THAT IS THE CREDO OF THE THIRTEEN COURT GUARD COMPANIES.

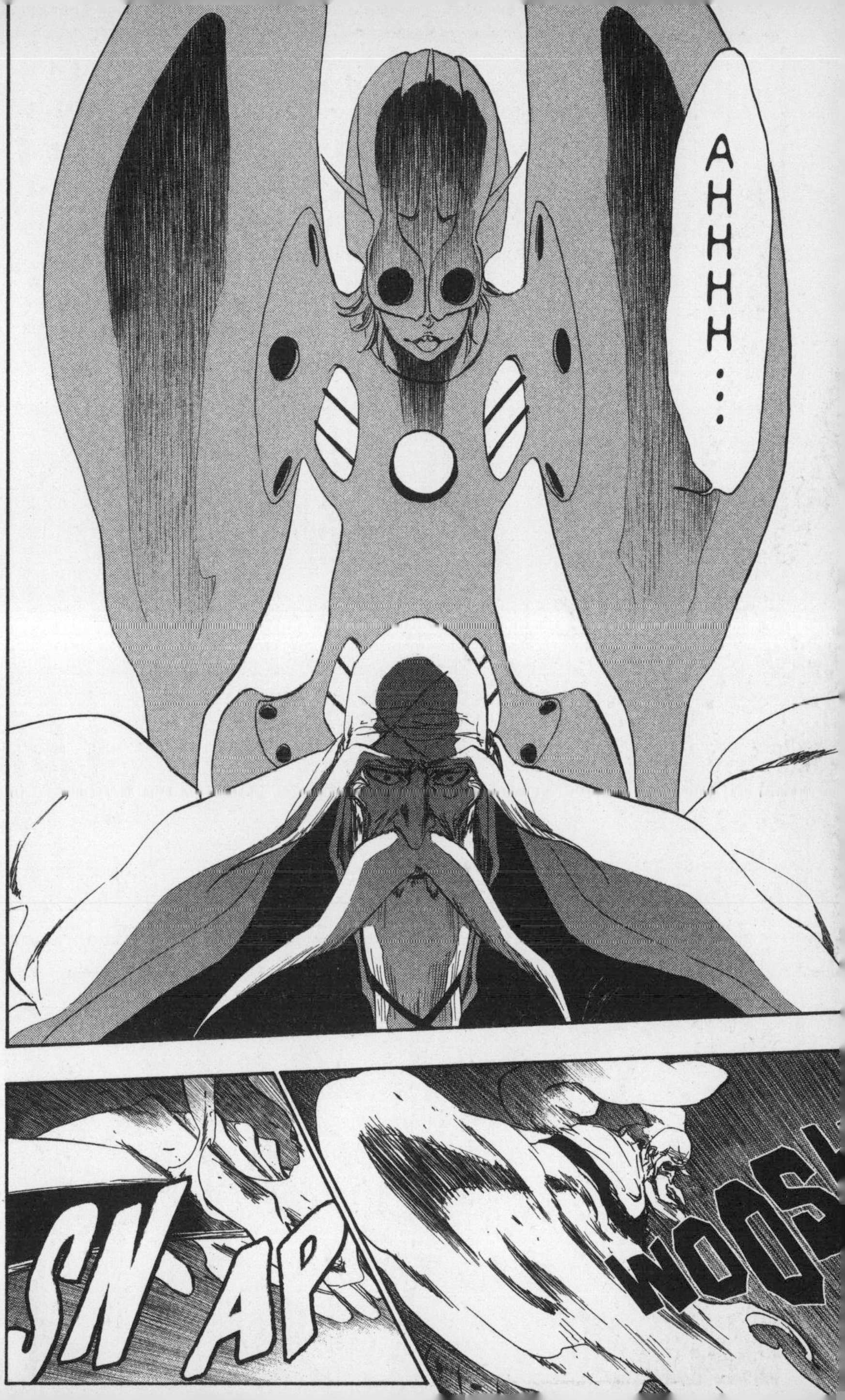
AHHHH...
WOOS
SNAP

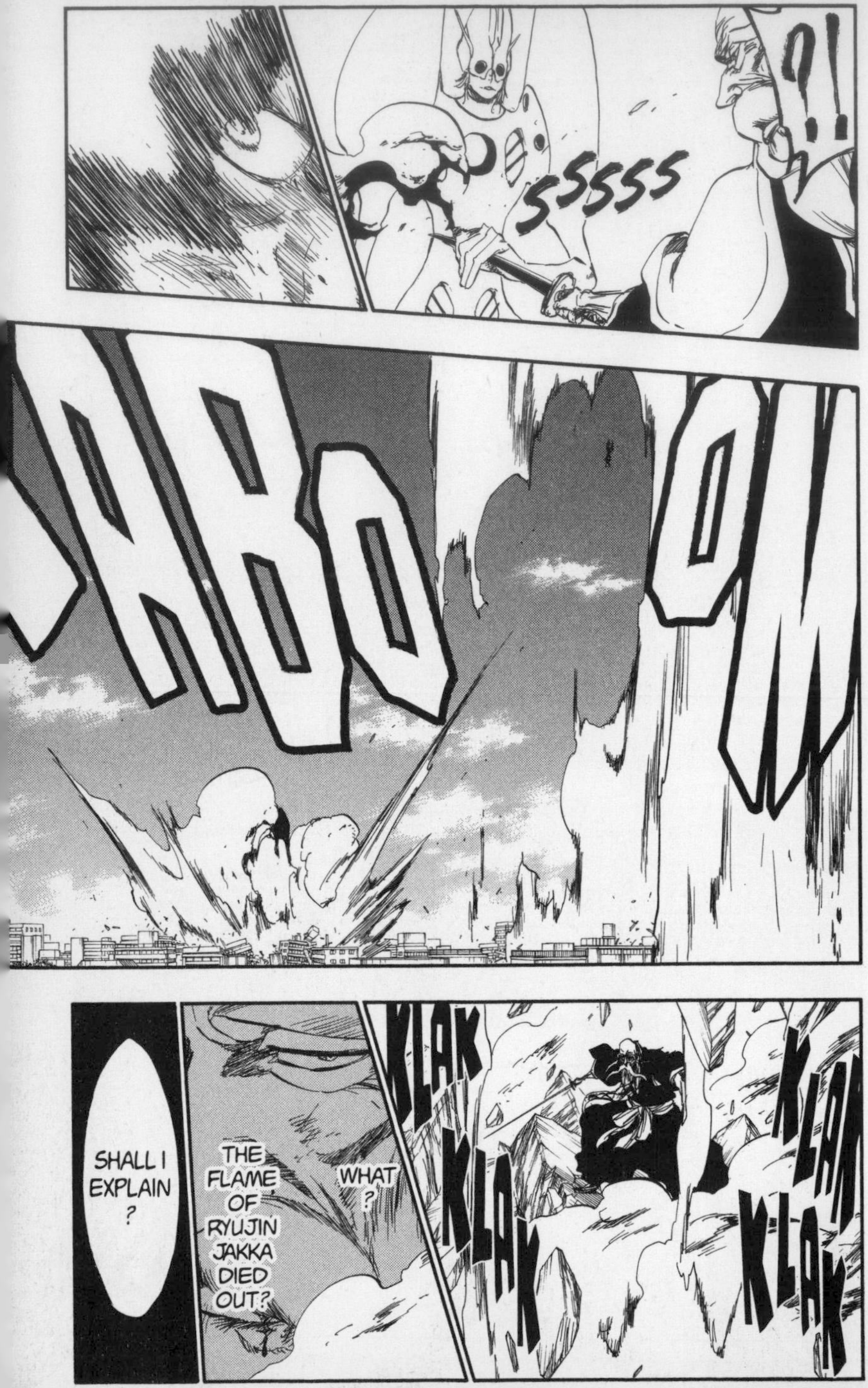
?!!
SSSSS
KLAK KLAK
KLAK KLAK
KLAK KLAK
WHAT?
THE FLAME OF RYUJIN JAKKA DIED OUT?
SHALL I EXPLAIN?

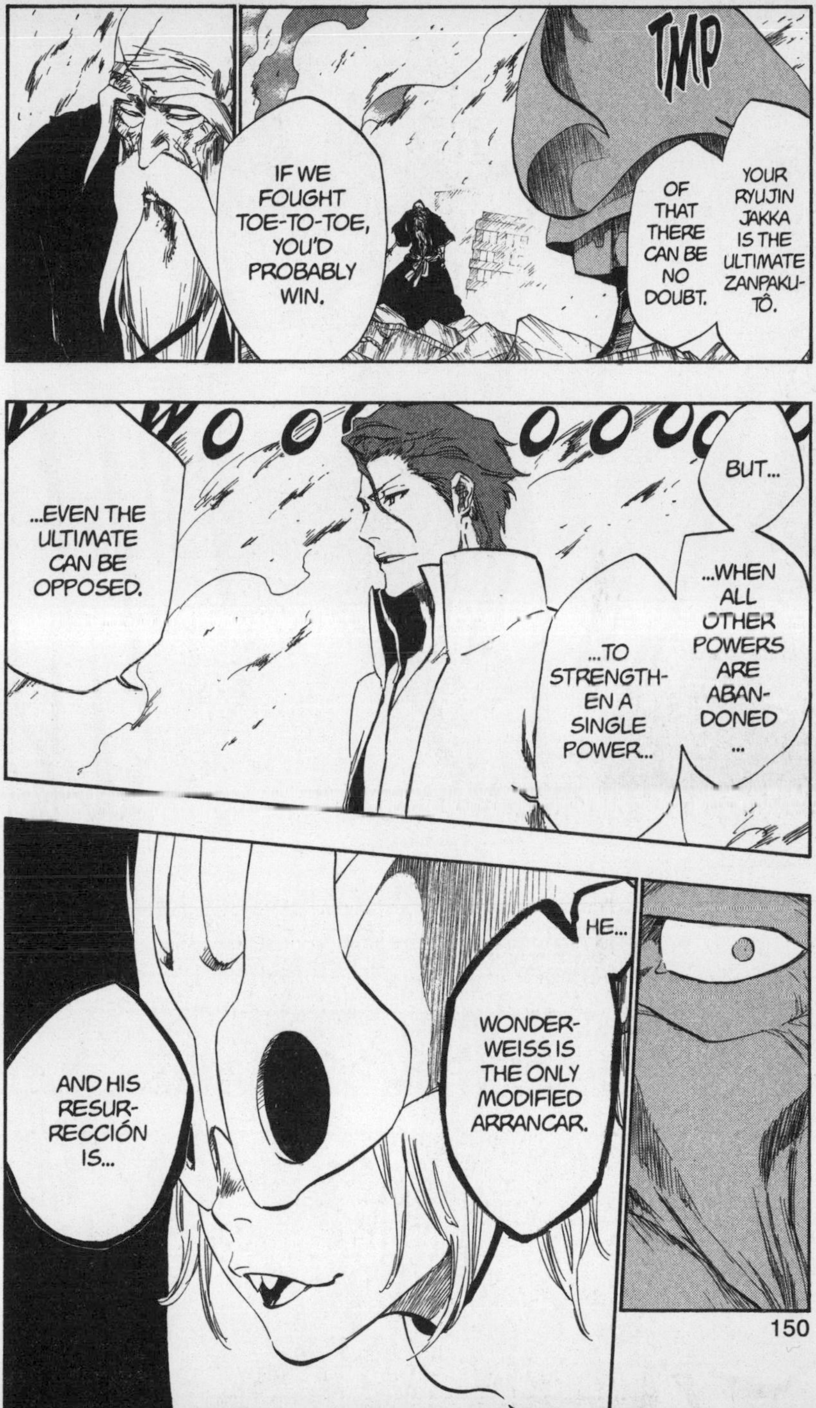
TMP
YOUR RYUJIN JAKKA IS THE ULTIMATE ZANPAKU-TÔ.
OF THAT THERE CAN BE NO DOUBT.
IF WE FOUGHT TOE-TO-TOE, YOU'D PROBABLY WIN.
WOOOOOOO
BUT...
...WHEN ALL OTHER POWERS ARE ABAN-DONED...
...TO STRENGTH-EN A SINGLE POWER...
...EVEN THE ULTIMATE CAN BE OPPOSED.
HE...
WONDER-WEISS IS THE ONLY MODIFIED ARRANCAR.
AND HIS RESUR-RECCIÓN IS...

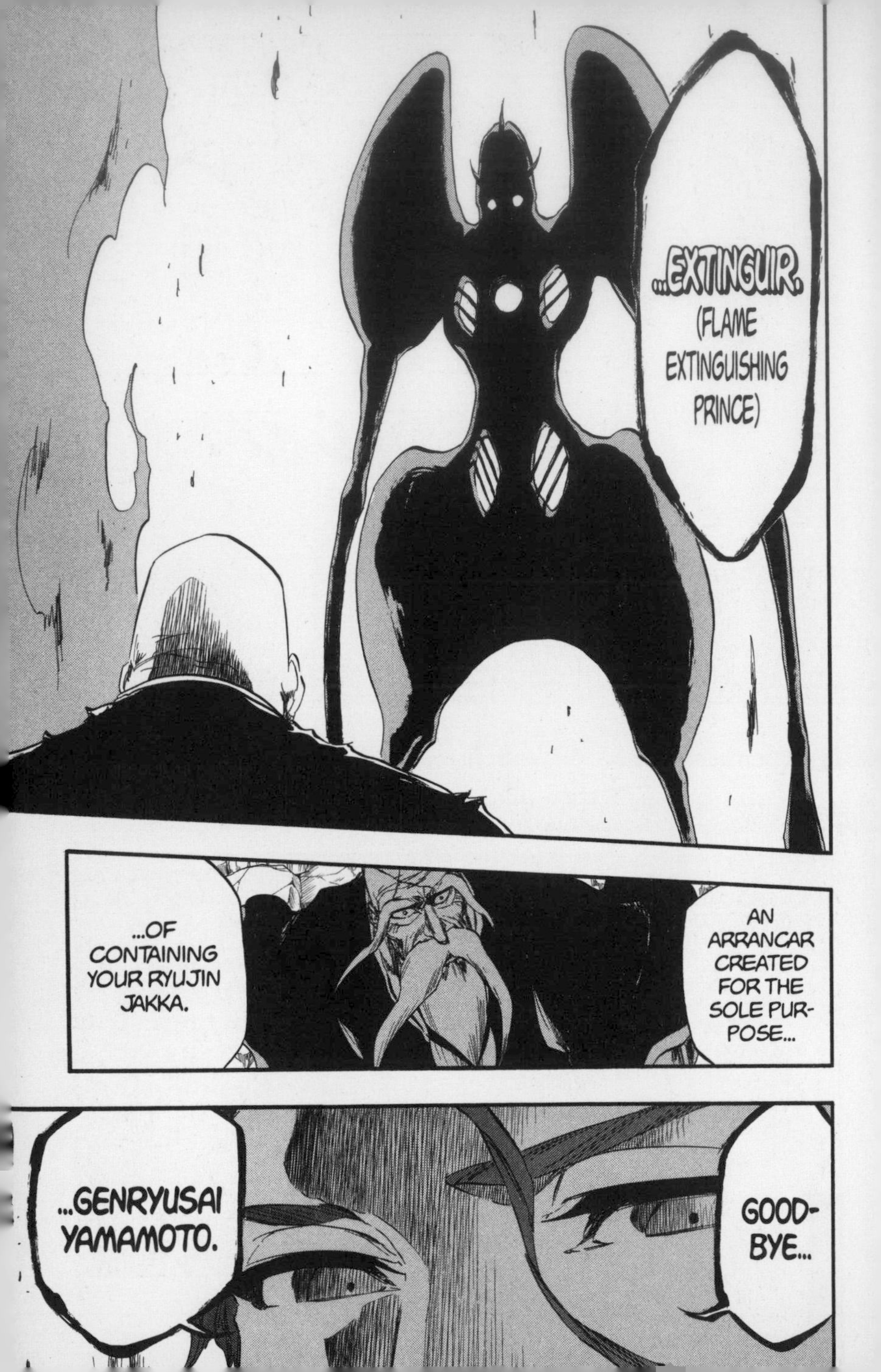
...EXTINGUIR.
(FLAME EXTINGUISHING PRINCE)
AN ARRANCAR CREATED FOR THE SOLE PUR-POSE...
...OF CONTAINING YOUR RYUJIN JAKKA.
GOOD-BYE...
...GENRYUSAI YAMAMOTO.

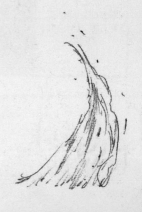

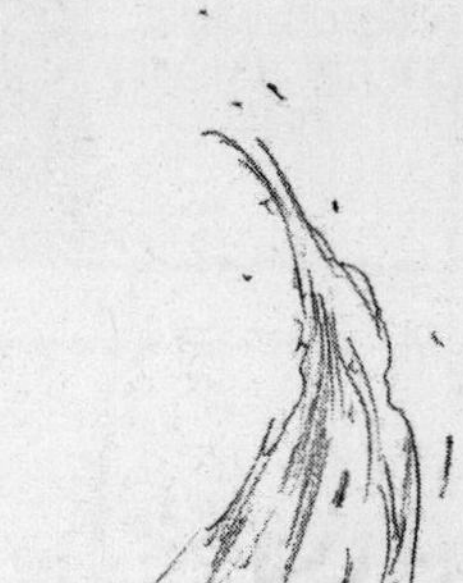

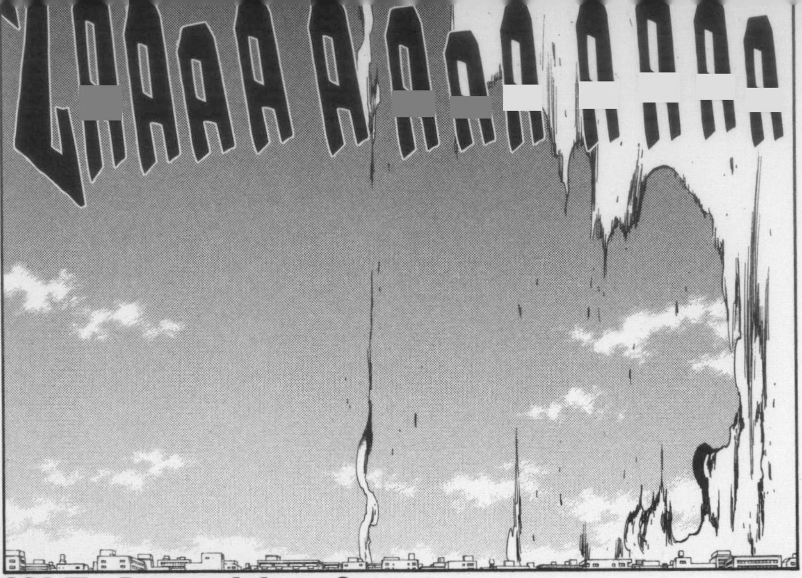

394. The Burnout Inferno 2

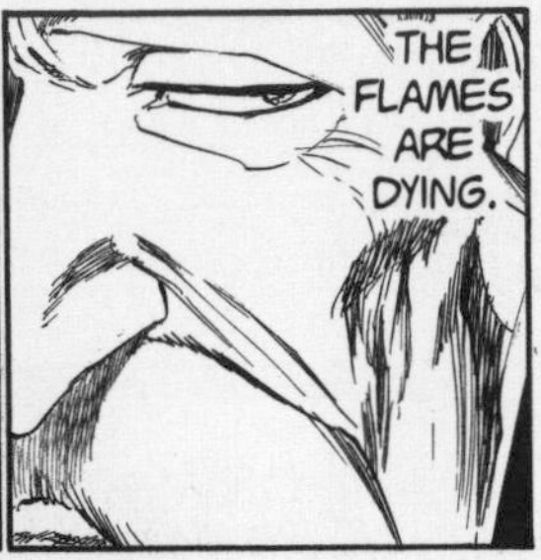
THE FLAMES ARE DYING.

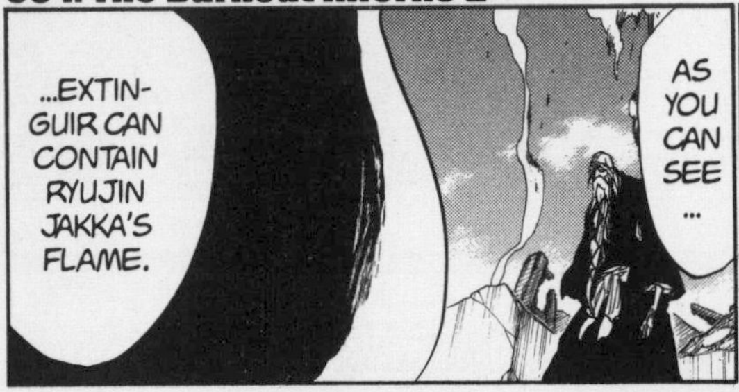
AS YOU CAN SEE...
...EXTIN-GUIR CAN CONTAIN RYUJIN JAKKA'S FLAME.

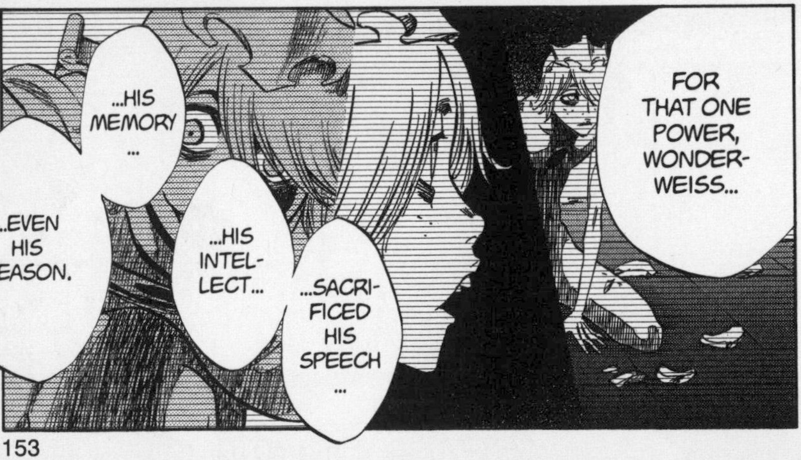
FOR THAT ONE POWER, WONDER-WEISS...
...SACRI-FICED HIS SPEECH...
...HIS INTEL-LECT...
...HIS MEMORY...
...EVEN HIS REASON.

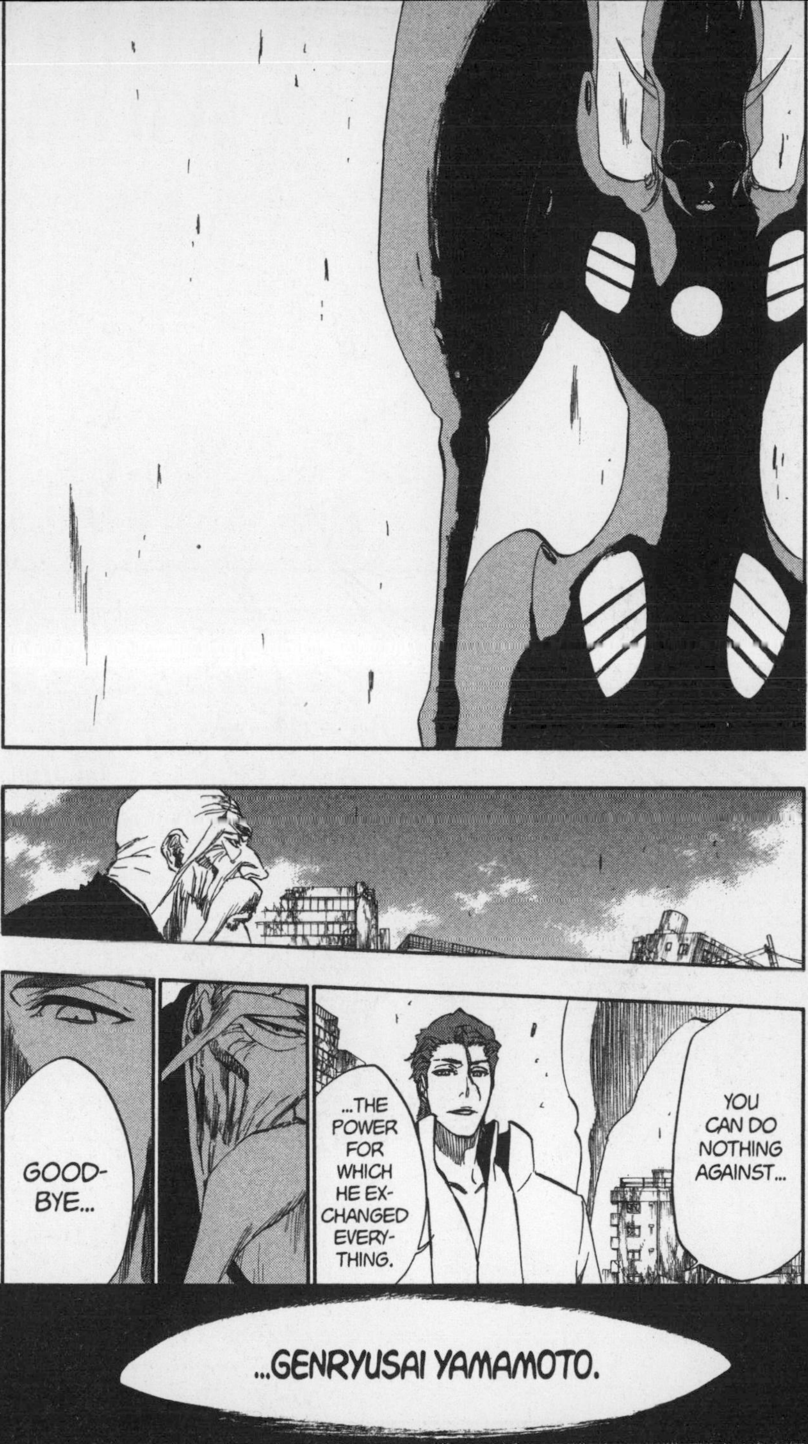
YOU CAN DO NOTHING AGAINST...
...THE POWER FOR WHICH HE EXCHANGED EVERYTHING.
GOOD-BYE...
...GENRYUSAI YAMAMOTO.

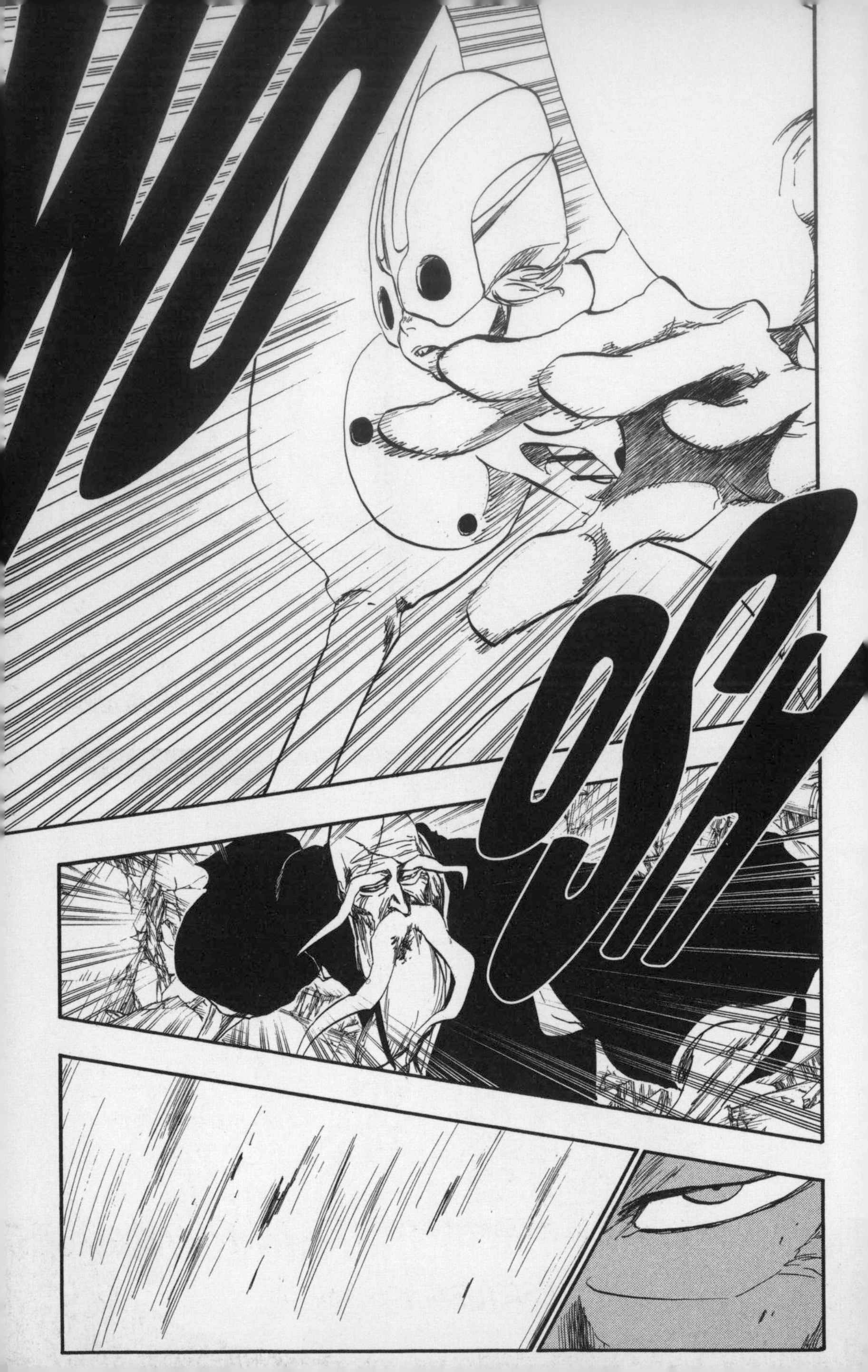
WOOSH

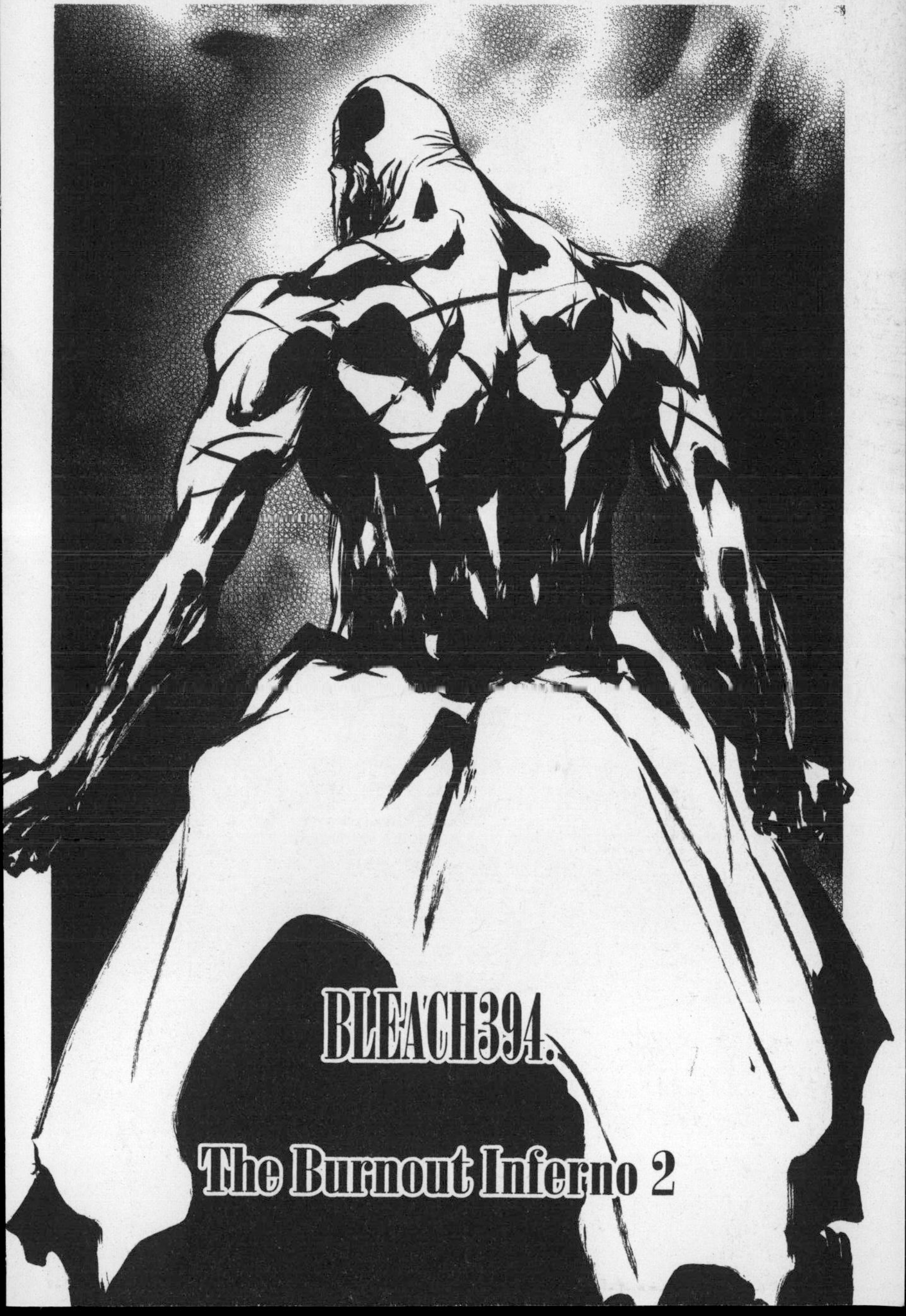
BLEACH394.
The Burnout Inferno 2

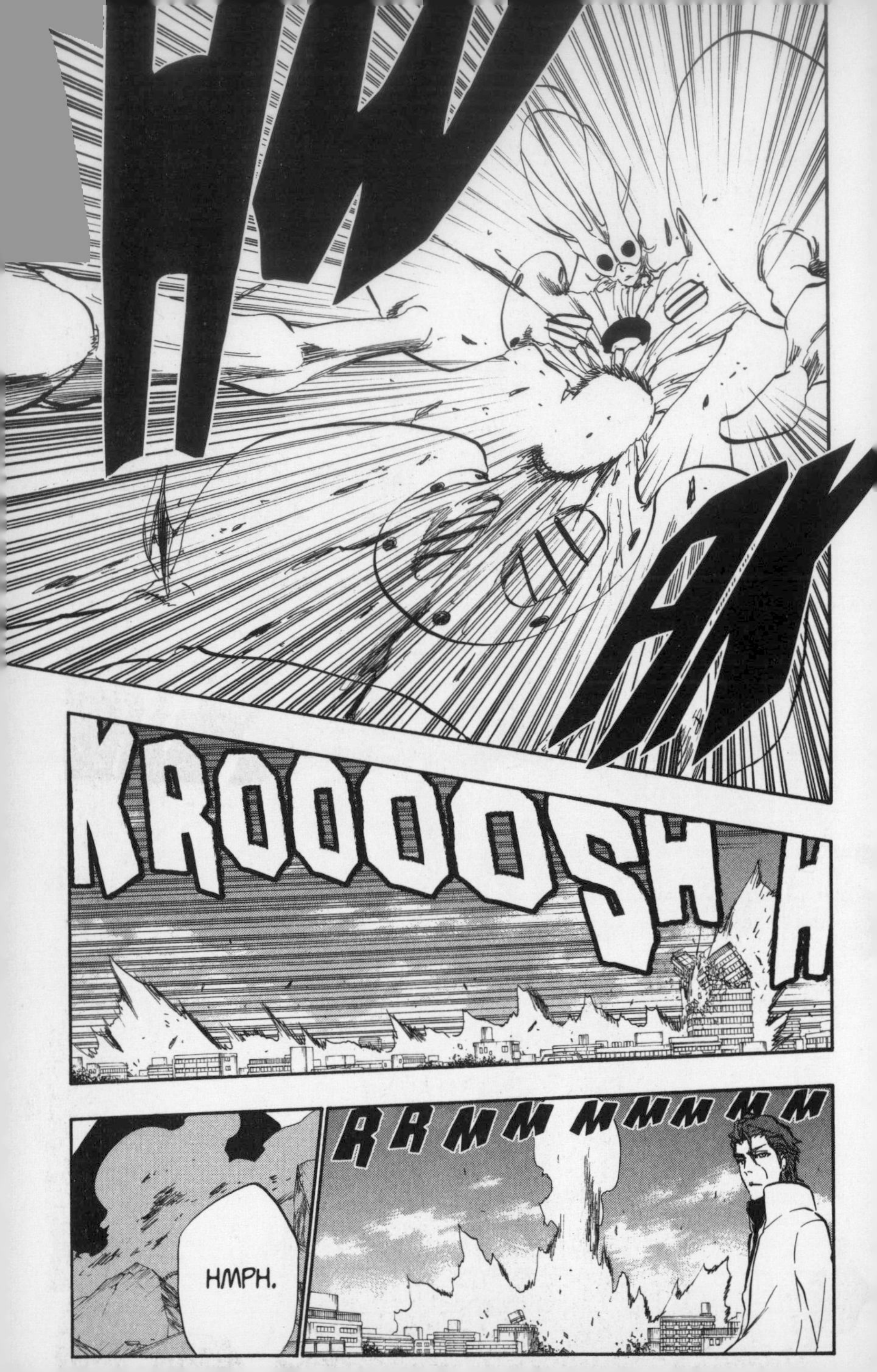
KROOOOSHH
RRMMMMMMM
HMPH.

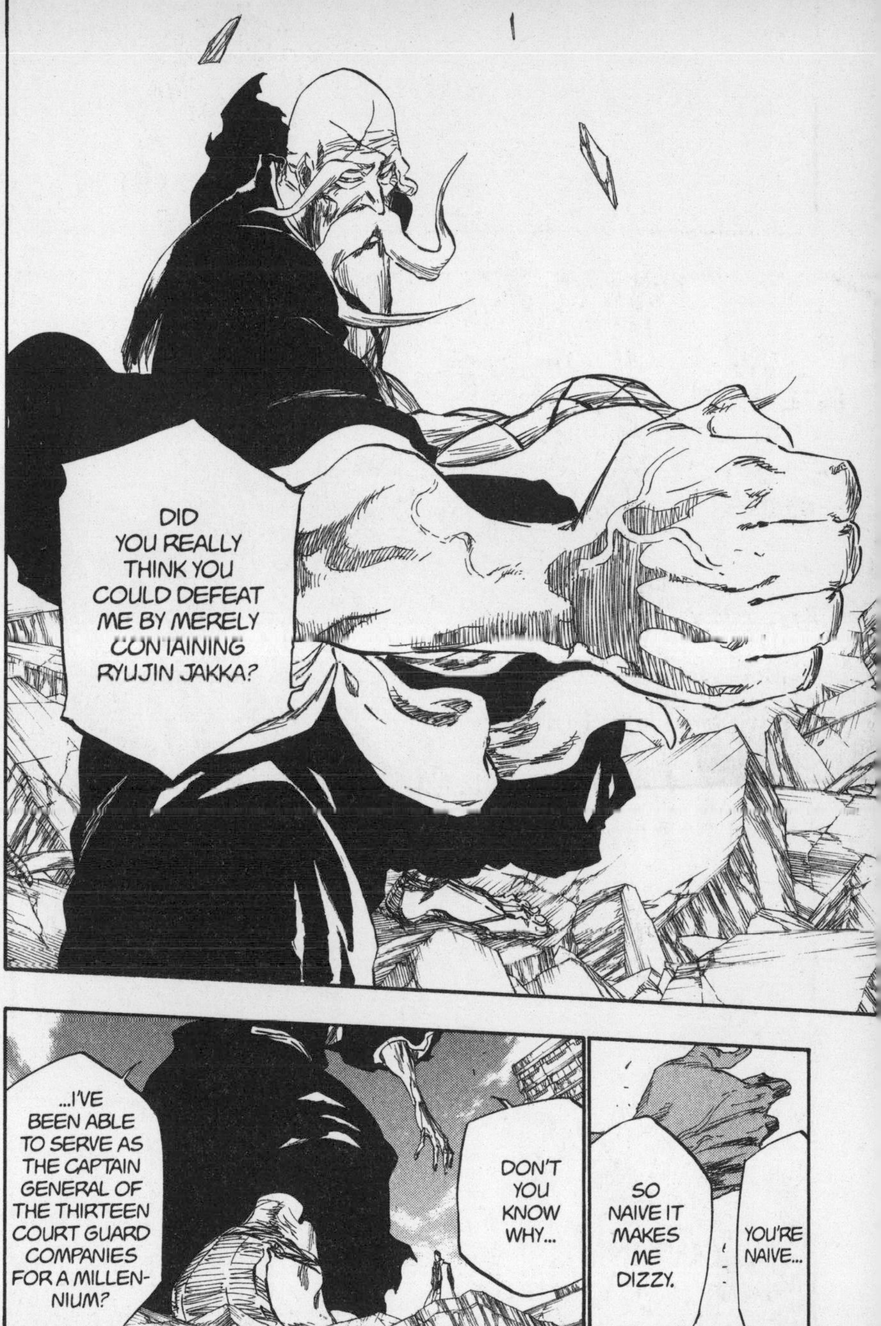
DID YOU REALLY THINK YOU COULD DEFEAT ME BY MERELY CONTAINING RYUJIN JAKKA?
YOU'RE NAIVE...
SO NAIVE IT MAKES ME DIZZY.
DON'T YOU KNOW WHY...
...I'VE BEEN ABLE TO SERVE AS THE CAPTAIN GENERAL OF THE THIRTEEN COURT GUARD COMPANIES FOR A MILLEN-NIUM?

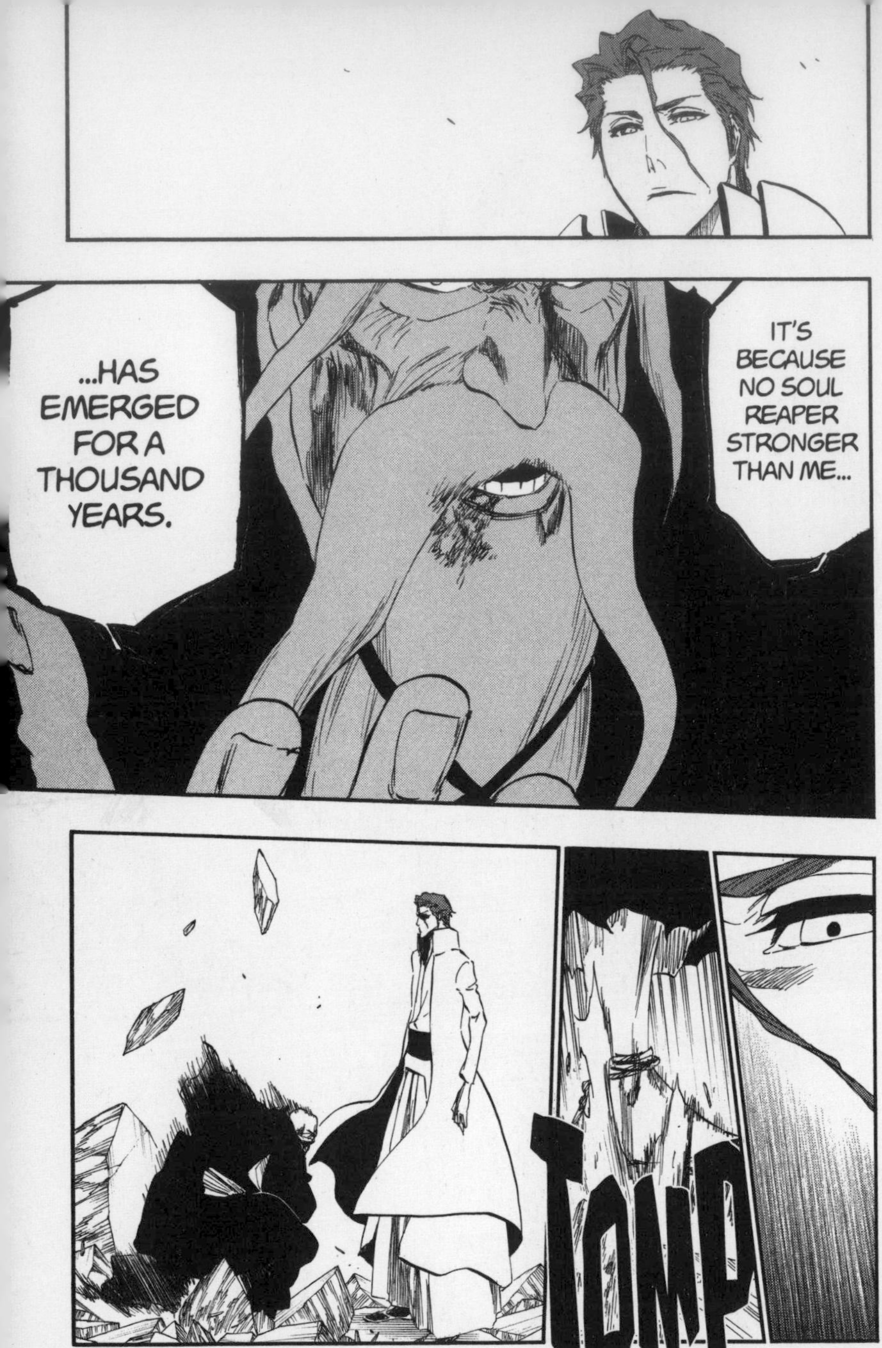
IT'S BECAUSE NO SOUL REAPER STRONGER THAN ME...
...HAS EMERGED FOR A THOUSAND YEARS.
TOMP

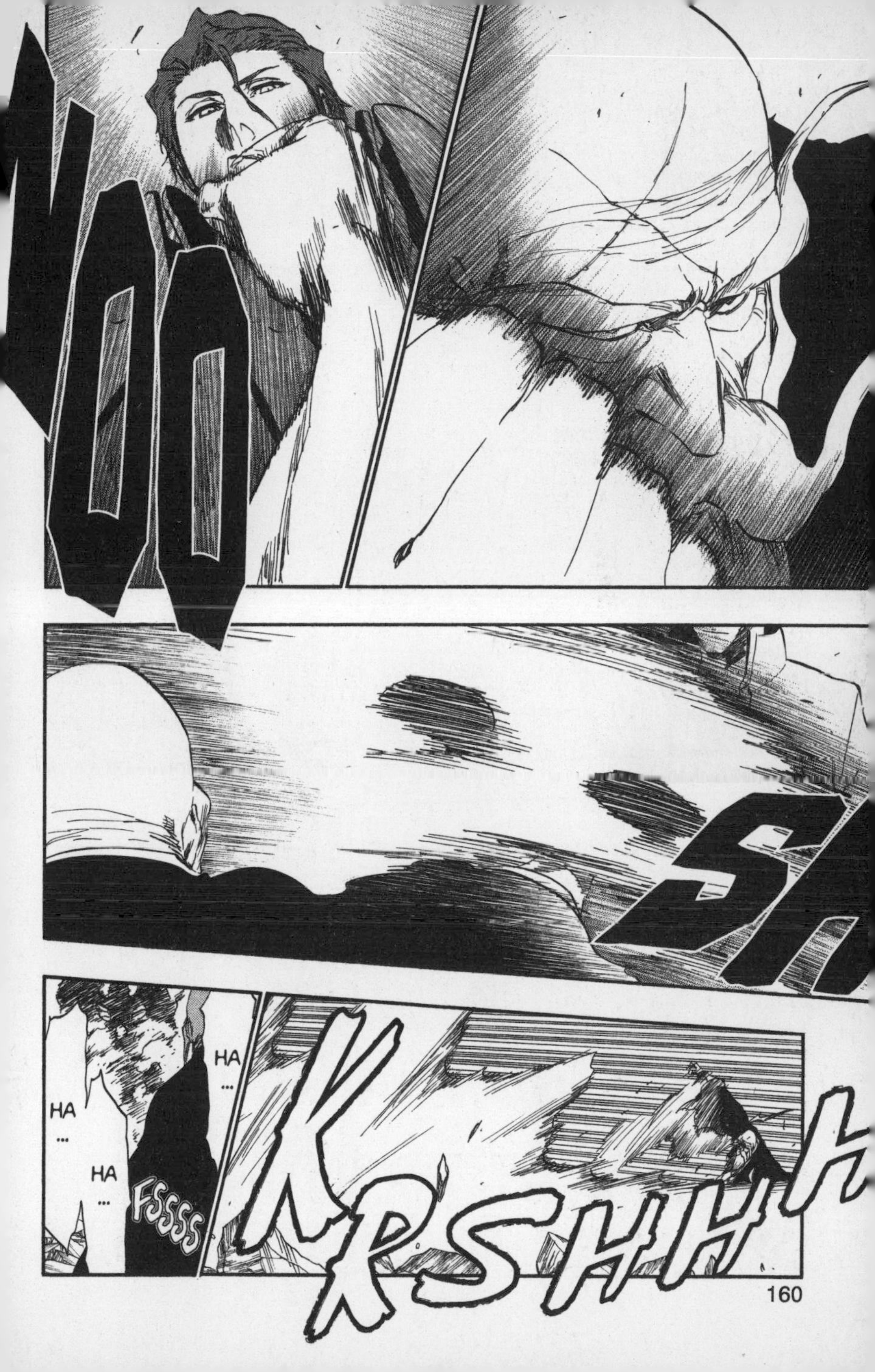
KRSHHH
HA ...
HA ...
HA ...
FSSSS

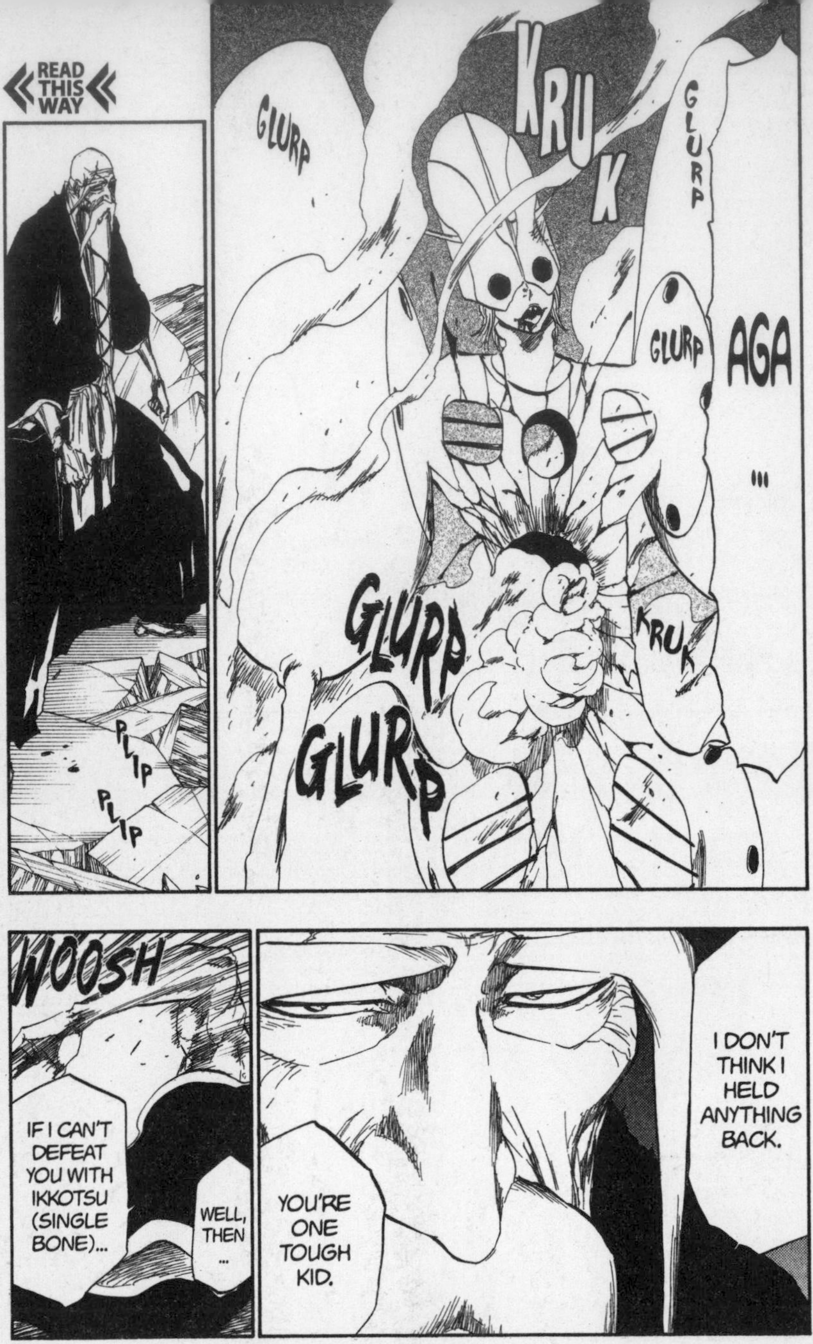
READ THIS WAY
KRUK
GLURP
GLURP
GLURP
AGA...
KRUK
GLURP
GLURP
PLIP
PLIP
I DON'T THINK I HELD ANYTHING BACK.
YOU'RE ONE TOUGH KID.
WOOSH
IF I CAN'T DEFEAT YOU WITH IKKOTSU (SINGLE BONE)...
WELL, THEN ...

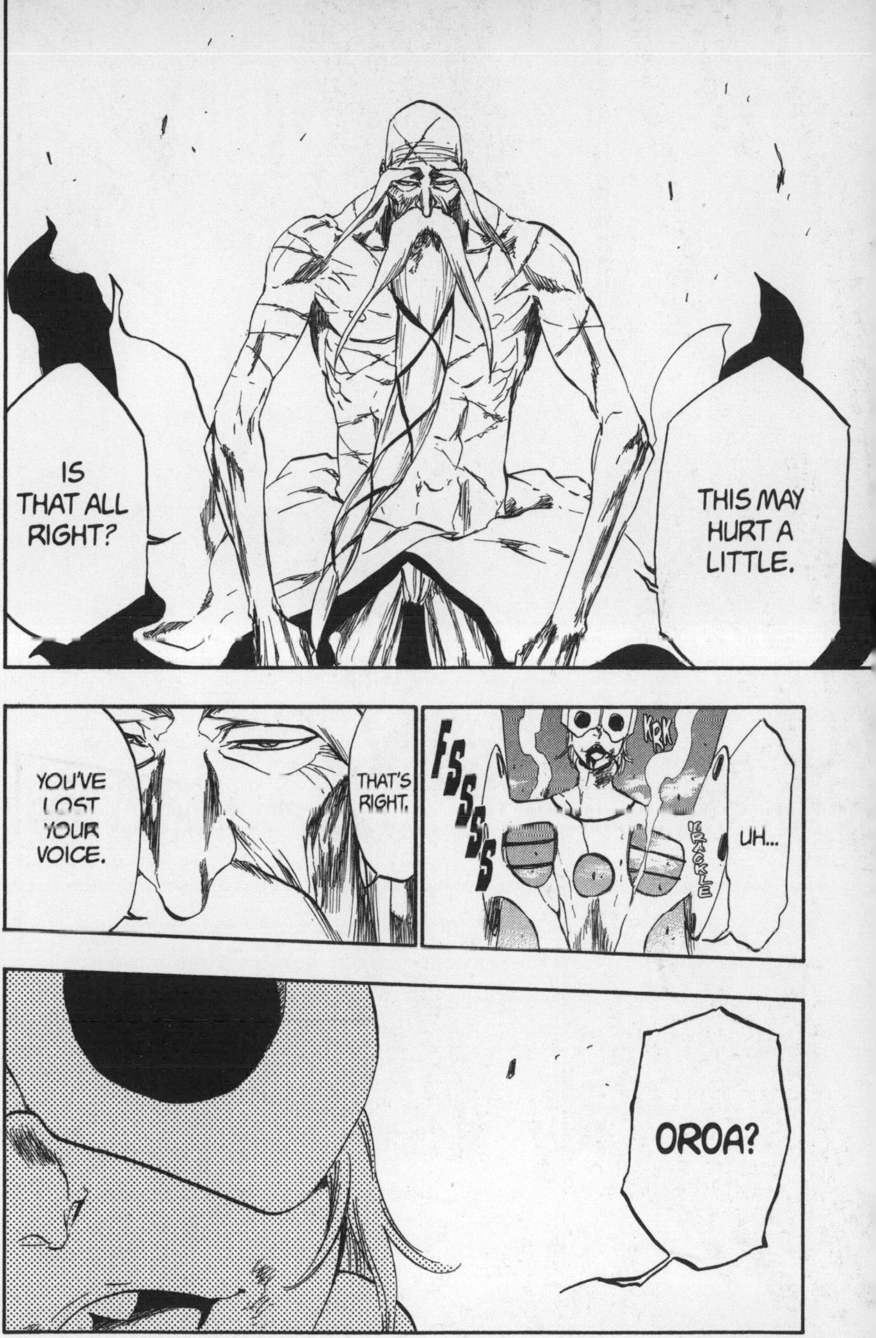
THIS MAY HURT A LITTLE.
IS THAT ALL RIGHT?
KRK
UH...
CRACKLE
FSSSS
THAT'S RIGHT.
YOU'VE LOST YOUR VOICE.
OROA?

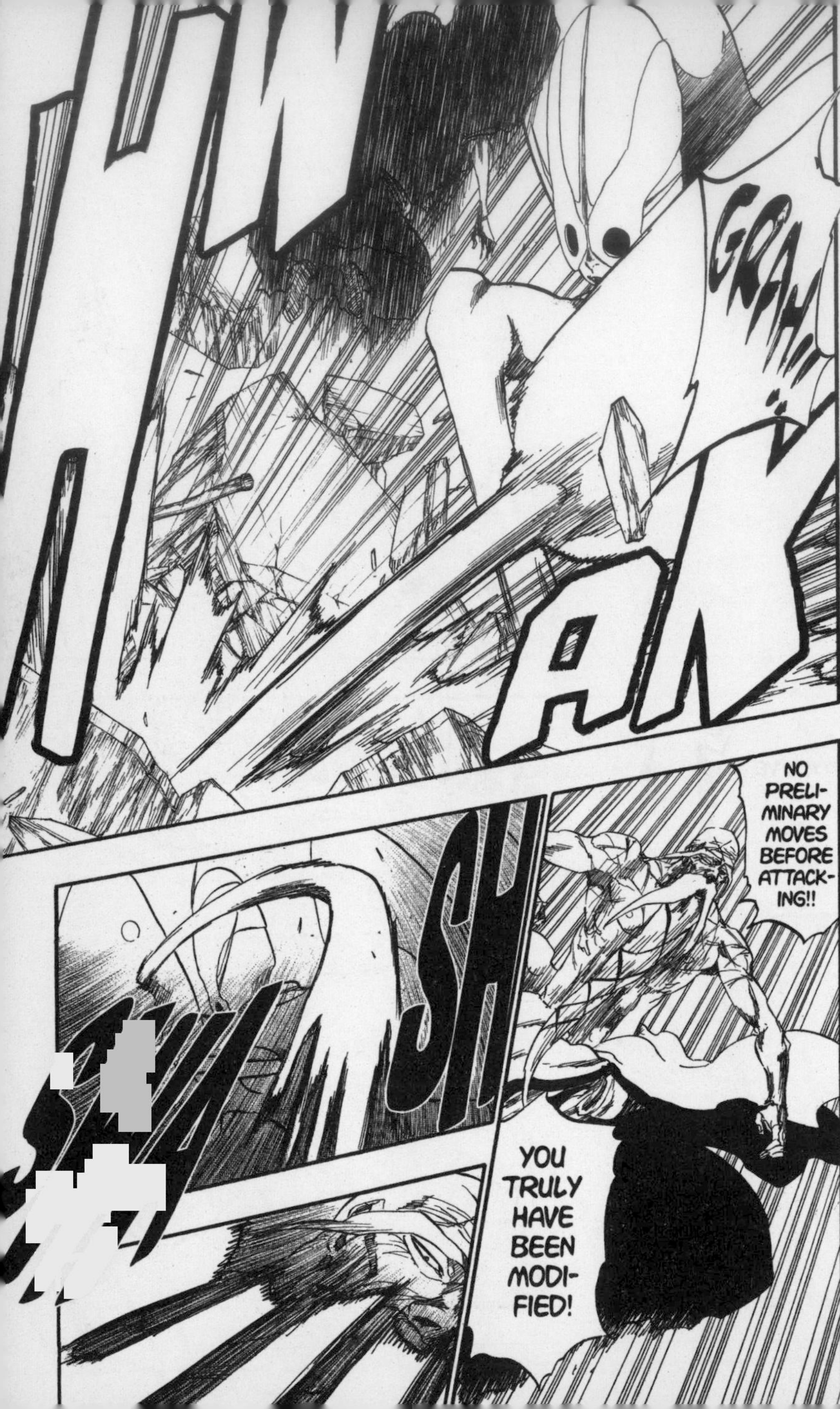
GRAH!!
NO PRELIMINARY MOVES BEFORE ATTACKING!!
YOU TRULY HAVE BEEN MODIFIED!

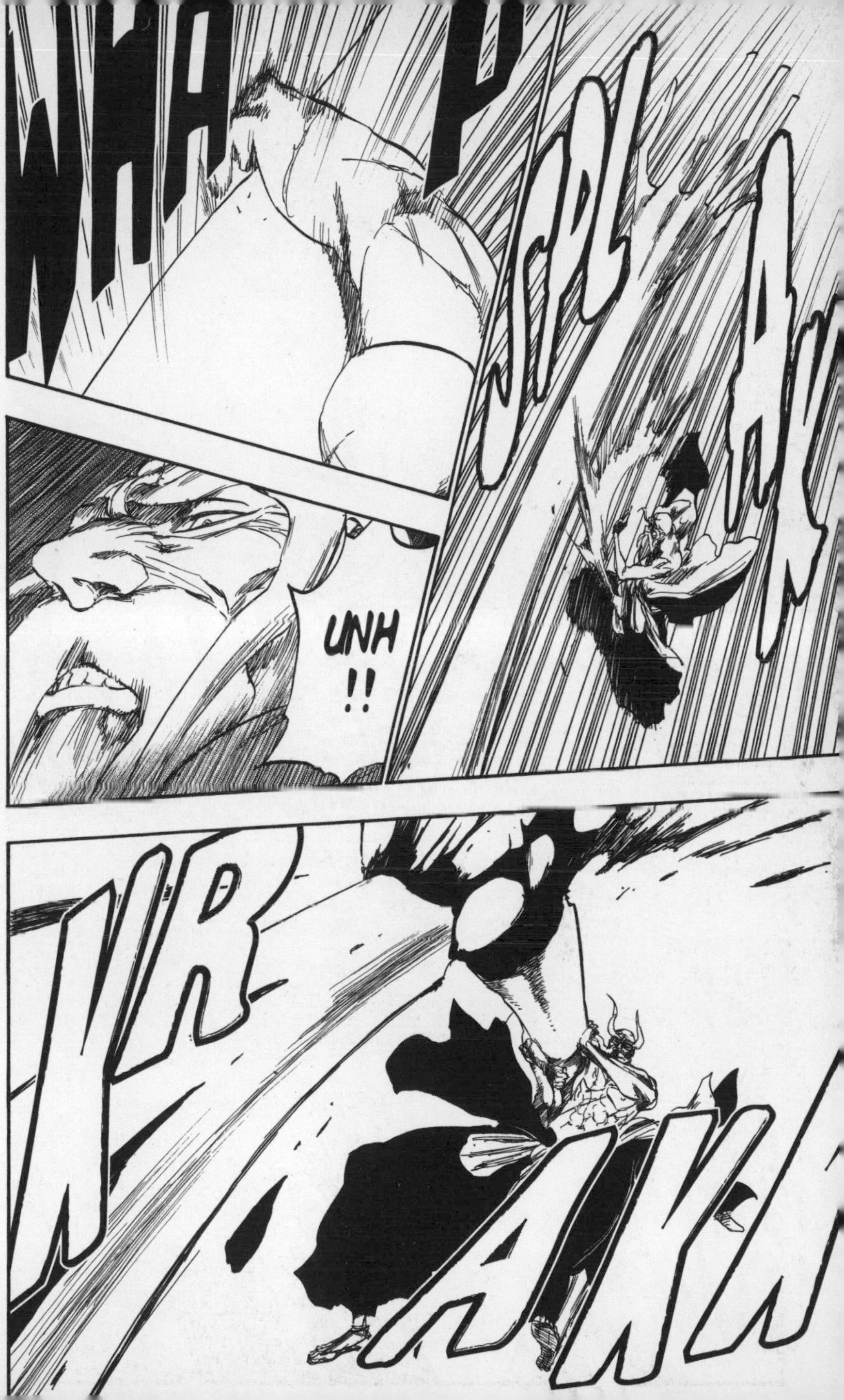
UNH
!!

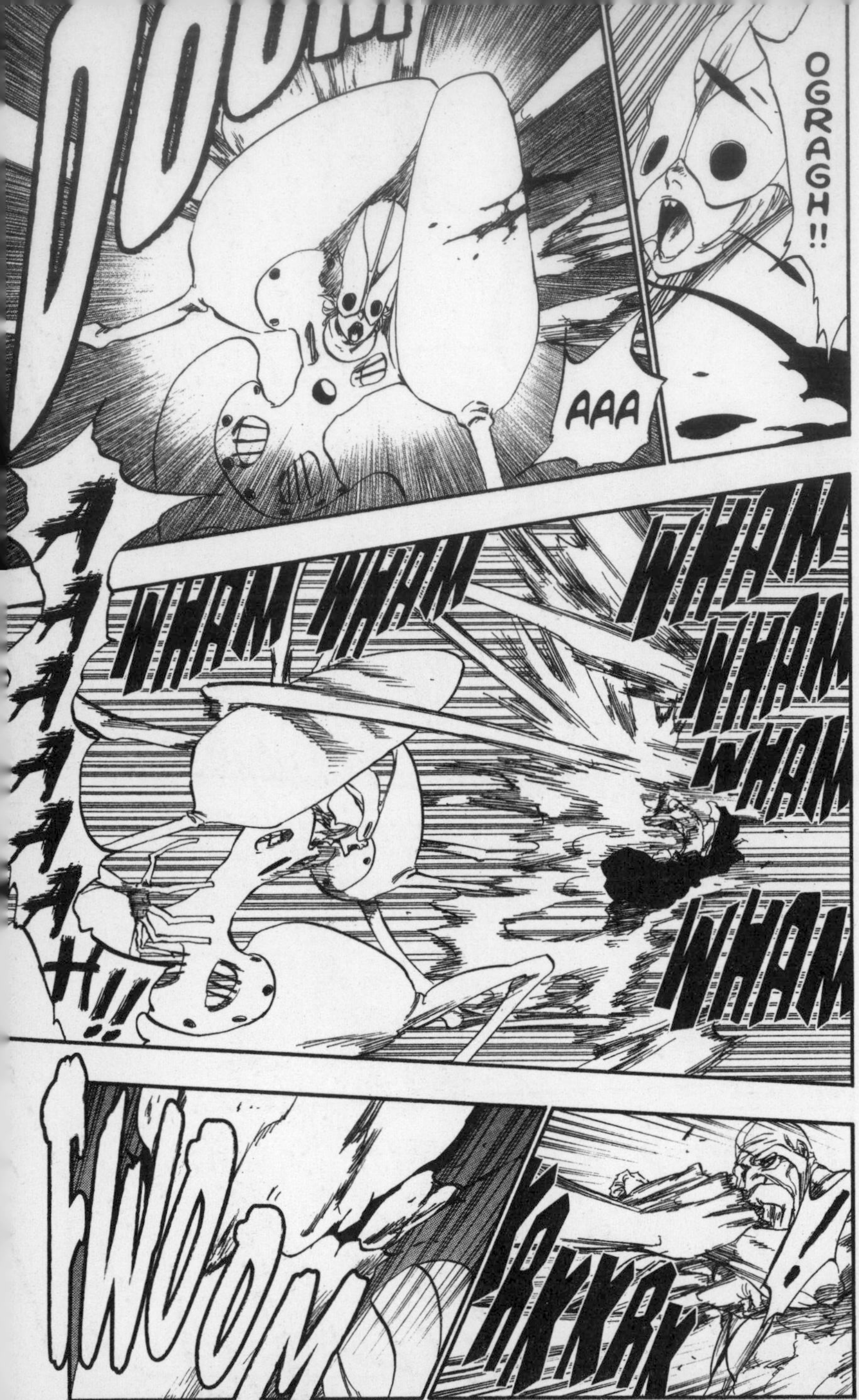
OGRAGH!!
AAA
WHAM WHAM WHAM WHAM
WHAM WHAM WHAM
AAAAAAAGH!!

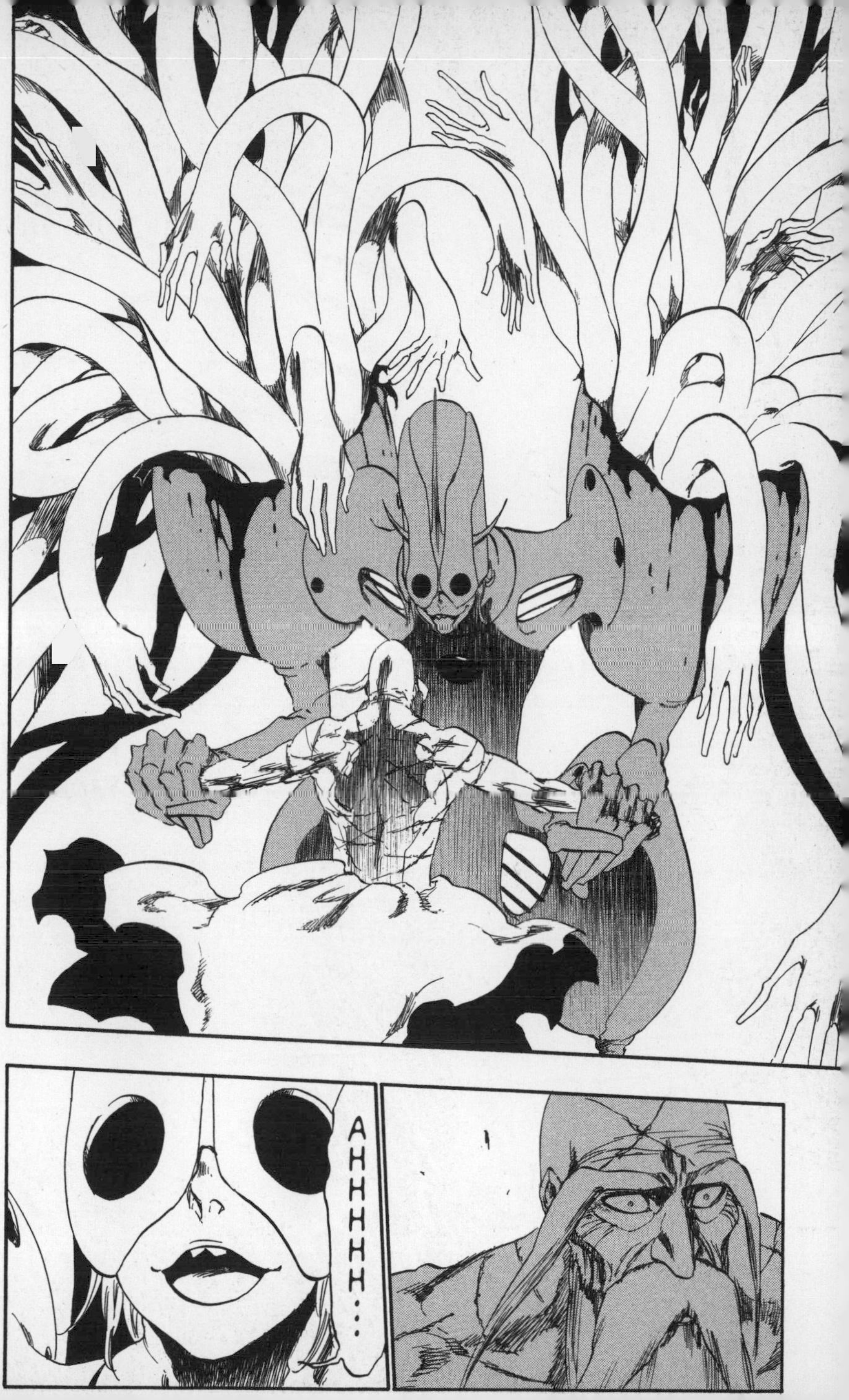
AHHHHH...

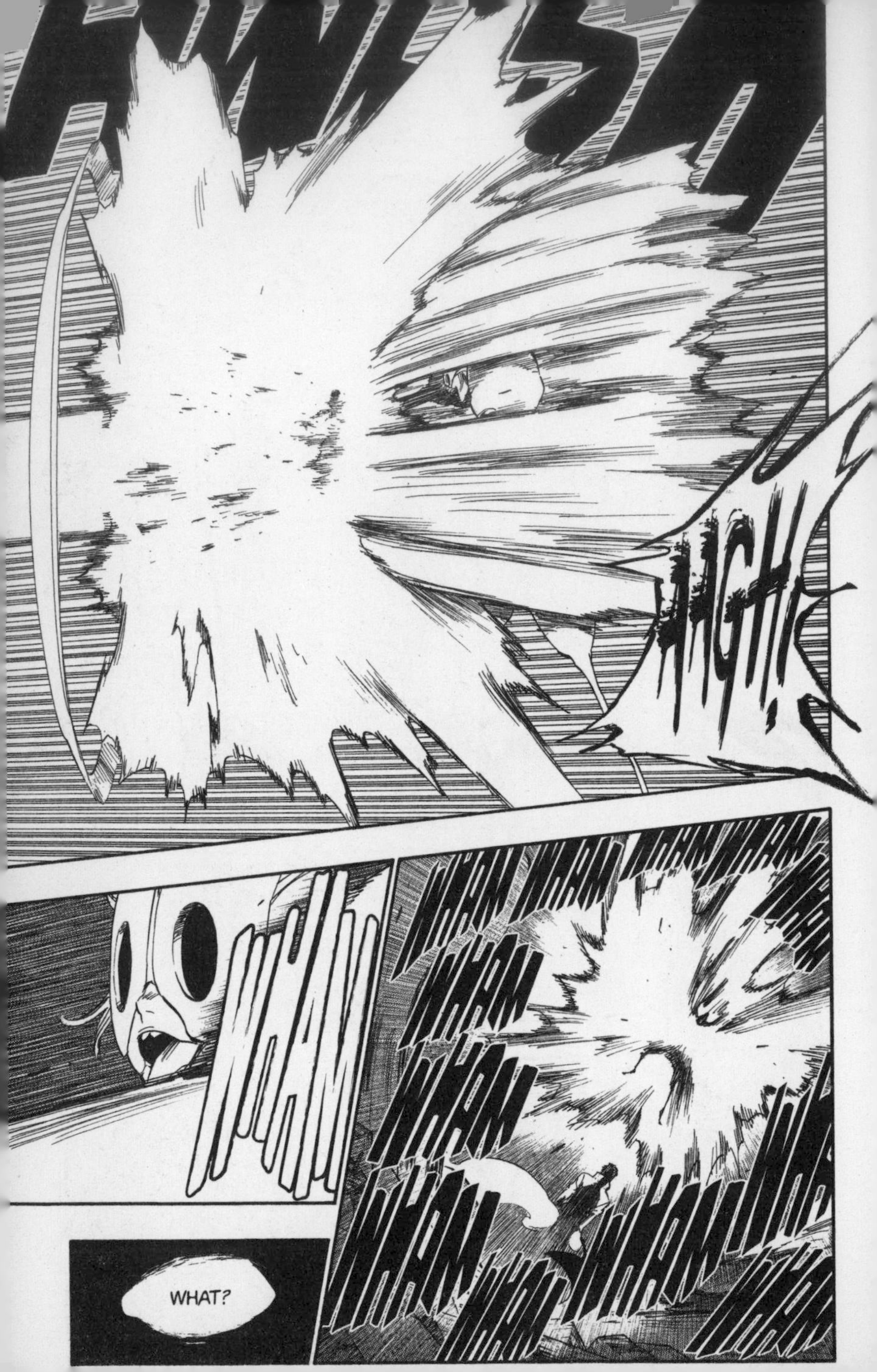
AAGH!!
WHAM WHAM WHAM WHAM
WHAM
WHAT?

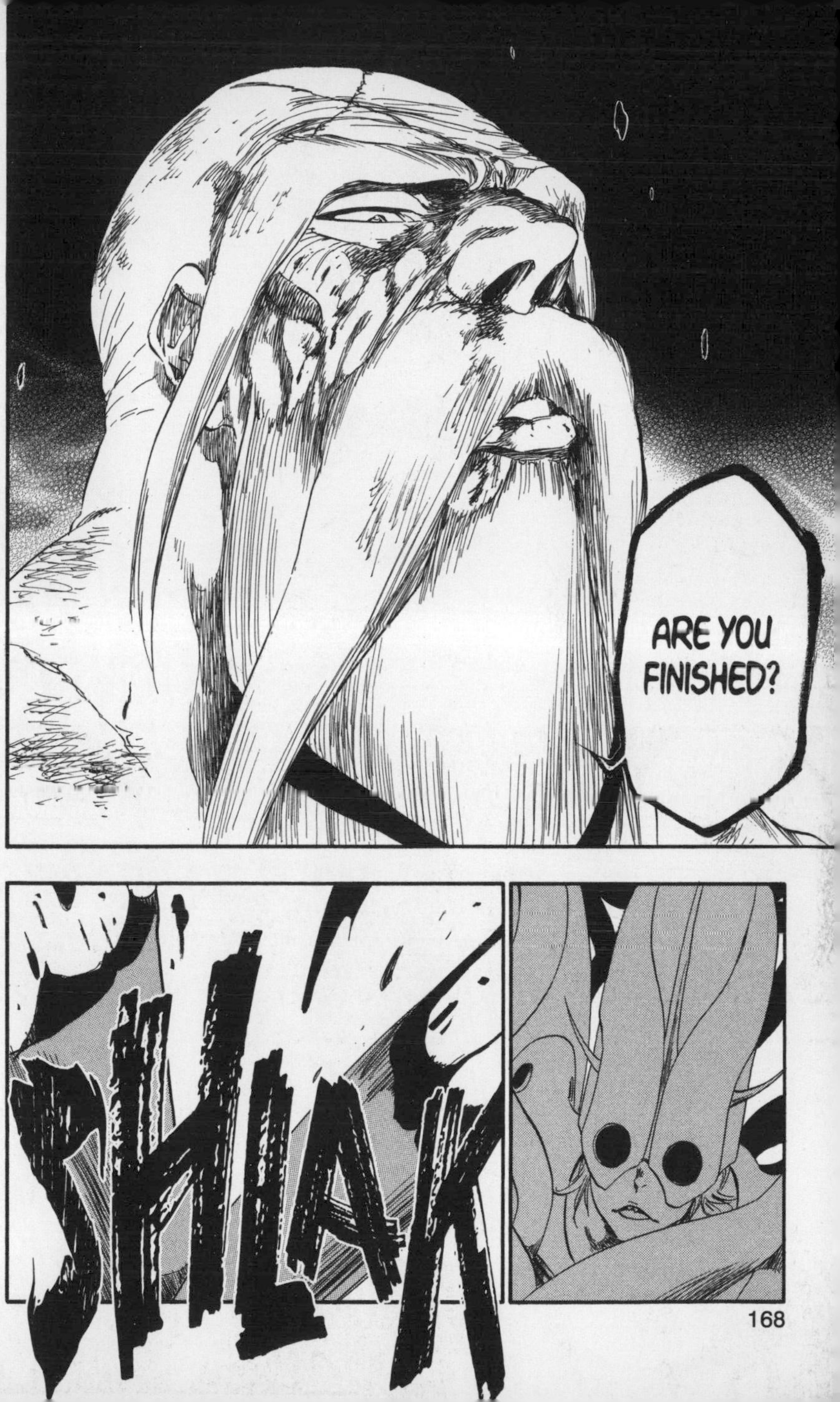
ARE YOU FINISHED?
SHLAK

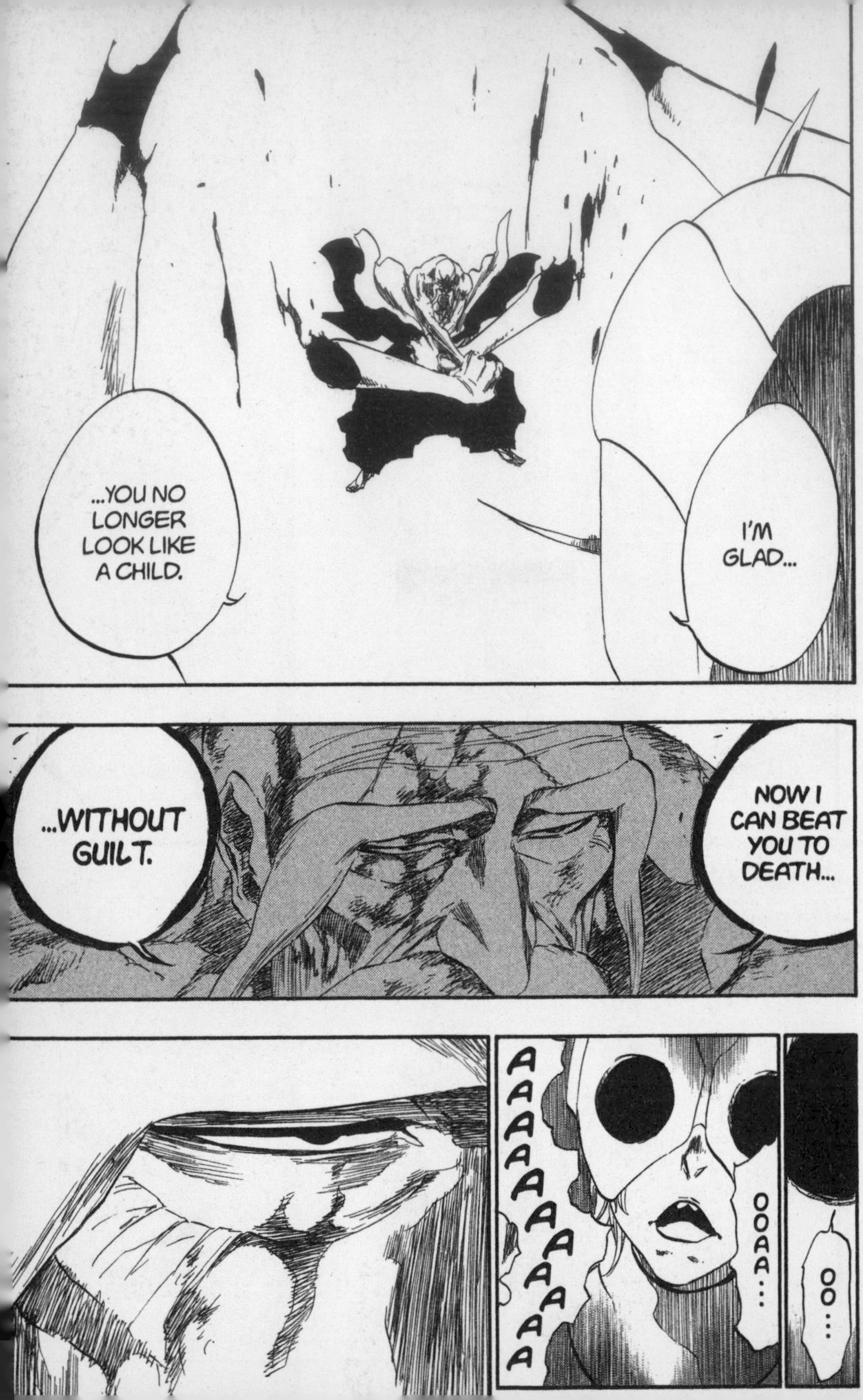
I'M GLAD...
...YOU NO LONGER LOOK LIKE A CHILD.
NOW I CAN BEAT YOU TO DEATH...
...WITHOUT GUILT.
OO...
OOAA...
AAAAAAAAAAA

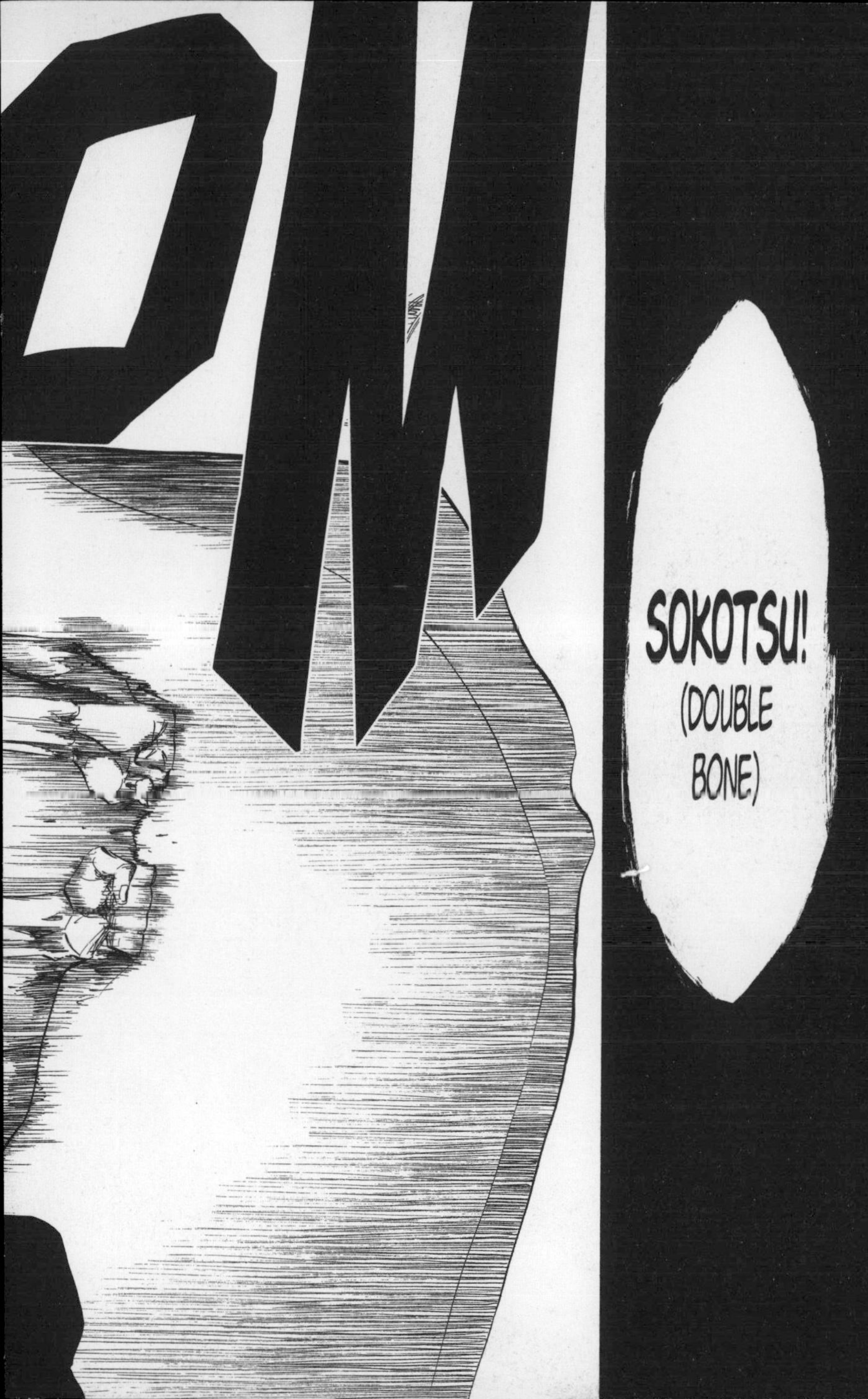
SOKOTSU! (DOUBLE BONE)

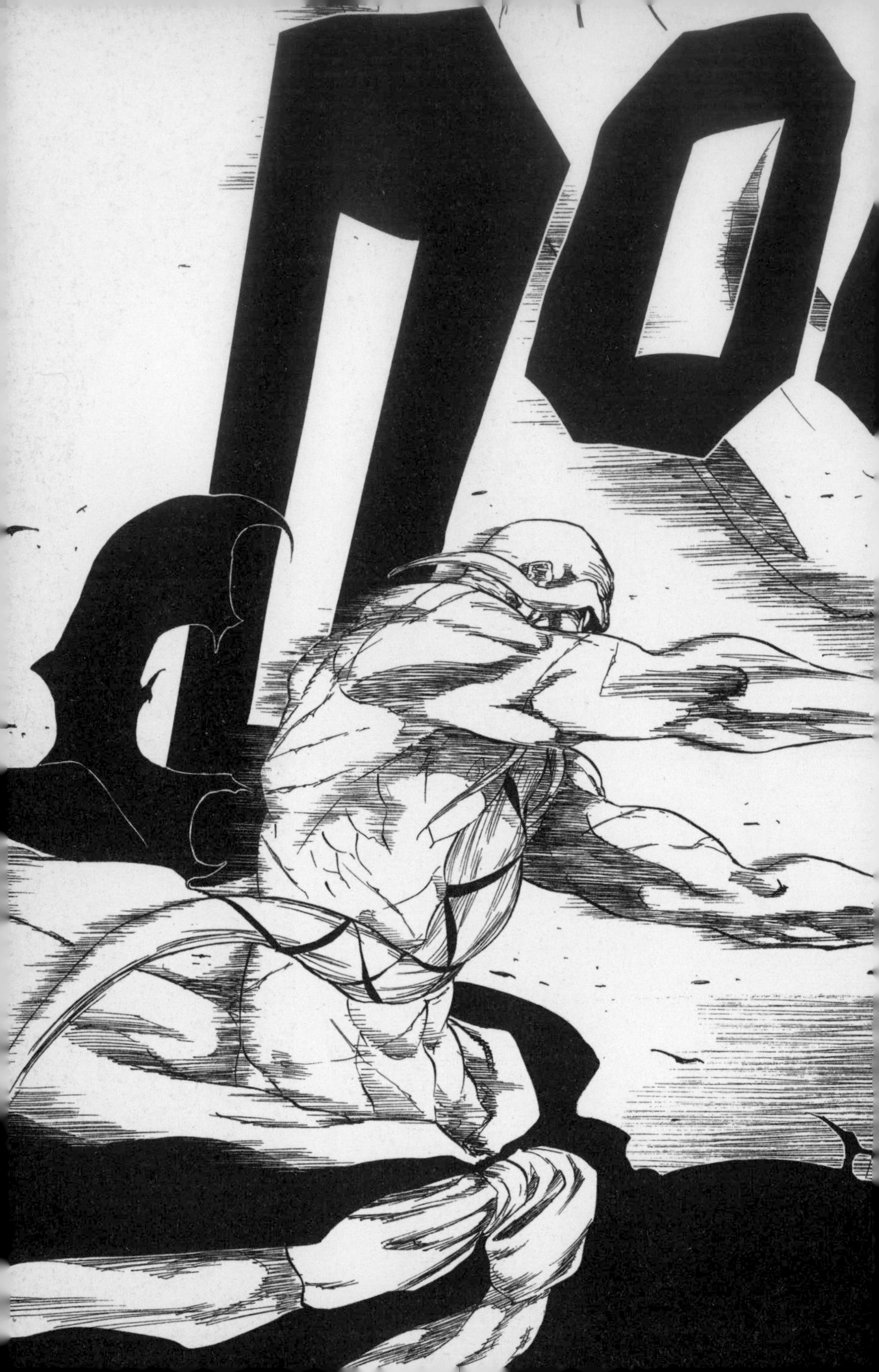
DO

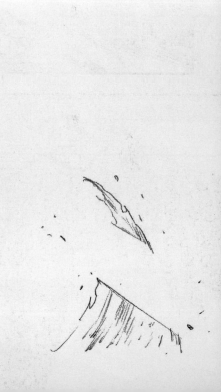

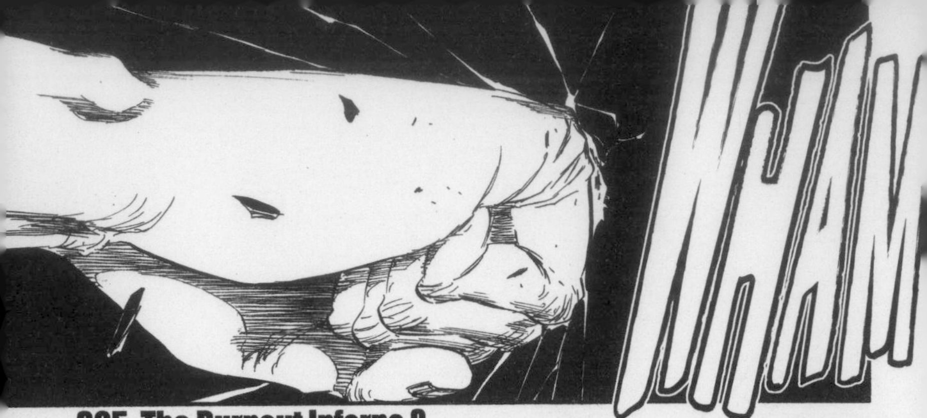
WHAM

395. The Burnout Inferno 3

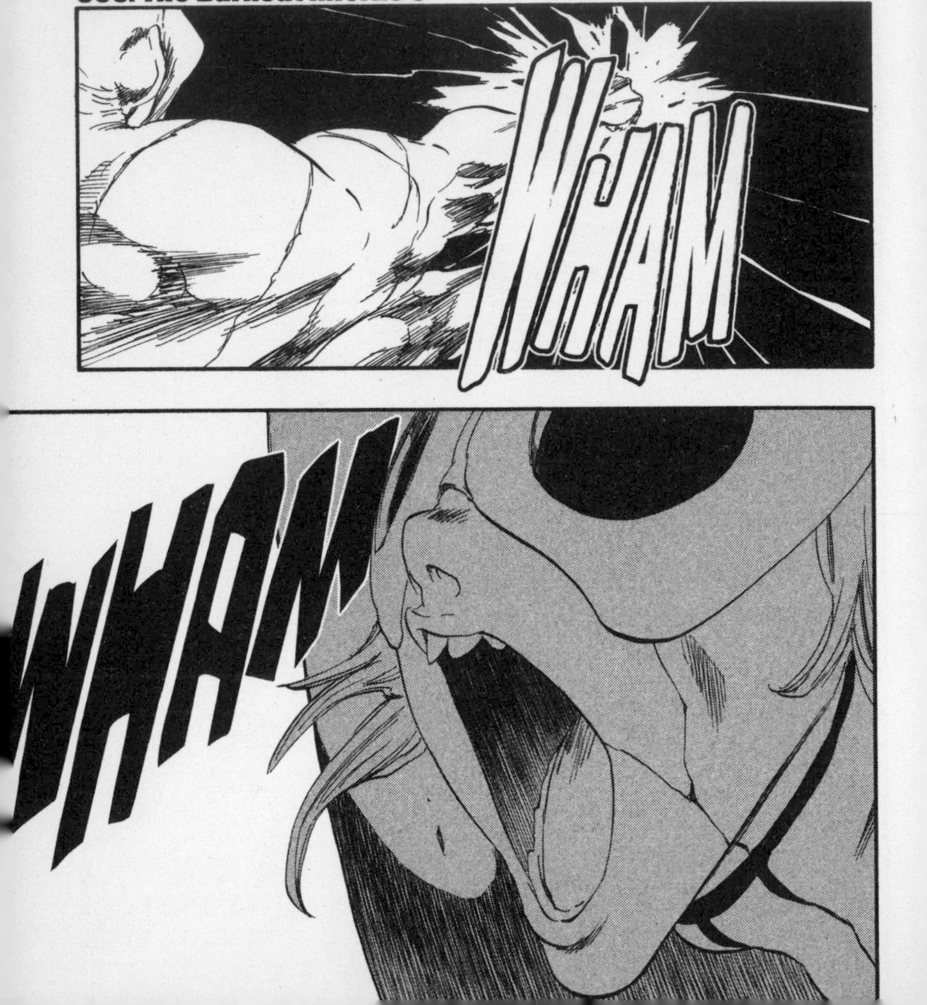
WHAM
WHAM

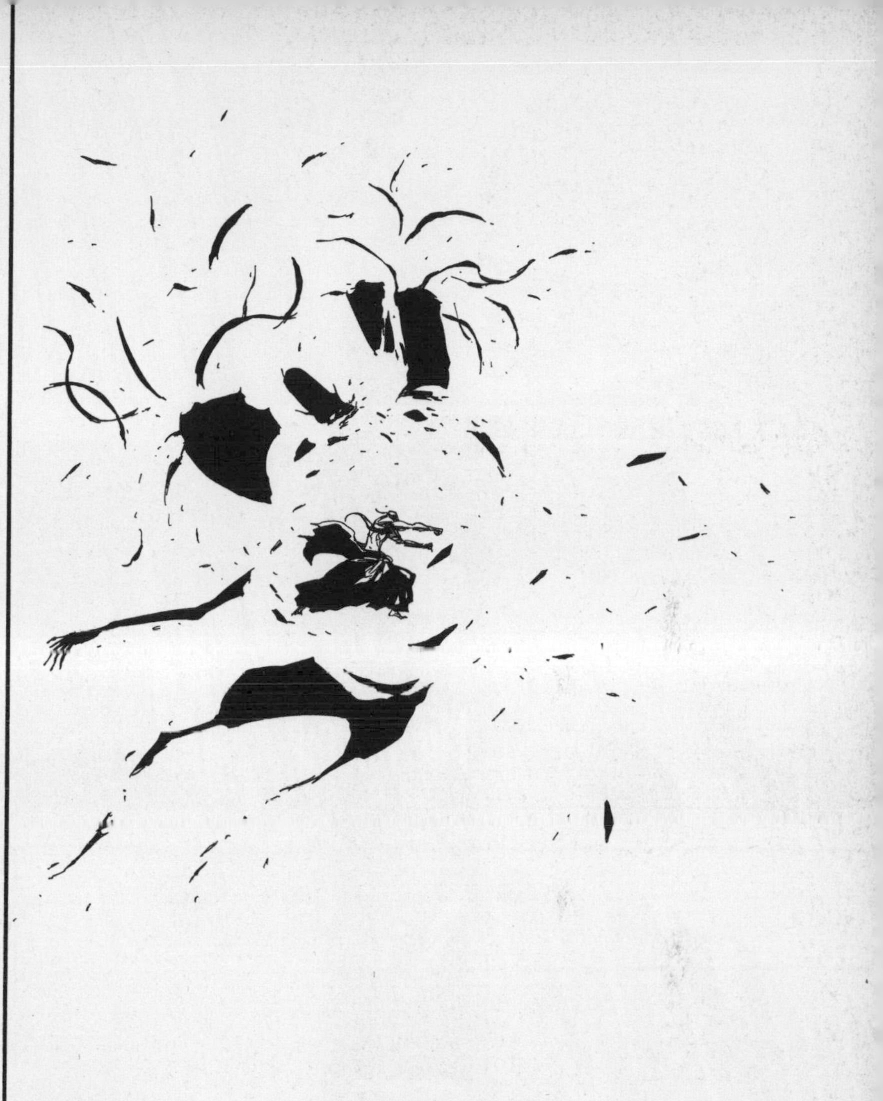
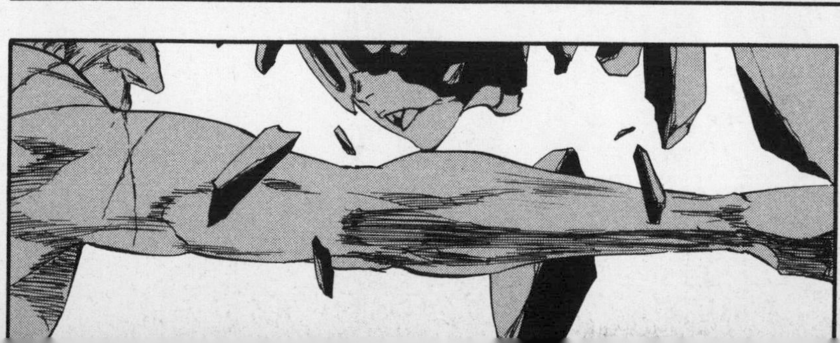

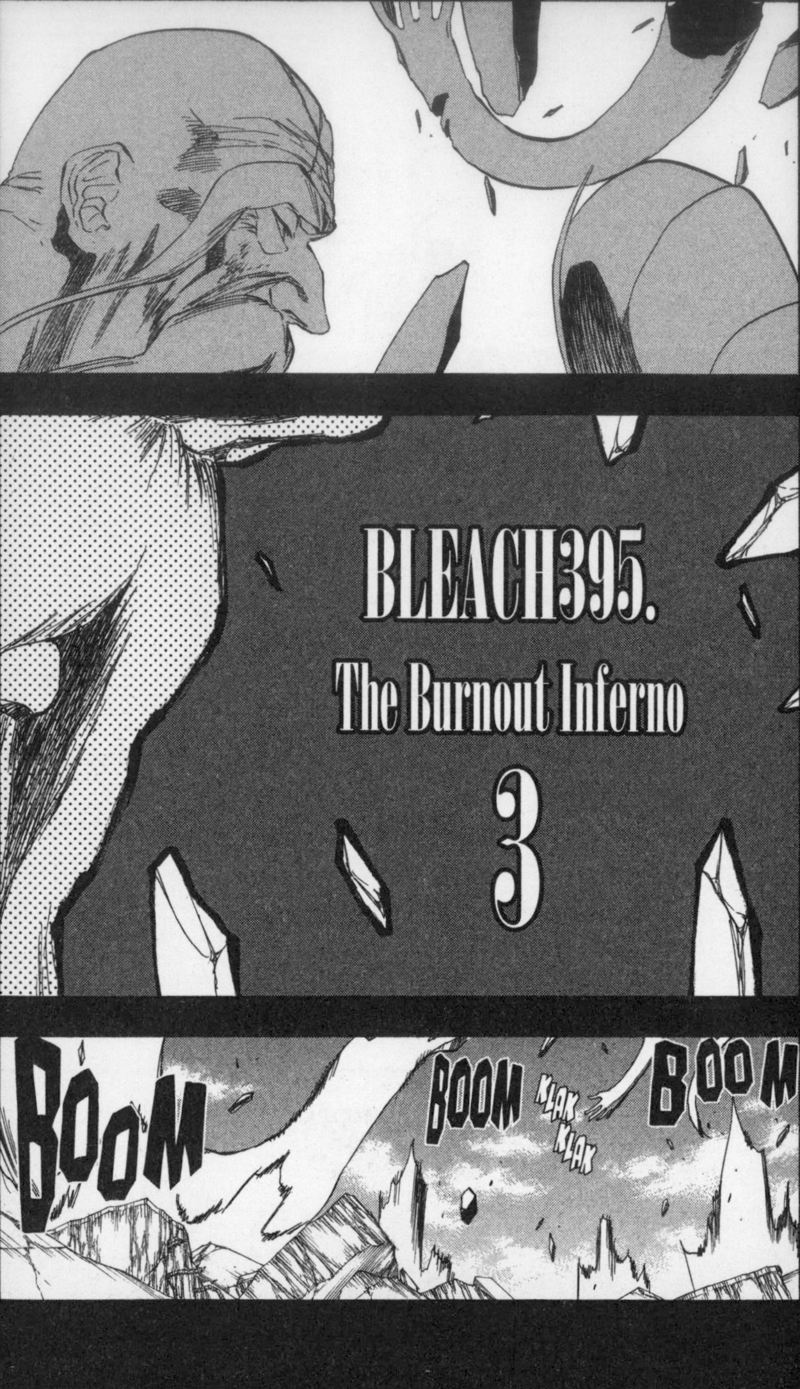
BLEACH395.
The Burnout Inferno
3
BOOM
KLAK
KLAK
BOOM
BOOM

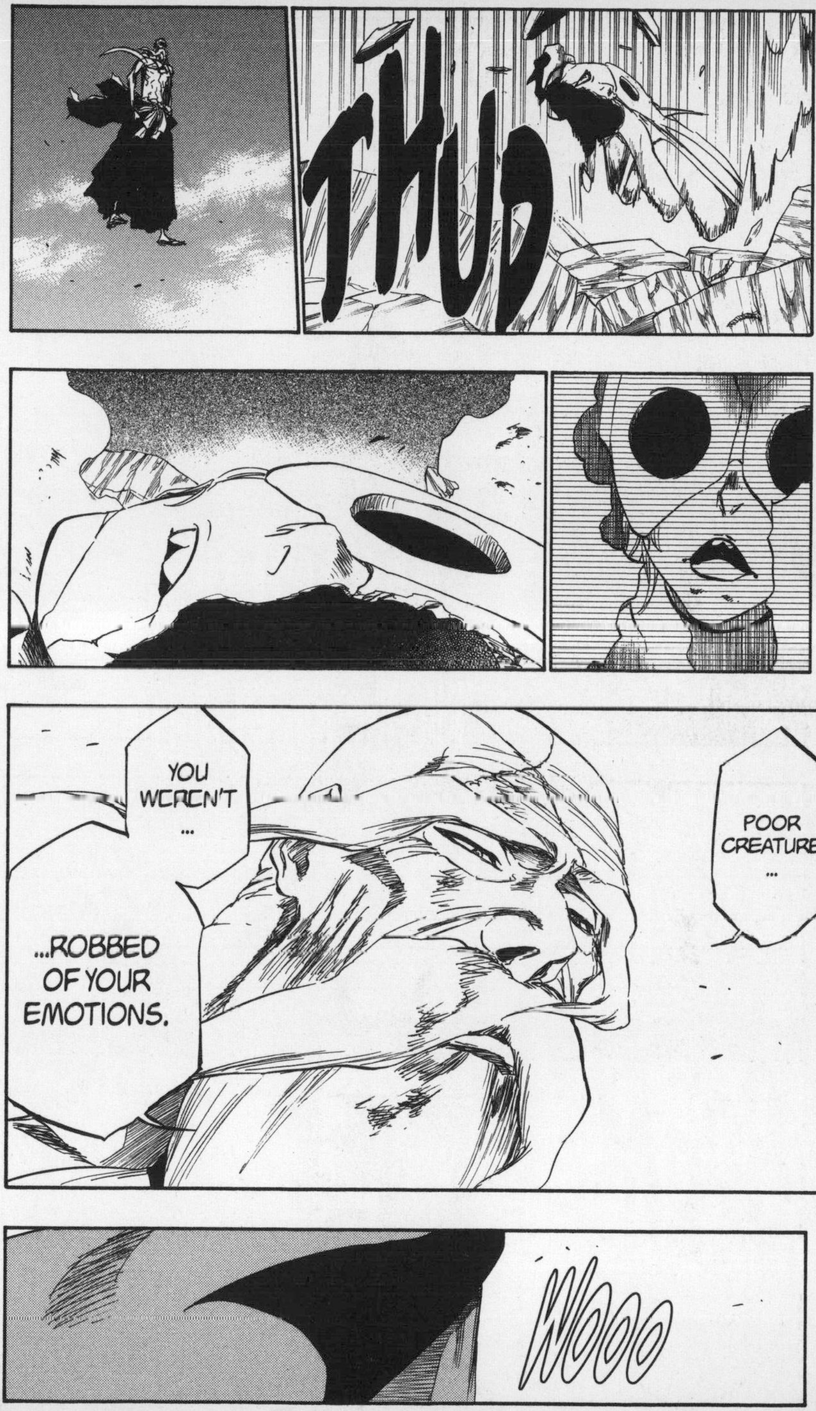
THUD
POOR CREATURE ...
YOU WEREN'T ...
...ROBBED OF YOUR EMOTIONS.
Wooo

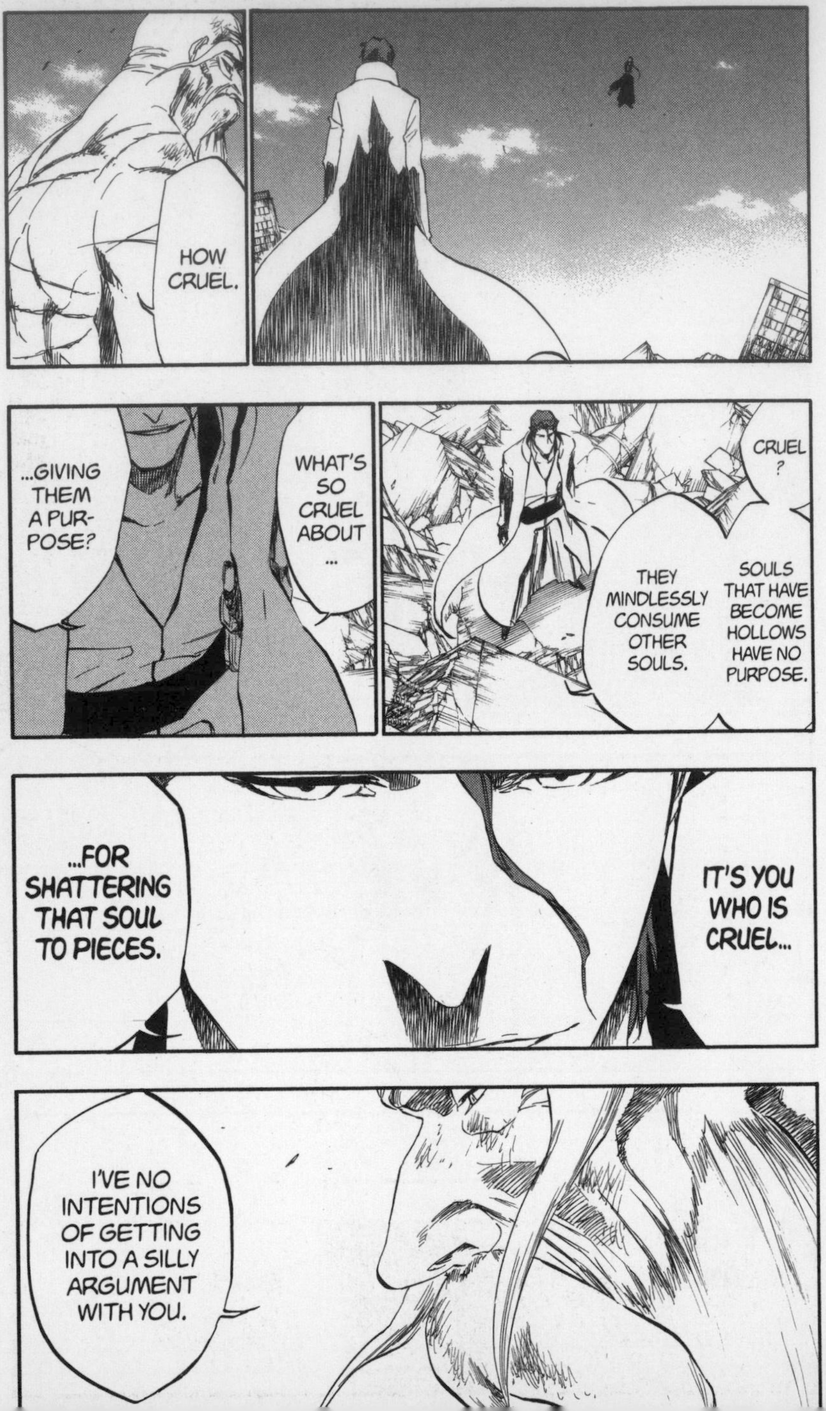
HOW CRUEL.
CRUEL?
SOULS THAT HAVE BECOME HOLLOWS HAVE NO PURPOSE.
THEY MINDLESSLY CONSUME OTHER SOULS.
WHAT'S SO CRUEL ABOUT...
...GIVING THEM A PURPOSE?
IT'S YOU WHO IS CRUEL...
...FOR SHATTERING THAT SOUL TO PIECES.
I'VE NO INTENTIONS OF GETTING INTO A SILLY ARGUMENT WITH YOU.

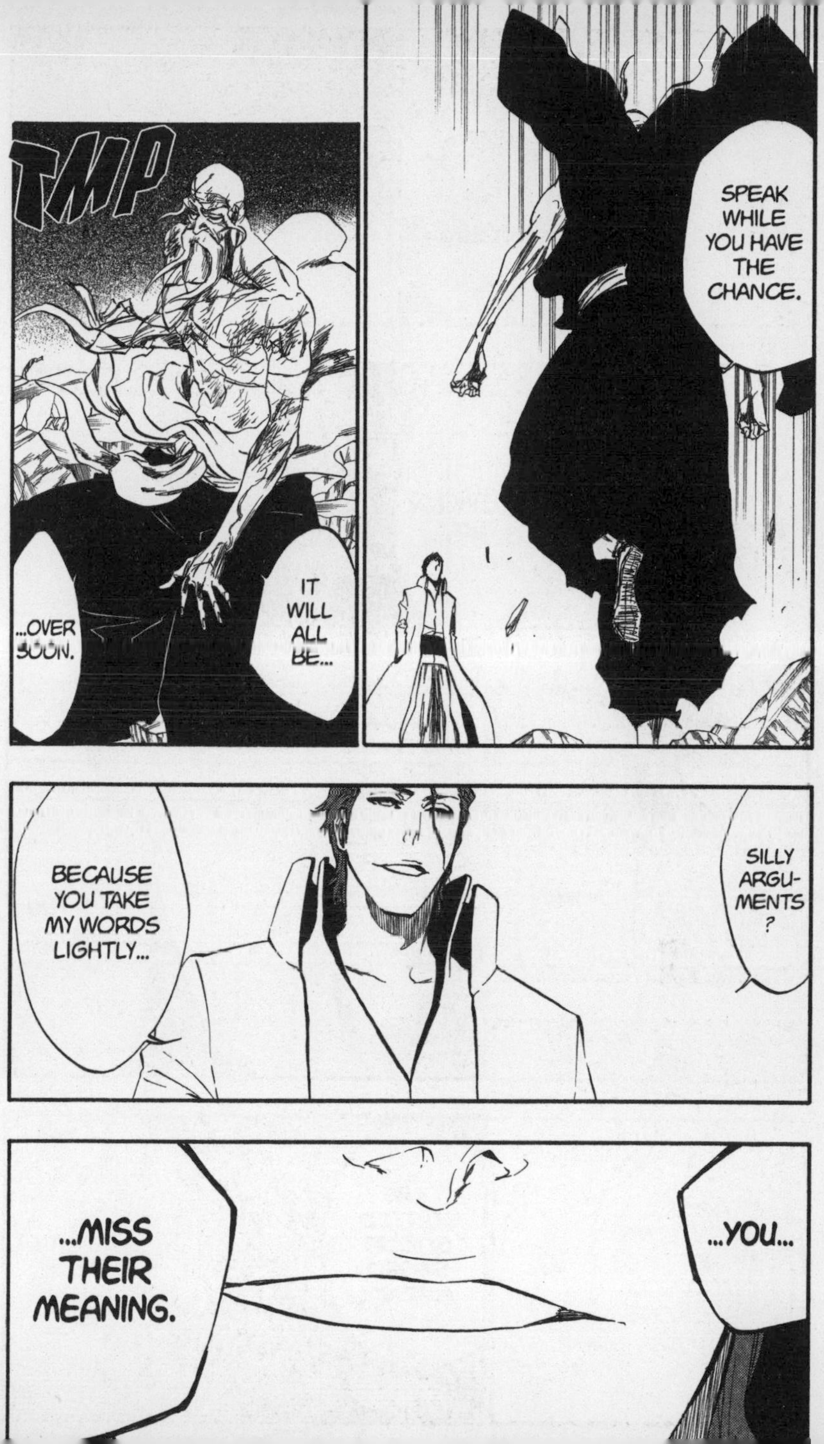
SPEAK WHILE YOU HAVE THE CHANCE.
TMP
IT WILL ALL BE...
...OVER SOON.
SILLY ARGU-MENTS?
BECAUSE YOU TAKE MY WORDS LIGHTLY...
...YOU...
...MISS THEIR MEANING.

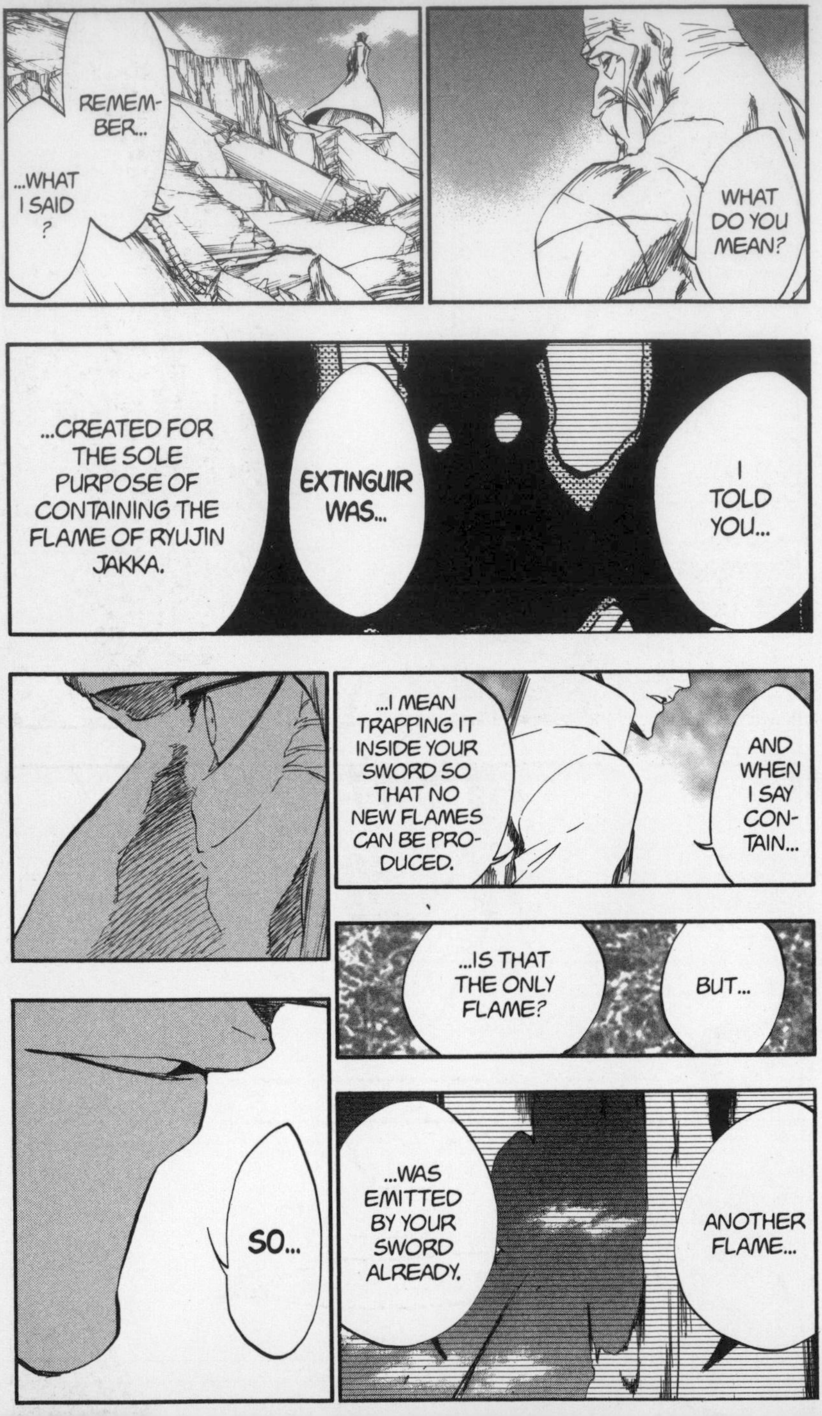
WHAT DO YOU MEAN?
REMEMBER...
...WHAT I SAID?
I TOLD YOU...
EXTINGUIR WAS...
...CREATED FOR THE SOLE PURPOSE OF CONTAINING THE FLAME OF RYUJIN JAKKA.
AND WHEN I SAY CONTAIN...
...I MEAN TRAPPING IT INSIDE YOUR SWORD SO THAT NO NEW FLAMES CAN BE PRODUCED.
BUT...
...IS THAT THE ONLY FLAME?
ANOTHER FLAME...
...WAS EMITTED BY YOUR SWORD ALREADY.
SO...

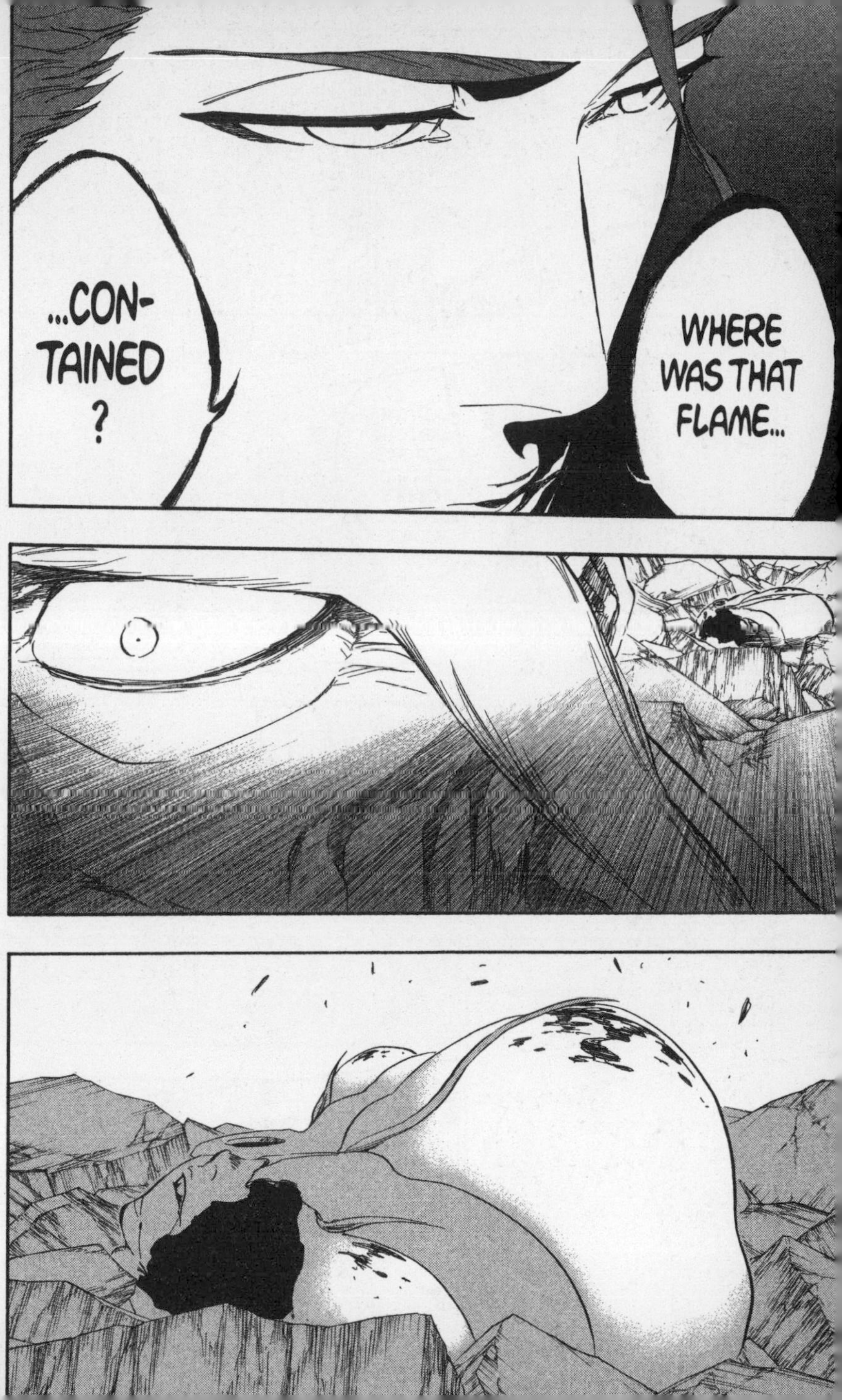
WHERE WAS THAT FLAME...
...CON-TAINED?

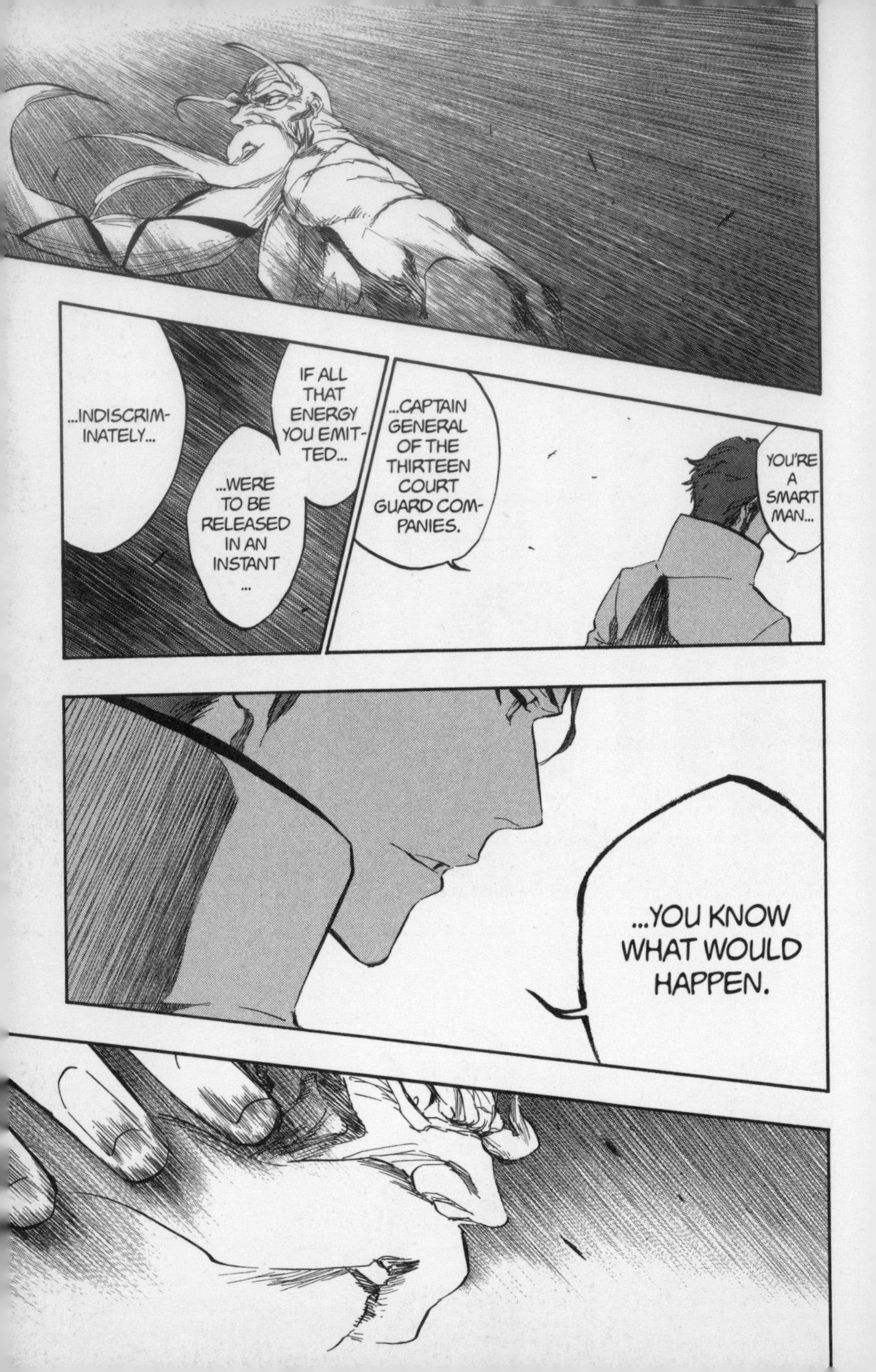
YOU'RE A SMART MAN...
...CAPTAIN GENERAL OF THE THIRTEEN COURT GUARD COMPANIES.
IF ALL THAT ENERGY YOU EMITTED...
...WERE TO BE RELEASED IN AN INSTANT...
...INDISCRIMINATELY...
...YOU KNOW WHAT WOULD HAPPEN.

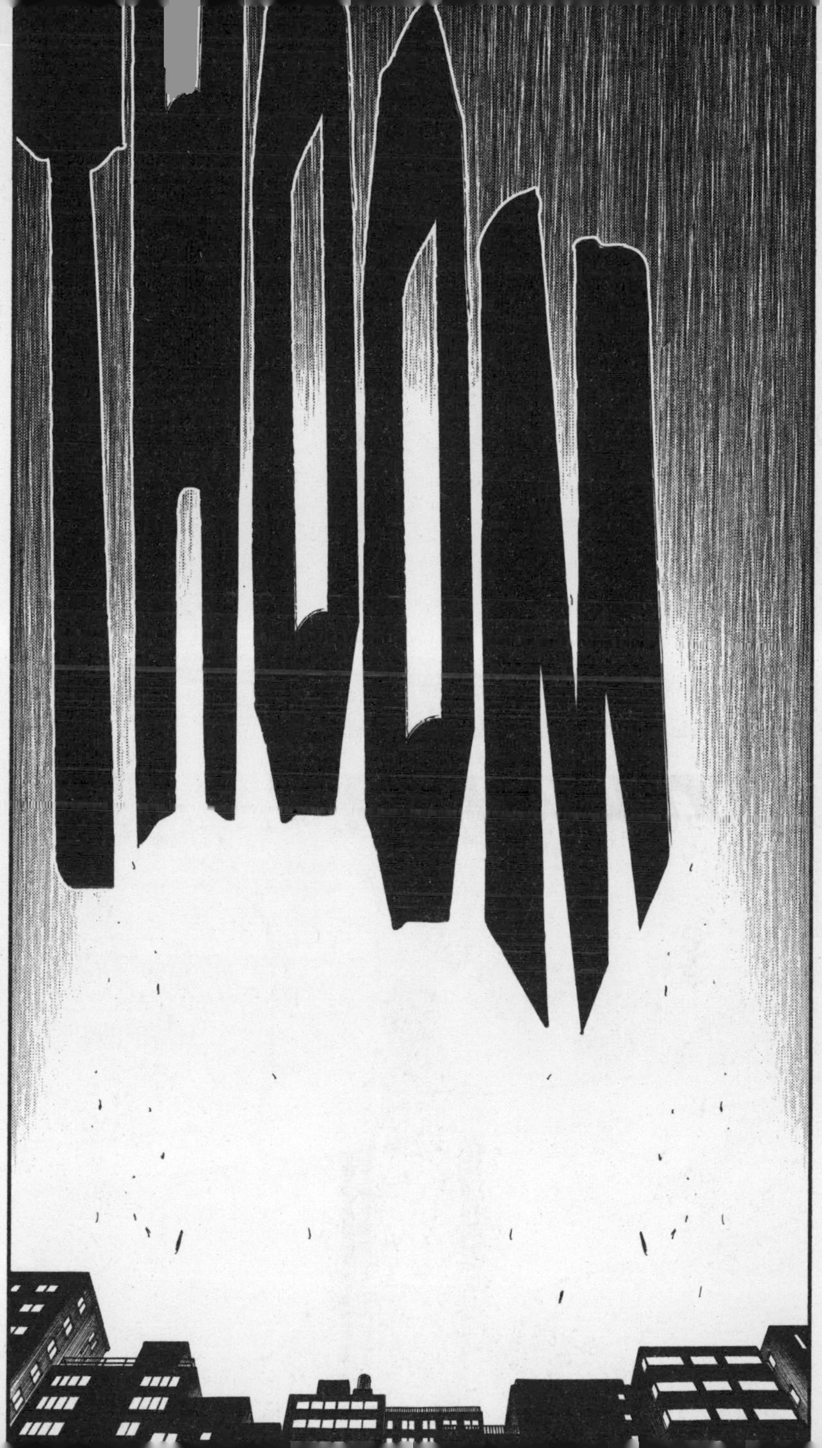
THOOM

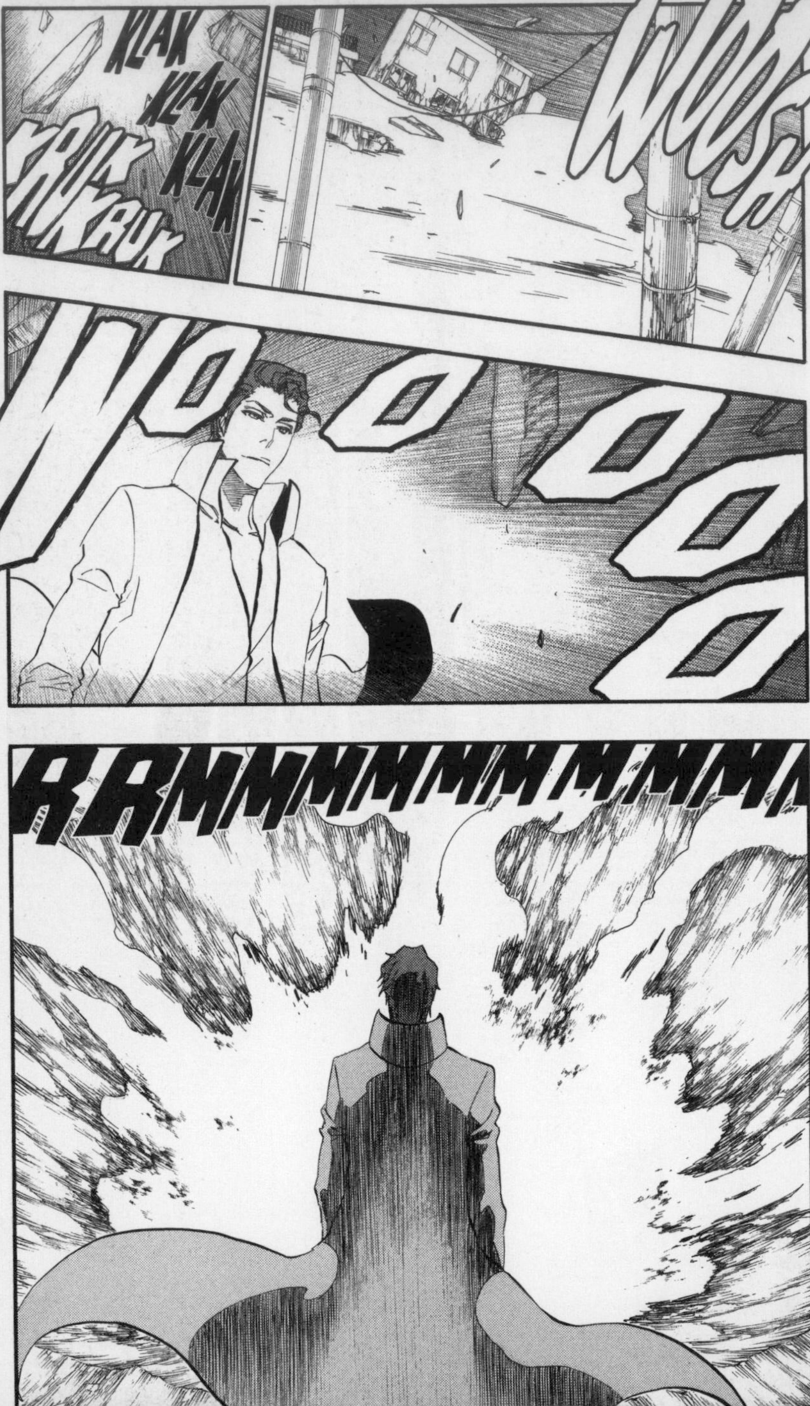
WUSH
KLAK
KLAK
KLAK
KRUK
KRUK
WOOOOO
RRMMMMMMMMMMM

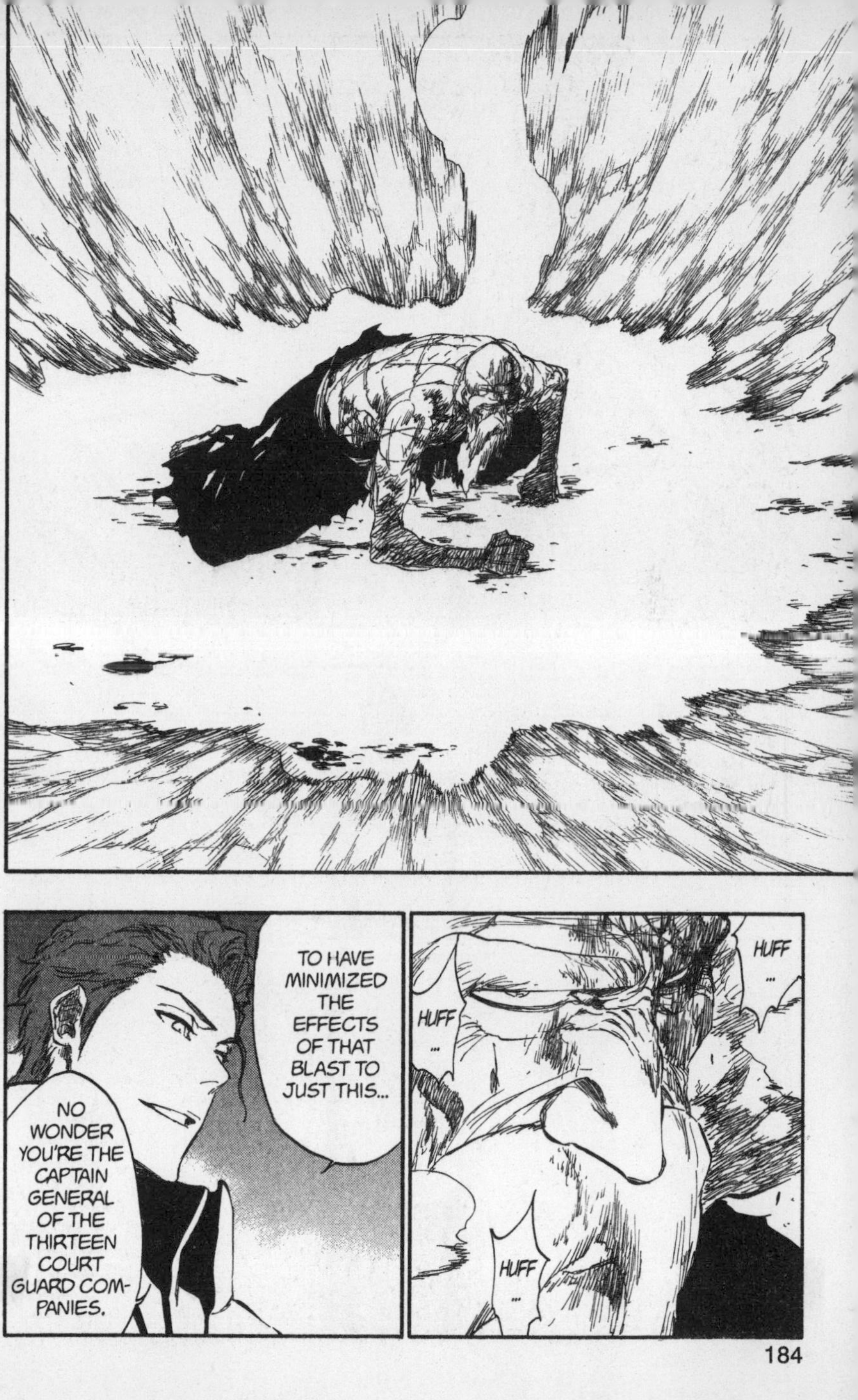
HUFF ...
HUFF ...
HUFF ...
TO HAVE MINIMIZED THE EFFECTS OF THAT BLAST TO JUST THIS...
NO WONDER YOU'RE THE CAPTAIN GENERAL OF THE THIRTEEN COURT GUARD COMPANIES.

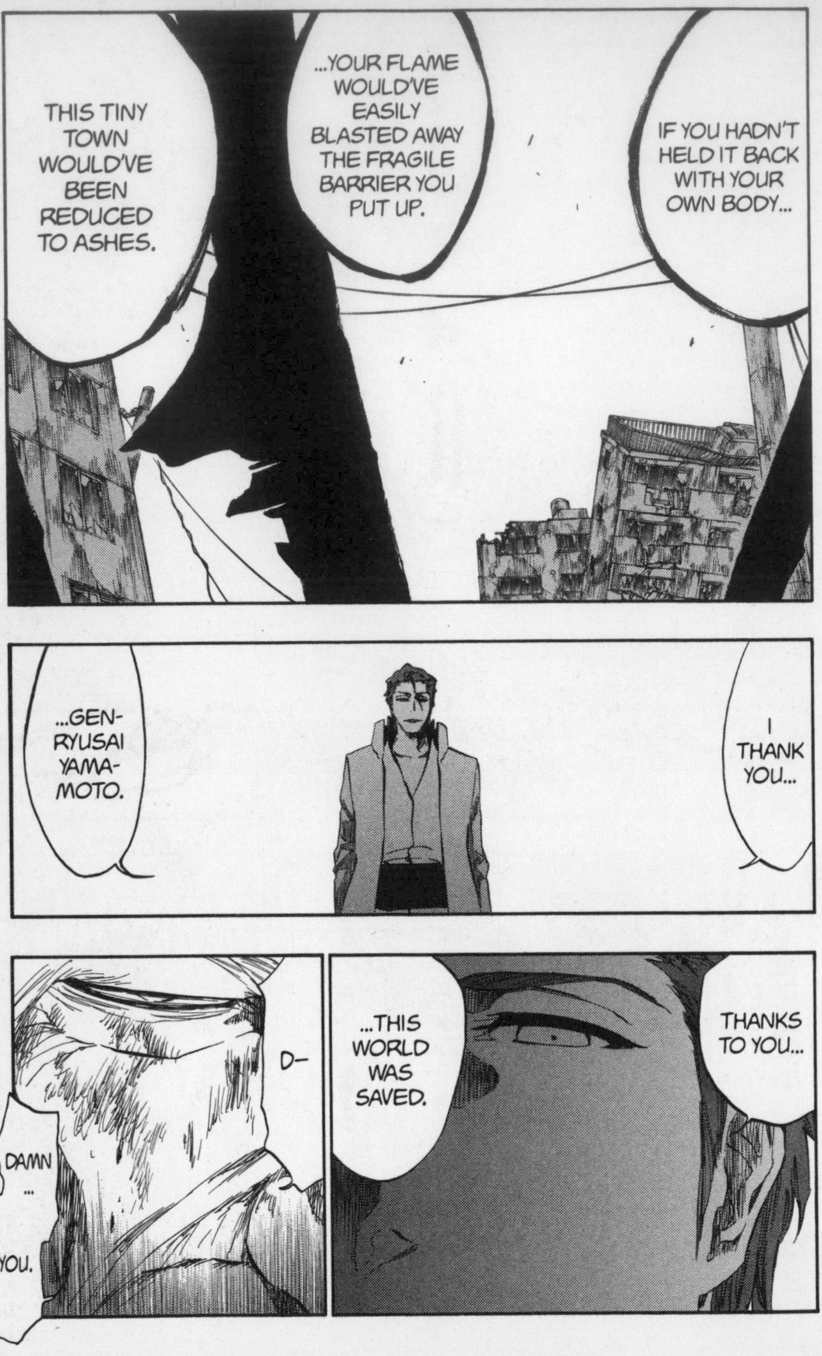
IF YOU HADN'T HELD IT BACK WITH YOUR OWN BODY...
...YOUR FLAME WOULD'VE EASILY BLASTED AWAY THE FRAGILE BARRIER YOU PUT UP.
THIS TINY TOWN WOULD'VE BEEN REDUCED TO ASHES.
I THANK YOU...
...GEN-RYUSAI YAMA-MOTO.
THANKS TO YOU...
...THIS WORLD WAS SAVED.
D-
DAMN ...
...YOU.

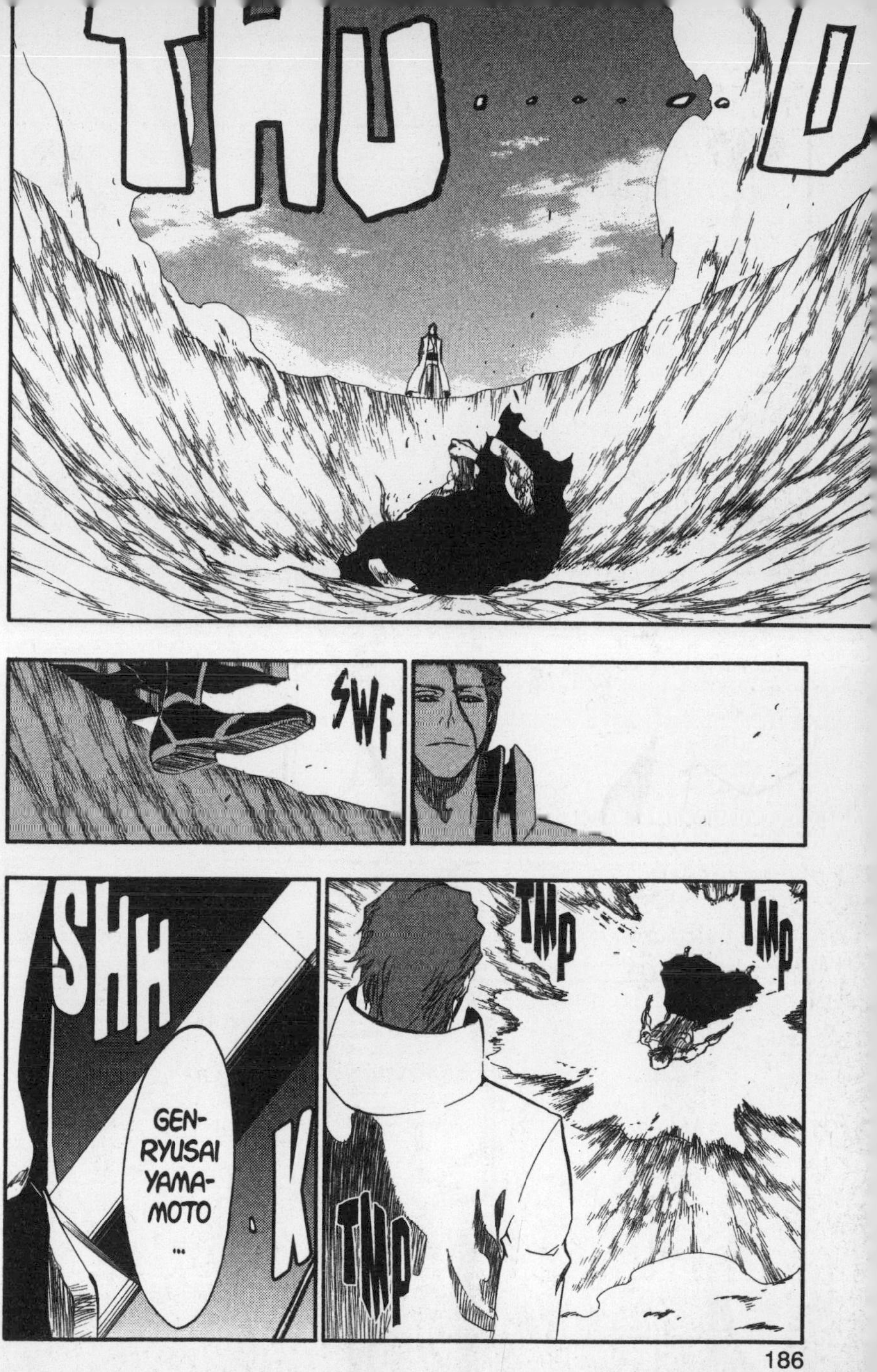

THU.....D
SWF
TMP
TMP
TMP
SHH
GEN-RYUSAI YAMAMOTO...
K

READ THIS WAY

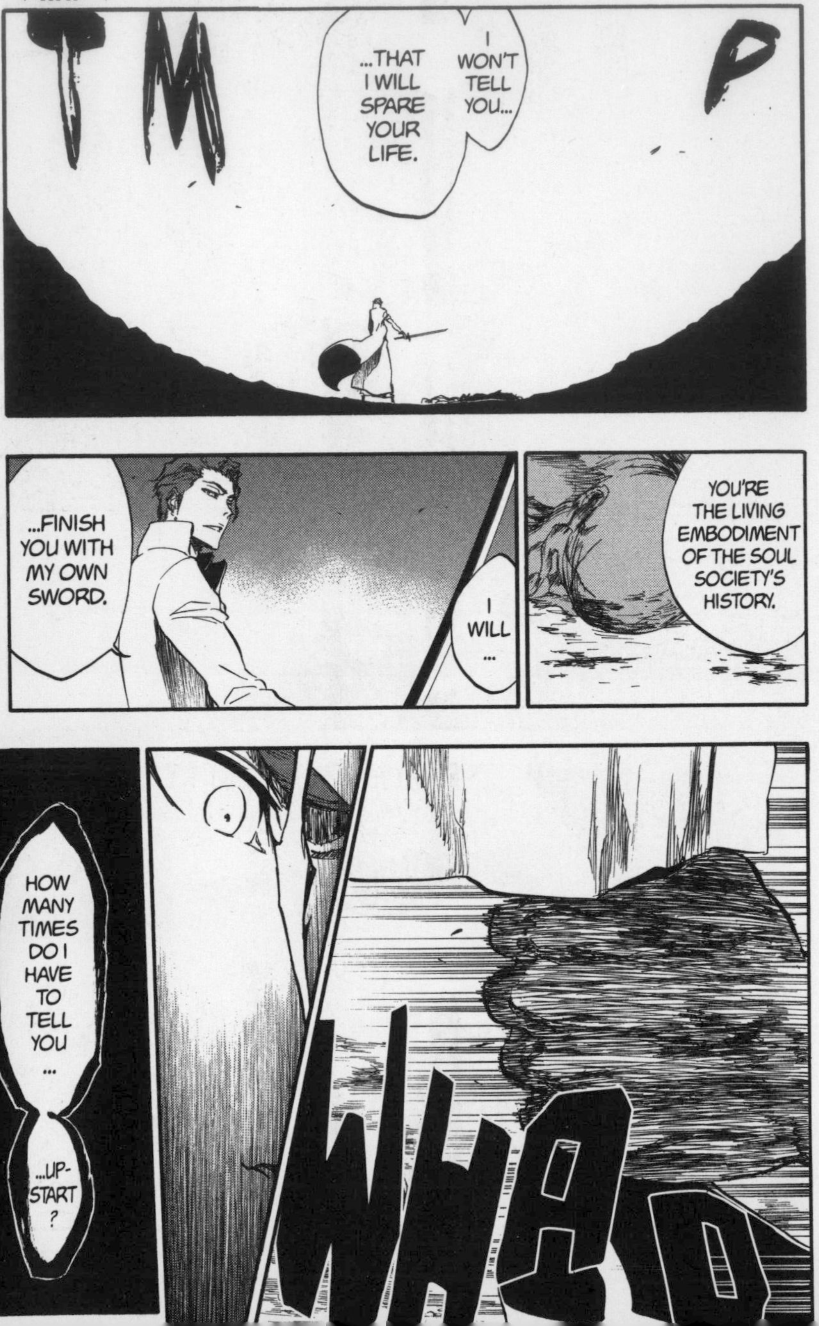
TMP
I WON'T TELL YOU...
...THAT I WILL SPARE YOUR LIFE.
YOU'RE THE LIVING EMBODIMENT OF THE SOUL SOCIETY'S HISTORY.
I WILL...
...FINISH YOU WITH MY OWN SWORD.
WHAD
HOW MANY TIMES DO I HAVE TO TELL YOU...
...UP-START?

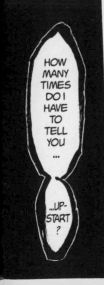

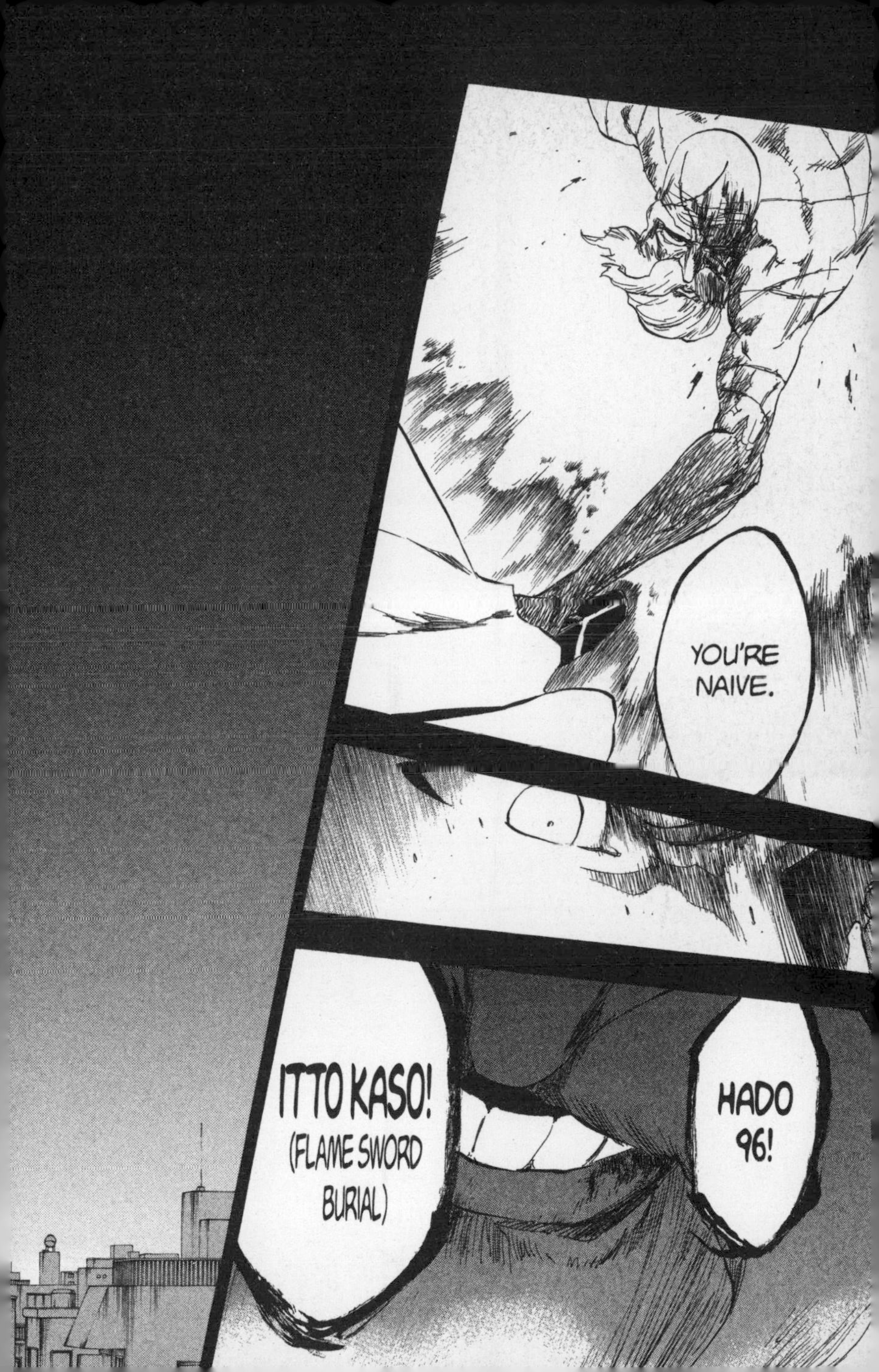
YOU'RE NAIVE.
HADO 96!
ITTO KASO! (FLAME SWORD BURIAL)

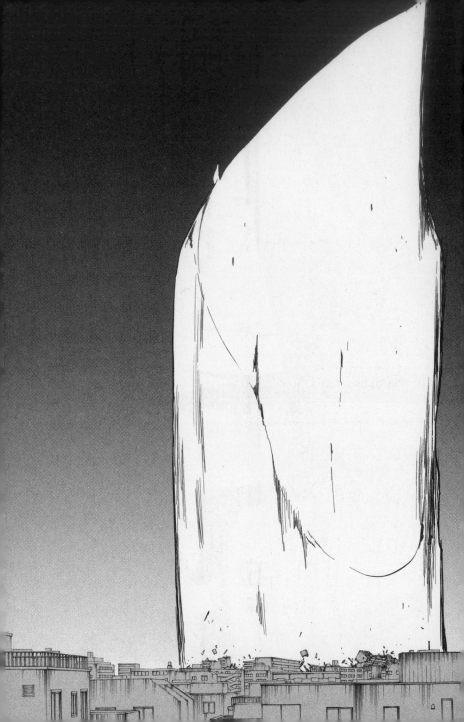

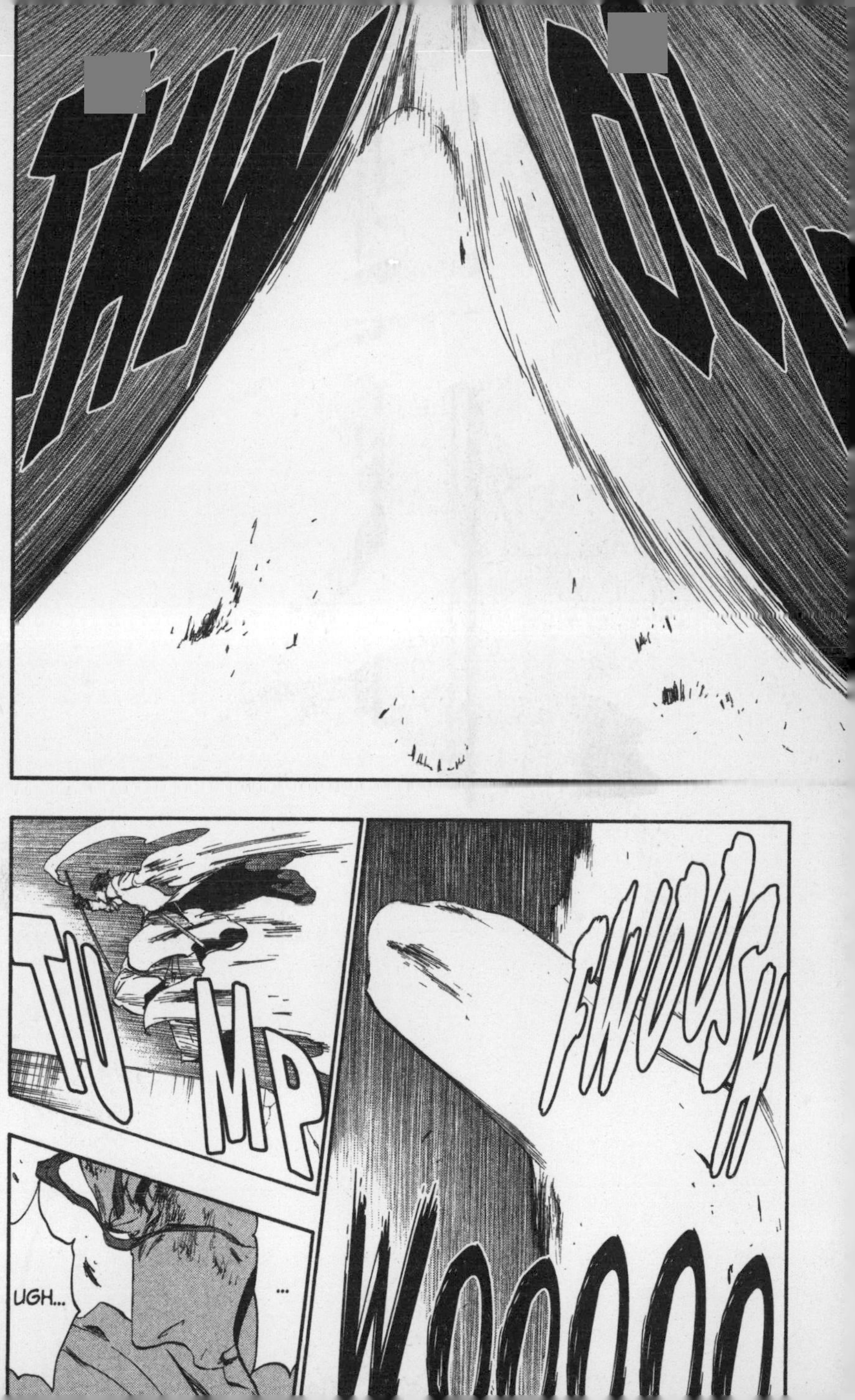
FWUSH
WOOOOO
THUMP
...
UGH...

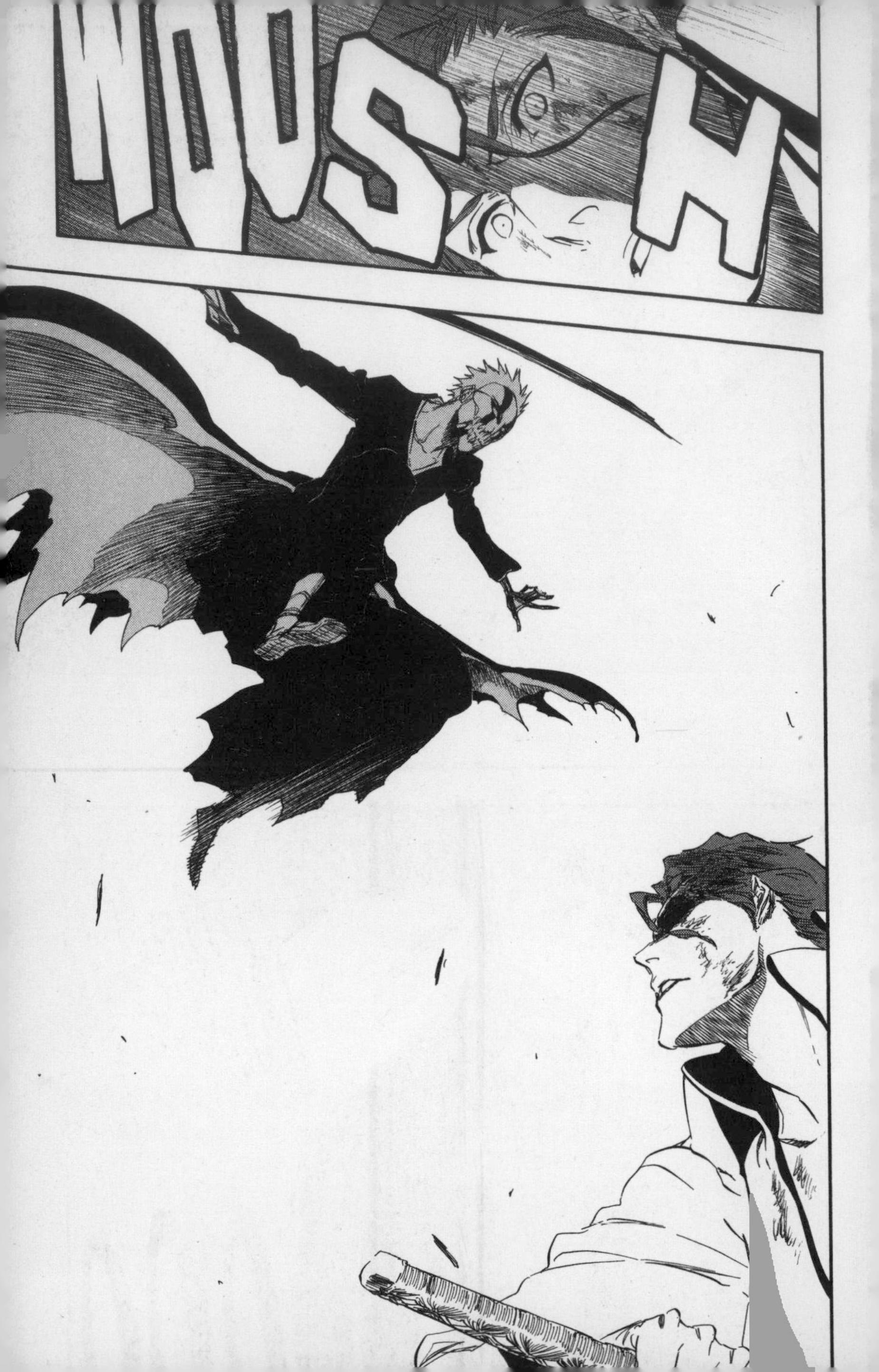
WHOOSH

Next Volume

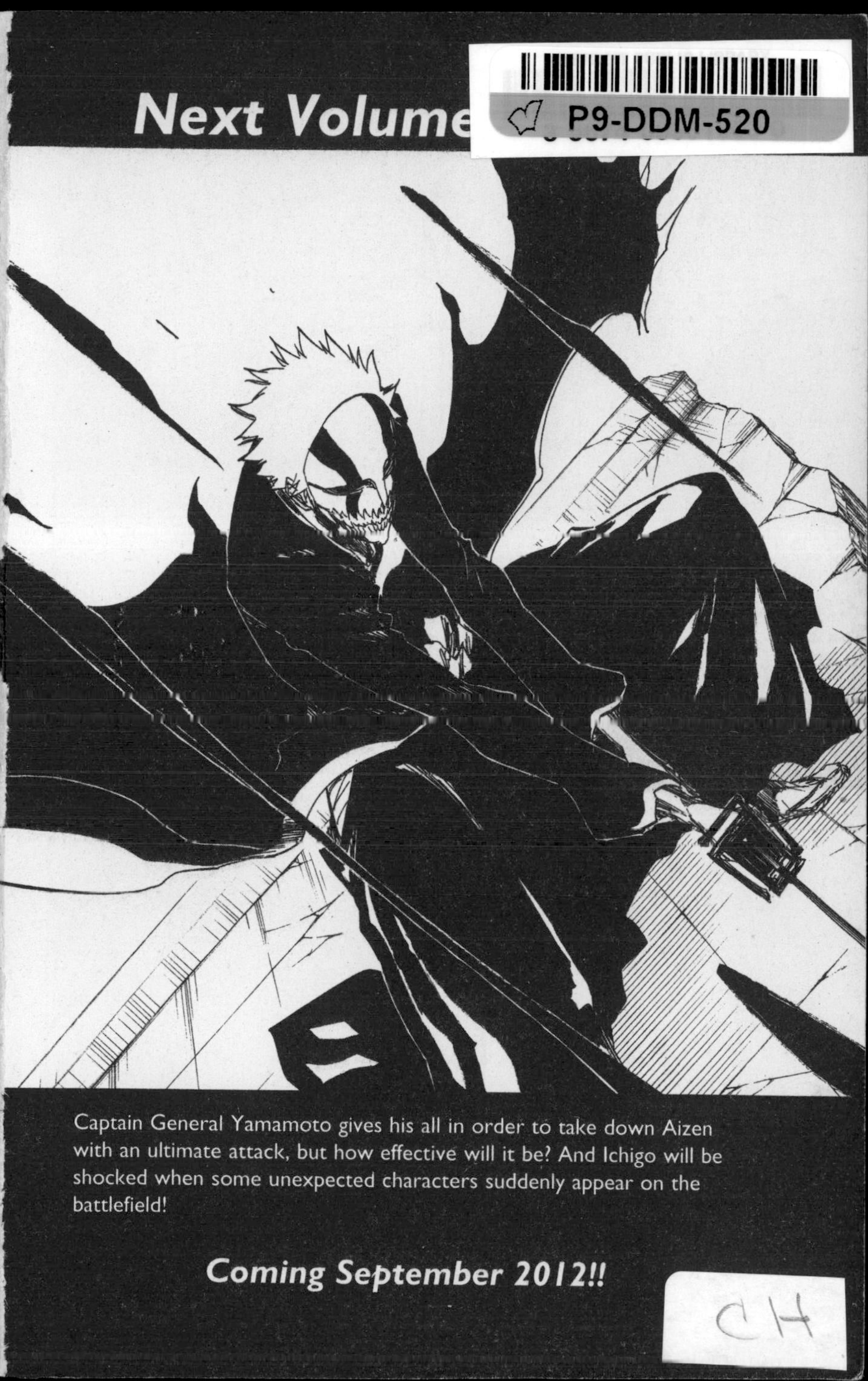

Captain General Yamamoto gives his all in order to take down Aizen with an ultimate attack, but how effective will it be? And Ichigo will be shocked when some unexpected characters suddenly appear on the battlefield!

Coming September 2012!!